DESPERATELY
SEEKING
PARADISE

DESPERATELY SEEKING PARADISE

Journeys of a Sceptical Muslim

ZIAUDDIN SARDAR

Granta Books
London

Granta Publications, 2/3 Hanover Yard, Noel Road, London N1 8BE

First published in Great Britain by Granta Books 2004

A CIP catalogue record for this book is available from the British Library.

1 3 5 7 9 10 8 6 4 2

ISBN 1 86207 650 2

Typeset by M Rules

Printed and bound in Great Britain by William Clowes Ltd, Beccles, Suffolk

For Mumsey: Hamida Bagum Sardar,
ever present, ever watchful

Contents

Chapter 1

PARADISE AWAKENED

As I walked in, a mixture of strong, familiar smells greeted me. It was past midnight; and most people in the mosque had gone to sleep. The aroma of their evening meal, the usual institutional concoction of biryani and lamb curry with the lurking sweet overtones of kheer (milk and rice pudding), hung in the air. It was infused with the miasma of an old, dilapidated, indescribably wretched building pressed into service as a mosque. The vestiges of spicy food combined with the mellower tones of damp walls, dry rot and carpets over which long parades of damp feet had walked, stood and prostrated. For anyone of a certain age raised in Britain, this aroma was instantly recognizable, homely and convivial, a compound everyday odour of sanctity. The 'anyone', of course, would need to be a Muslim, an intimate of mosques. Like this one in Glasgow almost all British mosques were initially established in any ramshackle building that could be appropriated with what cash was available. A mosque was the essential accoutrement for strangers desperate to build a home in a new land. In such places the air itself was a history of struggle and aspiration in inauspicious circumstances. Wherever there is a mosque there will usually be someone camping out for the night. It is the norm that when all else fails, the mosque offers a place of refuge: material and spiritual, real or metaphorical. The sight of several dozen men sleeping comfortably, snoring in unison, their suitcases and other belongings punctuating the prayer hall with chaotic symmetry, however, suggested something afoot.

These contented logs were not aimless travellers nor refugees nor desperate homeless vagrants. When they awoke these would be men on a mission. I, solitary and restless, found sleep elusive. At the ripe age of twenty I already had plenty of experience of various Muslim groups seeking to provide my life with dedication and purpose. None had been quite as bizarre and unsettling as the chain of events that delivered me to this company.

It was the summer of 1972, and just a few days previously I had been looking forward to a quiet Sunday morning when I was roused by the sound of the doorbell. Casual callers are rare on the seventeenth floor of a tower block of council flats. It is an unintended boon of the utopian vision of architects, planners and civic worthies determined to deliver the huddled masses from the squalor of Hackney's decaying streets into redeveloped bliss. Seaton Point, the tower block where we lived, reared over Clapton Pond, a pinnacle of the new East End of London, remade for a new era. But it was so dependent on the delicate mechanism of the temperamental and frequently inoperative lifts that none but the foolhardy, the dedicated relative or friend, or the utterly determined would brave the flights of stairs and just turn up on the doorstep. I opened the door to be greeted by an exceptionally warm salutation: '*As salamu 'alaykum wa rahmatullah*' ('Peace be upon you; and the blessings of God'). Two gentlemen in flowing *kurtas* (long shirts) and loose, baggy trousers, and resplendent with bushy, unruly beards, simultaneously stretched out their hands to grasp mine. 'Yes?' I said, releasing my hand from their joint clutches. 'By the Grace of Allah, we are here to guide you to paradise,' said the tall white man.

Dr Ahmad Zaman Khan was a vaguely familiar face. He was not actually a 'doctor' but a dentist. I knew him to be a Pathan from Northern Pakistan, more Caucasian than your average Englishman. When he spoke it was evident he had acquired an immaculate West Country burr. I had seen him in the distance at various Muslim gatherings, always engaged in animated conversations. Whenever I gravitated into earshot his speech appeared to be less conversation than a running commentary of pious utterances: *Bismillah* (In the name of God); *Alhumdulillah* (Praise be to God), I would hear him intone; *Mashallah* (What God has willed); *Inshallah* (God willing); *Astaghfirullah* (I seek forgiveness from God) often cropped up; *Nauza billah* (We seek protection from God); and, frequently, *La haula wa la quwwata illa billahi* (There is no power but in God). These overheard snatches suggested Dr Khan was a walking example of an old adage: the soul of a Muslim is like a mosaic made up of the formulae of the Qur'an in which he breathes and lives. It had not occurred to me that Dr Khan might have been eyeing and assessing my demeanour as I made my progress through these gatherings and marked me down as lacking in visible signs of piety.

I invited the guests in and offered them some breakfast. On the customary forms of cultural courtesy I was well trained and at least on matters such as feeding and watering of guests dedicatedly observant. Dr Khan introduced his companion. 'This is Masud Sahib,' he said. 'He has come all the way from Karachi to do *tabligh* here.' Masud Sahib, I learned, had left his spice business as well as his wife and eight children at home in Pakistan to travel around Europe inviting Muslims to the mosque. Doing *tabligh* is the exact equivalent of the actions of those earnest young Mormons who spend two years tramping foreign streets, ringing doorbells and engaging the innocent unsuspecting in pre-prepared Socratic dialogues designed to corral the mind into acquiescence with their particular worldview. I knew exactly what to expect and alerted my drowsy senses. As I poured tea, Dr Khan made his opening gambit.

'I have noticed, dear Brother,' he began, 'you are not mindful of your prayers.'

Well, that got me where it hurt. I nodded self-deprecation and shameful agreement.

'You know that *salah* [the five daily prayers] is the key to paradise. You must know how to perform the *salah* correctly.'

'Yes,' I said, 'I do know how to . . .'

'. . . pray in accordance with prescribed rituals?' Masud Sahib butted in before I could finish. 'You will be surprised, Brother, how many people think they know but cannot actually offer their prayer exactly in

the prescribed manner. Many of our brothers and sisters do not even
know how to perform their ablution correctly.'

'Yes, but I am not one of . . .'

This time it was Dr Khan who stopped me in mid-sentence. He
slapped me warmly on my back. 'Brother, Brother, you know it all too
well. It is not enough to say your prayers correctly and on time. A
Muslim must also perform *dhikr* [ritual remembrance of God]
frequently in order to purify the mind and inculcate a habit of
remembering our Creator all the time.'

'Exactly,' Masud Sahib concurred. 'But that too is not enough. We
have to take another step and invite our other brothers and sisters,
indeed lead them, to a life of prayer, remembrance and contemplation
of God.'

'Do you know, my young brother,' Dr Khan seamlessly continued
Masud Sahib's thought, 'that *dawa* is an obligation on every Muslim.
Allah Almighty . . .'

At the very mention of Almighty Allah, Masud Sahib began loudly
reciting a litany: 'the Sovereign Supreme, the Holy, the One with whom
all salvation rests, the Giver of Faith, the one who determines what is
true and what is false, the Almighty One who subdues wrong and
restores right, the One to whom all greatness belongs.'

Dr Khan paused reverentially to listen to the verse and then
continued. 'Allah Almighty has decreed that every Muslim must spare
time from worldly pursuits on a regular basis in order to travel,
following the footsteps of the Prophet, going from door to door, city to
city, and country to country, calling Muslims to the right path. You may
think that *dawa* is something that is limited only to professional *ulama*
[religious scholars]. No. It is the duty of every Muslim. You and I must
also undertake *dawa*. It is our route to paradise.'

'Yes, but . . .'

'Do you not want to go to paradise?' Masud Sahib intervened, taking
advantage of my hesitancy.

'Yes. Who doesn't? But I have to sit an exam in a few weeks' time,' I
offered lamely, hoping this would stem their onslaught. For an
immigrant community education was the key to getting on. It was even
true, in this instance. I was in my final year reading physics at City

University and exams were but weeks away. Masud Sahib was unimpressed. 'You worry about a mere worldly exam? Have you not considered the Final Exam? Are you prepared for *that*?'

'By joining us in *dawa*,' Dr Khan added in a reassuring and certain tone, 'you can, God willing, begin your preparation in earnest for the Final Exam before Allah on the Day of Judgement.'

My strategy was clearly in tatters. And I was becoming aware of a second front opening up in my rear. My parents were milling, eavesdropping on the conversation. I sensed my mother, by tradition and conviction custodian of religious education and observance within the family, ready to strip me of all defensive positions by spilling the beans: 'Not mindful of his prayer, you say,' I could hear her thinking, 'he doesn't even fast during the month of Ramadan.' And as for my father, he had a strong aversion to *Tablighi* types. Tablighis are but one among the many and diverse groups of Muslims, each of which has its own formula for paradise here and hereafter. Each represents a different lineage of thought and authority and thereby is a challenge to every other group. All contend with each other to attract adherents – and I, as a young seeker, was a legitimate target for all. While relishing this attention, I was determined not to be an aimless seeker. I wanted to experience for myself the different interpretations of Islam on offer, to question the propositions of each, and discover just what kind of paradise I was being ushered towards. These two uninvited guests were offering me an opportunity. And there was another thing to consider. At this stage in his life, my father had become an active supporter of a different, politically active Jamaat (or group) of Muslims. If he entered the game they would begin a new kind of jousting, after which sparks, diatribes and denunciations would start to fly. I had no intention of becoming the object of a tug-of-war between distinct approaches to Islam. How could one even think of paradise in the middle of a turf war? There was only one way to clear the board. 'All right,' I said with a mental shrug of resignation. 'I will join you in *tabligh*.' '*Alhumdulillah*' (Allah be praised), Dr Khan and Masud Sahib exclaimed in unison.

'You could start by volunteering for three days,' Masud Sahib said. 'And we are fortunate indeed: a big Tablighi conference is being held in

Sheffield tomorrow. So three days will not be enough. We would like you to volunteer for a full *chilla*.'

'*Chilla?*'

Masud Sahib saw that I was puzzled. 'Forty days of itinerant *dawa*,' he explained.

'Forty days!' I abruptly restrained my temper seeing my father, a villainous twinkle in his eye, bestir himself to join our conversation. 'Forty days it is,' I whispered, speedily corralling them out through the front door.

'But why are you ushering us out of house?' Dr Khan asked. 'You are coming with us!'

'You mean NOW?'

'Yes, Brother. *Now*. The conference in Sheffield starts tomorrow. There's no time to waste.'

'Paradise, like buses and trains, waits for no one,' Masud Sahib intoned with the self-satisfaction of a Cheshire Cat.

The scene shifts to the back of an old Triumph where I squatted while Dr Khan set course towards Sheffield. At least that's what I thought until we left London. Even my limited geographical knowledge alerted me to the fact that Dr Khan was going in the wrong direction.

'Dr Khan,' I said, 'I thought Sheffield was in the north.'

'Indeed,' he said, without taking his eye off the road.

'So why are we going south?' I asked.

'Because, dear Brother, we are going to Plymouth. We need to call on some brothers there. They will be coming with us to Sheffield. *Inshallah*.'

The way he said *Inshallah* was highly indicative. *Inshallah*, meaning 'God willing', is the most ineffable phrase. It betokens the infinite possibilities beyond human understanding. I had been informed that the brothers we were to 'call on' knew nothing of our coming. Nor had they the faintest intimation of joining us on the road to Sheffield and the Tabligh conference. My course in *dawa* had begun.

'Do you know anything about the Tablighi Jamaat?' Masud Sahib asked.

It had started to rain. Without looking at him I responded with an unthinking and truculent 'No'.

Masud Sahib seemed oblivious and began to fill the lacunae of our journey with historical detail. 'It started in 1926 in the town of Mewat, near Delhi. In those days the Muslims of India were in a very bad shape.'

'When have Muslims not been in a bad shape,' I mumbled to myself. How could someone like me be unaware of the sorry tale of decay, disorganization, fragmentation and dissension accompanied by all the ills of poverty, neglect and lack of self-determination that is and has been the fate of Muslims for generations? All those billions of Muslims, sure Islam is the one way, assured Islam has all the answers but without the faintest agreement on the questions to which to apply them. The events of the day summed it all up: running off on the spur of the moment for all the wrong reasons, in the wrong mood in quest of the ultimate prize with two earnest innocents who were as blown by the winds as me.

'Brother, Brother,' Masud Sahib turned a loving glance towards me and said softly: 'You must learn to listen. Your first duty as a student, as potential *dai*, as someone who calls others to right path, is to purify your soul from impurities such as cynicism. Unless and until physical body is purified from dirt and excrement prayer is not fulfilled, so unless and until mind is cleansed of doubt and sarcasm knowledge is not acquired.' He paused. Outside, the gentle shower was burgeoning into a monsoon.

As the shower fell, I let his history of Tablighi Jamaat wash over me. The movement was founded by Maulana Muhammad Ilyas in a region of Northern India inhabited by Rajput tribes known as Meos which, over the centuries, had converted to Islam. To the Maulana they seemed Muslims in name only. He considered their daily practice steeped in Hinduism: their birth, marriage and death rituals were based on Hindu custom, they celebrated Hindu festivals, even worshipped Hindu deities. Worse, this state of affairs made them natural targets for Hindu proselytizing movements, a politically charged turf war in the complex struggle to liberate India from colonialism and gather souls for the right road to paradise.

'Grass roots movement was needed to counter efforts of Hindu preachers, also to educate Meos about fundamentals of Islam,' Masud Sahib said and gathered himself to launch into more detail.

Dr Khan interjected: 'It is time for *Zuhr* [noon prayer].' As he spoke the car lurched onto the hard shoulder, juddered to a halt and in a single bound Dr Khan alighted, prayer mat in hand. Masud Sahib followed smartly.

'Are you not going to join us for *Zuhr*?' they asked in unison.

'But it's pouring down,' I said. 'Besides, we are travellers. We can postpone our prayers and say them later.'

'Do not seek the easy way,' Masud Sahib replied. And Dr Khan added thoughtfully: 'Our religion has been corrupted by people seeking the easy route.'

Reluctantly, I got out of the car. Masud Sahib began looking for a suitable place to spread our prayer mat while Dr Khan recited the call to prayer.

> *'Allah is the Greatest. Allah is the Greatest.*
> *Allah is the Greatest. Allah is the Greatest.*
> *I bear witness that there is no god but Allah.*
> *I bear witness that there is no god but Allah.*
> *I bear witness that Muhammad is the Messenger of Allah.*
> *I bear witness that Muhammad is the Messenger of Allah.*
> *Come to prayer. Come to prayer.*
> *Come to your salvation. Come to your salvation.*
> *Allah is the Greatest. Allah is the Greatest.'*

When Dr Khan finished, Masud Sahib enquired about the *qibla*, the direction we should turn to be facing Mecca. One might head north by travelling south but prayer time did not admit of deviation, then only one direction mattered and it had to be precisely located. Dr Khan pointed out that a compass was built into the prayer mat for utmost convenience and avoidance of all doubt. The trouble was we couldn't actually see it. The transition from the relative warmth of the car into the watery downpour outside was raising steam everywhere, including inside the convenient compass. The prayer mat was wet – we were all wet. Somehow, Dr Khan interposed his person between the rain and the mat, manoeuvring his head and upper torso in varied contortions, then straightened assuring us he had managed to read the precise declination of the exact south-easterly direction. The prayer mat was aligned accordingly and we all joined in the *Zuhr* prayer while the skies continued to pour their mercy upon us. A certain refrain of Noel Coward concerning the midday antics of Englishmen in the tropics came to mind as we performed our comparably bizarre observance to the astonishment of passing motorists.

Back on the road, Masud Sahib seamlessly recommenced his history of Tablighi Jamaat. He provided more than enough detail for me to locate where the *Tablighis* belonged in the vast array of Muslim movements. Each and every one of these is dedicated to revival and revitalization of the real and original Islam. Each has its own ancestry, its derivation from a particular school of thought within Islam that provides its particular aims, objects and mode of operation. Clearly, Tablighi Jamaat never had any pretensions to being an intellectual movement. On the contrary, it found the traditional system of education wanting because it produced religious scholars who could not or would not engage with the religious needs of the mass of the population who were peasant farmers. So the certainties of simple faith were condensed into a basic six-point formula, calling for rigorous observance of the fundamental rituals of Islam. These became their stock in trade, one they took with enthusiasm and conviction door to door, village to village.

'This proved great success. So Maulana Ilyas knew same method would work internationally. Now followers and supporters are all over Muslim world as well as in West. Last year, the Raiwind annual gathering of the Jamaat attracted over a million people,' Masud Sahib upped the ante in hopes of a reaction. 'We can honestly say it has become second largest religious congregation of Muslim World after Hajj.'

'*Alhumdulillah*,' Dr Khan could not contain himself. '*Alhumdulillah*. God is so Merciful. Which one of His mercies can we possibly deny!'

I could think of a few.

Soon enough it was time for *Asr* (afternoon) prayer; our sodden duty done, I immediately began to worry about *Maghrib*, the evening prayer. It was amazing how swiftly strict observance of the daily cycle of religious duties had become the major focus of my attention. Fortunately, and I was thankful for the mercy, we reached Plymouth just before *Maghrib*. Dr Khan steered us to a house not too far from Plymouth Polytechnic. It served as both mosque and student hostel and was managed by a Malaysian man, who, it soon transpired, was guilty of converting Dr Khan to the path of Tablighi Jamaat. Evidently he was also responsible for informing the good doctor that some of the resident students were failing in their religious duties and needed his benevolent attention. All this was made apparent as we bustled to join the congregation for prayer. When it was completed the Imam announced that a special guest from Pakistan was on the premises with a special message; he invited Masud Sahib to address the gathering.

'I have noticed, dear Brothers,' Masud Sahib began, 'that many of you do not perform the prayer in the prescribed manner.' The congregation, mostly Malaysian students, listened attentively as he continued his sermon, pointing out that prayer itself was not enough, that it was necessary to remember Allah and execute this remembrance in the way of the Prophet Muhammad, ending his peroration with the importance of *dawa*. This repetitive refrain was becoming familiar. It only remained for him to call on the assembly to come with us to the first Tablighi Jamaat conference in Britain. 'Sheffield will witness one of the greatest gatherings of Muslims in the history of Britain.'

I now witnessed one of the fastest disappearing acts in the history of Islam. One minute the congregation of students was there – listening attentively, nodding politely, sitting docilely. Next minute they were gone. It wasn't a mass exit. There was no hint of an actual movement. The worshippers simply evaporated. Many are called, but few it seems are sufficiently struck by the invitation to take time out to pay attention to the promise of paradise. All except one.

At first we did not notice her. She was sitting behind a curtain, in the area designated for women. Even on inspection she might have been mistaken for a pile of clothes strewn on the floor, draped as she was in her long, buttoned through coat that billowed formlessly around her as she sat and topped with a voluminous headscarf that enveloped most of her face. It was Doctor Khan who noticed her first and identified what lurked beneath the bundle. He poked his head over the curtain and shouted: 'What about you, Sister? Would you answer the call of Allah with us?'

'Me?' She sounded startled.

'Yes, you, Sister,' thundered Dr Khan. 'Would you join us in *Tabligh?*'

Sister Sofia, inhabitant of the swathes of material, was from Lancashire. We were soon apprised of her story. She fell in love with a Malaysian student and converted to Islam. They got married and moved to Plymouth where he was studying accountancy. But the marriage didn't last; although her devotion to Islam did. She appeared to me as the very personification of the ideal pious Muslim woman: dressed head to toe in regulation attire, she said little, and when she did speak it was quietly in sentences composed almost exclusively of pieties – *Bismillah, Alhumdulillah, Allah-u-Akbar* (God is great).

Early the following morning we set off at last in the direction of Sheffield. Sister Sofia, as was appropriate, occupied the separate eminence of the passenger seat up front alongside Dr Khan. Masud Sahib therefore joined me in the back. Due to lack of space in the boot, we were also accompanied by her suitcase. The night had been clear, the sky dotted with bright, shiny stars. As soon as we sallied forth on the motorway it started to rain again. How comfortable I would be, I thought, if God had created me as a legless dwarf!

We reached Sheffield, after numerous stops for prayer and lengthy delays for determined efforts by Dr Khan, very disappointed with his meagre catch in Plymouth, to find other Muslims in need of correction. Consequently, we made our arrival just as the Tablighi Jamaat conference was all but finished. Only the final speech of Maulana Inamal Hasan, the current spiritual leader of the Tablighi Jamaat, remained. Hazratji, as Maulana Hasan was popularly referred to, spoke in eloquent Urdu of our need to understand and propagate the *kalima*, literally 'the word', the basic creed of Muslims: 'There is no God but Allah; and Muhammad is the Messenger of God.' Emphatically he propounded the necessity of diligently observing 'the pillars' of Islam: five daily prayers must be offered punctually; fasting throughout the month of Ramadan must be undertaken vigorously; *zakat*, or the 'poor due', at least 2.5 per cent of one's annual income, must be calculated scrupulously and given promptly; and Hajj, the pilgrimage to Mecca, must be performed at least once in a lifetime. 'Pay attention to these basics' was Hazratji's insistent message. For the attention paid in this world will be rewarded in the world of the Hereafter. Hazratji added with utmost certainty: 'God will take care of the rest. In His Infinite Mercy, God will grant you paradise.'

So here was the essence of the *Tablighi* approach. Observance of religious practice was a quid pro quo with the Almighty, one merely applied the ready-made formula and one could relax, confident in the assurance that paradise would be the outcome, the consummation of a lifetime of duty done. It seemed the *Tablighis* neither offered nor considered they had to do anything particular about rampant injustice, the horrors of suffering and neglect that formed the circumstances and deformed so many lives in country after country, the Muslim world especially. They surveyed the ills of this world through the rosy glow of total complacency. Shouldn't we, I thought, be trying to make this present existence more of a paradise for all? The better we made this world the easier it would be to truly appreciate paradise when we got there.

The conference was not an end in itself. For all who attended there was a plan, an itinerary, a consequent course of action. We were divided into small groups, destined to be scattered to the four winds, each to make its way to various designated mosques throughout Britain. My group's mission was to proceed to Glasgow. If you have questions and you want answers evidence must be gathered, tested and carefully considered. Before I could dismiss the Tablighis it was incumbent on me to submit myself to the entire experience. So, Glasgow it would be.

Another car journey, intermittent rain, thanking God for British Summer Time which somehow managed to permit occasional dry halts at prayer time, and we were being greeted by Khalid Sahib. He was going to be the Amir – leader – of our group and had arrived before us in Glasgow. A lean man of about forty-five years, he sported a thin scanty beard and wore a black *sherwani* (long coat) and a black *topi*, hat. A lecturer in statistics at the Aligarh University in India, he stood barefoot on the old, worn-out carpet, greeting everyone warmly as they came in. Women were sent in one direction, the men in another. Sister

Sofia obediently disappeared from our sight. Ever polite, Khalid Sahib counselled us to have something to eat and turn in for the night.

Lying awake, the others snoring around me, I thought about Hazratji's speech. One part of it vividly stuck in my memory: his discourse on the nature of knowledge. The thirst to know, the imperative to think and reflect was the most resonant chord, the insistent theme I found running throughout the Qur'an. This urge to question and seek answers I had already taken as my basic creed and cure for all the ills of this world, and possibly the next. Knowledge was the Muslim heritage I imbibed if not with my mother's milk then definitely with her strictures that Islam was something to be not only performed in prayer but activated through learning. My attention homed in on Hazratji's words. The *ulema*, the learned Muslims, he declared, must understand the true nature of knowledge and should be able to distinguish between real and artificial knowledge. Real knowledge is distinguished by the fact that it can be put into practice, he asserted. It is not good enough for Imams and *ulema* to lead people in prayer; they must also have the ability to invite people to the mosque, 'Invite the Muslims to *dawa*,' he said. No wonder I found sleep so difficult. The speech described a closed circuit whose sole, obsessive concern was with the ritual obligations of religion. It made religion a reductive set of simple-minded observances that left the world and all its problems out of the equation. And the more I tossed and turned the less clear became the connection between all the effort and piety of the *Tablighis* and anything I could understand as paradise.

I was roused the following morning for the *Fajr* (dawn) prayer. British Summer Time allows but little rest with this dawn prayer clocking in before 4 a.m. We made a congregation of over fifty people with Khalid Sahib leading the prayer. After the prayer, Masud Sahib was invited with due ceremony to give the morning *dars* – a sermon. His chosen topic, which by now I expected: the Six Points of Tablighi Jamaat.

The sermon concluded with the announcement breakfast was ready. It was eggs and parathas – flat bread fried in ghee (clarified butter) – followed by semolina halva cooked with lashings of ghee. These were the days when everyone ate heartily and left their arteries to fend for themselves. After breakfast a large contingent from the assembled group moved on to Dewsbury, where Hazratji was addressing another big gathering. I detected the subtle hand of Dr Khan in the logistics that would deliver them from Sheffield to Dewsbury via Glasgow. I was thankful my group was to remain in Glasgow. If we stopped rushing about the country for a while perhaps I could discover if there was anything more to the *Tablighi* approach than constant repetition. We who remained were summoned for a consultation to chalk out the day's plan. Without further ado the leader assigned the day's work for each individual: some were given cooking duty, others were responsible for cleaning the mosque, some were appointed to the task of looking after the needs of the women. I was assigned to join the *talim*, an educational session by another name. For all their simple faith *Tablighis* seemed to have an inordinate talent for developing a whole host of technical terms to distinguish between phases of their repetitive procedures.

Dutifully I moved off to join the formal class in basic education. We formed a circle at the centre of which sat a man simply known as Hafiz Sahib – the term *hafiz* is an honorific indicating a person who has committed the entire Qur'an to memory – who described himself as a famous lock maker from Lucknow, India. He read aloud from an authorized *Tablighi* publication, selecting the chapter on prayer. For the last quarter of the session we divided into small sub-groups for more intense study where emphasis was laid on the correct pronunciation of Qur'anic Arabic. The leader appointed to oversee our sub-group was charged with ensuring we broke for prescribed prayers according to rule, that we bowed properly, sat correctly, and knew how to synchronize our movements with the entire congregation.

The noon prayer was followed by lunch: biryani with korma and lashings of ghee. I could feel the miasma of the building thicken along with my arteries.

We were allowed a brief rest after lunch before more classes. The evening session of this intensive day of basic education consisted of a sermon by another name, this one called a *bayan*. This time it was Hajji Sahib's turn. 'Consider a pickpocket,' he began. 'He regards his profession as unusual work and dedicates himself entirely and sincerely to his art. He trains hard and spends time perfecting his technique day in and day out. The establishment is against him; the public is against him; the police are on the lookout. But he bears all hardship for his work; and when it becomes unavoidable he even goes to prison. Now, my dear brothers, *Tabligh* too is necessary work. Find time for this duty and dedicate yourself to it – and you too will be as successful in the Hereafter as the dedicated pickpocket is in this life. Surely, God will reward you for your efforts and bring a revolution in your own life. By inviting others to Islam you too will become better Muslims.' After the *bayan*, Khalid Sahib announced, 'It is time we went on *gusht*.' I was beginning to get used to the *Tablighis'* vast technical vocabulary. 'We must make a trip around the town inviting people to *dawa*.'

The *gusht* contingent was comprised of me accompanied by Hajji Sahib and Khalid Sahib. They explained that members were required to tour the local area, meet the common folk, teach them the basics of Islam and invite them to join in *Tabligh*. There are six rules of *gusht*, he said. I would have expected nothing else. When you enter another person's home, say *As salamu 'alaykum* – peace be upon you – loudly and clearly. Do not enter the house unless you are invited in. Always be polite. Avoid arguments and controversy at all cost. Do not engage in idle talk. And never, never, discuss politics. Today, he informed me, we are going to call on two people who live just outside Glasgow.

Our first target was a medical doctor who came originally from Hyderabad, Deccan, in India. He received us graciously and invited us to join him for tea. Khalid Sahib began by asking if he was regular in his prayers.

'I try to be,' he said.

'That is good news.'

Hajji Sahib looked visibly enthusiastic. 'So you would not have any objection in joining us for *Tabligh*,' he asked rather impatiently.

'I do,' said the Doctor. 'Many.'

'Many?' Khalid Sahib and Hajji Sahib were aghast in unison. 'Surely, you know that *Tabligh* is a duty imposed by God on all Muslims?'

'How many Muslims are there in the Indian subcontinent?' the Doctor asked.

Khalid Sahib thought for a minute. 'All together, both in India and Pakistan, I would say we are about half a billion,' he replied.

'And each one of them with a problem,' said the Doctor, 'and instead of correcting their ways, showing them the right path, trying to solve their problems, you have come thousands of miles to preach here, to show us the errors of our ways. Should you not be putting your own house in order?'

Khalid Sahib looked at me. I was examining the contents of the Doctor's bookshelf. 'Charity begins at home,' I said without thinking.

Khalid Sahib must have noticed the book I was perusing: *Khilafat-o-Mulukiyat* (Caliphate and Monarchy) by Maulana Abulala Mawdudi, the ideologue and leader of another brand of politically active Muslim revivalism. In one deft movement he jumped up, grabbed the book from my hand and placed it back in the bookshelf as if dealing with a hot potato.

'You don't like Maulana Mawdudi?' the Doctor asked.

'It is not a question of like and dislike,' Khalid Sahib answered. I made a mental note of *gusht* rules three to six coming into action. 'It is much better to pay attention to the fundamentals than get involved in politics and polemics.'

'But how can we do something about the injustices of the world if we do not get involved in politics?' the Doctor retorted.

'If Muslims were diligent about their prayers and remembered God and their place in the cosmos, there wouldn't be any injustice.' Having observed the niceties of the rules of engagement Khalid Sahib was not about to wait for a reply. '*Alhumdulillah*,' he said. 'It was a great pleasure to meet you. It is time for us to move on.'

Our next call was to a labourer from the Punjab who had been in Britain for many years. Khalid Sahib politely asked if he had paid attention to his prayers and if had experienced any difficulty in practising Islam while living in the West. 'No,' the labourer replied emphatically. The brothers in *Tabligh* were taken aback in unison. Khalid Sahib composed himself and began to talk about *Iman* (faith).

'Faith,' he began, 'is the key to paradise. It is essential for Muslims to have the right *Iman* and to practise their *Iman* in the correct manner.'

'How do you know that I do not have *Iman*? Or that my *Iman* is weak? Do you carry an imanometer around with you? Where's this device for measuring my *Iman*?' the labourer enquired with a mischievous twinkle in his eye.

'All I am saying, dear Brother, is that faith, sincere submission to the will of Allah, is the key to all understanding and a prerequisite for entering paradise.' Khalid Sahib had clearly seen the gleam but was intent on being conciliatory.

'Do you know the story of the prostitute?' the labourer asked.

'Prostitute? What prostitute?' Khalid Sahib clearly could hardly believe his ears.

'One day,' the labourer began warming to his task, 'the Prophet Muhammad saw a prostitute walking past a well. As she went by she noticed a dog dying of thirst near the well. So she took some water out of the well, poured it into one of her shoes, and gave it to the dog. The Prophet was moved by her act of kindness. For this act of gentleness, he said, all her sins would be forgiven and she would enter paradise.'

'What is your point?' Hajji Sahib asked impatiently. It seemed to me rule four might be coming under severe threat.

'If I am neglectful of my prayer like the prostitute, what makes you think I will not be forgiven for something that I have already done or will do and therefore carve out a piece of paradise for myself?'

Khalid Sahib clearly felt a change of tactics was necessary and determined to fight narrative with narrative, rule four notwithstanding. 'Let me, my beloved Brother, also tell you a story from the life of Prophet Muhammad.' He drew his chair nearer to the labourer. 'One day the Prophet was sitting outside among a group of people when a man, all dressed in white and with a long white beard, and who showed no sign of fatigue, came to him and asked: "What is *Iman*?" The Prophet replied: "*Iman* is that you believe in Allah and His angels and in meeting with Him and believe in His Messengers and that you believe in the Hereafter." Then, the man asked: "What is Islam?" The Prophet said: "Islam is that you worship Allah and do not associate anything with Him and that you keep up prayers, pay the *zakat* as ordained and fast in the month of Ramadan." The man then asked: "What is *Ihsan* [goodness]?" The Prophet replied: "That you worship Allah as if you see Him; for if you do not see Him, surely He sees you."' Khalid Sahib paused. 'You know, the man was Archangel Gabriel.' After a few heartbeats for emphasis, he added: 'Surely, you would rather follow the Prophet than a prostitute?'

Hajji Sahib beamed at me as if to say 'that's clinched the argument'. The labourer looked at each of us one by one.

'Let me,' he said, 'relate to you another saying of the Prophet Muhammad. "What is *Iman*?" he was once asked. "*Iman*," he replied, "has over sixty or seventy branches. The most excellent of these is saying There is no God but Allah; and the lowest of them is the removal of harmful objects from the way of others." I am a cleaner. That's all I do all day. I clean the streets five days a week, year round in all weathers. So my *Iman* is solid. It doesn't need confirmation or check-ups."

Khalid Sahib was speechless. Wearily, he rose to his feet, we muttered our salutations and beat a hasty retreat.

As we made our way back to the reassuring precincts of the mosque Khalid Sahib remarked how argumentative the Muslims have become. 'You must beware,' he said affectionately and in all innocence to me, 'or you could end up following their footsteps.' It has never been my practice to kick a man when he's down so I listened sympathetically as he advised me to pay particular attention to the six points. 'You have much to learn. You must spend much more time with us,' he kept saying. It seemed clear to me that more time would simply mean more repetitions of exactly the same truncated pieties, the same six points. I felt no nearer to paradise nor clearer in my ideas about paradise than when they stormed my flat that fateful Sunday morning. All I had learned was that their formula could not be mine.

En route to the prayer hall I caught sight of Sister Sofia. She waved to me and made a figure of eight in the air while uttering something soundless. I was momentarily distracted and when I looked again she was nowhere to be seen. On reflection, I concluded she wanted to meet at eight o'clock, just when the evening prayer would be in session. I lingered over my ablutions, the ritual washing of face, arms and feet before prayer, until everyone else was safely forming their lines in the prayer hall and instead of joining them I slipped out and began to look for the sister. She was nowhere in the other rooms or corridors of the mosque so I stepped outside to look around the car park. A stray billow of cloth told me Sister Sofia was standing behind a van, waiting for me. We greeted each other warmly. 'Are you thinking what I am thinking?' she asked. 'I certainly am,' I replied eagerly. 'Then, let's get the hell out of here.'

Chapter 2

THE BROTHERHOOD OF SALVATION

Sister Sofia and I headed straight for the coach station and conveyance south. True to form, she said little during the journey; we sat quietly at the back of the coach. Then, for some reason, she took off her scarf and started to brush her long, blonde hair. Categorically, my brain raced to reassign her. She ceased being a 'sister', and for the first time I classified her definitively as a member of the opposite sex. Having completed her toilette she took hold of my right arm with both her hands, placed her head on my shoulder, and promptly went to sleep. The coach appeared to have taken lessons from Dr Khan. We reached London, via a convoluted route, in the small hours the following night. I invited Sofia to my home.

All was quiet at Seaton Point. The lights were off and everyone was clearly asleep when we reached the door of my flat. It has never been my habit to carry extraneous items at any time, let alone when flying out of the house on *Tabligh*, so I had no door key. I rang the doorbell. It reverberated around the tower block. We waited. A light went on, and my mother opened the door. She was wearing her white nightgown. 'Mumsey,' I said, my eyes fixated on the ground, 'this is Sister Sofia.' Mumsey looked at me; Mumsey looked at Sofia; Mumsey turned to me again, her gaze coming to rest on entirely the wrong conclusion. In the resounding silence I stole a sheepish glance at Mumsey and watched as her complexion slowly merged into the whiteness of the nightgown.

By the time I woke the following morning, Sofia had already left. How and in what way she was spirited from the premises I was never to learn. Curious and inquisitive as my nature might be, there are some questions it is neither politic nor sensible to pursue. And, anyway, I had another problem to preoccupy my mind. It was evident the *Tablighi* route was not for me, but I could not dismiss the matter of paradise as easily. My restless night in Glasgow turned over a new awareness that paradise was a motif deeply woven into culture and society, politics and art, Muslim and British. It was an ideal operating in and through the identities that framed my life. Paradise transcended and perhaps interconnected the worlds of belonging that were mine. And in both worlds it was pregnant with implications and usages from the banal and idiomatic to the profound. In both it implied a state of mind afflicted by an ongoing dissatisfaction with how things are, a dissident search for ways to make things better. Dr Khan and Masud Sahib had issued their invitation and its effect had been like that of a pebble thrown into the still waters of my consciousness. Whatever limitations I saw in their six points, the question of paradise – what it is, what it means and how it is to be achieved – was limitless. In future, I could never take it for granted.

I grew up questioning most things – an appropriate by-product, you might say, of my birth and times. I was born in shifting circumstances in the rural backwater of the Punjab. The village of my birth was, at the time, a contested area. Forceful efforts were being made to determine where a new frontier should be drawn to separate parts of my heritage that had previously been a complex whole. Would I be a Pakistani or an Indian? This application of force, the open warfare between two new identities anxious to recruit me, was the latest round in a long-running partitioning process. It waxed and waned over the landscape, swallowing and disgorging the village where I was born. Partition of India was a cause that involved me in a complex history of contentious identities long before I was born. Partition was about attempts to distil what I should regard as my heritage into some new singular and potent essence. But no sooner had the international frontier across the subcontinent been settled and new identities begun to assert themselves than my family relocated. My village was confirmed as part of Pakistan, which was defined by Muslim identity and engaged in nation-building. But meanwhile my father was recruited to help rebuild the very nation whose parting gift as the Empire retreated was the fracturing of the subcontinent. He left my mother and his three children back home in Pakistan while he joined the ranks of workers invited to help reconstruct Britain's war-ravaged economy. He established himself in his job at a car factory and found a small flat in a ramshackle terraced street before summoning the family to join him. We had to begin the process of defining our identity all over again.

In the anonymity of the great metropolis I was instantly recognizable as an unknown quantity and found independence thrust upon me. The adaptability of children pushes them to the forefront of the struggle to make a home in a new environment. I was sent off to school across the treacherous streets of Hackney. 'Paki bashing' was the latest vogue, a game I often suffered from. Being and becoming a Muslim, shaping an identity, was a contested arena wherever I lived, in London or in a divided India 'back home'. The independence I was forced into did not come merely from attending school. I had the language of this new land and thereby acquired responsibility as negotiator, interpreting for my mother with the new species of shopkeepers, bus conductors and myriad officials who now impinged upon our lives. And it was my appointed task to seek out the newly emerging nooks and crannies where people like us were setting up the infrastructure of continuity and belonging: the halal meat shops, the proto-corner shops selling spices, lentils, *atta* (flour) and convenient, normal-sized humongous bags of rice. I had to go out and about; it was my role in the process of resettling our family life on a sustainable pattern.

The growing child I was had to quickly master the rules of the new game plan of survival. It is immigrant children who bring home the vital information about the strange new world. Unlike adults they take the new and wondrous for natural phenomena, and therefore see them in more rounded fashion. Parents, whose normality was fashioned otherwise, are more resistant to new influence. Effortlessly, children bring the norms of the public space – school, the streets, television, the latest craze, the modes and manners of the times – to the established pattern of domestic usage. My parents frequently filled the house with friends and the evening would always develop into a *mushaira*, these are the poetry recitals that are an institution for literature-loving, Urdu-speaking families. The themes for the evening would often be chosen in homage to a particularly fine line, word or idea my mother picked up on regular visits to the Indian cinema. Most Sundays I would escort her and a gaggle of her friends across London to attend a double-feature of cinematic offerings from the classic era of Indian movies. In the darkened space I reconnected with and internalized the unified heritage of a subcontinent where I no longer lived. All of these films were alive with songs, all of them written by recognized poets with a love of language. My parents and their friends would make their own efforts to compete with these poems, in the genre of Urdu where poetry is musical words. This too was in the mix of my normality. Children are amalgamators. They add bangers and mash and fish and chips to sag gosht and parathas, not noticing the joins. What is normal for the child is to say: all this I am heir to, all this belongs to me. This is the world that nurtures me.

I was the newest kind of explorer because I existed across so many worlds of belonging. But the worlds I lived in barely recognized each other, and knew precious little about each other. From all sides there was pressure to compartmentalize, to make exclusive each of the worlds I belonged to and thereby deny their profusion of possibilities. On the other hand, I am part of that golden generation of the post-Second World War baby boom that, in my British incarnation, was bequeathed new horizons. Here was the seedbed of questions I would spend the rest of my life harvesting. In my new existence I was inheritor of the welfare state of opportunity; I grew with the rising tide of consumer abundance never before known to the common herd. I was forged in the white heat of the technological revolution. I was the kid from Brooke House Secondary Modern School in Clapton Pond who became Science Editor of *Sixth Form Opinion*, a national magazine for school students. It came about quite by chance. On one of my forays out and about I met the nice old gentleman who was the moving spirit of the magazine. I asked could I join in. What could be more enticing than a licence to investigate and interrogate the world of my belonging?

We published, I recall, a long interview with Tony Benn on the revolutionary technological paradise he sought to popularize. We reflected a time when contested meanings, contending ideas and conflict were reshaping my generation. Revolting became the mass participant sport for all young people: protests, marches, sit-ins, little red books and Che Guevara T-shirts. As my own form of protest, I established an Islamic Society at my school. This, in turn, brought me in contact with FOSIS. Technically FOSIS, or, to give it its full title, the Federation of Students Islamic Society in UK and Eire, was an organization of university students. But due to the fluidity typical of the structure and operative practice of Muslim organizations everywhere, I became a participant in their activities while still at school.

By the time I had my adventure with the *Tablighis*, FOSIS had been part of my life for some years. Attending a FOSIS function in the early 1970s, one had to be blind not to notice what a motley crowd we were. The Muslim students in Britain were a microcosm of the Muslim world in its ethnic and geographical extent as well as its disparate relations to tradition, modernity, revolution and reform. There were two main categories of members: expatriate students from various Muslim countries pursuing their higher degrees in Britain; and a string of indigenous and American hippies who, often after a long and arduous search, had arrived at Sufism and converted to Islam. The third wave was not yet a dribble. I could count myself among the first few droplets of the coming tide: Muslims born of immigrant parents who had been born or brought up and educated in Britain and actually made it to higher education.

The organization was established in Birmingham in 1962 by students from various British universities who wanted to coordinate the work of Islamic societies across Britain. The Federation captured the imagination of the British Muslim community by conforming to the general temper of student times and protesting. But FOSIS did not make its name by taking up the vanguard in the anti-Vietnam demos or sitting-in for student empowerment. Our attention was turned to the overlooked, unfashionable issues that struck a chord and mattered to Muslims. We organized a series of important protests:

after Sayyid Qutb, the chief ideologue of Muslim Brotherhood in Egypt, was executed by the regime of Gamal Abdel Nasser in 1966; after the occupation of Palestine in the wake of the Arab–Israeli war of 1967; when Al Aqsa mosque was burned by the Israelis in 1969; and after Hindu–Muslim riots broke out in several parts of India in 1969. By 1970, it had acquired a permanent head office in Kilburn, London, from where a network of around thirty constituent organizations was managed, and Winter Camps and Annual Conferences – two major events in the Federation's calendar – were organized.

Those who became my mentors were a good indication of the multiverses that composed the membership. There was Abdullah Jabreel Oyeken, a Nigerian with an infectious sense of humour, who was studying Industrial Chemistry at Imperial College. Ebrahimsa Muhammad, a gentle, totally selfless Malaysian, was studying Law. Abdul Wahid Hamid, an introspective historian from Trinidad, was studying at School of African and Oriental Studies. Muhammad Raziq, who was working to qualify as a chartered account, was a self-effacing Sri Lankan. Ghayasuddin Siddiqui, a Pakistani who always spoke with considerable hesitation, was doing his postgraduate work on industrial pollution. Muhammad Iqbal Asaria was a quiet Ugandan Asian reading Economics at the University of Manchester. Abdullah Naseef, an exceptionally well-mannered Saudi easily provoked to a winning and generous smile, was working for a PhD in Geology at Leeds University. The youngest of all, another of the droplets of the coming tide, was Jamil Sharif, a self-assured Pakistani studying Chemistry at City University in London.

With the intensity of student friends we lived in each other's pockets. We often prayed and worked together, and ate at each other's homes, providing my mother with a stream of eager mouths. Like so many student organizations of this era we shared a tremendous feeling of duty: to each other as well as the wider community; a moral fervour that infused all we did. In many respects, we fulfilled the prescription laid out by the celebrated Muslim scholar Al-Ghazali during the eleventh century, in *On the Duties of Brotherhood*: 'Know that the contract of Brotherhood is a bond between two persons, like the contract of marriage between two spouses. For just as marriage gives rise to certain duties which must be fulfilled when it is entered into, so does the contract of brotherhood confer upon your brother a certain right touching your property, your person, your tongue and your heart – by way of forgiveness, prayer, sincerity, loyalty, relief and considerations.' And if that was not enough, we arranged actual marriages.

Marriage has always been the province and prerogative of the matriarchs. The senior women of the family in Muslim households the world over jealously guard their right to investigate, analyse and pair off all individuals who come within their purview. It is a traditional skill combining consummate mastery of the deepest mysteries of personality profiling, sociological sensitivity and understanding, psychological insight and quantifying of variables well beyond the most sophisticated computer-dating software. The ideal arranged marriage seeks compatibility, the kind that develops, grows and flourishes in and for the lifetime of two people who, even if close relatives, officially have no previous idea of each other's existence. Arranging marriages is an art form, but one that does not travel well. In Britain of the 1960s and 1970s, the women of the Muslim community had been uprooted. They were removed from stable environments where they were interconnected over generations with entire villages or neighbourhoods. In their new setting in Britain they had more truncated networks, more circumscribed access to the contacts and information that were essential to perform the arcane rites of arranging marriages. The steady business of building circuits of visiting, connecting with people from similar backgrounds, identifying the right kind of people from within the limitations of the 'Asian' community, sniffing out the not suitable kind of *badmashes* and making sense of all the new environment's influences and effects and how they worked on young people was in its infancy. And that was how neophyte inepts in the subtler mysteries, mere young men having only extensive acquaintances among people of an age and character to need spouses, came to do a roaring trade in matchmaking. Making sure that those who needed a wife got one was not the least duty of brotherhood we felt obliged to fulfil.

If the causes FOSIS adopted seem marginal to the great swell of mainstream protest this was more illusory than real. Out in the mainstream, Third World issues were a hot new topic. Colonial guilt was coming home to roost. It was the era of independence, when so many former colonies became new nations only to inherit poverty and the inability to develop. Concern for the starving was beginning to stimulate questions about the structural injustices of an unequal world. The failure of development was beginning to be seen by some as a systemic inevitability, not an unfortunate mistake. To the membership of FOSIS these new ideas were hoary old chestnuts. We knew all too well the shortcomings of classic development theory and all it chose to ignore, all the complex realities it was ignorant of, all the false premises and specious ideas it compounded, because it was the world we inhabited, from which we sprang, to which, in various permutations, we belonged. We had our suspicions about the alternative-lifestyle brigade not because alternatives were not urgently required but because they seemed to take a romantic view of tradition. And the one thing we scions of the underdeveloped world, we FOSIS members, knew, that no one else was yet ready to acknowledge, was that putting it right, changing these times, would be a lot harder than the spirit of protest dared to confront.

It was this often unexpressed tacit understanding that bound us even more closely. We knew, with certainty, that our generation of Muslims did not have the option of dropping out. Our moral fervour, our protest, our determined search for pragmatic alternatives would be crucial. We really did have to work it out. More importantly, we had to get it right. It fell to us to set the juggernaut of Islamic history back on the rails. Many FOSIS members who obtained their qualifications and returned to their respective countries would become captains of industry, prominent politicians, noted academics or administrators. All the aspirations and sense of earnestness diffused across the mainstream of our generation of student protest was concentrated and heightened among our membership. We were the future of the worldwide Muslim community, longing for its former glories to be revived. The hopes and aspirations of genuine self-determination and independence across the Muslim world had been suffused with appeals to the former glories of history. We had all grown up on stories of how Muslim civilization long ago had been the ornament and pinnacle of human achievement: rich, powerful and splendid, learned and wise. We were the pivotal generation that came after the first flush of independence had failed to deliver its glorious new horizons. We were courted by all shades of opinion, anyone and everyone who had a plan, a dream or an alchemical formula for the future of the Muslim world.

Prominent scholars and members of the Islamic movement were queuing up to contribute to the pages of our magazine, *The Muslim*, and speak at our conferences and winter gatherings. Said Ramadan, the former Secretary of the Muslim Brotherhood who was now the Director of the Islamic Centre in Geneva, was a regular. Malcolm X stopped to have dinner with us, 'No knives and forks for me: I eat with my big, black hands!', on his way to Mecca for pilgrimage. The Algerian scholar Malik Bennabi, seen by many as one of the most profound and eminent Muslim philosophers of the post-Second World War period, came to present his thesis of 'colonizibility': to be colonized, he said, a society has to be in a physical and mental state which makes colonization almost inevitable. Bennabi, an electrical engineer, studied in Paris and had spent over three decades in Europe. His profound understanding of western culture and civilization led him to the conclusion that Europe's military superiority and imperialistic tendencies were not enough to explain the colonization of the Muslim world. Colonization was not the basic cause of Muslim decline, as many Muslim scholars had argued. It was the phenomenon of colonizibility, which had set in centuries before, that made the Muslim world ripe for colonization. His thesis shattered the myth of the invincibility of Europe by focusing attention on the weaknesses of Muslim societies themselves, and thus appealed to students. It turned our attention to domestic issues, things we should be able to get to grips with, a task we could undertake with our own hands.

In particular, we were courted by the Islamic movements. Across the Muslim world the quest to decolonize, to achieve independence, had been nurtured, advanced, supported and fought for in multiple senses by organizations that drew their inspiration from Islam. The true meaning of freedom, such organizations argued, would be returning society as a whole to the path of Islam. They said that Islam had all the principles and answers to stem the long decline of Muslim civilization, that a return to the full social, political and economic ideals of Islam in practice was the only proper course for genuine nation-building. Two of the most influential organizations of the global Islamic movements vied with each other to capture our souls: the Muslim Brotherhood of Egypt and Jamaat-e-Islami of Pakistan.

Khurshid Ahmad was the most prominent of the Jamaat-e-Islami personalities. A heavily built man, he arrived in Britain in 1968, sporting a neat, rounded, regulation Jamaat-e-Islami beard. Jamaat-e-Islami had been formed in August 1941 in Lahore by Maulana Sayyid Abulala Mawdudi as a revivalist political party devoted to establishing an Islamic state. Mawdudi, who worked as a journalist, had been reflecting on the condition of the Muslims for decades before reaching the conclusion that no Muslim party was likely to succeed unless it followed the high standards of Islamic ethics and morality and urged Muslims to be morally upright and adhere to their religious convictions without compromise. The fact that he had been imprisoned at least four times between 1948 and 1967, and sentenced to death in 1953 by a Martial Law court for writing a seditious pamphlet, made him into a living martyr for students.

Khurshid Ahmad, a high-ranking official in Jamaat-e-Islami, spared no opportunity to enhance the reputation of his mentor. He was himself, it seemed to us, following in the footsteps of Mawdudi: going to prison for nine months for 'the cause', writing and speaking about Islam and continuing the political struggle through the ballot box for the establishment of an Islamic state. Mawdudi, he always insisted, was an ideal model of an Islamic scholar worth emulating in every detail: from personal piety and righteousness to his political activism, his devotion to Islam and his unflinching adherence to truth in face of all adversity.

Then, in the winter of 1969 I met him. He came to London for medical treatment; and I, along with thousands of students, went to Heathrow Airport to welcome him. FOSIS organized a huge reception in his honour at the London Hilton. During his time in London, Mawdudi was overwhelmed by a continuous stream of visitors, wanting to shake his hand, ask about his health, and generally shower him with admiration.

He was interviewed at length for *The Muslim*. He was asked about his own adventurous life, about the role of Muslim immigrants in Britain, about nationalism and the Islamic movement, about socialism in Pakistan, about student power, the problems of sighting the new moon for Ramadan, and, most important of all, about armed revolt. 'Do you think,' the Maulana was asked, 'that the Islamic state can be established by an armed revolt?' 'I do not think this is the right road for us to pursue,' he replied without a moment's hesitation. 'Such a policy, instead of producing any good, may prove to be highly harmful.' The Maulana elaborated: 'Even if you establish an Islamic state through armed revolution, it would not be possible to run the state and carry on its affairs in accordance with the Islamic way, for the simple reason that society and its different sections have not been properly prepared for the moral transformation that Islam wants. Armed revolution as a means to power is open to others as well – so there is a danger that Muslim countries will become ensnared in a vicious circle of revolutions and counter-revolutions and of conspiracies and counter-conspiracies. Moreover, to bring about armed revolution, you have to organize your movement on the pattern of secret societies. These have a temperament of their own. They admit to no dissent and disagreement. The voice of criticism is silenced; and free, fair and frank discussions become conspicuous by their absence. Another demand of the inner logic of secret societies is to permit workers to resort to deceit, lies, forgeries, frauds, bloodshed and many other things, which are forbidden in Islam. It is also in the nature of revolutions brought about by the bullet that they can be maintained only through the bullet. This produces a climate where a peaceful switch-over towards an Islamic order becomes virtually impossible.'

I was impressed. Here was a subtle reading behind the headlines of what was happening – and could happen – across the Muslim world, indeed the whole of the Third World. It sounded like a call to an alternative dimension of political, social, moral and ethical thinking, a way into a new dispensation, a passport to paradise.

So I started to read everything I could get hold of by Maulana Mawdudi. I found his most popular writing to be reformative, rather than revolutionary, concerned with improving the citizens' understanding of

Islam. He saw Islam as a total system that touched every aspect of an individual's life and shaped society as a whole. He placed a great deal of emphasis on character building, personal reformation of the individual, suggesting that change ultimately depends on increased personal piety initially unaided by structural reform; Islamic order is established in society only after the individuals themselves have been transformed.

But I soon encountered some serious problems. Mawdudi's portrayal of Islam as a total system, covering society, economy, politics and international relations, seemed a touch utopian. It was not evident to me that Islam, as we understood it, had all the necessary principles to tackle the dilemmas of the modern world. It was a debatable point, the point where I wanted more discussion and thought rather than assertion of unquestionable certainty. His arguments remained inconclusive, insufficiently tested against the challenging realities of contemporary society. While he suggested, again and again, that traditional scholars had lost touch with the modern world, Mawdudi himself, it seemed to me, was offering more of the same. For him, the Shariah – Islamic Law – was a ready-made framework which could solve all problems. There was nothing in his thought that could provide us with a way of gaining a fresh understanding of the worldview of Islam. Could it really be the case that an old system of law that had not been in effective operation for an entire society for hundreds of years could just be taken off the shelf and dusted down and then provide answers for complex questions about governance, development, modernity, questions that were by no means settled and the subject of earnest debate even in modern developed societies?

Most of all, I was deeply disturbed by Mawdudi's views on women. Here was the essential touchstone, the infallible indicator of a writer or thinker's position on the scale of reformative thought. The status and role of women in Islam, the fate allotted to half the Muslim people, was the iconic issue. It most clearly demonstrated any thinker's willingness to question the bounds of traditionalism as inherited and currently constituted in Muslim society. It was also an acid test of their stance towards and understanding of western society where the feminist movement was rapidly revising, rephrasing and rethinking the whole question of women's life chances. And it was here I found most explicitly that the Maulana seemed to have absolutely no understanding of the world I inhabited, let alone the world, outlook and attitudes of my mother and sister, nor of the diverse women of my acquaintance from schoolteachers, nurses, sundry officials and functionaries to classmates and fellow students. Despite all the string and sealing wax he uses to tie up his arguments, in such works as *Purdah* ('The Veil') and *The Status of Women*, the fact remained that he saw women as innately inferior, creatures who should be wrapped up in shrouds and confined within the four walls of a house because by their inherent nature they are a moral threat to the health of society! The more I read the more it became obvious that most of Mawdudi's opinions were uninformed, his reasoning rather shabby, and the utopia he had constructed just that: a non-place for non-people.

There were two other things that I found quite perplexing. Despite its emphasis on intellectual jihad (sustained struggle) and dedication to knowledge, many members of the Jamaat I met were positively ignorant, in the deepest sense of the word. And I was appalled at the guru syndrome that dominated the Jamaat-e-Islami. Mawdudi was not only the founder and lifelong leader of the movement, but the ever-present, ever-shining sun that illuminated everything its members did. I often wondered whether Khurshid Ahmad's narrow loyalty to his guru, his unflinching obedience to the vision of the founder, had not truncated his own intellectual growth, turning him into a rigid and mechanical devotee.

The other major component of the Islamic movement, which also courted us assiduously, was the Muslim Brotherhood. It was founded in Egypt in 1928 as a youth club by Hassan al-Banna, a young elementary school teacher. Al-Banna saw Islam as much more than religious observance. For him Islam was, as we students tended to repeat endlessly, a complete way of life in which religion and state were a single entity and the Qur'an and military jihad were two sides of the same coin. He made it a requirement for the members of the Brotherhood to add military training to their traditional Islamic education. By the time the Brotherhood was transformed into a political organization in 1936, some of its members were already participating in uprisings against Zionist settlements in Palestine. Al-Banna himself had a rather simplistic view of Islam. In *What is Our Message?*, the only pamphlet he seems to have written, he sees the development of Islam in five stages. The first stage is the era of weakness, defined as a time when the Muslim community is weak and 'a group amongst the noble and respected class' is in 'the servitude of a tyrant who is disobedient to Allah'. The second stage is that of leadership: now a leader emerges to challenge the rule of the tyrant. The third stage is confrontation between the forces of light and the forces of darkness. The fourth state is 'adherence to truth with patience, perseverance and tolerance in the face of disgrace'. And the final stage is triumph, when God delivers the faithful from their enemies. Al-Banna saw the final stage as the triumph of the Shariah – Islamic Law – which he believed to be absolute and perfect: 'the Islamic Shariah and the rules framed by Muslim jurists are such that many defects have been removed and all requirements have been met so that every need is satisfied'. He saw culture, in its multifarious forms, as anarchy to be rooted out from 'every road, in every place of assembly and in every winter and summer pleasure resort'.

While Al-Banna was father to the Muslim Brotherhood, its true intellectual spirit was Sayyid Qutb. Qutb was trained as an educational administrator but established a formidable reputation as a literary critic. He was the first critic to recognize the talents of Naguib Mahfouz, winner of the 1988 Nobel Prize for literature, and the two became close friends. Qutb was also close to Gamal Abdel Nasser, the leader of the revolution, who became President of Egypt in 1956. Sayyid Qutb was transformed, so the story goes, by a two-year sojourn in America in the late 1940s. In Colorado, he discovered an America far from the image he had acquired from the study of American literature and popular culture. He found Americans to be primitive: 'it is astonishing to realize, despite his advanced education and his perfectionism, how primitive the American really is in his views of life', he was to write later. 'His behaviour reminds us of the era of the caveman. He is primitive in the way he lusts after power, ignoring ideals and manners and principles.' While there was no lack of churches in Colorado, Qutb found Americans to be totally lacking in spirituality. Indeed, he noted, it was sometimes difficult to differentiate between churches and places of entertainment. By now, the Brotherhood was getting increasingly involved in violence. During the mid-1940s its members were implicated in terrorist activities inside Egypt; in December 1948 the then Egyptian Prime Minister, Mahmud Fahmi Nokrashi, was assassinated by a member of the organization; in retaliation, Hassan al-Banna was himself killed by government agents in Cairo in February 1949. Qutb was horrified at the ecstatic reception America gave to news of the assassination of al-Banna. Until this point, he had not totally identified himself with the Brotherhood; but his experiences in America were to prove decisive.

Sayyid Qutb's best work, *Social Justice in Islam*, was published while he was still in America. In it, Qutb paints a picture of Islam as a global civilization based on a law that 'consists of mercy, love, help and mutual responsibility between Muslims in particular and all human beings in general'. His emphasis is on social change which, he argues, can only be accomplished through political action. Social justice, he suggests, has to be based on freedom of conscience and human equality, and accomplished through economic justice. But those with wealth and power do not give up their ill-gotten gains easily. So jihad has to be an instrument of social justice. Islam prescribes 'holy war in the way of Allah', he writes, 'as a responsibility incumbent on every one who is able for it' because it brings 'justice and glory' to a society: 'Allah has purchased from the Believers their persons and their wealth, for the price of Paradise reserved for them; so they fight in the way of Allah, so they kill and are killed'. (The Qur'an, 9:111.) It was a thesis and philosophy not very different from the ones being advocated by the wavers of the *Little Red Book* and wearers of Che Guevara T-shirts. In my time there were those who graduated from protests and sit-ins on campus to outright urban guerrilla terrorism of the Baader–Meinhof and Simbionese Liberation Army variety. How much more likely, then, that Qutb resonated with Muslim students whose acquaintance with economic and social injustice was more intimate and direct?

Within a few years, Qutb had radicalized the whole Islamic movement in Egypt and his influence spread beyond the Arab world to the Indian Subcontinent and South-east Asia. But the Brotherhood's destiny was radically transformed on the fateful night of 26 October 1954 when a member of the organization attempted to assassinate Nasser as he spoke before an immense crowd in Alexandria. Nasser responded by summarily executing six conspirators and arresting over a thousand activists of the Brotherhood, including Qutb, who was sentenced to fifteen years' imprisonment.

In prison, Qutb, already in ill health, was regularly tortured. During his famous show trial before three judges, including future president Anwar Sadat, Qutb tore off his shirt to display the marks. He was released in 1964 only to be rearrested on charges of sedition. The prosecution's case was built largely on the inflammatory passages contained in Qutb's last book, *Milestones*. Written while he was in prison, the book was already in circulation, in manuscript form, before being published in Cairo in 1964. A truly appalling translation, complete with legions of typographical errors, was published in Kuwait and distributed free to members of FOSIS. My well-thumbed copy of the book seemed to suggest that his experiences in Nasser's prison had made Qutb an angry and vengeful man, who had lost all perspective. The entire world, Qutb now declared, including all Muslim countries, was the abode of *jahiliyya* – absolute ignorance. The Muslim community no longer existed; it had disintegrated into darkness, unbelief and ignorance. 'Islamic civilization' was now equated with the totality of humanity; human values could only be attained through Islamic civilization; and the rule of God's law must be the way of the world. There was no notion of difference, of any kind, in *Milestones*. Jihad was now all-out war between the Brotherhood and everyone else. Qutb was sentenced to death and hanged on 29 August 1966: 'I performed jihad for fifteen years until I earned this martyrdom.' On 6 October 1981, the members of the Muslim Brotherhood took their revenge by assassinating President Anwar Sadat.

The trials and tribulations of Sayyid Qutb resonated and had a very real meaning for us. Many older members of FOSIS had not only witnessed the events of Qutb's life but lived their own lives through them. We constantly read his commentaries on the Qur'an, *In the Shade of the Qur'an*, and chanted the slogans of the Brotherhood:

Allah is our objective.
The messenger is our leader.
The Qur'an is our law.
Jihad is our way.
Dying in the way of Allah is our highest hope.

Except, on reflection, mark me down as not keen on death. Definitely, I was one who preferred to explore the option to live for Allah, and understood the Divine not so much as my 'objective' as my Creator. And it was too much of a stretch of my imagination to see 'the Qur'an as our law' since law is a dynamic, changing institution and the Qur'an contains remarkably few legal injunctions. A book of eternal guidance, as the Qur'an describes itself, cannot be reduced to a fixed set of laws. And I remained convinced that there were other ways to solve problems besides militaristic jihad. Indeed, during the twenty-three years Muhammad was a Prophet he spent only a few months engaged in such jihad. All the rest of his life was an alternative kind of jihad, literally a word meaning exertion or effort, the effort to build a just society among the realities of his time and place. It was those more extensive efforts that, in my view, had more bearing and more to teach about how to tackle the kind of problems we faced in the modern world. When I thought about it, the mindless slogans appeared to me nothing more than a prescription for totalitarianism.

Most of the members of the Brotherhood I met verged on the boundaries of fanaticism. The sole exception was Said Ramadan, whom I liked very much; his deep passion and sharp intellect left its mark on everyone he met. But there was something in his eyes that was not quite right; something I detected in other members of the Muslim Brotherhood such as Mohammad Qutb, the younger brother of Sayyid Qutb, whose book, *Islam the Misunderstood Religion*, was very popular amongst students. What was that something? It became clear the day I met Ramadan on one of his visits to the FOSIS head office.

He had recently published an article in *The Muslim*. In 'A Lesson from the Battlefield', Said Ramadan recounts a dialogue between one of his friends and an Israeli officer. The friend was captured in the 1948 Arab–Israeli war. Just before his release, he meets the Israeli officer.

'Would you permit me,' he asks, 'to ask you about a matter for which I, as a soldier, could find no satisfactory explanation?'

'Please do. Perhaps I will be able to answer you,' replies the Israeli officer.

'Why did you not attack Sur Bahir?' Sur Bahir was a village near Jerusalem, surrounded on both sides by two strong settlements, Tell Buyut and Ramat Rahel.

'A good question. Do you want a *frank* answer?'

The friend nods agreement.

'We did not attack Sur Bahir because it contained a large force of volunteers from the Muslim Brotherhood.'

'What difference does that make? You often attacked other positions defended by much larger forces, under conditions more difficult for you.'

'The fact is that the volunteers of the Brotherhood are completely different from your regular troops. For them, fighting is not a duty which they fulfil within the bounds of tactics and of orders received, but a passion to which they devote themselves with wholehearted enthusiasm. In this respect, they are similar to our own soldiers who are fighting for the sake of Israel. But the difference between us and them is that we are fighting to found a national state to live in, whereas they want to die! To attack people who are not only unafraid of death but actually *aspire* to die with an enthusiasm bordering on madness, as if they were savage demons out to challenge mankind itself, to attack such people is like attacking a thicket full of wild beasts. It is a risk we prefer to avoid.'

'What do you think it is that has afflicted these people so that they are infatuated with death and have become transformed into a demonic force which defies all reason?'

'The magic effect of religion on the minds of simple people,' replies the Israeli officer. 'The poor wretches are still prey to those fertile delusions about paradise awaiting them after death, with milk and honey, wine and women . . . They present a danger not only to us but also to you, and to you in the first place . . .'

The friend tells Ramadan that he felt elated by the conversation, 'as if I was reborn. I realized the power of that terrible weapon which is stored in the concept of belief and martyrdom'. Ramadan tells his readers that the incident transformed his friend's life and he became a pious Muslim (and, by inference, a member of the Brotherhood). I had serious problems with this variety of piety. While acknowledging the bravery of the Brotherhood's fighters, I sided with the Israeli officer. 'Isn't the pursuit of death for the sake of death, even at the expense of tactics on the battlefield, a sign of cultivated unwisdom, born of some men's despair of their own enlightenment?' I asked Ramadan on his visit to the UK.

'No. No. No,' he said. 'It's a sign that faith has become the centre and axis of one's being.'

'But it is a blind faith, devoid of all rationality. Is the Israeli officer not correct in pointing out that individuals fired by such an insane notion of faith will turn on their own kind, judging the faith of their brothers to be less worthy than their own?' Ramadan did not reply.

'If faith is turned into a "terrible weapon",' I continued, 'what is there that prevents it from being misused like all weapons? And, as a weapon, does faith not cease to be faith?'

'It is all about the power of faith,' Ramadan replied. 'The eyes of the Brothers shine with the light of certainty and faith.'

His own words unravelled the mystery. This is what I detected in his eyes; and the eyes of so many members of the Muslim Brotherhood: 'the light of certainty and faith'. Except faith is never certain; by its very nature it hovers constantly near doubt. My own faith went up and down like a yo-yo! As an imperfect individual, I thought, I could only have imperfect, but dynamic, faith that keeps me constantly on the verge of doubt. Only perfect people can have perfect, certain faith. And that was my problem with the members of the Brotherhood. They saw themselves as perfect; they were certain of everything. In short, they were ideologues: Islam, for them, was an ideology that allowed for no imperfections, no deviation, and, in the final analysis, no humanity. This is why I found so many of them so repugnant.

The writings of the leaders and followers of the Muslim Brotherhood and Jamaat-e-Islami were the basis of the debates and activism that motivated my generation. More fundamentally, they spoke to me as a

Muslim, the core around which all my complex identity existed. By the negative impressions and unanswered questions I gathered from them they intimated and threw into relief the kind of solutions I wanted to find. What I had to resolve was what kind of Muslim I could be; and how to be a Muslim for and in the better world my generation was committed to creating.

After my experience with the *Tablighis*, and my new thoughts about paradise, I turned to the one place Muslims always turn to in times of crisis: the Qur'an. Could I find any answers there?

Chapter 3

A TALL FRUIT-BEARING TREE

During my childhood, I, like most young Muslims, was taught to read the Qur'an by my mother. It is the way the Word of God becomes part of the fabric of one's growing consciousness. It began in Pakistan, where the sound of Islam fills the air: the muezzin's call to prayer punctuates the passage of the day, marking the movement of light from dawn to dusk and into night. Prayer itself consists in remembrance of God's Word, repetition of verses of the Qur'an, through one's mind, voice and body. In this atmosphere mothers begin by teaching simple phrases of the Arabic scripture before children celebrate learning to read their first verse of the Holy Book.

The daily sessions of learning the Qur'an spanned the momentous removal that brought my family from Pakistan to Hackney in London where the air, the light, the sounds and passage of the day were different. I was nine years old and the normality of Islam as warp and weft of everyone's daily life was removed. Now only the private space at home found regular time for the Word. My parents' expectations for my education in Islam did not alter with the alteration we made in our lives. Every evening, in the cramped quarters of the ground-floor flat in the terraced house in Hilsea Street, our first British home, after I had finished my homework, my mother would sit with me for half an hour or so, taking me from verse to verse of the Qur'an, correcting my pronunciation, occasionally explaining the meaning of a word or a verse. By the time I was fourteen, I had read the whole of The Book in original Arabic. There was a small celebration to mark the occasion; and from then on I was expected to read it frequently myself and consult it whenever I felt the need. For me, as for every believing Muslim, the Qur'an is not just another book on the shelf. It is the Word of God, a direct contact with Allah Himself. In essence, this is the definition of a Muslim. It is the Book, the Qur'an, the unchanging source of the message of God to which Muslims turn for inspiration, guidance and to seek answers to pressing problems.

I well remember my mother frequently quoting the words of Muhammad Iqbal, the great poet of the Indian Subcontinent, that you should read the Qur'an as if it was revealed to you. So it is to the Qur'an I turned for an answer to the matter of paradise, the pertinent but newly perceived set of questions, paradoxes and dilemmas. What exactly did the source of my religion have to say about paradise?

This is a delicate matter. I had performed the essential rite of passage by reading the Qur'an in its unchanging Arabic. But along with the vast majority of Muslims in the world I am not a native Arabic speaker. My mother tongue is Urdu, that glorious fusion that flourished in Mughal India, a compound of Turkish, Farsi, Sanskrit and Hindi with a rich infusion of Arabic words. In preparation for our relocation to England my father made dedicated efforts to encourage me to master English. To this end he provided me with a large supply of classic novels published in a series shamelessly glorying in the title 'The Great Books of Mankind', the sort that furnish a well-rounded English book collection. My existence is rich with words yet finding answers in the Qur'an brings one face to face with the question of language and understanding. It is not quite the impasse it seems. Indeed, over the years I have come to the conclusion it is a prudential advantage. Approaching the Qur'an through translations makes understanding a struggle with language and words in quest of their meaning. Far from being a passive process it becomes an exertion of the brain cells, an active engagement to gain insight as well as information.

I read the Qur'an in translation; and the translation I used most frequently was by Mohammed Marmaduke Pickthall, one of those eccentrics Britain produced in abundance during the era of Empire. He was a novelist who converted to Islam, became a polemicist and produced the first translation of the Qur'an by a Muslim whose mother tongue was English. I checked Pickthall's translation for the verses on paradise. The precise Arabic word for paradise – *firdous* – occurs only twice in the Qur'an, though the English word 'paradise' occurs more frequently in translations, a function of the wrestle with words. On one occasion, *firdous* is used in conjunction with gardens ('Verily, as for those who attain to faith and do righteous deeds – the gardens of paradise will be there to welcome them', 18:107); and on the other it stands alone ('[these are the heirs] who will inherit paradise; there they will abide', 23:11). Of course, that is not all the Qur'an has to offer on the subject; rather, just as I had always assumed, the idea of paradise is implied, suggested, inferred, described and interconnected in multiple ways throughout the text as a whole. Perhaps that's why the *Tablighis'* direct approach homing in on paradise in obsessive and splendid isolation had given me such a jolt. The Qur'an uses the metaphor of the garden a number of times to signify paradise. Verse 35 of Chapter 13 – Surah Ar Ra'd, 'Thunder' as translated by Pickthall, reads: 'A similitude of the Garden which is promised unto those who keep their duty [to Allah]: Underneath it rivers flow; its food is everlasting, and its shade; this is the reward of those who keep their duty . . .' I asked my mother what she understood from this verse.

'The description of paradise as a garden with rivers flowing in it is clearly stated as a parable,' she said. 'But the use of the word *jannah* – garden – for the abode of bliss has a deeper significance, a significance that we must tease out, since the true blessings of paradise cannot be perceived by physical senses, by us in this life, for it is not of this world.' My mother relished, as she always does, the wrestle with words and meanings. She paused for thought. 'As the Qur'an tells us elsewhere, "no soul knows what refreshment of the eyes is hidden for them: a reward for what they did". The Prophet himself provided an explanation of this verse when he said: "Allah says I have prepared for my righteous servants what no eye has seen and no ear has heard, and what the mind of man has not conceived".'

'But this doesn't really help me to answer my immediate question,' I said impatiently. 'What if I was looking for a few blessings of paradise here and now?'

'Then look at the similes within the parable.'

'Such as?'

'Take the word *zill*,' she said. While I was struggling with the translation, she was trying to grasp the significance of the original Arabic.

'You mean the word for shade?'

'*Zill* does mean shade,' Mumsey allowed, 'and the Qur'an does say that *zill* is one of the blessings of paradise.' She paused to recall an appropriate reference: ' "Those who kept their duty are amongst shade and fountains". But *zill* does not in all its Qur'anic usages mean shade. Indeed, we are clearly told that there is no sun in paradise: "They will see therein neither sun nor intense cold". There is thus no question of shade as such.'

With the skill of an F.R. Leavis, the aplomb of a master of literary criticism, my mother was very good at confusing me. Once again, I thought, she has succeeded ably. She saw my thoughts reflected on my face.

'How many times I have told you,' she said. 'The Qur'an is an integrated text.' My mother was becoming more proto-postmodern in her literary criticism by the moment. 'You must not approach it atomistically, picking a verse here, and a verse there. You have to approach it holistically.'

'Yes,' I said in the matter-of-fact way one does to oft-repeated conventional wisdom whose meaning has not yet penetrated one's inner recesses.

'*Think* about it. In the context of the Qur'anic paradise, *zill* signifies protection. The idea underlying the notion of shade is *protection*. The garden of paradise that the Qur'an speaks of also provides "everlasting food". Again this is a simile. What need would we have of food in heaven anyway! The groceries being indicated here refer to the sustenance we need for our inner self. That's why prayer is also called sustenance.'

The discussion had taken positively the wrong turn. My mother had a knack of being both proto-postmodern and unfailingly Socratic in directing all arguments to a simple, indisputable assertion: I was quite neglectful of my prayers. It was time to use another of her favourite tactics, the argument from authority, to steer the conversation back to more comfortable terrain.

'But one cannot be sustained by prayer alone,' I said. 'I mean you'd soon be climbing the wall if you had to eat dal [lentils, the staple diet of the poor] every day! Anyway, isn't *ilm* – knowledge – also a form of prayer? Did the Prophet not say, "an hour's contemplation is better than a year's worship"? "To spend more time in learning is better than spending more time in praying"? Can we not be sustained by the pursuit of *ilm*?'

'For sure,' her response was immediate. 'The fruits of paradise are not the kind of fruits you buy at the grocer's but the fruits of deeds done. And *ilm* is crucial in distinguishing good from bad deeds. So we can say the sustenance on offer in the garden of paradise is achieved through knowledge.' Mumsey picked up steam on this new heading. 'And this interpretation receives further support from the metaphor of fountains. The garden of paradise is full of fountains – the fountains of knowledge.'

'So it is settled,' she said with finality after taking a deep breath. 'If you want to transform this wretched earth into a paradise you need to seek shade, something that can protect you, and the sustenance of knowledge that leads to good deeds, the seeds which grow the trees of the next life.'

Throughout this conversation my father remained silent. His speciality was sitting quietly and fuming. Sometimes his existential condition would take on physical manifestation. Plumes of smoke would emanate from his person and wreathe his favourite chair in swirling mists. It was merely incidental that these emanations originated in his pipe, which he never learned to light properly, and which, mercifully, he gave up after his first heart attack. He could remain dormant for long periods, but it was always folly to assume his inner fire had cooled; he was never inert. His seismic cycle was linked in comfortable, connubial fashion to the pattern of my mother's discourse. He would sit there, an Etna occasionally sending out smoke signals but otherwise just forming the scenic backdrop, until my mother had finished. At which point his tectonic plates would realign, causing a perturbation in his magma chamber that would generate a potent lava flow. His eruptions were made only to contradict – and every now and then to disparage – what she had said. Like an assured vulcanologist I sat quietly waiting for his intervention.

'To live the metaphor of shade,' he began after some time, 'you need two things: a teacher, like a tall and strong fruit-bearing tree, under whose protection you acquire the knowledge of classical disciplines. If you are seeking a profession, like law or medicine, you go to an institution where you are educated and provided with appropriate skills. If you are seeking paradise, you have to go to someone who is qualified enough to show you the right direction.'

I expected my father to say something like this. My father's life had been made up of journeys, relocations, disjunctions and radical shifts both physical and spiritual. When he was in his thirties, he acquired a *peer*, a guru, a mystic teacher; and he remained loyal to him for much of his life. A picture of his *peer* would always adorn one of the walls of his room. And occasionally, during moments of solitude, he would read the *shajrah* – the chain of names that connected his teacher to the Prophet Muhammad. He would start with his own *peer*, 'the clear Proof of the Beauty of Islam, the Perfect Teacher', and work backwards citing names of saints and mystic teachers, ending with Prophet Muhammad, and Jibreel (Gabriel) 'The trusted archangel', and 'The One whose sublimity is majestic and whose Names and Attributes are utterly pure, God, the Lord of the Worlds'. The expected statement was, nevertheless, utterly unexpected in its import. Through the differences in their ways of thinking and expressing themselves I had uncovered a rare topic on which my parents were in agreement.

Where my mother's discourse was a fencing match in which she relished the cut and thrust, the parry and riposte of literary dissection, my father's discourse delighted in narrative. He liked to tell stories – mostly of saints and scholars.

'But a good teacher is not enough. You must also know the best way to learn, which reminds me of a very instructive story about Imam al-Ghazali,' he continued. 'The great author of *The Book of Knowledge* went to a university in Gurgan at the south-east corner of the Caspian

Sea, where, during his four-year course, he studied metaphysics, philosophy, mathematics – everything that could be learned there. On his way back from Gurgan, he joined a caravan, as individual travellers had to do in those days. The caravan was attacked by a set of Bedouins who robbed them of everything. Al-Ghazali had kept all his course notes in a little leather bag, which was about all he had, and they took that too. So he went to the Bedouin chief, caught his stirrups and begged him to return this bag, saying that it was of no use to the Bedouins who could not read and that it contained all the knowledge he had gained in Gurgan. The Bedouin chief threw the bag at him and said, "I thought you went to the university to learn, not to take notes." Al-Ghazali was very struck with this and went back to the university for a further four years, taking no notes at all but really thinking about it all to such good purpose that he became one of the leading scholars of the Islamic civilization.'

'I get the message,' I said. 'But what is the other thing that I need?'

'A man was visiting the Sacred Mosque in Mecca. As he went round and round the Kaa'ba, in the manner prescribed, he started to pray aloud. "O God," he said, "Grant me a few good friends. O God, grant me a few good friends." Another man heard his prayer and cornered him. "This is the House of Allah," he said. "You should be asking for forgiveness; you should be asking God to grant you paradise. Not for a few good friends." "You need forgiveness," the man replied, "You ask for forgiveness. I need good friends. Only good friends will keep me away from bad deeds. This is the only way I know of getting into paradise."' My father paused to make sure I understood the parable before adding: 'Find yourself a few good and loyal friends to protect you.'

By now I had realized that neither the Jamaat-e-Islami nor the Muslim Brotherhood was going to provide me with the shade and sustenance I looked for. Their pre-packaged unwisdom left me cold. I read avidly, read according to recommendations of my FOSIS friends, and read whatever I could find. But my reading had no real direction; the kind of knowledge that would take me to paradise seemed elusive. Then, I met Jaffar Shaikh Idris.

Jaffar was a Sudanese theologian working on a doctorate in

philosophy at Cambridge. A tall man, his face bore what he called 'beauty marks': tribal scars consisting of two vertical cuts on each cheek. If such marks were intended to inspire awe and intimidation, on Jaffar they added to his overwhelming aura of humility and warmth. He smiled generously; and his eyes, far from reflecting monolithic certainty, refracted a mischievous curiosity, one that combined good humour and innocence with the alertness of a deceptively sharp intellect. When he dressed in the conventional Sudanese robes of a scholar – loose, flowing white cotton kaftan topped by a white turban – he looked positively angelic. I imagined him as the man in the famous tradition of the Prophet, 'all dressed in white, who showed no sign of fatigue', and who asked: 'What is Islam?' At the end of our first meeting I asked Jaffar: 'Can you provide me the shade I seek?'

'What do you think?' he enquired bemusedly. 'Am I a tree?'

'Yes,' I replied. 'I see you as a tall and strong fruit-bearing tree under whose protection I can acquire the knowledge of classical disciplines.'

'A teacher seeks students,' he said. 'And if the student thinks the teacher is a tree, then let the teacher provide the shade.'

Thus began my education in traditional Islamic disciplines, the writings of the masters of Islamic law, philosophy and exegesis. It seemed the logical next step. On all sides there were organizations and movements urging the fundamentals of Islam as their own panacea, claiming authority over a tradition they presented in their own image for their own ends. It was time to examine in detail what tradition spoke unmediated in its own words.

I established an *usrah* group. The word *usrah* literally means 'family': it is a study group reflecting the moral and social solidarity of a family. During the 1960s and 1970s *usrah* groups became a popular institution amongst various components of the Islamic movement; the Muslim Brotherhood in particular encouraged their formation amongst its members. It was not the fashion but the teacher, I suspected, that mattered. A few friends joined me; and we met weekly, in turn at each other's homes. Jaffar became our *Nageeb* – leader, teacher, tree – under whose guidance we studied the classical texts. He suggested we should follow the instruction of the Prophet and walk according to the steps of our weakest; so our study programme was regularly readjusted to reflect the needs of the least knowledgeable amongst us – which often turned out to be me.

We started with the obligatory things: the Qur'an and Hadith, the records of the sayings and actions of the Prophet Muhammad. Muslims make a sharp distinction between the Qur'an, which is the Word of God, and Hadith, which are the words of a mortal human, although a divinely inspired one. Reports of the Prophet's words and deeds began to circulate in oral and written form almost immediately after his death. They became a yardstick by which the expanding Muslim community, that so rapidly assumed control over vast swathes of territory beyond Arabia, debated, determined and set policy, and evaluated its actions. By the ninth century the vast corpus of reports were a subject of intense study and were collected in what could be called the canonical editions that remain a basic resource of all Islamic scholarship. So, we studied famous classical commentaries on the Qur'an and then moved to the great collections of Hadith compiled by Imam al-Bukhari, who died in 869, and Imam Muslim, who died in 875, and the later compendium produced by Al-Baghawi in the twelfth century and revised in the fourteenth as *Mishkat Al-Masabih*. We studied *The Life of Muhammad* by Ibn Ishaq, who was born in 704 and became the Prophet's first biographer in our modern sense of the term. And other histories of the eighth and ninth centuries. Then, we read commentaries on commentaries. After that, we began to tackle the classical jurists. Then, we moved on to philosophy and read theologians and thinkers who flourished in the Golden Age from the ninth to the twelfth centuries and whose works had an immense impact not only on Muslim civilization but on Europe as well. When Jaffar could not attend the meeting, another Sudanese scholar, Tayeb Abedin, took his place.

The *usrah* meetings always started with a reading of a particular verse (or verses) of the Qur'an, followed by the consultation of two or more famous commentaries on the meaning of the relevant verse(s). We would then look at the life of the Prophet Muhammad and his authentic Hadith to discover if they could illuminate the verse(s) further. As this programme of study developed and Jaffar took us through the biography of the compilers of Hadith and the great Imams who codified Islamic Law, I encountered an outlook that was startlingly fresh. It became evident that these great luminaries were not at all like the contemporary leaders of the Islamic movement who had been opening and then foreclosing paradises on me. These authentic voices that became traditional authority were more critical and less certain of their opinions. They thought and wrote as men of their own changing times, not as monuments of imperishable stone.

I was deeply impressed by how gentle and moderate the classical scholars really were. Take Bukhari, the compiler of one of the major collections of authentic Hadith. An exceptionally polite and mild-mannered person, Bukhari in fact pioneered the science of Hadith criticism, a vast field of research combining ethics, morality, sociology, law, politics, economics and logic into a unique discipline of intellectual inquiry. At the centre of Hadith criticism is the notion of *isnad*, or attestation. It concerns tracing each link in the chain of narrators, those who reported a saying or action of the Prophet. Nothing was taken for granted, critical inquiry required investigating the qualities of each link in the chain as regards memory, accuracy, truthfulness, examining their competence as reliable witnesses whose testimony would be accepted in the court of civil law and tracing the chain right back to Prophet Muhammad himself. But even that was not good enough. Time and geographical circumstances had to be investigated to establish that it was physically possible for individuals in the chain of narrators to have met. Moreover, further investigations were needed to ensure that the Hadith was not against reason or established historical fact; or against the teachings of the Qur'an; or that it did not express a partisan view; or that it did not contain warning of heavy punishment for ordinary lapses of conduct or mighty rewards for ordinary acts of piety.

Bukhari, who had a passion for archery, began his study of Hadith as a young boy (in his native city – Bokhara, as his name testifies). By the age of sixteen, which would have been about the year 825, he had memorized early texts, knew the chain of narrators of thousands of Hadith and had learned the biography of the transmitters. Then he began to travel extensively, meeting scholars, collecting Hadith and discussing the techniques of Hadith criticism. He would take a bath and pray every time he examined a particular Hadith – given that he had collected around 600,000, it is not surprising it took him sixteen years to compile his collection of authentic Hadith: the *Sahih*. Often, as one of his students reported, he would wake up a number of times in the middle of the night, light his lamp with a flint, make some notes, and then go back to sleep. The student asked: 'Why did you not call me instead of suffering all these things alone?' 'Because', Bukhari replied, 'you are young and I did not wish to disturb your sleep.' Of all the Hadith he examined, he included about 7,000 in his book and labelled only 2,602 as authentic. Having compiled the *Sahih* he was still not satisfied; he revised the text three times. When it was finally published, Bukhari's reputation spread far and wide. In Baghdad, where he had settled, scholars queued up to test his prodigious memory. On one occasion ten men were assembled to stage a kind of quiz show: each was told to recite ten Hadith, but mix up the *isnad* and the content. Bukhari patiently listened to the recitals, on each occasion saying he did not recognize the Hadith. But he was definitely not the weakest link. When they had finished, he repeated the performance placing the correct *isnad* with the corrected Hadith.

Scholarship, in its authentic traditional guise, was definitely more than prodigies of memory; that was merely the technique – the computer software of the times – on which thought depended. It was the quality of the thought on offer that was capturing my imagination. Consider Imam Malik. The School of Islamic Law this Medinan scholar inspired is said to be the most rigid, extreme and uncompromising. Yet Malik himself was anything but rigid and free from doubt. He was asked by the Caliph to write a book that would be distributed throughout the Muslim world as a guide to Islamic law. Anyone differing from this book could then be prosecuted. Malik rejected the idea outright, declaring his opinions were not certain. Anyway, he said, the Companions of the Prophet were to be found all over the Muslim world, and people could learn from these individuals, rather than from a single book. Imam Malik insisted there was more than one way to practise Islam; and that people should be free to go to any fountain of knowledge they deemed fit.

Much the same can be said of Imam Shafi'i, a disciple of Imam Malik, who went on to establish his own School of Thought. The story goes that Shafi'i went to the governor of Medina with a letter of introduction from the governor of Mecca, demanding an audience with Malik. The governor took Shafi'i to Malik's house, and Malik, impressed by his intelligence, took the young man on as one of his students. Shafi'i, a handsome and generous young man who gave most of his earnings to the poor, remained in Medina until Malik's death – by which time he was a brilliant jurist in his own right. After visiting Iraq, where the jurists followed the School established by Imam Hanafi, another mild-mannered individual who favoured personal reasoning rather than total reliance on Hadith and analogy. Shafi'i concluded that Maliki theories had many weaknesses. But after debating with Hanafi scholars, he concluded that the Hanafi School too was flawed. He devoted the last years of his life to producing a synthesis of the two Schools of Thought which appeared as *Al-Shafi'is Risala*. After a life of debating and challenging received opinions, Shafi'i, who never shied away from disagreeing with anyone, died at the hands of followers of Imam Malik who beat him to death. The legal opinions of these scholars, the substance that forms the body of Islamic Law, was never meant to be absolute, comprehensive or eternal, let alone the ultimate understanding of what constitutes the Law in Islam. They themselves saw, and emphasized, that their personal opinions were just opinions, which they changed frequently, and never intended to be Eternal Law. To claim, as for example Hassan al-Banna did, that the Imams had solved all problems for all time, amounts to attributing divine authority to gentle, unassuming, unsure men. Who can say that Islamic Law, as it exists, is the final word on everything?

Jaffar carefully avoided the differences in various Schools of Thought and stayed away from controversial issues. 'Learn the basics,' he would say, 'then you can judge for yourself.' When we had covered the 'fundamentals', the *usrah* sessions became a forum for questions and answers and general discussion on the nature of belief. Jaffar would sit on a chair, surrounded by his students sitting in a circle on the floor. He would begin the session with a proposition and ask one of the students to defend and another to oppose it. Sometimes we would end with a debate in which Jaffar was on one side and the students on the other.

By the time Jaffar returned to the Sudan, he had negotiated our path to a reasonably good grounding in classical thought. I owe an immense debt to this gentle giant who opened my mind to a sustaining diet of critical thought. And his educational influence was not solely confined to classical Islamic scholarship. He studied philosophy under Karl Popper and was just as erudite and insightful on the currents of contemporary thought, adept at relating his classical Islamic scholarship to these latest trends. When one debated with Jaffar one was not compartmentalized but liberated to consider the great questions of human existence with tools refined from multiple discourses ancient and modern, Islamic and western. Why was a teacher of his calibre not elevated to a fountain head, leading a prestigious academic institution, and made the protective shade and teacher for a generation desperately in need of knowledge and skill in critical consciousness? But Jaffar's influence was all too limited; indeed, the young Jaffar I knew in London seemed to me to be quite a different proposition from the one I met years later, after he had taken up a teaching position in Saudi Arabia. What Jaffar had to offer was deeply unfashionable. It was a path less travelled that languished, overgrown and neglected, when it should have become a main road, the high road. From the shade of my Sudanese fruit-bearing tree it became increasingly apparent that collectively, my group of Islamist friends were short on two things: self-doubt and forgiveness. The first led many to see the world in black and white. The second sowed the seeds of discord amongst us.

My alienation from FOSIS, and from the Islamic movement, centred around the question of absolute certainty. Doubts arose when *The Muslim* published the 'unanimous verdict of the Pakistani ulema' – a fatwa – that socialism is *kufr* (unbelief) and that 'any help rendered to a socialist is *haram*' (forbidden). The word *kufr* literally means 'obliterating, covering' or 'concealing benefits received' or being 'ungrateful to God'. But in contemporary parlance *kufr* has also come to signify 'the enemy' and the term is often used to differentiate 'Us' from 'Them'; to divide the world into two perpetually warring blocs. I just did not, could not, see the world in such black and white terms. I had no problem with the premise that many socialists did not believe in

God; but how could that mean one should regard them as an enemy or that working with them should be expressly 'forbidden'?

Indeed, throughout my mid-twenties, I led a double life. During the week I was an 'Islamic activist' in the sense that I circulated among the various activities of FOSIS and the doings of the Muslim community this led me to engage in. But at weekends I became a socialist, active in the Hackney Citizens' Rights Group. I manned an 'advice stall' in the Ridley Road market every Sunday. Later, I got involved with a local project that helped establish a youth club called Centreprise, which later became a thriving community centre. Weekdays or weekends, I met and mingled with idealist young people like myself, all with a burning desire to change the world for the better. I shared the goals of my socialist friends of fighting poverty, structural injustices and the abuses of class and racism. How could these goals not qualify as Islamic in the purest sense, even if that was not the motivation of my socialist collaborators? Was Islam a test of blood line, a natural endowment handed out by the accident of one's birth; or was it, as I believed and as Jaffar's teaching had encouraged me to think, a moral quality to be discerned according to criteria of right and wrong, beneficial or harmful, better or worse for the fate of individuals and society as a whole? However, the absolute certainty of the brothers influenced by the movement led them to declare that associating with *kufr* was itself *kufr*. There was even a new *kufr*, thundered an article in *The Muslim*, the *kufr* of condoning *kufr*: 'The choice is very plain. One is either on "good terms" with Allah and His faithful servants, or on good terms with *kufr* . . . The division is clear-cut and cannot be blurred or smudged: Islam and *kufr*, like light and darkness, cannot coexist in the same place.' Not for these brothers the reality of quantum space, the reality of my world, the one I inhabit across belongings, of being everywhere at one and the same time.

I could not enter their cordon sanitaire. I imagined God to be a socialist, rather than a capitalist: this surely was a logical consequence of both the attributes of the Divine and the guidance commended to us. The potency of socialism was that it offered people a convenient, circumscribed, political vehicle, a means to follow and establish the ideals and teaching of religion, the Message, in the context of the modern world. So I didn't see the choice in such 'plain' terms. Indeed the terms offered seemed abysmally short on both rational thought and understanding. Neither did I believe, as the article went on to argue, that 'all the heads of all the countries of the world today, including the Muslim countries, are *kuffar* [unbelievers]. They, as well as all others who freely associate with them, aiding and abetting them in ruling contrary to what Allah has directed, and those who fail to denounce them as such, are all disbelievers, oppressors and debauched.' Surely there were some men on this earth, despite their less than certain beliefs, who were not disbelievers, oppressors and debauched? By such standards who was there pure enough to consort with? Was I the only one who heard the distant rumble of the tumbrel, or perceived over the horizon the first glimmer of the purge that would consume even those currently considered fit to compose the ranks of the elect? People with absolute certainty have an absolute passion for not being forgiving. I was soon educated in the enormity of this truism when, as General Secretary of FOSIS, I published what should have been the innocuous, underwhelming and entirely inoffensive *The Muslim Student's Guide to Britain*.

During my tenure as General Secretary, the President of FOSIS was a Welsh Muslim studying international relations at the University of Kent in Canterbury. Dawud Rosser-Owen had converted to Islam while serving with the army in Malaysia. But he hated being called a 'convert': I am not a convert, he would say, I have only returned to my natural state. 'I was born in a naturally good and pure state, free from all blemish, in the state of Islam,' he would reply to anyone who asked: 'When did you embrace Islam?' 'It was my parents who made me a Christian. By embracing Islam and becoming a Muslim I have simply returned to my natural disposition. So, I am a returnee – not a convert.' Rosser-Owen traced his lineage to the long history of distinguished British Muslim 'returnees'. Indeed, his goal was to establish a community consisting exclusively of white newcomers to Islam. He spoke fondly of the century-old community of Yemeni Muslims in Cardiff, who were sailors on ships coming into the docks, and who settled just off Wharf Road. They had converted many to Islam. They married local Welsh girls, who became Muslims, and a thriving community developed, occupying three or four complete streets and

with its own mosque (an old chapel converted to look like a mosque –
even on the outside). He frequently mentioned a British Muslim called
Quilliam who established a community in Liverpool in the 1880s. He
once caught me reading *Arabian society in the middle ages: Studies from
the Thousand and one nights* by the famous nineteenth-century British
Orientalist Edward William Lane. 'You may think he is a good writer,'
he told me. 'But he showed fanaticism and intolerance towards British
Muslims. He went out of his way to write vituperative articles against
Quilliam. He got Christian authorities so worked up against Quilliam
that they launched a crusade against him and his group.' But the English
Muslim convert he identified with most was Lord Headley al-Farooq,
the man who established the Woking Mosque in Surrey. Rosser-Owen
himself behaved very much like a lord: expecting other (non-white)
Muslims to run errands for him and show deference to him. And it
seemed to me that I did most of the work, while Rosser-Owen stood
there scratching his beard.

The point was far more mundane. Forget for a moment the wrongs
of history or the global predicament of Muslims everywhere, our office
was constantly bombarded with urgent requests for the address of
prayer places, halal butchers, reliable restaurants and other needs
essential to the quality of life of overseas Muslim students. The answer
to all the big questions of our time seemed to hinge on the bare
necessities of keeping body and soul together. So Rosser-Owen and I
decided to put all that we knew into a booklet. The *Guide* was a modest
success in keeping with its eminently modest, utilitarian objective.
However, we soon discovered, thanks to the omniscience of some of our
more circumspect brothers, that many of the halal meat shops we had
listed were not actually selling halal meat; neither were many of our
'reliable restaurants' all that reliable. It was no good being utilitarian if
you could not at the same time be punctilious – and never, on any
account, believe anything written on a shop sign. The senior FOSIS
brotherhood demanded we pulp the book instantly. Unable to believe
that our trusting innocence, even if it was wrong, could actually consign
anyone to perdition or imperil the entirety of Muslim civilization as we
wished it to become, we argued for a new, revised edition. The hatred
our *Guide* had generated was quite unimaginable to me: copies of the

Guide with pages marked with black crosses were frequently found on my desk. Stern judgement applied not only to the *Guide*; now I was treated as inherently unreliable. An inner cabal of brothers sat in judgement on this weightiest of matters and barred me from editing *The Muslim* and, as befits such purging, my name was duly expunged from history, so that the issues I did edit do not carry my name!

I continued to work for FOSIS for a number of years as I continued my education as a postgraduate student. But the incident of the infamous *Guide* left a bitter taste. If such rigour attached to such a little thing, what, I wondered, would the brothers make of my other imperfections? I had reached my conclusion on the strictures of the Brotherhood and Jamaat but I could not withdraw from the body of Muslim students any more than from the British Muslim community or the worldwide community of Muslims, the *ummah*: they were part of my belonging. My quest was about finding new ways to relate to them that offered prospects of change for the better all round. Then, one day while discussing the nature of *kufr*, Rosser-Owen quoted a verse by an Arabic poet: 'So long as belief and unbelief are not perfectly equal, no man can be a true Muslim.' He went on to suggest I would be much happier with a different, 'less arid', more tolerant and humane variety of Islam. So I agreed to accompany him on a visit to Sheikh Nazim.

Chapter 4

THE MYSTERIES OF MYSTICISM

There was a lot of mysticism about in the 1970s; it was trendy. Any and all mystic traditions chimed with the desire of the peace and love generation for a gentler, more forgiving and indulgent outlook on life, a more esoteric, yet simpler, vision of existence. Mysticism, or more appropriately its Islamic variant, Sufism, was part of both my heritage and my upbringing. My great-great-grandfathers, I was told by my parents, were notable Sufis. I took this to be a general state of affairs for all Muslims: Sufism is such an integral part of Islam that it would be difficult to find a Muslim family, almost anywhere in the world, that does not boost a fully blown mystic in its lineage. I grew up, like so many Muslim children, listening to stories of prophets and saints on my mother's lap. When I learned to read, I read stories from the Masnavi of Jalaluddin Rumi, saint, mystic and poet of the thirteenth century; then graduated to the enthralling *Conference of the Birds* by Fari ud-Din Attar, the twelfth-century Persian mystic. My parents' room was full of mystical works in Urdu – discourses, stories, poems – and I read them liberally. But it was my father who really pushed me towards Sufism. I had seen his own life revolve round a Sufi Sheikh who had clearly taught him much. Maybe a mystical teacher would take me beyond the classical education I had received from Jaffar?

So, despite my questioning nature, I was drawn – almost naturally – towards Sufism. Dawud Rosser-Owen endlessly filled my ears with talk of the many 'miracles' his Sufi Master performed: a gaze from the Sheikh is enough to melt any heart; people embraced by the Sheikh see the Prophet in dreams; junkies and tramps convert to Islam within minutes of meeting him; his devotees, running into millions, include presidents, prime ministers, sultans and princes. They were not unlike the stories my father told of his own Master. I agreed to go and see his Sheikh, and for good measure decided to allow my younger brother to tag along. With Rosser-Owen as my guide, an enjoyable reversal of the colonial motif I thought, we hiked off . . . all the way to Newington Green in north London.

Sufism has a long and distinguished history in Islam. The first Sufi is said to have been the great ninth-century saint, Rabiah al-Basri, originator of the doctrine of 'disinterested love of God', which she made the basis of her entire life. The word 'sufi' comes from the Arabic word *suf* or wool: the rough woollen clothing worn by early Sufis who emphasized simplicity and lived an austere life. Conventional wisdom has it Sufism emerged as a reaction against the austere Puritanism of those obsessed with the minutiae of the Shariah. But many Sufi Orders insist that the Shariah is an essential part of *tasawwuf*, the technical term for Sufi mysticism. Sufis see themselves as being on a spiritual path to God; the journey, referred to as the *tariqah*, eventually taking them close to God in paradise. But this intimacy with God is attained not just after death in the Hereafter. It is also possible, by following a strict discipline, to experience this closeness, this paradise, while one is alive. This, in essence, they argue, is the purpose of creation. In the early days, Sufism was not recognized as a separate path but was identified with Islam proper. All Sufi Orders went back either to Abu Bakr, the closest companion of the Prophet and his immediate successor as Caliph, or to Ali, the Prophet's cousin and the fourth Caliph of Islam. Most of the classical Sufis, such as the tenth-century mystic Al-Junayd and the twelfth-century Indian Master Abd al-Qadir al-Jilani, acquired fame throughout the Muslim world in their lifetimes. Imam Shadhili, who flourished in the thirteenth century, was renowned for developing an intellectual approach to Sufism. When Sufism came to be recognized as something quite distinct from orthodox Islam, it led many Sufis to declare: 'In the beginning Sufism was a reality without a name, today it is a name without a reality.'

There are as many definitions of Sufism as there are Sufi Orders. Great Sufis of history are frequently asked, 'What is Sufism?' And each has answered the question in his own particular way. The tenth-century mystic Abul Hasayn an-Nuri, for example, replied: 'Sufism is neither external [experience] nor knowledge, it is all virtue.' Al-Junayd, who is credited with formulating the Sufi path, answered: 'Sufism is that you should be with God without any attachment.' While Sahl ibn Abdullah al-Tustari, who flourished in the later part of the ninth century, responded: 'Sufism is to eat little, to seek peace in God and to flee from the people.' The enigmatic Samnun, who prospered in Iraq towards the end of the ninth century and described himself as 'the liar', said: 'Sufism is that you should not possess anything nor should anything possess you.' An alternative approach to pinning down Sufism is to define it in terms of its central experience – *fana*. *Fana* literally means to be dissolved, to be annihilated. Junayd suggested it is the experience you have when 'you die to yourself and live by Him'. Essentially, it is the negation of the Self: negation of will, existence, self-consciousness and being; forsaken for union with God, assimilation into His will, His attributes and finally His being. The discipline that leads Sufis to *fana* is *zikr*: the act of remembering Allah. *Zikr* can consist of elaborate procedures but usually involves saying 'Allah' loudly, stretching the word as it is pronounced, and saying it with all the force of heart and throat. It also involves negation and affirmation of God, saying *la ilaha illa Allah* (there is no god except Allah). Even more elaborate *zikr* consists of meditating on certain verses of the Qur'an – such as 'He is with you wherever you are' (57:4) or 'Whichever way you turn there is the face of Allah' (2:115) – where the Sufi imagines God is before him, sees him, and is with him clearly and vividly but places Him above space, and concentrates on it till he is completely absorbed. This is where *fana* begins; where it leads no one can tell.

For Mansur al-Hallaj, the radical Sufi who lived in the second half of the ninth century, *fana* led to a permanent state of ecstasy. Al-Hallaj provides the most celebrated example of the experience of *fana* in Islamic history. He was first introduced to me by my father. It was apparent to me quite early on that I owed a good deal to my father's youthful attraction to this notorious Sufi with unorthodox views and behaviour. Later, I read the French Orientalist Louis Massignon's massive multi-volume study of *The Passion of Al-Hallaj* and was bowled over by its description of the depth and breadth of his vision. He was born in the ancient province of Fars, in southern Persia, and became a disciple of Al-Junayd. Al-Hallaj seems to have reached the state of *fana* rather early in his mystical career, and from then on he spent most of his life intoxicated with the love of Allah and seeking total destruction by becoming one with His Beloved. Al-Junayd, his Master, counselled the young mystic to seek solitude and silence. But Al-Hallaj courted publicity, going out and about in a state of oblivious ecstasy, uttering these verses which my father was particularly fond of quoting:

> *I am He Whom I love, and He Whom I love is I.*
> *We are two spirits dwelling in one body.*
> *If you see me, you see Him;*
> *And if you see Him, you see us both.*

Not surprisingly, orthodox Muslims and even more moderate Sufis were scandalized and turned away from him. Many accused him of heresy. So he was advised by Al-Junayd to travel. Al-Hallaj travelled far and wide, visiting Mecca, Baghdad, Khurasan, Transoxania, Sind, even China. But wherever he went, his passion went with him. He was constantly on fire, regularly creating controversy and attracting accusations of heresy. In his famous mystical text, *Kitab at-Tawasin*, Al-Hallaj draws parallels between the tradition of the Prophet, 'Die before you die', and the moth that is attracted to a flame. The moth circles the flame, each circle taking it closer, until it flutters so close it is burned. Al-Hallaj declared himself to be like the moth which wants neither light, nor candle, nor its heat, but only to throw itself into the flame. This analogy became a central motif of Urdu poetry; both my father and mother often wrote poetry incorporating it. The *Tawasin* also contains the fateful line which earned Al-Hallaj his martyrdom: *ana'l haq* – 'I am the Truth'. Al-Hallaj was not content simply to publish this; he stated it, repeating the line at almost every opportunity. When he knocked on Al-Junayd's door and Al-Junayd asked: 'Who is there?' Al-Hallaj replied: 'I am the Truth.' Al-Junayd warned his disciple again and again to keep the 'Secrets of Allah' to himself, and not reveal them to those who could not understand. Al-Hallaj was either oblivious or enjoyed subversion. Eventually, the orthodox had their way; and even Al-Junayd sided with them. Al-Hallaj was executed as a heretic. Folklore has it that even after his execution, Al-Hallaj's corpse continued to utter, 'I am the Truth.'

Truth to tell, there was nothing to suggest that the converted building in Newington Green was a centre of subversion, nor an exotic conduit to ecstasy. It was just another Victorian house in streets of such houses. We entered through the side door, leading by a narrow alleyway to the back of the building. A rickety, latched door stood ajar and we went into a dark back room devoid of furniture where dust hung in stray shafts of sunlight mingling with the familiar heavy musk of incense. Sheikh Nazim Adil Haqqani, a Cypriot Sufi, first arrived in Britain in the early 1970s. Within a year or two, he acquired a huge following among British Muslims and established his headquarters in north London. He claimed to be the fortieth Grand Sheikh of the Naqshbandi Sufi Order, which traces its lineage, in a 'golden chain', right back to Abu Bakr, the first Caliph of Islam. Educated as a chemical engineer at Istanbul University, Sheikh Nazim traced his own lineage, through his father, to the great tenth-century Indian Sufi Abdul Qadir Jilani and, through his mother, to the thirteenth-century Turkish Sufi Master Jalaluddin Rumi, the founder of the Mevlevi Order, better known as the Whirling Dervishes.

We proceeded to another, darker room, once more without furniture but full of carpets and cushions, where the Sheikh was sitting in a corner. To his left sat a host of devotees, looking impressively mystic in green turbans and baggy pants. As my eyes acclimatized to the scene, I found myself engaged in an earnest disquisition concerning an old, familiar theme: facial hair. Its dynamics are no simple matter, not if you are a Muslim. To have facial hair is an endowment of nature, what to do with it is the action of free will. But more than this, it is the consciously unconscious exercise of a state of being. In surveying the galaxy of faces, be-turbaned in green, I was suddenly struck by the variety of aspirational facial hair arrayed before me. Muslim men indicate, almost unfailingly, their allegiance to schools of thought, organizations, groupings, factions, trends, ethnicities and cultures in their cultivation, by the nature and nurture of their facial hair. The turbans were superfluous, by their beards I would have known them. The Sufi beard, a sign of piety, cleaves to chin and jowls but eschews the upper lip. Here was a gathering of men with near naked upper lips, huddling near the source, seeking illumination and motivation, their gaze turned to a man of small stature, with deeply set eyes and a long, wispy, white beard, also with naked upper lip. Sheikh Nazim looked serene in his white turban and long *jubba*. Rosser-Owen, already his devotee, with regulation if straggly facial emoluments of gingerish hue, openly aspired to become his deputy, and rushed to kiss his hand. He introduced me to the Sheikh, and then introduced my brother. We said *As salamu 'alaykum* with one voice. He welcomed us and asked us to sit next to him.

There was no doubt Sheikh Nazim had a strong spiritual presence. His face reflected deep calm and serenity. Rosser-Owen often spoke of his *barakah* (blessings), which I now understood to be his aura of spirituality. We sat there quietly as the Sheikh began one of his metaphysical talks.

'A seeker should be someone who has left himself and connected his heart with the Divine Presence. He stands in His Presence performing his obligations while visualizing the Divine with his heart. Allah's Light has burned his heart giving him a thirst for the nectar of roses, and withdrawing the curtains from his eyes, allowing him to see his Lord. If he opens his mouth it is by order of the Divine Presence. If he moves it is by the order of Allah, and if he becomes tranquil it is by the action of the Divine Attributes. He is in the Divine Presence and with Allah,' said Sheikh Nazim, looking towards us.

'The Sufi.' Now he looked towards the rows of his disciples: 'The Sufi is the one who keeps the obligations that Allah has conveyed by the Holy Prophet, and strives to raise himself to the state of Perfected Character, which is the Knowledge of Allah, Almighty and Exalted.' He paused for a moment. 'The Sufi seeks *tasawwuf*,' the pauses were elegant punctuation points. '*Tasawwuf* is the purity of progressing to Allah's Divine Presence, and its essence is to leave this materialistic life.' The disciples listened in rapturous silence. '*Tasawwuf* is a knowledge from which one learns the state of the human soul, praiseworthy or blameworthy. If it is blameworthy one learns how to purify it and enable it, by becoming praiseworthy, to journey to Allah's Divine Presence. Its fruits are the heart's development: Knowledge of Allah, Glorious and Sublime, through direct experience; salvation in the next world; triumph through gaining Allah's pleasure; the attainment of eternal happiness; and illumination and purification so that noble matters disclose themselves, extraordinary states are revealed, and one perceives what the inside of others is blind to.'

'Praise be to Allah,' the disciples murmured.

The Sheikh continued. '*Tasawwuf* is not a particular type of worship, but is rather the attachment of the heart to Allah. Such attachment demands that one adheres to the standards of the Sacred Law, and follows its guidance.'

Then, Sheikh Nazim addressed my brother directly. 'Beware of this world,' he said. 'To gain this world is humiliation; and to achieve the next world, the Hereafter, is honour. What do you prefer: humiliation or honour?'

My brother looked bashful and bemused, and remained silent.

'The aim of people today,' Sheikh Nazim continued, 'is to collect zeroes. But what's the point of all this wealth? Are you going to show your cheque book to Allah? Allah has created you for His Divine service. The service of this world is not for Allah. As Muslims we must devote all our time to reflecting on Allah's verses in the Holy Qur'an and His signs which cause love to evolve in us; thinking about His Promise to reward us, which will generate and bring forth in us yearning; and thinking about His Warning of punishment, which will keep us away from the wrong path.'

Now, the Sheikh turned his attention towards me. 'There are three big snakes that harm human beings,' he said. 'Beware of them: to be intolerant and impatient with the people around you; to be dependent on something you cannot leave; and to be controlled by your ego.' He paused, looked at me directly. Were his words and his gaze directed to my upper lip? Had my fulsome moustache betrayed me? There is a body of opinion that regards forgoing of beards in favour of a moustache as a sign of arrogance. Impatience is certainly apt, I was born almost devoid of patience. But intolerance, that certainly grated. I was here fleeing from intolerance, a condition and attitude that revolts me. Then the Sheikh said something I found quite astonishing: 'I am the collector of souls. I polish souls till the ego has evaporated.' He took a breath. 'There is too much information in the head of young seekers. You must empty your mind of all that you know. Only then can you begin the journey towards *tasawwuf*.'

Abruptly, the Sheikh rose and left us to go to the women's section. As he stood up, he indicated to one of his deputies to take over. Now there is an important distinction between information, knowledge and wisdom. We can be bamboozled, swamped and perplexed by too much information, the mere welter of facts. Knowledge is the product of processing information, asking questions, scrutinizing, discerning among and between bits of information, seeing patterns and seeking conclusions; wisdom is the insight that results from utilizing knowledge thoughtfully and well. Wiping oneself clean of information and knowledge seems a perilous path, a giant leap into the void, even if the objective is a form of wisdom. Unprepared to leap, I reverted to my usual procedure of asking questions, chatting to one of the deputies, a former English hippy who had embraced Islam and rapidly risen amongst the ranks of Sheikh Nazim's disciples. 'Tell me,' I asked innocently, 'something about the Sheikh.'

'Where can I begin?' the deputy said. 'Quite simply, he is the Imam of the People of Sincerity, the Secret of Sainthood, who revived the Naqshbandi Order at the end of the twentieth century, with Heavenly guidance and Prophetic ethics. He infused into the Muslim Nation and the Planet, love of God and love of the lovers of God, after they had been darkened with the fire and smoke of tribulation and terror, anger and grief. He is the Unveiler of Secrets, the Keeper of Light, the Shaykh of Shaykhs, the Sultan of Ascetics, the Sultan of the Pious, the Sultan of the People of the Truth. He is the Chief Master without peer of the Divine Knowledge in the late twentieth century. He is the Rain from the Ocean of Knowledge of this Order, which is reviving spirits in all parts of this world. He is the Saint of the Seven Continents, his light having attracted disciples and students from all quarters of the globe. He wears the Cloak of the Light of the Divine Presence. He is unique in his time.

He is the orchid planted in the earth of Divine Love. He is the Sun for all the universes. He is known as the Saint of the Two Wings: the external knowledge and the internal knowledge. He is a Miracle of Allah's Miracles, walking on the earth and soaring in the Heavens. He is a Secret of Allah's Secrets, appearing in His Divinity and Existing in His Existence. He is the Owner of the Throne of Guidance, the Reviver of Divine Law, the Master of the Sufi Way, the Builder of the Truth, the Guide of the circle, the Lyric Poem of All the Secrets. He is the Master of Saints and the Saint of the Masters. Seekers circle the Kaa'ba of His Light. He is a Fountain always flowing, a Waterfall continuously cascading, a River always flooding, an Ocean endlessly cresting and breaking on infinite shores. He . . .' 'I get the point,' I interjected as he took his first pause for breath. That was quite enough information for one visit.

Around this time the Sardar household moved from Clapton Pond to Warwick Avenue, from one council flat into another. On my wanderings to get acquainted with our new enclave I discovered that a group of Sufis had taken over a squat in Bristol Gardens, not too far from our block of flats. The coincidence was too convenient to be miraculous, but it provided another opportunity to seek answers to the questions Sheikh Nazim had left hanging in my mind. The charismatic leader of the group who had opened a Sufi Zawiya (a place, akin to a mosque, for Sufi meditation and ritual) was Abdul Qadir. I became a regular – and the only non-white – visitor to the mystic community's prayer room and religious school. I first met Abdul Qadir in 1972, when he was plain old Ian Dallas, a Scot born in Ayr, who, after a sojourn in Fez, Morocco, embraced Islam and joined the Darqawiyya Sufi Order. He had published an autobiographical novel based on his experiences in Morocco. The lyrical power of *The Book of Strangers* had quite a profound effect on me. It opened with the memorable words: 'Today I am leaving. I am leaving the Library, my house, my friends, the city where I live. I do not know where I am going. Strangest of all, I am leaving the Library to find a book.' And went on to describe a quest for meaning and knowledge that ends with an encounter with a Sufi Master. In the key passage of the novel, the protagonist is invited to a meal with the Sufi Sheikh:

The meal began. No one pressed me to eat, as had previously been the case, and when a piece of food was placed in front of me, I ate it, as was the custom, with a whispered '*Bismillah*'. During the meal, I felt a tremendous warmth grow in me for the old man at my side. It was not affection; it was something richer and more solemn, something sacred. I did not think, for my thinking apparatus was suspended, but from my new consciousness, which moved moment by moment, it came to me that I was fed, so too I must share with this man beside me. I took from the large bunch of grapes on the table the finest, rosiest grapes I could see and placed them before him, whispering the Divine Name. No sooner had I done this than the hand of Sayedina Sheikh moved across the table and placed in mine what seemed even larger and more perfect grapes. I looked up at him and took the grapes. He gazed at me, and in the depths of that look, I saw. Everything connected in my mind. A flash, a tremendous, stunning second that must have been filled with angels' voices, and the man beside me and the room and the poverty and the table and grapes given and grapes received were unified in that blessed, blessed moment that lies forever beyond any words, as indeed does every moment of our existence, waking and sleeping. Sayedina Sheikh sat back on his divan, a task among so many accomplished, while I remained unmoving beside him, gently drifting to the shore, but changed, never to be the same again. The meal was over.

The Book of Strangers convinced me that Abdul Qadir was a seeker like myself, who, after a meeting with a remarkable man, had acquired some deep insights. Maybe I could learn from him what he had learned from Sayedina Sheikh? So I joined the *fuqara* (literally, beggars) of the Habibiyya Sufic Tariqah, as they were called, on Thursday nights for their *zikr*.

The sessions began with a 'discourse' by Abdul Qadir. He would start his deliberations with a question, definitely a more promising way to my heart and imagination. What is matter? What is form? What is 'tree' before it manifests and is 'bud'? What is man? Where do we come from and where are we going? What is the nature of dream experience?

What is the death process? What are jinn? Are angels a metaphor or reality? The answer to each question came from the world of the Unseen. 'Know,' Abdul Qadir would say, 'the difference between a Mumin [a true Muslim] and a modern Muslim. Modern Muslim has shut himself off from the World of the Unseen. He is opaque, solid in this world, arrogant of "his" Islam, and with no awe radiating from him as his experiential reality of existence. The Mumin, in contrast, is open to the World of the Unseen. Therefore, there is a certain transparency, a certain luminosity that comes from his awareness of being encompassed about by the mysteries of the Unseen.' The modern Muslim, we learned, has lost *ilm al-yaqin* (knowledge of certainty), which is based on the Unseen. In the modern Muslim, the whole confrontation with his own nature has been conveniently filed away in the pursuit of worldly pleasures. With no sense of the Unseen, no sense of the mystery of creation and the angelic order, the jinn, and the nature of forms, the modern Muslim has to repress his own inner world, so that he is totally alienated from himself.

The discourse was followed by the *Isha* or night prayer. After the prayer, the disciples fully initiated into the Darqawiyya Order will sing the Greater *Wird*, the sacred and secret prayer of the Order, which was intended to purify the soul and unite the reciters with Reality. Occasionally, they sang the Lesser *Wird*, which reads:

In the name of Allah, the Merciful, the Compassionate
Oh Allah, we ask You by the secret of the essence and by the essence of the secret. He is You and You are He. I have veiled myself with the light of Allah and the light of the Throne of Allah and all the Names of Allah from my enemies and the enemies of Allah. With one thousand 'no power, no strength but through Allah' I have set a seal upon my self and my Deen [religion] and upon everything given to me by Allah with the seal of Allah with which He has sealed the Heavens and the earth. Allah is enough for us and He is the best guardian, the best protector, the best helper. The blessings of Allah be upon our lord and master Muhammad, and upon all his family and companions and great peace. Praise belongs to Allah, the Lord of the worlds.

The *Wird* would accelerate the spiritual pulse of the assembly. One of the disciples would start to sing a devotional song in praise of their Sheikh. Many of Abdul Qadir's followers were musicians. There was Richard Thompson who sang with Fairport Convention; Ian Whiteman who was with Mighty Baby; Roger Powell who was with a group called The Action; and Peter Sanders, a photographer with a beautiful voice. In fact, the Zawiya was a veritable den of stunning voices. In no time, the *zikr* session would be raised to another, more ethereal plane. Then the *fuqara* would stand up, form a circle holding one another's hands, and be led by a high-ranking member of the Zawiya, standing in the middle of the circle, in chanting *La ilaha illa'llah* ('There is no God but Allah'), *La ilaha illa'llah, La ilaha illa'llah*. The dancing disciples would inhale with *La ilaha* and collectively exhale with *illa'llah*. The chanting would start gently but as it gathered pace, the circle would become more of an octagon, and *fuqara* would begin to sway, throwing themselves backwards as they drew deep breaths for *La ilaha*, thrusting forwards as they expelled their breath with *illa'llah*. When the chanting reached frantic pitch the walls of the Zawiya would reverberate with *La ilaha illa'llah*. Soon, the assembly would be in a state of total frenzy. Finally, *Allah*, uttered sixty-six times, would bring the exhausted assembly to a serene calm. Quiet would fall over the gathering.

It was powerful, intoxicating stuff. And no one seemed to me to be more intoxicated than Abdul Qadir himself. He now started to call himself Sheikh Abdul Qadir. He declared he had authorization – *Idhn* – from his guru, Sheikh Muhammad ibn al-Habib in Morocco. Then he announced further authorization from a certain Sheikh Muhammad al-Fayturi Hamudah who 'by his authority had joined together the two separate branches of the Habibiyya and the Alawiyya Orders in the Darqawiyya Order'. Abdul Qadir was now the Muqaddim – the representative – of this Order in the West. 'Allah has singled me out with sciences and secrets which only the unique man of Muhammad possesses.' In recognition, his name became Sheikh Abdul Qadir as-Sufi.

The disciples were ordered to purify themselves with the water of the Unseen. Their hearts had to be cleansed of the ailments which veiled them from the presence of the Knower of the Unseen. The purification involved the Sheikh – Abdul Qadir – who was 'purified of fault', pouring the water of secret sciences that flowed from the presence of the Unseen into the heart of the devotees. Those who refused to be cleansed in such a way lacked the inner sight to recognize the qualities of the Sheikh. Abdul Qadir was now the absolute master of the Bristol Garden community. He chose husbands for his female devotees, ordered male disciples to divorce their wives, and generally regulated all aspects of the lives of all his followers.

I began to detect a pattern. The information was forming itself into discernible knowledge. The pattern was not merely Sufi, it was much more general – it seemed to materialize wherever mysticism lured eager souls. The Beatles, famously, sought their Maharishi. The Orange Energy brigade settled in at Rajneesh. The Moonies proliferated. And whatever mind-expanding consciousness individual seekers personally acquired, their physical world became circumscribed by the diktats of the guru. This was the age when Indian mystics of various stripe and hue made millions in hard currency from the otherworldly, non- or anti-materialist longings of their followers. The guru syndrome was becoming a general epidemic. One could argue that it's the followers and not mysticism itself who are at fault. But I was beginning to suspect that there was something at the core of mysticism – all mysticism – that was deeply flawed.

And I did not have to leave home to diagnose the condition. While I was getting acquainted with Abdul Qadir, my brother had returned to Sheikh Nazim. Shortly thereafter he took *biyah*, accepted Sheikh Nazim as his teacher, and became his disciple. He started visiting the Sheikh frequently; first it was once or twice a week, then he was there almost every day. On the Sheikh's advice, he resigned from his promising job as an economist, and became a carpenter: 'It is much better to work with your own hands,' the Sheikh had said. In due course, my brother married a woman approved by the Sheikh; and as time wore on the Sheikh chose the names of his children. He withdrew from normal life; and the Sheikh came to dominate every aspect of his existence. My soul, on the other hand, wasn't free to be handed over to a 'collector'; and I sought not so much to empty my mind as to cram it as full as possible. In quest of knowledge I observed, and I read.

As everyone knows, reading can be a dangerous undertaking. Especially dangerous for those certain they are 'purified of fault', I observed as Abdul Qadir discovered a 'new book'. He was wandering in the streets of Rabat, the story goes, searching for Islamic works in various bookshops, when he came across a book on the life of the Prophet Muhammad by Qadi Ayad. He was electrified, for the book represented a picture of Islam that was 'all but obliterated by two thousand years of corrupted religious scholars from every direction'. It presented 'the best and purest Islam' as opposed to 'Jew-tolerant' westernized Islam. The book, 'which could not have been found in a library' and was a discovery made 'possible while struggling in the way of Allah', emphasized the importance of the Maliki School of Thought. Following the way of Malik's people, Abdul Qadir insisted that his followers became 'Arab speaking'. He declared that all other Schools of Thought were innovations based on error and deviations from Islam. Malik's jurisprudence spoke of a 'clear Islam, which had in it no innovation, no element that could be debated by anyone but a Jew or an unbeliever'. There was no option: the Muslims had to accept this 'survival-kit Islam'. So, Abdul Qadir modified his name once again: he now became Sheikh Abdul Qadir as-Sufi al-Maliki.

The Bristol Garden community broke up in recrimination. Abdul Qadir's interpretation of the Maliki School was not one I recognized from the learning circle that clustered around Jaffar Shaikh Idris, nor, I suspected, one that would have been familiar to Malik. I left Abdul Qadir's circle and followed his career from a distance, as great a distance as I could manage. Or as Fitzgerald made Omar Khayyam say, 'evermore came out by the same door as in I went.' Abdul Qadir took his dwindling band of followers to Norwich to establish a pure 'Muslim village' which turned out to be a retreat-cum-military garrison; and published his manifesto, *Jihad: A Ground Plan*, a programme to establish the rule of Islam all over the world. From Norwich, he moved to Granada to create a 'new species' of 'Islamic man who was a fitting follower of the Messenger'. The new species turned out to be the Murabitun. The original Murabitun were an eleventh-century hereditary cult of living saints, individuals who often played the role of hereditary arbiters among the rural tribes of North Africa. They built a *ribat*, or fortress, at the mouth of the Senegal River, from where warriors were sent to spread their version of puritan Islam throughout the western Sudan. These warriors themselves acquired the label of Murabitun, signifying 'those dwelling in the frontier fortress'; the term has also given us the Spanish form *Almoravides* and the French word *marabout*, 'holy man, local saint'. The Berber warriors were also known as 'the veiled ones' as they wore veils over their faces. Eventually, the Murabitun conquered the whole of North Africa as far as Algeria, made incursions into Spain and established a dynasty, the Almoravids, which lasted about a hundred years. During this period, the Murabitun developed a coinage system, issuing a gold Islamic dinar that became the standard throughout the region. Following in their footsteps, Abdul Qadir issued a call for the currency system in the Muslim world to be replaced by a gold dinar and changed his name to Sheikh Abdul Qadir as-Sufi al-Maliki al-Murabit.

I watched in astonishment as the new Murabitun spread to North America, South Africa and other parts of the world; joining hands with other, more established, puritans in the Middle East. It seemed to me that where previously I had one problem now I had a whole collection. Men with rigid certainties in their eyes were multiplying and coming at me from all directions. The problem of cults was born. It flourished, developing into a full-blown sociological phenomenon. It spawned a voluminous literature, from tabloid headlines to scholarly studies. It produced its own reaction in the spread of self-help organizations specializing in kidnapping cult members and deprogramming them.

All I was left with was questions. I wondered about the man, Sheikh al-Habib of Fez, who had launched Abdul Qadir on his new trajectory; and whether authoritarianism was an intrinsic part of Sufism. So I decided to go to Fez myself.

In Old Fez, I stayed at Palais-jamais, a hotel set at one of the highest points in the city: from here the city appears laid out before you as a composite whole, white houses rising amongst glittering green inside the reddish brown city walls. The walls, although slightly weather-beaten, were as sturdy as ever and conveyed a lasting impression of age-old integrity and beauty. Built in about the eighth century, Fez, of all the great Islamic cities, has preserved its traditional character best. The tradition of town planning that gave it birth has all but disappeared. Water played a large part in those plans, not only because most Muslim cities arose in regions with an arid climate but also because clean running water is a basic requirement in the ablutions all Muslims perform before their obligatory prayers. The site of Fez was certainly determined by the presence of a river; the city flourished as a link in the great trade routes connecting the vast extent of the Muslim world of the day. The heart of the city, as with most Muslim cities, is the great main sanctuary, and typically it is adjacent to the main market. In its historic days, Fez was a major centre of culture and learning. On me, the city had a powerful hypnotic effect. I wandered enveloped in history, within a time warp in which the parallel universes of past and present appeared to coexist. Mysticism and spirituality seem to ooze from its very walls and narrow cobbled streets. Little wonder it had attracted so many world-weary truth seekers and become a hub for a new generation of Orientalists longing for release from the constricting conventions of their western world. This was the era of Paul Bowles and his exotic coterie of writers.

It did not take me very long to locate Sheikh al-Habib. But I did not want to introduce myself to him; or to obtain his blessings. I merely wanted to observe him and his followers from a distance. Every evening I would walk down from Palais-jamais to their Zawiya, join the congregation for prayer, and watch. Occasionally, someone would suggest that I should sit next to the Sheikh, or become his disciple, or join their Sufi Order. I would tell them I was only there to learn; that I was not ready to be initiated. During the day I just wandered and watched. One afternoon, I watched a man in the Medina making a comb out of a goat horn. I sat in a café across the street from his workshop sipping mint tea while he continued to chip away at the horn, slowly transforming it into the recognizable shape of a comb, totally unaware that he was being watched. He seemed literally and metaphorically absorbed in his craft. As I watched, I slowly began to realize something. Not in separation from his life but in pursuance of his living the worker was performing *zikr*: remembering Allah. He wasn't reading some secret and mystical *Wird*, or dancing to the chants of '*Allah Uh*', or performing any other ritual discipline of Sufi Orders.

He was simply being himself: he and his craft were one. It is a classic Orientalist image, a common everyday event, a lost world, a standard promise made by every travel brochure and a living, lived experience. There was and is eternity in that moment: the very act of carving and watching encapsulated the entire universe. As one workman allowed his Ego, his Self, his very entity to dissolve in his craft, this was the moment of *fana* – the annihilation that the disciples talked so much of in the Zawiyas of Fez. If, as Sufi philosophy argues, this state of consciousness – what Eliot called the 'moment in and out of time' – is the purpose of creation, the most irreducibly ultimate human experience, then it must be within everyone. God, who is God, is an equal opportunity Creator, or ceases to be the God I believe in. So the search is not long, and does not lead to the feet of a mystic master, but within.

Suddenly, I began to think that all I had observed of Sufi Orders was little more than role reversal, an inversion of what we should be remembering. The whole panoply created by Sufi Orders complicated, making different, special and abstruse what should be effortless and openly available, marking off a territory for themselves on what should be common land. And there was something more. The whole idealization of simplicity, the primitive, the Oriental idyll of the noble peasant, was another red herring. Here I watched a man pursue his livelihood in a state of grace. The state of grace was in the man and expanded from him to all in his activities and surroundings. Surely, I thought, the trick, if trick it be, is not in leaving our modern life to find grace but bringing this sense of grace into our life wherever that be, whatever our environment. If it ennobles the craft of this man here in Fez what could it not do in a factory in Luton? In Fez this worker and his work were a unified whole, in Luton everyone had convinced themselves it was impossible, and that appeared to me the single solitary difference. In which case, the only Sheikh worthy of having a following was the one who was not aware he was a Sheikh; who sought no followers and who wanted nothing except to lose himself in prayer by doing what he did best.

I dallied along, mooched my way past a carpet shop. It was a huge traditional house, with an open courtyard, full of carpets. The man inside the shop started to show me his wares. I did feel the need for retail therapy. Directly opposite the carpet shop, there was a public fountain set off by brilliant *zillige*, the tesserae of coloured ceramic tiles cut into small shapes then fitted together to form enchanting geometric patterns. Adjacent to the fountain was a public bath that seemed heavily oversubscribed. I could see two small stone canals, barely sixty centimetres across, one bringing clean water from the local river to the bath and the other carrying away the used water. They employed nothing more than the power of gravity to perform their function. The noise of flowing water was being drowned by the murmurs of children learning to recite the Qur'an nearby.

Next to the Qur'anic school was a small bookshop. I walked over and looked at a few books. Modern Arabic titles were tightly packed on cramped shelf space alongside old, handwritten manuscripts. I picked one up and asked about it. 'It is a treatise *On Being and Craftsmanship*. My father wrote and calligraphed it,' said the shopkeeper, a young man whose hair had prematurely turned white, seated within the dingy interior of his booth, immersed among the books. 'He was a Master Craftsman. And a very religious man.'

'Do you do calligraphy as well?' I asked.

'I am working on a book on the metaphysics of Sufism. Would you like to see it?'

He pulled out an unfinished manuscript and handed it to me. It was exquisitely written: I was too lost in the beauty of the form of the written words themselves to think about the meaning behind them. 'Do you work from notes?'

'Not really. The book is in my head. I calligraph it as I go on.'

'Would it not be better to have the book printed?' I enquired.

'It would be. But then who would keep the traditions of my great-grandfathers alive?'

I smiled and stretched across the barrier of shelves to hand the manuscript back. I hovered, vacantly, preparing to move off. The calligrapher took hold of a rope hanging from the ceiling of his booth and in one seamless movement swung himself out of his shop, effortlessly carving a parabola that avoided all the shelves and books in his path. He landed right on my toes and even before regaining his balance, presented me with a small manuscript. I was impressed by his agility; but totally overwhelmed by the manuscript. It was a leather-bound, illuminated biography of the Prophet. I could not take my eyes from its pages. 'It's yours,' said the calligrapher with premature white hair. 'Give me whatever you can.'

I bought the book and sauntered off through the labyrinthine white streets and lanes, dodging the local human and animal traffic, stopping now at a lumber yard overburdened with the fragrance of cedar wood, now at a metal works where dozens of workers clattered their mallets on sheets of tin or brass, now at a *fonduq*, an inn, still being used after serving tired travellers for over a thousand years, now pausing for yet more mint tea outside a pottery producing pragmatic art of exquisite beauty. Eventually, I stepped into the house of a merchant, another carpet seller.

Beyond the magnificent entrance hall, decorated with eye-catching ceramics, was a small square courtyard with a fountain. The richly painted woodwork integrated with the polychrome tiling to supplement the harmony of the archways framing the entrance to rooms with high ceilings. For a split second I was in ninth-century Morocco, then my eye caught the crude sign on the wall proclaiming that 'Visa Cards' were welcome in this establishment. I was stuck with real time. I did not buy the fine Moroccan carpets on offer but did ask the merchant's young son, who was studying in the local university, to explain how the water system in the city works. Exoticism really does not move me. But plumbing . . . now there's a topic I can really get excited about.

'You know,' he said, 'that Fez is situated in a valley between two plains at different levels; the water from the upper plain, which has many springs, has to flow across the city. Since the valley is curved, it is like a shell, it is possible to distribute water over practically the entire extent of the valley from its highest edge. There the Wadi Fez is first taken over and divided into several branches traversing the various quarters of the city in canals above and below ground. Conduits lead from these canals to each house. The used water is collected into other conduits and led back to the same canals which, from a certain point downwards, assume the function of sewers. Think of the whole system in terms of circulation of blood in the human body with its separate arteries and veins.' And you thought plumbing had nothing to stir the human imagination? If you thought beauty and wisdom exist only in what is termed Art, think on. Art, sympathy and beauty in science – the truly unified field theory – once it was and here it still is, in Fez, why not elsewhere in the workings of the modern scientific world?

There had to be more to Sufism than simply submitting one's will to the will of a Master, being high on the aura of a guru. Perhaps I was trying to drink from streams and tributaries – maybe I ought to go to the mouth of the river itself. Perhaps, I thought, I will find satisfaction in Konya, the Turkish city of the renowned Sufi sage and poet, Jalaluddin Rumi, a centre of mystical thought, a place marked since the beginning of time for an extraordinary numinous destiny. There was definitely something to be said for covering distance to explore the worlds that were within me. So a few weeks later, I flew to Konya, via Istanbul.

I found Konya to be as peaceful and spiritually alive as I had imagined; if touched with a tinge of sadness. Ancient records tell us Konya was the first city to emerge from the Flood. And certainly one could feel the presence of a great deal of history in the city: I was ready to believe that Rameses II married one of his daughters here, that the Apostle Barnabas and his disciple Timothy taught the Gospel here, and that this city and its surrounding areas saw the birth of the first Christian communities and the meeting of the first synods. But you had to search for that history. The Konya of Rumi's time, on the other hand, was all too evident. 'In Konya,' wrote the author of the *Mathanwi*, 'the leaders and the lords and the dignitaries have thousands of houses, castles and palaces. The merchants and the bourgeois have houses more magnificent than those of the artisans, the palaces of amirs are more magnificent than those of the merchants and the domes and the palaces of the sultans are more magnificent than all the others.' I located a couple of the monuments Rumi knew. Alauddin Kaykoad's palace, said to be the palace of 'Aladdin' of *The Thousand and One Nights*, had only one intact wall. But the truly sublime mosque within the city walls that bears Rumi's name was completely intact. The splendour of the city could be judged by the Mevlevi Museum, a network of halls, courtyards, gardens and mausoleums, which incorporates Rumi's own tomb, the Green Mausoleum. Why is such living history turned into a museum, set aside and labelled 'dead', I wondered? Just as *The Thousand and One Nights*, a living, changing, oral text, had been transformed into a fixed, frozen and authentic written text, so Rumi's heritage had been frozen in history, isolated, surrounded and turned into a museum. Once again, I was returning to my central problem with Sufism by another route. Rumi himself was against the idea of being entombed in a mausoleum. When he heard that his disciples wished to build a mausoleum in his honour, he admonished them saying, 'How could there be a better mausoleum than the sky itself?' Nevertheless, after his death on 17 December 1273, his son gave permission, and the Persian architect Bedrettin built the monument on four columns appropriately called 'elephant feet'. Numerous sultans and noblemen have added to the original construction.

I entered the Museum through the 'Gate of the Dervishes', passing through a row of cells where the novice mystics must have lived, indicating that this was a monastery. Rumi rests under a turquoise dome surmounted by a ceiling covered with green tiles. His coffin, standing on a platform and surrounded with a low railing in what I assumed to be solid silver, was covered with a green cloth, richly embroidered in gold with Qur'anic verses. A number of inscriptions, neatly framed, from the *Mathanwi* and *Divan-I-Kabir* adorned the *Huzur-i-Pir*, as the tomb is known:

> *Come, come, whoever you are*
> *Believer or unbeliever, Magian or pagan, come*
> *Come into the house of hope.*
> *And,*
> *Either seem as you are*
> *Or be as you seem.*

I sat and read the *Fatiha*, the opening chapter of the Qur'an, which according to tradition is the appropriate thing to do in front of the tomb:

Praise be to Allah, Lord of the Worlds,
The Beneficent, the Merciful.
Owner of the Day of Judgement,
Thee (alone) we worship; Thee (alone) we ask for help.
Show us the straight path,
The path of those whom Thou hast favoured;
Not (the path) of those who earn Thine anger nor of
   those who go astray. (1: 1–7)

I lingered in front of the tomb in a state of semi-meditation, the kind where ideas pass in ranks but conclusions fail to bring up the rear. My attention was attracted by a group of men in long trench coats and turbans offering their prayers. I watched them for a while; and when they began to leave the mausoleum, I followed them. They set off gently, then walked hurriedly, and then began to run. I kept pace. We bundled our way into a mosque. Inside the mosque, numerous other men, in the same uniform, all congregated towards the front. I sat beside them. The *Azan* (call to prayer) was called and I joined in the prayer. Afterwards, as the other worshippers left, the turbaned men gathered around an old, frail man: he had a thick long nose, small deeply set eyes, a long bushy white beard, but no moustache; unlike the others, his turban had a red band around it. They all stood respectfully in front of him and took their turn in shaking his hand. Some of them kissed his hand reverentially. Eventually, they all took their places seated in a large circle around the old man. He led them in chanting the ninety-nine names of God: *ar-Rahman* (the Beneficient), *ar-Rahim* (the Merciful), *al-Jameel* (the Beautiful). This went on for some time and I sat back, outside the circle, observing them. When they finished, I felt intoxicated and strangely drawn to the group.

Without thinking, I got up, walked towards the old man, and sat next to him – on the right – and greeted him by placing both my hands in his. He received me warmly, smiled and then closed his eyes. For several minutes the old man, still grasping my hands, sat there with his eyes closed. I found myself unable to move. Then the old man spoke. He said something in Turkish. I shook my head to indicate I did not understand. A disciple got up and came to sit on my left. 'Sheikh Ahmad says he knows why you are here,' he translated. 'You can ask him any question you like.'

I could not think of a question to ask. My mind had gone totally blank. Eventually, I muttered, 'What is Islam?' It was the only thing I could think of. I felt silly.

'Islam is wearing a beard, a trench coat and a turban,' replied Sheikh Ahmad.

The mosque reverberated with a mortifying silence. All the whispering, the constant praying – the ever-present, background noise – disappeared. The very air itself came to a standstill. Suddenly, from being almost invisible, I became the focus of all attention. What kind of answer was that, I thought. I tried to speak. But nothing came out. My throat was dry and, for a moment, I felt as though I was sitting on hot sand in the middle of a desert with the sun directly above my head. Was the old man, the congregation of devotees in long trench coats and turbans, the mosque itself – playing some sort of trick?

Sheikh Ahmad broke the silence. 'What don't you understand?'

'You cannot reduce Islam to dress,' I said, clearing my dry throat. Then I remembered that Kemal Atatürk, the founder of modern Turkey, had actually banned the beard, the turban, and, I think, the trench coat. 'Are you not defining Islam in opposition to Kemalism?' I added.

Sheikh Ahmad listened but said nothing. He sat there with his elbows on his thighs, palms together, beard, chin, mouth, nose, resting in his joined palms, looking intently at the intricate calligraphy and arabesque patterns on the walls – endless curves and zigzags moving rapidly, from infinity to infinity; from every corner of the mosque a line veers off, engages, disengages, plunges in again, wheels round and skips lightly out of range; then once again it faces a morass, gathers velocity, rapiers through and see-saws out leaving ricocheting angles behind. Would his concentration hold to follow the antics of the arabesques? Or maybe he was reading something in them? Something I could not read? Maybe they spoke to him in a language only he understood?

His silence gave me time to gather my thoughts. 'Sheikh Ahmad,' I began respectfully, 'it seems to me that you have reduced your faith to a set of symbols. These symbols have no meaning for me.'

'The human individual is not just motivated by physical needs and appetites,' Sheikh Ahmad replied through the interpreter, 'but also by a shared perception of reality within which a community exists. In our community this shared perception is provided by a set of symbols. In this symbolic world the individual is no longer merely a biological animal but also a social entity. These symbols may look ridiculous to you, but they give birth to our symbolic self. They are an integral part of our identity as Muslims. But if they mean nothing to you then you must look for your own symbols.'

I knew Sheikh Ahmad was not being dismissive. He uttered the words with some calm. He continued, 'The paradise you seek' – I understood the word *firdous* without the need of translation – 'is a symbolic paradise. Full of gardens, rivers of milk and honey, the Throne, the Lote Tree. You make what you will of these symbols.

'But here we do not seek *firdous*. We seek something higher. We seek *ridwan*, or proximity to God. The *ridwan* of God is greater than paradise.'

'But the whole function of paradise is to give us proximity to God,' I replied perplexed.

'No doubt one will be close to God in paradise,' Sheikh Ahmad replied. 'But we seek *ridwan* here and now. Paradise is a relative term. In its highest sense, Paradise denotes the Unsurpassable, and this is the Paradise of the Essence. At this stage paradise and *ridwan* become one: All is the Absolute, the Infinite, the Eternal.' Sheikh Ahmad paused; and then recited a verse from the Qur'an that I instantly recognized. 'O soul at peace, return unto thy Lord, content in His good pleasure. Enter thou among my servants! Enter thou my Paradise' (89:27–30). After another pause, he continued. 'The Paradise the Qur'an speaks of here is the Paradise of His good pleasure. The Paradise of the Infinite. Nothing can be added to the Paradise of the Infinite; so only nothing can enter it. We seek to be nothing here and now. As a Sufi sage once said: "I went in and left myself outside." We seek to annihilate ourselves in the Infinite.'

Sheikh Ahmad took both of my hands in his. This time he spoke directly to me; and I understood what he said without the aid of translation. 'This is not to be your fate. The Master you seek knows not that he is the Master. And he takes no disciples. You must chalk out your own route to paradise. Your destiny lies elsewhere.' Then he paused for a little while.

'Peace be on you,' he said loudly. The disciples echoed his words. With this Sheikh Ahmad got up, someone handed him his walking stick, and with a group of his followers, he left the mosque through a side door. Suddenly, I was the only one sitting in the mosque.

For the next day or so I walked around Konya as though in a stupor, visiting mosques, more mausoleums, and witnessing a *semah* ceremony, during which the whirling dervishes perform their dance. I kept repeating Sheikh Ahmad's words to myself. Whatever did he mean? Was he saying that I was too sceptical ever to experience mysticism – too rationalist ever to let go of myself entirely, to reduce myself to cipher and annihilate myself into the Infinite? Was he implying that I was my own Sufi Master – though I knew it not? Or that the kind of Master I was seeking does not exist? Unable to resolve these questions, I took a taxi to Aksehir, some 130 kilometres north-west of Konya, to visit the mausoleum of Mullah Nasruddin.

In Turkey, one could hardly go anywhere without encountering an anecdote or two from the life of the philosopher and humorist Nasruddin Hoca. 'Hoca', or Hodja, means teacher; and 'Nasruddin' means 'helper of the Faith'. And Nasruddin, at once wise and foolish, crafty and naive, teaches us how to resolve many and diverse dilemmas of life. His proverbs are used for teaching not just children but all those who seek to resolve the complexities of existence. Maybe, I figured, he could teach me a few things, help this particular faithful, and shed some light on my encounter with Sheikh Ahmad.

Not much is actually known about the life of Hodja. He is said to have lived in the thirteenth century, although some scholars place him in the fourteenth or even the fifteenth. Perhaps it is not even important whether Hodja actually existed at all. What really matters is what he is recorded as saying; told in simple and spare terms, following an impeccable logic, his stories were based on a common sense that can hardly be bettered or gainsaid: 'Give praise to Allah, O believers, for if He had provided wings for the donkey our roofs would come tumbling down!' Hodja lived, if and whenever he lived, in a period when whatever was authentic was universal; and whatever was universal was usually anonymous. So a lot of stories attributed to Hodja surface in other Muslim cultures: the roly-poly turbaned figure of Hodja is not too far removed from the Juha of the Arabian tales, or Mulla Dopaiza of India, or Bahlul the wise fool of the Middle East. Indeed, it is suggested that Cervantes's Sancho Panza, the sidekick in *Don Quixote*, may have been based on the Anatolian Mullah himself.

Hodja is said to have lived at a time of war and turbulence when Anatolia was conquered by the ruthless Mongol king Timur. But his stories are not about blood and glory – their purpose is to deflate power: 'What is my true worth?' Timur once asked Hodja. 'About twenty gold pieces,' Hodja replied. 'Why, just the belt I am wearing is worth twenty gold pieces,' retorted Timur. Nasruddin nodded. 'I included that when I gave you my estimate,' he said. He was equally concerned with exposing the pretensions of class: one story tells how Hodja is invited to a banquet. He arrives in his everyday work clothes. No one pays any attention to him. So he goes back home, puts on his finest clothes and a fur coat and returns to the banquet. This time he is met at the entrance, treated with great respect and given a choice seat. When the soup is served, Hodja dips the lapel of the fur coat in the bowl saying, 'Please have some. Eat, my fur coat, eat! Eat, my fur coat, eat!' The dinner guests are amazed and ask why he is doing this. 'It is the fur coat that has been received with attention and dignity. So, the fur coat should eat.'

Hypocrisy, fanaticism and self-righteousness were dismissed by Hodja with equal candour: 'Listen carefully to those who know. If someone listens to you, be sure to listen to what you are saying.' In a famous story, Hodja suggests that every argument has more than one side: two men involved in a quarrel ask Hodja to settle their dispute. When the first man tells his version, Hodja says: 'You are right.' The second protests, demanding to tell his version, after which Hodja remarks: 'You're right.' His wife, who has been listening, intervenes: 'But they can't both be right.' Hodja promptly replies: 'Woman, you're right, too.' Muslims everywhere need a character like him to lean against; someone who is a projection from deep within the universal Muslim psyche; someone who can point out the absurdities of their situation; someone they can believe and laugh with.

By the time I reached Hodja's mausoleum, it was late afternoon. I found myself standing in front of a huge gate, a grave clearly visible through it. I could read the gravestone from where I stood: 'Here lies

Nasruddin Hoca.' There was a ridiculously huge padlock on the gate. It seemed that the gate had never been opened; indeed, it appeared to have been designed not to be opened. Then I stepped back and noticed there were no walls. A parting joke? I could feel the Mullah rolling with laughter. The point of my stories, he seemed to be saying, is to persuade people to look away from the logically obvious to the blatantly evident. I sat by Hodja's tomb smiling to myself. I am not quite sure what happened next. I must have nodded off. I must have dreamed. Or maybe I had a mystical experience – the only such experience of my life. It was as though I was asleep but conscious and aware of what was happening around me.

I found myself standing by a lake. The shimmering water looked inviting and I felt the urge to scoop some in my palms. But as I bent down to take the water, it and my hand dissolved into nothing. I tried again; and again the two, water and palm, merged and annihilated each other. My desire to touch and feel the water increased; and I tried again and again, with the same result. I noticed a figure standing on the other side of the lake. The setting sun was casting a huge shadow. It made him look ethereal, unreal. I started to walk around the lake. As I moved towards the figure, I noticed I was not getting nearer. I thought I had misjudged the distance, perhaps he was much further off than I assumed, and lengthened my stride. Still the distance between us remained exactly the same. Yet all this time, the figure remained motionless. 'Why can't I get near you?' I shouted. Even though I could not see him clearly, I felt as though I knew him. More: I felt that he knew what I was feeling. He seemed to have moved a few centimetres closer. But I still could not see his face. Stubbornly, I kept my eyes on the figure. He appeared to bend down and pluck a blade of grass. He broke the two ends of the blade so that it was the length of a pencil. He then moved to a nearby tree and plucked a large leaf; and proceeded to write with the grass-blade pencil on the leaf. He seemed to be taking considerable care in writing, and was reciting his words as he wrote. I tried to move closer to see if I could hear what he was saying. But it seemed the gravitational force of the earth had increased several-fold; my feet were glued to the ground. I was standing fixed to this spot while the earth was going round me. Was he getting closer to me? I remember he pressed something cold into my hand and words echoed in my head: 'You will know what to do.'

When I regained full consciousness a small Turkish boy was hovering over me trying to sell me something. He was carrying a tray loaded with worry beads, local guides, and other trinkets – standard tourist fare. But he was pressing a calligraphic picture into my hands. It was an illustration of a huge vine leaf, the sort Turks use to wrap rice and minced meat when they make dolma, with an inscription on it that I recognized to be a verse from the Qur'an. I bought the illustration; and quivered with fear and anticipation as I read out the verse:

Allah is the Light of the heavens and the earth.
The similitude of His light is as a niche wherein is a lamp.
The lamp is in a glass. The glass is as it were a shining star.
(This lamp is) kindled from a blessed tree, an olive neither of
the East nor of the West, whose oil would almost glow forth
(of itself) though no fire touched it. Light upon light, Allah
guides unto His light whom He will. And Allah speaks to mankind
in allegories, for Allah is Knower of all things. (24: 35)

My own mystical experience meant that I couldn't reject Sufism per se. There is something deep and quite intoxicating at its core. But my encounters with its contemporary manifestations were far from enlightening. My problem was a problem of forms, the forms in which Sufism today has been made into a business of Masters, mystery and obfuscations. I saw how Sheikh Nazim's Sufi path led my brother to economic ruin, neglect of his family and finally to total disenchantment: after following the Order for two decades, he left complaining that the Sheikh had totally taken over his life. Individual Sufis – the likes of Al-Hallaj and Al-Junayd – are one thing. But as a collective spiritual path, Sufism does not produce a viable and equitable social order. The tendency to degenerate into authoritarianism and become a cult of the Master is ever present. It could not be my route to paradise. Where contemporary Sufi Masters of various kinds led I was not about to follow.

Chapter 5

THE CRADLE OF PARADISE

In classical Islam the quest for knowledge had always been intimately linked with extensive travel; a fact endorsed by none other than Al-Ghazali. The eleventh-century philosopher and theologian is a towering figure in Islamic history. During his lifetime, Al-Ghazali, whose full name is Abu Hamid ibn Muhammad ibn Muhammad al-Tusi al-Ghazali, was known as 'the Proof of Islam' and 'the Renewer of the Religion'. Born in Tus (now Khorasan), he studied at a famous college in Nishapur under Al-Juwayni, a prominent theologian of his time. At the rather early age of thirty-four, Al-Ghazali obtained a full professorial chair at the celebrated Nazamiyah University of Baghdad. It was during this period that he produced his greatest treatise: *The Incoherence of the Philosophers*, a formidable attack on Greek philosophy and its Muslim champions. Al-Ghazali believed that religion could be neither proved nor disproved; such efforts were doomed to incoherence and amounted to little more than pseudo-justification for belief. But after writing his celebrated text, Al-Ghazali suffered an acute spiritual crisis, gave up his position at the University and began to travel. For over a decade he wandered throughout the Middle East, visiting Mecca, Medina, Damascus and other cities. When he finally settled down, he produced what is undoubtedly the most influential work in Islamic history: *The Revival of Religious Sciences*, a massive text containing forty books that provide a route map to Islamic paradise. Al-Ghazali was a grand synthesizer and *Revival* – or *Ihya* as it is known in Muslim circles – synthesizes theology, law, ethics, philosophy, and mysticism in a formidable attempt to teach logic to mystics, spirituality to logicians and mathematicians, and rhetoric and philosophy to theologians, and usher all and sundry towards the balanced road to paradise.

Al-Ghazali is the classical author most Muslims turn to in despair. And he certainly knew a few things about despair: while writing about certainty, he was perpetually on the edge of doubt, always searching for truth, moving from one fit of scepticism to another. 'No one believes,' he said, 'until he has doubted.' The most interesting thing about Al-Ghazali is that he is an equal-opportunity doubter, a very rare breed. He ends up doubting instrumental reason itself, a leap of doubt and willingness to interrogate one's beliefs secular-minded modern-day adherents schooled in scientific method are remarkably loath even to contemplate. Throughout my FOSIS period, and many years after that, Al-Ghazali's *Book of Knowledge*, the first book of the *Revival*, was my constant bed-table companion. I dipped into it religiously every night before going to sleep. After my return from Konya, I turned to the *Book of Travel*, the seventh book in 'The Management of Life', the second quarter of the *Revival*.

For Al-Ghazali travel is an essential component of belief. He links thought and travel to the common theme of seeking knowledge. Both worldly knowledge and inner knowledge of one's Self and one's position in the cosmos are acquired through travel. Knowledge is the gate of paradise; and travel is the key that unlocks that gate. 'From my early youth,' he tells us in his autobiography, *Deliverance from Error*, 'since I attained the age of puberty before I was twenty, until the present time when I am over fifty, I have ever recklessly launched out into the midst of these ocean depths, I have ever bravely embarked on this open sea, throwing aside all craven caution; I have poked into every dark recess, I have made an assault on every problem, I have plunged into every abyss, I have scrutinized every creed of every sect, I have tried to lay bare the inmost doctrines of every community.' He did all this through travel, he says, to 'distinguish between truth and falsehood'.

Al-Ghazali distinguishes two general categories of travel: *rihla* and *safar*. Both words simply mean 'travel' but signify different orders of endeavour. *Rihla* is outward, physical travel, professionally undertaken, for the sake of learning and discovery. Islam's great travellers, such as Ibn Jubayr, who flourished in the twelfth century, and Ibn Battuta, who travelled the globe during the fourteenth century, produced magnificent *Rihlas* or Travelogues. Ibn Jubayr travelled throughout the Arabian peninsula and produced a book that became the source of invaluable information on medieval Islamic art and architecture. He travelled like a magpie, accurately recording and describing what he saw. The *Rihla* of Ibn Battuta is also a catalogue of weird and wonderful things he saw and a chronicle of his breathtaking adventures. To safeguard the idea of *rihla*, Muslim scholars insisted that the truly great traveller had to produce a compendium of what he had discovered and show how travel had enhanced his own knowledge and learning. But Al-Ghazali was not interested in this kind of travel. For him, travel was not just a physical, outward journey, but also an inner journey. *Safar* involved physical exertion as well as inner transformation, liberation and attainment. In particular, Al-Ghazali suggests, *safar* involved 'motion' and 'mixing'. Motion is the physical movement of the journey as well as the changes the journey brings within hearts and minds. The journey must transport the individual towards new experiences and encounters and force him to perceive the interconnectedness of all things around him. Mixing involved social interaction: it is not the things that the traveller encounters that matter but the people he meets. The traveller learns from mixing with ordinary people who force him to constantly re-examine his own assumptions, his accustomed routine of activity and thought, thus transforming him from the inside and producing a new synthesis.

You can make a philosopher into a traveller, but you can never entirely eradicate the philosopher in the one who travels. So, of course, Al-Ghazali is not content with two categories of travel. He goes on to define whole classes of travel and travellers and generate a typological schema with some politically prescient categories. It's not entirely his fault. Classification, typology building, was a basic requirement, the intellectual instrument of classical Islamic thought. These guys were taught to think and think lucidly for a purpose. His schema for travel is rather like the Victorian train system: hierarchically organized into first, second, third class and the cargo hold. The first-class traveller goes in search of knowledge that eventually transforms him and leads to paradise. The second class, as one would expect, is occupied by sturdy, sensible, middle-class worthies bent on improving themselves: those who travel for the sake of worship, going on a pilgrimage to Mecca, from where they return purified, with a new active religious consciousness, humbled by their experience and more conscious of their social duties. These are the praiseworthy classes of travel. Third class contains the upwardly mobile, aspiring working classes and refugees: travellers who are escaping from persecution or economic misery – they seek changes in their material well-being as well as in their ability to practise their faith. This is a 'permissible' class of travel. In Muslim sensibilities it is rather more, in fact. The very first Muslim community was formed by just such asylum seekers: the Islamic calendar begins in the year 622 CE with the migration or Hejira of Prophet Muhammad and his followers from Mecca to Medina to escape persecution and economic sanctions. The fourth class, those lurking in the steerage hold, are 'problematic', comprising travellers who are escaping from things that are harmful to the body such as a plague or what depreciates wealth such as inflation – this travel is not permitted and can actually be blameworthy or undesirable: fleeing a plague will not prevent one from catching it but could actually spread it. I will spare you the detailed analogy with latter-day political rhetoric. Suffice it to say, I chose to travel first class, like a mystic or a vagabond, in search of knowledge.

The ostensible excuse for my next round of travelling was to gather material for my first book, *Science, Technology and Development in the Muslim World*. I persuaded a few friends and family members to finance a trip around the Middle East to visit science institutions, to examine research programmes and the development plans of various Muslim countries. Development, through the acquisition of modern science and technology, had for decades been touted and promoted, packaged and purveyed as the one and only route to the earthly paradise of modernity.

Why the Middle East? The region is a veritable Clapham Junction of routes to paradise. Apart from being the birthplace of three major world religions: Judaism, Christianity and Islam, it saw the beginning of a few lesser ones, such as Zoroastrianism, as well. Furthermore, the region also gave us the idea of Eden, the Earthly Paradise, the point of origin from which humanity began its perverse career through history. Eden is an immensely potent idea, relentlessly deployed, reworked, secularized, fashioned into utopias of various stripe and hue in numerous traditions of thought. And the road to the alternative earthly paradise fashioned by the rise of science and technology also begins its career in the Middle East. The region is the hearth around which civilization, as we know and define it, was invented. Here mankind began that particular process of making itself: domesticating plants and animals, developing agriculture and metallurgy, inventing writing and the literary arts, developing long-distance trading systems, coming together in cities and shaping state systems of governance.

What is the relationship between the land itself and the vision unleashed in these lands? – this is a question any first-class traveller must explore. The landscape, places and history of this region belong to billions of people around the globe in an intimate and real sense despite the fact that they have never and may never set foot there. The entire region is overlain by a superstructure of cultural reference. The inferences constructed from its landscape and history are infused with meaning and perpetually meaningful to billions of strangers, living in their aspirations, dreams and fantasies.

The Middle East is the land of forefathers, the Patriarchs, the Prophets for Jews, Christians and Muslims. It is the land where miracles happened. It is not only the land of parables, narratives told to illustrate a moral principle; it is also a land of fables, narratives that subvert reality, told through fabulous incident that stretches human credulity. This is a storied land in many senses, many meanings of the phrase. Here be marvels is a basic quality of the very first travel books produced by Europeans who made pilgrimages to the holy places of the Middle East. Their works are generically known as Book of Wonders. All the pilgrims who came after seem to have brought marvels with them and found these marvels reflected in the lands they visited and the peoples they encountered. The fables grew in the telling until nothing is beyond belief out East in this intimately known, impossibly imagined Orient. The Middle East is not only long in story, it's a tall story the European literary imagination cannot entirely dispense with. And for the people of Europe this land, so central to their image of self, was lost, it passed from their control. I can trace a unitary line through the history of the Middle East from the beginning to myself. Not so Europe. With the rise of Islam in the Middle East, conceptually Europe had to confront a second expulsion from Eden, a new dispersal of peoples from the Tower of Babel. And the fabulous explanations of why and how this happened have shaped my life in Europe, they enfolded me and surrounded me with fables of who and what I am.

I began my journey in Tehran. It was the summer of 1974. Just a few years earlier, in 1971, the Shah had amazed the world with his obscenely magnificent celebrations at Persepolis. On that occasion his modernization plan for a profoundly Muslim nation was cast as a celebration of 2,500 years of Empire traced back to Cyrus the Great. The lavish splendour of the ceremony, mostly furnished by Parisian designers, from the Lanvin uniforms for the cast of thousands to the Limoges china and even the food and wines served thereon, looked like a hybrid cross between a Hollywood epic and scenes from *The Arabian Nights*, also beloved by Hollywood.

I had the perfect contact, an old student friend. Reza had just finished his doctorate in Islamic history and was an emerging expert on the history of the Ismaili branch of Islam. After returning to Tehran, he tried, unsuccessfully, to get a job at the university and then at the Imperial Iranian Academy of Philosophy. The reason for his rebuff, I soon discovered – apart from the fact that his specialist subject was not the kind of history currently in vogue – was that he was active in the growing underground of opposition to the Shah. Not getting a job meant he had even more time to spend clandestinely distributing speeches and tapes of Ayatollah Ruhullah al-Musavi al-Khomeini. The tapes were smuggled through an elaborate network from Iraq where Khomeini was living in exile and directing the struggle against the Shah of Iran. When I arrived in Tehran, there was a palpable tension in the city, people were wary and watchful. Walking the streets of the thoroughly modernized areas of north Tehran, redeveloped in homage to Parisian boulevards, I felt as if I was inside a gathering thunderstorm watching the pressure rise.

'We are on the verge of a revolution,' Reza told me confidently when he picked me up from the airport in his old Chevrolet and drove me to his family home in the poorer, unmodernized southern part of the city. He was a tall, well-built man, with a neat, closely cropped full beard. He spoke softly but passionately; and there was an air of cultural sophistication about him, but not the urbane kind that had washed across the news coverage of Persepolis. The following day he took me to a demonstration against the 'Political Immunity Act'. 'The act was passed in 1963,' Reza explained. 'It limits the jurisdiction of Iranian courts and prevents American citizens from being tried by our courts. Thus, Americans enjoy total immunity; while our religious leaders and students are terrorized and tortured.' Reza paused and cast his eyes down. I followed his gaze: a small column of ants tortuously made its way through a crack in the pavement towards a discarded crumb of bread. 'Many of my friends have been arrested on false charges. They have suffered unbelievable tortures. It is only a matter of time before it is my turn.'

The demonstration was noisy, there were some arrests, but no violence. Reza pointed out that we were being photographed by SAVAK, the Shah's secret police, who already had an awesome international reputation. Among agit-propers everywhere they had become a byword for brutality. 'Congratulations!' he said without a hint of jubilation. 'You too are a marked man.'

During the next few weeks I visited several research institutions and talked to numerous scientists. I sampled the atmosphere of approaching storm in the north and the south of the city. I engaged with civil servants, the merchants in the bazaar, and professors, writers and thinkers in the universities. Everyone talked of the coming revolution in hushed tones. The overwhelming majority of people I spoke to were convinced it would usher in perfect justice and equity; and build a divine paradise on earth. But while Reza and his associates dreamed of revolution, my mind was wandering in another direction.

Earthly utopias always begin with a dream; but the reality often turns out to be a nightmare. Not far from Tehran, several centuries ago, there was another group of revolutionaries who dreamed of an earthly paradise. The more I heard about the coming revolution, the more I began to think about the 'Order of Assassins', the extreme and violent sect that flourished from the eleventh to the middle of the thirteenth century. I kept drawing parallels between these erstwhile seekers after paradise and the revolutionaries I met in Iran. Both were determined to create an earthly utopia; both were more than willing to use violence to secure their goals; both were being directed by a charismatic religious leader. When I realized that Reza was uniquely qualified to guide me to the Alamut valley, the site of the castle from where Hasan al-Sabbah, the leader of the sect, founded the order, I became quite determined to visit the Valley of the Assassins.

Like me, the Assassins were seeking paradise. It was their propensity to seek paradise with a dagger in their blood-drenched fists that made them such a thundering good story reverberating down the centuries. The main ingredients of the legend can be traced back, via Freya Stark, to the *Travels of Marco Polo* and beyond. According to Marco Polo, who passed through Persia in 1273, the Assassins trained their young men from childhood for the sole purpose of turning them into fanatical killing machines against their enemies; they used drugs in the indoctrination process, and taught them total obedience to their Sheikh, the so-called 'Old Man of the Mountain'. Central to this legend is the idea of a wonderful garden, a Paradise on Earth, in which the young assassins, according to Marco Polo, 'had what young men would have; and with their own good will they never would have quitted the place'. When we set off from his house Reza kept looking around to see if we were being followed by SAVAK agents. Only when we left the city and were on the narrow road to Qazwin, did he begin to relax.

'Did the Ismaili Assassins actually invent assassination?' He laughed. I realized with a sudden jolt that this was the first time I had heard him laugh since my arrival. As a short summer storm releases the tension in the air, so the laugh seemed to soften him immediately into conversational mode. 'So you too have swallowed the Orientalist propaganda. I didn't expect this from you.'

There was silence while Reza concentrated on overtaking a lopsided truck that seemed dangerously overloaded.

'No. The Ismaili Assassins did not invent assassination,' he resumed with what might have been a chuckle. 'Assassinations have been around from the dawn of human history, what age or nation has been without them? Even the course of early Islamic history was changed by assassinations. Have you forgotten that three of our four Rightly Guided Caliphs were themselves assassinated? And throughout the so-called Golden Age of Islam, during the Abbasid dynasty and the period of Harun-al-Rashid, the Muslim community regularly witnessed the assassination of its leaders.'

'But they did lend their name to it.'

'Yes, they did. But that too is based on an erroneous assumption.' Reza took his eye off the road and looked directly towards me. 'It is the product of the propaganda perpetuated by your lot!' He smiled as he turned his eyes back on the road. 'Unable to grasp why the Assassins were so effective, you Sunnis attributed their success to the use of hashish. *Hashishin*: those who take hashish. It was the Sunni way of deriding them. The members of the sect would be shocked to hear themselves described in this way. They called themselves Nazaris.'

Soon after the death of the Prophet Muhammad, we had the first major division in Islam, which produced the Sunnis and the Shia. The Shia wanted political power to remain in the family of the Prophet. Sunnis did not. Then, the Shia split into two major factions: the Twelve-Imam Shia and the Ismailis. The former assert that power in the Muslim community, in which esoteric guidance and spiritual leadership are inseparable elements, belongs to Ali, cousin of the Prophet and fourth Caliph of Islam. They also believe that according to the specification of the Prophet, the Imams of the Household of the Prophet, that is legitimate inheritors of power, are twelve in number. Throughout my Islamic education, the Shias were never mentioned. Indeed, even when I learned about the various 'Schools of Thought', the main Shia legal school, the Jafari jurisprudence, was totally ignored: as though it just did not exist. Still, that was better than what most Sunnis actually learn about Shiism: in most Sunni circles, the Shia are painted as dark outsiders who denigrate the Rightly Guided Caliphs, and venerate Caliph Ali, the cousin of the Prophet, beyond his station, even suggesting that he – and not Prophet Muhammad – should have been the true recipient of God's revelation. Sunni hostility towards the Shia has produced a whole genre of derogatory literature designed solely to locate them outside the boundary of orthodox Islam.

The landscape changed drastically. From the austere mountain scenery that surrounds Tehran we had burst into a valley lush with spring. The tang of growing things lifted my spirits and the scent of green growth reminded me, as it always does, of my home village in Pakistan where I played in the fields of sugar cane as a young boy. We were both relaxing into our former selves.

'The Ismailis emerged during the time of Imam Jafaar Sadik, the fifth Imam,' Reza explained to me. 'His elder son, Ismail, died during his lifetime. Imam Jafaar summoned the elders of the community to witness his death. But some of the witnesses believed that Ismail did not die but went into occultation and will appear again as the promised Mehdi, the redeemer who would appear at the end of time. They believed the next true Imam was Ismail, and not his brother, Musa al-Kazim. These people became the Ismailis. The Ismailis believe that God is neither existent nor non-existent, intelligent nor unintelligent, powerful nor helpless. They're of the opinion it is not possible for anything or any attribute to be associated with God for he is the maker of all things, including all names and attributes. They believe the earth can never exist without a Proof of God. The "Proof" is of two kinds: "speaker" and "silent one". The speaker is a Prophet; and the silent one is an Imam or Guardian, who is the executor of the testament of the Prophet.'

'For Ismaelis, the principle of Proof of God revolves constantly around the number seven. A Prophet, who is sent by God, has the function of prophecy and esoteric power of initiating men into Divine Mysteries. After him there are seven executors of his testament who possess the power of initiation into the Divine Mysteries but do not have the power of prophecy. The eighth in the succession, however, acquires both these powers and becomes a Prophet in his own right. The cycle of seven executors is then repeated. The Ismailis established the Fatimid dynasty in Cairo, deriving their name from Fatima, daughter of the Prophet and wife of his cousin, Imam Ali. In rivalry with the Abbasids, who ruled from Baghdad, the Fatimids proclaimed themselves to be the true caliphs, but the majority of their subjects remained Sunnis. For seven generations, from 909 to 1036, the Fatimids ruled North Africa, Egypt and Syria without any divisions. At the death of the seventh Imam, Al-Mustansir billah Muidd ibn Ali, his sons, Nizar and Al-Mustali, began disputing the succession. The dispute over both the caliphate and imamate, both political and spiritual power, ended in bloody battles. Eventually, Al-Mustali won, captured his brother, and imprisoned him. Nizar died in prison. Are you with me so far?'

'Yes,' I replied. 'But I am beginning to realize why you need a PhD to understand this stuff.'

Reza explained that the Ismailis were divided into at least two parts. The followers of Al-Mustali continued Fatimid rule in Egypt till 1171, when they were conquered by Salah ad-Din (Saladin) who, apart from sorting out the Crusaders, established the Ayyubid dynasty in Egypt. They disappeared from Egypt only to reappear in India – nowadays they are known as the Bohra Ismaili community of Bombay. Those who sided with Nizar came to be known as the Nizaris. A close associate of Nizar was a man called Hasan al-Sabbah. After Nizar's death, Al-Mustali expelled him from Egypt. He came to Persia and after a short while appeared in the Fort of Alamut near Qazwin, where he established his rule and began inviting people to join the Nizari cause.

We were approaching Qazwin. My tutorial was over for the day. My mind swimming in the detail of history, I turned my eyes to the city. It was as if our conversation had transported us back through time and space, our words delivering us into the landscape of *The Arabian Nights*. There were minarets, domes, arches, portals, tombs, baths, arabesques, calligraphy, engraved woodwork and dazzling doors everywhere. This bustling city was alive with spectacular buildings, including the Jamia Mosque, said to have been built by the Abbasid Caliph Harun-al-Rashid in the eighth century. It retained the ambience of a glittering caravanserai, a way station on that fabled route James Elroy Flecker dubbed the Golden Road to Samarkand, the Silk Road that connected the trading world of Asia from west to east and east to west. And here, still, were souks selling miniatures, textiles, carpets and crafts of all description. Dreams and reality are not always separate and distinct, sometimes you can walk through reality that is dreamlike and feel the connective tissue of time. But even a wide-eyed traveller should observe the proper courtesies. In this town my mentor, the traveller first class Al-Ghazali, ended his earthly journey. On my request, Reza took me to the grave and we both said a little prayer.

I wanted to linger in the bazaar and let my thoughts wander through the realities of an earlier global economy, the trading world before upstart Europe determined it must control and own everything. Reza was eager to proceed; he still had the unfinished business of the future to return to. After a quick meal and a prayer at the nineteenth-century Sardar mosque (no relation) we resumed our journey. We left Qazwin, and it was as if the dream evaporated. The road stretched out across a dusty featureless plain before it began to climb the range of jagged hills that would take us to the Chala Pass. As we wound upwards the way narrowed to a convoluted dirt road, and Reza had to concentrate hard to insinuate his cumbersome vehicle around tight bends. Sometimes, he had to go backwards to advance, shifting into reverse to create the space to get around the corners.

When we passed the village of Chala the road became more forgiving. And our thoughts turned back to our immediate objective. Reza took up the thread of his lecture at precisely the point where the Assassins entered the scene.

'When Hasan al-Sabbah arrived in Alamut,' he said, 'Persia was ruled by the Saljuqs. The Saljuq state was run on strictly hierarchical lines, with the supreme Sultan supported by a Persian bureaucracy and a multinational army managed by Turkish commanders. Naturally, the Saljuqs were not very happy with this upstart who was trying to establish his own empire in the north. Al-Sabbah, who was fired by a simplistic but militant faith and led an abstemious life of religious piety, saw the Saljuqs as an evil empire out to destroy him. And he had a ready-made constituency in the turbulent and disaffected population, with a strong local tradition of personal loyalty. His problem was simple: his followers were rather few while the Saljuq army was numerous and mighty. He needed an effective weapon to fight the Saljuqs.'

'He was giving recognition to the Shia principle of justified revolt against an oppressive tyrant or sinful leader.'

Reza corrected me politely: 'After the assassination of Caliph Ali, the Ismailis as well as the Shia in general believed that it was not the rulers who were being killed but their Imams. So the Ismailis saw ritual murder as an act of defiance as well as an act of piety. And the element of piety meant that the assassin himself had to be willing to give his life.

Al-Sabbah relied on ordinary people who had nothing to lose and therefore "loved death more than life". Each victim was chosen with extreme care to cause the maximum disruption to the established . . .'

'You mean Sunni,' I interjected.

'. . . order. They had two groups of victims: princes, officers and ministers; and religious leaders and scholars who had condemned their doctrines. And they always killed their victims using a single weapon, which depended upon the particular Nizari group. Some used daggers, some strangled, some clubbed their victims to death. They never used poisons or missiles even though those would have been a far safer option.'

We now arrived at the place where the Taliqan and Alamut rivers converge to form the Shah River. The road submerged into their waters, we splashed our way through the shallow bed of the Alamut River. A few kilometres further on, we spotted where the road reappeared. We drove for a few more hours until we reached a village called Shahrak. It was getting dark and Reza suggested we find a place to spend the night. We slept on the veranda of a coffee shop, where a determined army of whining, whirring, dive-bombing mosquitoes kept me awake most of the night.

The following morning, we set off on foot. Reza left his car at a petrol pump and paid the attendant to look after it. We followed a path beside the Alamut River.

'This is the valley,' Reza said, 'from where the Nizaris ruled their theological kingdom.' It looked an innocent enough enclave. The local farmers were growing rice, so much of our path was waterlogged.

'Just how many people did they actually kill?' I asked.

'Well, quite a few but not as many as the legend would have us believe. You have to remember that the dynasty of the Grand Masters of Alamut lasted well over 150 years, from 1090 to 1256. Hasan al-Sabbah was succeeded by seven other Grand Masters before the Mongols captured Alamut and brought their rule to an end. But the extremism and violence of the Assassins had subsided by the time of Grand Master Hasan III, who was converted to Sunnism by the Abbasid Caliph an-Nasir, around 1166. So the actual period when the assassins operated is less than sixty years. But the assassinations did cause considerable havoc in the Sunni world. This is why the Sunnis created a heady mixture of myth and fantasy that exaggerated the power of the Assassins far beyond their limited capabilities.'

'So, it is all the fault of us Sunnis!' I observed.

'I am glad you accept the responsibility,' Reza shot back.

We crossed the river by means of a precarious 'bridge' which consisted of nothing more than two supple wooden poles. We were walking in the shadow of the central Alborz mountain range. Waterfalls, cascading down from the heights, dotted the landscape.

'The Sunnis needed a villain,' Reza resumed once we had safely crossed. 'A sort of internal demon Other, and Hasan al-Sabbah provided just the right ingredients. Take the story of his friendship with Omar Khayyam, the legendary Persian poet and mathematician, and Nizam al-Mulk, the famous intellectual Vizir of the Saljuq Empire. The narrative goes that Al-Sabbah went to school with these two figures – all three destined to greatness. They became close friends and swore a solemn oath: whoever achieves greatness first will advance the career of the other two. It so happened, Nizam al-Mulk achieved his ambition first and rose to become an important figure in the Saljuq Sultanate. Remembering his oath, he offered provincial governorships to his school buddies. Omar declined the post, accepting a regular stipend from Nizam instead. Hasan refused because he thought the post was beneath him. Nizam offered him a higher post, which he accepted, and excelled in his work. Soon, Nizam began to see him as a threat; consumed with jealousy he turned on Hasan who was forced to flee. When Hasan himself became successful and founded his Order at Amalut, his first victim was Nizam al-Mulk.'

'What's wrong with the story? It seems perfectly plausible to me.'

We were passing near a small village and Reza waved to the children playing in the field.

'It's a great story. It provides Al-Sabbah with ambition and desire for vengeance. But the three men grew up in different parts of Persia and lived nowhere near enough to each other to go to the same school in their youth. Besides, when Omar Khayyam was born, Nizam al-Mulk was already thirty. We do not know when Al-Sabbah was born; but unless he was over a hundred years old when he died – and we do know that he died in 1124 – he was not the same age as Nizam al-Mulk. But stories like this played a key part in building up the legend of Al-Sabbah and attributing to him superhuman qualities: hatching his evil plots in a magical castle and sending forth his murderous emissaries drugged with hashish all over the globe. His victims were to be found not just in Persia and Syria, but also in Iraq and Egypt. He was even blamed for certain murders in Europe as though Europe needed any help in that direction.'

'The Assassins needed nothing more than religious belief to perform their dastardly acts?'

'The Nizari faith did have a strong mystical flavour. The intoxication of the assassins was, if anything, their brand of mysticism that associated Truth with certain individual persons. They may have used hashish in their mystical ceremonies. But the young assassins themselves, who were highly educated, fluent in a number of languages, very patient and were excellent planners, needed nothing more than religious devotion to carry out their tasks.'

We now reached the village of Qasir Khan by a small tributary of the Amalut River. It was an idyllic vision of rural paradise. Neat, flat-roofed houses everywhere, their brightly painted doors pleasing the eye. Some of the houses nestled among orchards that gave off a subtle, inviting, fragrance. Some had vines growing on their roofs, seeming to envelop the man-made structure and integrate it with the landscape.

'Look behind the village,' Reza said, pointing towards a mountain. 'That is Mount Haudegan. And this,' he now pointed towards a smaller hill dwarfed by the great mass behind it, 'is the site of the Castle of Amalut.' Distance plays havoc with perspective, whether in time or space. Only when I got closer to the Rock was it possible to appreciate how imposing it is. From one line of approach where it presented a defiant sheer rock wall to the world, it was clearly impregnable. The castle itself had all but disappeared, only a few broken teeth of stones were evidence of its former existence. I could also pick out various channels criss-crossing its face.

'Just over there,' Reza said, pointing at the top of the Rock, 'is the Vine of Hasan al-Sabbah.'

'And these folks,' I said, pointing to the villagers who were staring at us with some curiosity, 'are what's left of the Assassins?'

'No. No. No,' replied Reza in agitation. 'These people have nothing to do with the Assassins. After the Mongol invasion, the Assassins totally disappeared from here only to reappear in your country.'

'England?' I retorted.

'Yes,' Reza replied bursting out in laughter. 'And Pakistan. The Assassins were reborn as the Aga Khanis. The Aga Khan, that well-known playboy of the western world, is a direct lineal descendant of the Grand Masters of Alamut. They don't assassinate people any more; but the cult functions in exactly the same way.'

By now we were surrounded by an interested and exceptionally friendly crowd of villagers. Reza negotiated a well-deserved meal of pastry and rice. As we chatted inconsequentially one of the villagers agreed to guide us to the top of Amalut hill. We climbed through a passageway where the hill joins the main mass of Mount Haudegan and wandered about examining the ruins of the castle.

'Where is the famous garden?' I asked Reza.

'Well, if there was a garden, it would be over there,' he pointed to the farther end of the hill. 'It is not visible from here,' he said, 'you have to climb down.' I wandered in the direction he indicated and arrived at a precipice and found myself staring into the pit that might once have been the garden of paradise. The vertiginous cliff face looked devoid of ledges but our guide insisted that it was easy to climb down.

'What is this I see,' Reza said in a sarcastic tone. 'You've come all the way to see the garden of paradise and now you don't want to climb down to actually see it?'

I stood there transfixed. 'I have come to see,' I said. 'Not to die.'

We climbed a few steps down from the summit, sat at the mouth of a tunnel and feasted our eyes on the panorama before us.

'This is how Hasan al-Sabbah must have seen the Alamut valley,' Reza said.

I nodded. I did not wish to speak of the thoughts that made me dizzy as I stood on the precipice of this particular vision of paradise. I had said 'I want to live, not die.' But it was so much more than that. I wanted a paradise that fosters a living garden – what was the point of one that inculcated the willingness not only to die but to kill?

We spent the night at Qasir Khan; and started our walk back to

Shahrak early in the morning. There was nothing now to keep Reza from his eagerness to return to Tehran. We rejoined his trusty old Chevrolet the following morning and began retracing our route back to Qazwin. And he was released from his role as history lecturer and guide to talk of his real passion: the coming revolution and Imam Khomeini. I listened.

'I don't understand this Imam business,' I said. 'If you combine spiritual and political leadership in a single man you are asking for trouble.'

'But the Imams are *masoum* – totally innocent – they can do no wrong,' he said.

'That's the trouble,' I replied. 'How can a man be totally innocent? If he is he's not a man, but an angel. What if Imam Khomeini turns out to be another Hasan al-Sabbah?'

I turned my face to Reza and saw his had turned red. He brushed the question aside and launched into a learned discourse on Imamology – explaining the meaning of Imam, his role in the exposition of 'divine sciences' and the history of the twelve Imams. The more he explained, the more sceptical I became. When he started to explain how the twelfth Imam went into occultation and would reappear as the Mehdi, I could take it no more.

'What if,' I said, 'the twelfth Imam did not go into occultation. What if he just got lost? Say, fell in a well where no one could find him?'

That was a question too far. The old Chevrolet came to a screeching halt as Reza stepped on the brakes. 'Brother Zia,' he said, taking a deep breath, 'you have two problems. You are a coward. You come all the way to see the Paradise of Al-Sabbah but are afraid of climbing down a hill. Yes, it was a bit steep; but you could have at least made an effort. And you just can't keep your mouth shut.' Reza offered no opportunity for me to open said orifice. 'Please take your suitcase and get out of my car; and find your own way to Tehran.'

And there I stood. Rebuffed. Alone, suitcase by my side, on a dusty road that might lead to Qazwin.

I stood not knowing what to do. I had no idea how far I was from Qazwin. It is a serious limitation for a traveller first class to have as little sense of geography, distance and direction as myself. Then, in the distance, I became aware of a vehicle approaching. More than a vehicle, a whole caravan of lorries. We are on the Silk Road, I reminded myself, a major artery that throughout history has carried trade, people and ideas across the face of the known world. Of course it's a caravan coming my way. I stuck out my thumb. A driver stopped. 'Tehran,' I said, 'Tehran.' He shook his head: 'Kermanshah,' he replied, 'Kermanshah.' He who knows not geography will take any port in his abandonment. Did it matter where or in what direction? I climbed aboard.

The truck driver, a well-built man with several days of unshaved stubble, was in high spirits. He took two cigarettes out of a pack with his mouth, lit them both while leaving the driving wheel unattended for what felt like a very long time, passed one on to me, and threw the match, still burning, out of the window. 'No, no,' I said, 'I don't smoke.' But he kept insisting; so I took the cigarette and pretended to smoke it.

'What are you carrying?' I asked. He replied. I am not quite sure what he replied because I did not understand a word. But he was talking incessantly, lighting cigarettes two at a time, and smoking them with lightning speed. Eventually I got hold of the word 'paraffin'. He was carrying paraffin. And he was smoking like a chimney; and throwing lighted matches out of the window. I was travelling on a powder keg. With no idea of exactly where I was going. The truck driver was blithely unconcerned; he was fully engaged in telling me his life story. I did my very best Hodja impersonation, pretending to understand every word, shaking my head vigorously in agreement, laughing when he laughed, replying to the questions I imagined he had asked. Gradually, it occurred to me that my driver was not in high spirits – just high. This thought must have occurred shortly before I realized I too was high, which would have been shortly after I had eaten various things he passed to me. Shortly thereafter, I lit two cigarettes, gave him one, and threw the live match out of the window.

We passed mountain after mountain; stopped at a place called Hamadan for refuelling; and continued meandering through the mountainous region. Eventually, I fell asleep. When I woke up, hours later, I was in Kermanshah. It transpired I had been following the Dr Khan theory of geography. Kermanshah is a good 600 kilometres south-west of Tehran. We were in a truck depot. My truck driver was involved in an animated discussion with several other truck drivers. I knew instantly that they were talking about me. I joined in the conversation. By now, I too sported a few days of stubble and looked like one of the truck drivers; they, in turn, seemed to have adopted me. Soon we were eating together like long-lost friends. The conversations continued; despite the lack of a mutually intelligible language I slowly began to grasp a sense of the issue under debate: who would take me to Tehran. No offers appeared forthcoming but I gathered some trucks were on their way to Baghdad. It made perfect sense to 'Fare forward' to the fabled city and not retrace my steps to Tehran. Baghdad, I intoned like a mantra until everyone got the message. And so it was settled. My driver took my suitcase from his truck and placed it in another. When it was time to move, I climbed on the new truck. In less than eight hours, I was in the city of Harun-al-Rashid.

Chapter 6

PRESIDENTS AND PEASANTS

I came to ground in an area of Baghdad called Alawi Alhilla. The hotel did not look very inviting. Nevertheless, I went in and enquired if they had a room. 'For sure,' replied the reception clerk. He took my money and I followed him upstairs into a large, rectangular room. He pointed towards the corner.

'That's your bed,' he said. 'I know it is a little shabby, but you will have a restful night on it.'

'Shabby!' I said. 'It's not a bed. It's just a foam mattress. And what's that red thing crawling on the pillow?'

'Sorry about the bedbugs.' He was clearly embarrassed. 'We can't get rid of them. But they don't bother strangers. Something to do with foreign blood.' He paused for a moment to gauge my reaction. 'You will be safe. But I can't guarantee anything about your suitcase.'

I had no energy to begin a search for a more appropriate place. 'I suppose this will have to do,' I muttered with disconsolate resignation. This theme of classes of traveller, travel and now accommodation was losing its whimsy – rapidly.

'Good,' said the hotel clerk. 'Have a good night. But remember to look after your luggage. We've had many thefts lately.'

I placed my suitcase under the pillow and fell onto the mattress. Two occupants of mattresses at the other end of the room were talking and reciting poetry just loud enough for me to hear. I could see the man who was reciting sitting on his mattress, shaking his head from side to side as though in ecstasy. He was reciting a poem by Abu Nuwas, a ninth-century local resident:

> *Ho! a cup and fill it up, and tell me it is wine,*
> *For never will I drink in shade if I can drink in shine.*
> *Curst and poor is every hour that sober I must go,*
> *But rich am I whene'er well drunk I stagger to and fro.*
> *Speak, for shame, the loved one's name, let vain disguises fall;*
> *Good for naught are pleasures hid behind a curtain-wall.*

I turned on my other side and closed my eyes and lingered on the fringes of sleep. Every bone in my body was aching, and the bedbugs had deemed me local not foreign by blood. I tossed and turned for over an hour. Eventually, I began to dream. I dreamed that I was standing in front of an endless wall. I was trying to climb it, but it was too high. It appeared to be touching the sky. I kept on trying to climb it but to no avail. Suddenly, I was distracted by laughter. It was Abu Nuwas. He was pointing at me as if to say, 'You fool. There is no way you can get over that wall.'

'You scoundrel! I will show you. Nothing is beyond me,' I said angrily.

'I was deserted first by my father, and then my mother. See how well I have done on my own. I am highly respected among the learned circles of Baghdad and am the favourite poet and companion of Caliph Harun-al-Rashid. Stop climbing the wall and let yourself be. You will carry less luggage and go much further. Who knows, you may acquire a reputation like mine.' He laughed again, a loud, boisterous laugh.

'Not likely,' I said, and chased after him.

I turned round to scratch a back bitten by bedbugs and confronted an empty room. All the guests had gone. I slipped my hand under the pillow to make sure that my suitcase was still there. It was.

It was a new day and time to explore. I left the hotel and crossed the Tigris on Jasr Atiqh, said to be the oldest bridge in Baghdad. I was looking for the Baghdad of Harun-al-Rashid, the enormous ninth-century world of royal cities-within-a-city I had read about in so many stories and legends surrounding that magical monarch. I wanted to find the Baghdad where classical Muslim civilization began. As a village, Baghdad probably dates back to antiquity. The whole of Iraq is littered with sites whose occupation stretches back to the very beginning of that thing we call civilization. Archaeologists know them as tells, from the local term for a hill. It always strikes me that 'tell' is a fitting name best left untranslated for the extra meaning it conveys in English. These hills were raised above the surrounding area by generation after generation of residents building on the ruins of previous occupants, a chain of rebuilding stretching right back to the first people who took up a settled agricultural life. The hills tell of the accumulated physical record of human existence and much about change, progress and the continuities of human life as a result. Baghdad itself is just a few kilometres from the site of the ancient city of Babylon, a centre of empire with 2,000 years of history when Athens was just beginning to fashion itself as a city with an inflated sense of self-importance. Reality and dreams, the Tigris has seen so much as it washes its way to the sea.

It was Caliph Abu Jafar al-Mansur, the second Abbasid caliph known for his knowledge and wisdom, who built Baghdad to be the capital city of the Abbasid Empire. By the reign of Harun-al-Rashid in the later eighth century, the city – now second in size only to Constantinople – had become a thriving world centre of commerce and learning. The Abbasids built libraries, colleges and hospitals as well as canals, dikes and reservoirs, and drained the swamps around the city thus freeing it of malaria. Harun-al-Rashid's son, Al-Mamun, founded the famous Bait al-Hikma, 'the House of Wisdom', in the ninth century, and launched a scientific and cultural revolution unparalleled in history. The House of Wisdom's first director, Hunayn ibn Ishaq, translated the complete medical and philosophical works of Galen, the physics of Aristotle, and the Greek Old Testament, before his death in 873. Ibn Ishaq's numerous students translated Plato, Aristotle, Hippocrates, Ptolemy, Euclid, Pythagoras and the neo-Platonists into Arabic. One of the city's early inhabitants, a certain Abu Jafar Muhammad ibn Musa al-Khawarizmi, discovered algebra at the beginning of the eighth century. Another, Al-Kindi, the first Arab philosopher, worked tirelessly to promote the use of reason and reconcile the ideas of neo-Platonism with Islamic revelation. Yet another, the philosopher and medic Al-Razi, produced a monumental medical encyclopedia. And, of course, Al-Ghazali occupied one of the most prestigious academic posts in the city, the professorial chair at the Madrasa al-Nizamiya, Baghdad's first great school of religious law, founded in 1067.

What remained of that Baghdad, I wondered? The Baghdad of fountains of knowledge. The Baghdad at the centre, the fulcrum of a globalized culture that went on to humanize Europe: the Baghdad that taught Europe the distinction between civil society and barbarism, the difference between medicine and magic, and the importance of experimental method; the Baghdad that trained the West in scholastic and philosophic method, drilled it in making surgical instruments, told it how to establish and run hospitals and provided it with the model of a university complete with curriculum and syllabus, terminology and administrative structure; the Baghdad that schooled Europe in the importance of biography, the novella, the history of cities and historical and textual criticism. In short, the Baghdad that gave Europe its most prized possession: liberal humanism. By what intellectual conjuring trick had Europe self-servingly made the reality of its cultural debt disappear into a fairy-tale dream of Sinbad, Aladdin, harem ladies in diaphanous veils, the subject matter of pantomime and other such dissembling misrepresentations?

I walked and walked but found little that was more than a few centuries old. The thirteenth-century Al-Madrasa al-Mustansiriyah (Mustansiriyah School), once a highly esteemed university, was still there, even if in a bad state of repair. The Abbasid Palace, built in the same era and architectural style, still stood overlooking the Tigris. The rest was modern architectural desolation. I turned into Souk-al-Sarai and discovered an enchanting book market, a few shops displaying old manuscripts. Across the road on the west side of the souk, a cloth market contained a mixture of Arab and western garments. I carried my suitcase over to Souk-Safafir and saw a few craftsmen at work. A man was working hard to turn a sheet of brass into a flowerpot. Another was making a jug, working with a natural rhythm. Then I walked towards Shourjah where I was greeted by the fragrance of a multitude of teas and spices. Another turn, and I was on Rashid Street.

I noticed the street was becoming emptier and emptier. Suddenly, it was completely devoid of life. People were running from side to side, shopkeepers were pulling their shutters down. I noticed a man standing in front of a shop in a perplexed state. Two soldiers appeared from nowhere, picked him up by his arms and threw him inside the shop, which immediately closed its doors. Up above the small dwellings, a helicopter hovered. I was pushed inside a furniture store; its doors closed behind me. Through the window, I watched as a presidential entourage of cars zoomed by: 200 cars and counting, it seemed to go on for ever.

'Some president?' I said to a man standing nearby.

'President Ahmad Hasan al-Bakr,' he replied in a matter-of-fact way. 'He became president after the Ba'athist coup of 1968.'

We introduced ourselves. He turned out to be a Professor of Political Science at the Waziriyah University in Baghdad.

'He is a Ba'athist? What does that mean?' I enquired innocently, in an unashamed attempt to stimulate his teaching instincts.

The word *Ba'ath*, he told me, means to resurrect. The Ba'athists argue that to reverse the humiliations visited upon the Arab people, they have to go back to their roots, to resurrect themselves, as a united Arab Nation. Their sacred and eternal mission – the *risalah khalidah* – is to unite the Arab people under the banner of socialism. They seek regeneration through Arab Nationalism. This mission is conceived in opposition to Islam. The Ba'athists conceive their sacred mission in natural terms transcending all phases of Arab history, including the history of Islam.

'So Ba'athist ideology is basically a theory of salvation, a route to an earthly paradise?' I asked.

'That is a good way of putting it,' he replied. Michel Aflaq, the teacher who is considered the spiritual leader of Ba'athist ideology, I was told, formulated his ideas in esoteric and Messianic terms. The word *Ba'ath* itself is used in Arabic for the Christian belief in the resurrection of Jesus, and indeed Easter is termed the *yawm al-ba'ath* – the day of Resurrection. When Aflaq used the term *Ba'ath* for the party he helped establish, he meant to convey the idea of eternal, almost divine mission of the Arab people, one above and beyond the call of Islam. The three pillars of the Ba'ath ideology, unity, freedom, and socialism, Aflaq said, are akin to the Holy Trinity in Christian theology. To my surprise, he suggested the Ba'ath are great believers in freedom. 'The Ba'ath constitution declares "freedom of speech, freedom of assembly, freedom of belief, and freedom of art are sacred things which no authority can diminish".' But they envisage this freedom rather like the Communists. The freedom of speech, publication and assembly belongs to the state – the citizens are at its mercy!

'How do they envisage Socialism, then?' I asked.

'The Ba'ath ideology sees itself as scientific socialism plus spirit,' he replied, and then went on to explain that the spirit of revolution guides everything. Aflaq argued that revolution is both a political and social programme as well as a prime propelling power, a mandatory struggle that will lead to Arab reawakening. For him, revolution meant changing the people rather than the system. He envisaged the role of the Ba'ath in revolution as one of an elite vanguard whose task it was to convert the people, to lead them along the road that would end in the construction of a new, vital society in which the Arab people would enjoy all their just glories in an independent united state of Arabism. Whether the people actually followed the elite vanguard was irrelevant.

The Ba'ath will lead the Arab Nation to the promised land whether they like it or not; and will not allow anything to stand between them and their goal – which is to achieve power. Lacking a mass base, the Ba'athists had little vote-getting appeal. So they relied on assassinations. The history of Ba'ath parties in Iraq and Syria is a history of coups and counter-coups, assassinations and violence.

All of this reminded me of the Order of Assassins. 'It should,' I was told. 'But much remains to be seen yet. If you think President Hasan al-Bakr is problematic, you should keep an eye on his Vice-President.'

'Who is that?' I asked.

'Saddam Hussein,' he shot back. His eyes darted sidelong glances around the shop. 'This conversation is getting dangerous,' he murmured. 'It was good talking to you. My Salaams,' he said, darting rapid looks to check the road was clear of police and presidential entourage, and hurriedly walked out of the store.

The street was coming back to life. I continued my exploration, walking along Jamhuriyah Street till I encountered the Mosque of

Khalifahs, a simple but elegant rectangular structure, encrusted with ceramic tiles, as is its conspicuous dome and slim, statuesque minaret. I entered the compound and met a beggar by the fountain. He stretched his left palm in front of me.

'Look after my suitcase and shoes while I pray and you'll get a dinar,' I said to the man, who looked much healthier than most people I had seen in Baghdad.

'But it's not prayer time yet,' he observed with surprise.

'Oh, I'm offering a special prayer for surviving a horrific night and managing to hold on to my luggage.'

The beggar sighed. 'Thieves and assassins have taken over this city. Give me two dinars for looking after your luggage and shoes.'

I agreed and went inside the mosque. After offering my prayers I spent a little time admiring one of the rare remnants of Abbasid architecture. When I came out the beggar was nowhere to be found. He had gone. And taken my suitcase and shoes with him. My loss is not the only reason this mosque is etched on my consciousness. Now it is the backdrop used by every foreign correspondent to report every twist and turn of the continuing saga of Iraq. It has the misfortune to stand directly in the camera shot of the hotel roof from which CNN, and every correspondent since, broadcast the war on Iraq for everyone's television viewing pleasure.

I bought a pair of cheap flip-flops, a shoulder bag and some provisions; and recalled the advice Abu Nawas had imparted in my dream. I was to carry no luggage; so I could go much further. I decided to move on to Syria.

After a long, exhausting bus journey I arrived in Aleppo. When Baghdad was a citadel of learning, Aleppo was a major centre of trade in the Muslim world. It rivalled Sijilmassa in Morocco, Alexandria in Egypt, Nishapur in Eastern Iran and Samarkand in Central Asia as a great emporium and transit point for further destinations, where goods of every conceivable description changed hands. It was the trade centre for Europe, the portal through which the riches of the trading world percolated to that impoverished peninsula tangential to global history, the Levantine gateway used by merchants from Venice, Amalfi and Genoa. It was a consumer's paradise. That, and the fact that the

University of Aleppo was about to set up an Institute for the History of Arabic Science, propelled me towards Aleppo.

I found Aleppo's covered bazaar to be one of the few traditional Arab markets to have escaped the ravages of time and modernity – it was still functioning, with a few minor modern trappings, as it had always done. Walking round the bazaar was like losing yourself in an elaborate labyrinth, there was a surprise at every turn, and every turn took you closer towards the hidden treasures of the bazaar. There was almost nothing in the market that was not fashioned out of centuries of craftsmanship: the sweat and labour of the craftsmen produced objects that interwove art with utility, traditional technology with creativity, and infused human expression into inanimate objects. Most of the products on sale were for daily use – rugs, cloths, lamps, plates, jugs, incense burners, but even the most simple had been turned into rich and exciting works of art. In one segment of the market I saw an entire family at work turning sheep's fleece into wool. Nearby, another family was using the same thread to weave rugs. In an enclave opposite, yet another family was using the leftover bits from the two businesses to make multicoloured floor coverings. This symbiosis was also reflected in the architecture of the bazaar: each dome seems to be supporting every other dome, each tunnel linking several others. I played a game which involved entering the bazaar through one of its many entrances, and then trying to retrace my route back to the same entrance. I tried this several times. Each time I found myself emerging from a different doorway in a different part of the town. It was relatively dark inside the bazaar, except inside the shops which were artificially lit, and I was convinced the ventilation holes, permitting parallel beams of sunlight to hit the walls, were designed to lead wanderers astray. One day, tired and frustrated by trying to master the intricate route-map of the bazaar, I decided to go and sit inside a rug shop.

'*Ahlan wa sahlan.* This is your house,' the shopkeeper, sitting cross-legged on the floor, greeted me the moment I walked in. In the background someone was weaving.

I sat on a large pile of rugs next to him. 'Make yourself at home. How are you?'

'Tired,' I replied. 'It's exhausting wandering around the bazaar.'

'Yes,' he replied. 'Newcomers roam around for hours. It's not easy for them to find their way without some help. Would you like some tea?' Arab hospitality and generosity have also survived, I thought. So much so, in fact, that many people have been financially ruined because they have carried it a bit too far. Even the poorest of Arabs will insist 'my house is your house' and that you must have tea or dinner with him, even stay overnight. If you don't accept his invitation he may be hurt; and if you do, you can, ninety out of a hundred times, be sure he will kill his only goat to feed you. I knew shopkeepers were no exception.

A little girl with two long braids of hair resting on her shoulders brought the tea on a small, round tray. I sat there sipping sweet, syrupy tea from a small glass, watching the man attending to his other customers. As soon as my glass became empty he would pour some more tea, never giving me a chance to say no. Almost an hour later, in between conversation about the differences in life between Aleppo and London – 'You run after time, while we let it flow through us,' he told me – he slipped in the question: 'Is there anything that interests you?'

I almost blurted out: 'I'm only here for the tea,' but caught myself in time. I felt overcome by a strange impulse. Perhaps it was sheer politeness, which in itself would be a novelty for me, I reflected. I picked out an item and pointed towards it, 'I like the subtle use of colour in that cushion cover.'

'Ha, ha,' he replied with suppressed laughter, 'it's not a cushion cover. It's a donkey saddle. How about some coffee, now?'

'I ought to be going,' I said. 'Perhaps I will come across your shop again. I promise I'll drop in for some coffee.'

'It's past *Zuhr* [the midday prayer], it will be very hot outside. Stay until *Asr* [the late afternoon prayer], by then the sun will have gone down. During midday the bazaar is the coolest place in town. You'll be much more comfortable here. Anyway, we are about to have our lunch and it would be an honour for me if you joined us.' There was a polite insistence in his eyes.

Just before lunch he told me that the donkey saddle was 500 liras, around twenty dollars, but he would let me have it for 450. After lunch we had some Turkish coffee and he suggested I should lie down on a rug and have some rest.

I did as he said and within a few minutes was sound asleep. When I woke up I knew the sun had set. As soon as I opened my eyes I was served tea. The little girl had now become quite friendly. She sat on my lap and put her arms round my neck.

'Now that you have become a family friend,' said the shopkeeper, pausing for a smile, 'you can have the donkey saddle for only 250 liras.'

'Tell me,' I asked, looking him straight in the eyes. 'Has anyone ever left your shop empty-handed?'

'Not after they have accepted my tea,' he replied, chuckling.

As I walked out of the shop with the donkey saddle thrown over my shoulder, I heard the little girl ask her father: 'If they don't have donkeys in London, what is he going to do with the saddle?'

'I expect, like the rest of them, he will hang it on the wall of his house,' replied her father.

Through the corner of my eye, I enjoyed the look of amazement on the little girl's face.

It was getting towards midnight as I traipsed out of the old bazaar and walked towards my hotel. I hadn't shaved for a few days and decided it was time to tackle my incipient beardedness by collecting some razor blades. I took a detour to the new bazaar. It was still bustling with activity. I was picking up a piece of ceramic that caught my eye just to admire when I heard the rat-tat-tat. I am no munitions expert but there is something instantly recognizable about machine-gun fire. Pandemonium enveloped me. Shoppers were scattering wildly in all directions. Rat-tat-tat. An entire row of stalls crammed with ceramic goods burst into fragments in the blink of an eye. I ran and hid behind the steel door of a tourist shop. Rat-tat-tat. More gunfire followed by the crashing and cascading of more rubble. Between bursts of fire an eerie silence held the empty streets. I was hardly breathing as I hunkered down behind the doors, nestling among a tangled group of bodies who were likewise barely breathing. After a longer pause I cautiously popped my head around the door to see what was going on. A tank was standing in place of the stalls. The street was full of soldiers. They were all looking at the top of a building. Rat-tat-tat. I heard fire coming from that direction. By the time I looked down towards the street again the tank had opened fire. Minutes later, the building looked like an ancient ruin. Still nestled behind the door, each of us gasping, taking in sudden deep breaths, we all waited and watched. They dragged out a body. He was wearing a turban that hid most of his full bearded face. His once white *toupe*, long white robe, was now red. I could hear murmurs amongst the spectators. 'Akhwan al Muslimeen' – the Muslim Brotherhood – 'Akhwan,' 'Akhwan.'

The following morning, still unshaven, with the donkey saddle over my left shoulder, I took a taxi to Damascus. There were seven men in the taxi. Four, including my squashed self, crammed in the back seat, three in the front. Though the taxi hurtled towards Damascus at over seventy kilometres an hour, it too showed serious signs of neglect. The man sitting next to me seemed as agitated as the cramped conditions permitted and kept casting nervous glances in all directions. He offered me a cigarette. As I politely declined his offer, he pushed his packet of cigarettes towards the taxi driver. The taxi driver drew my attention. He was murmuring something. Everyone looked back. I followed. There was a military vehicle following us. They signalled; and the taxi came to a jerky halt.

Two soldiers brandishing Kalashnikov rifles leaped out of the vehicle and covered us. A third soldier shouted orders. We came out of the taxi one by one with our hands on top of our heads. A fourth soldier opened the boot and threw all the luggage out. The soldier giving the orders asked which suitcase belonged to me. 'I have no luggage,' I replied. He asked for my passport. He took the passport in his left hand, looked at the picture, and felt the stubble on my face with his right hand. He looked at the donkey saddle on my shoulder, smiled, and handed my passport back. He had obviously concluded that I was an idiot. Systematically, with deliberation and immensely slowly, he looked at the identification of each of the other passengers. The soldier looking through the luggage suddenly produced a shrieking noise that must pass for the local equivalent of Eureka. He threw a suitcase in front of his colleagues. He'd forced it open and as it fell it disgorged its load of rifles. The man who'd been sitting next to me was not anxious any more. I saw one of the soldiers hit him with the butt of a rifle. Once the guns were discovered very little was said by anyone. Everyone seemed to know who was who and what was going on. The only two words uttered were said by the soldiers: 'Akhwan' and 'Hamah'. As the soldiers drove him off, the man gave me a long backward glance.

The traditional Muslim city of Hamah was midway between Damascus and Aleppo. As the taxi took us around the outskirts, I saw what looked like a whole battalion of tanks moving into the city. The Syrian Ba'athists were preparing to wipe the city of Hamah, stronghold of the Muslim Brotherhood, from the face of the globe, as easily as one wipes chalk from a blackboard.

Damascus turned out to be as grey as Baghdad. Perhaps it was my state of mind. I forced myself to visit the University of Damascus and its famed School of Medicine, the only institution in the Arab world to actually teach medicine in Arabic. I made the inevitable visit to the Mausoleum of 'Saladin', covered in a red dome and set in the gardens of the Umayyad Mosque, which is itself opposite the Souk al-Hamadiyyah in the Old City, which is surrounded by a Roman wall. I prayed at the Takiyyeh as-Sulaymaniyyeh Mosque, built in the Ottoman style in 1554, and admired its slender minarets and alternate layers of black and white stones. Was I praying for dead and distant history or deadly reality? History in Damascus cast me a look that was dead and distant. The city was plastered with portraits of President Hafez al-Assad who was busy building a Ba'athist paradise. Wherever my eyes turned, President Assad looked back at me – till I could bear to look no more.

Only when I reached Amman in Jordan did I become aware I was breathing normally again, and that gave me the heart to let my eyes linger on what was around me. My gaze was rewarded by what turned out to be one of the most serene and beautiful cities of the Middle East. The oil wealth had begun to trickle down to oil-less Jordan; and the capital had acquired a sophisticated elegance unique in the region. From the lovingly restored 2,000-year-old Roman Amphitheatre, standing at the centre of the city, to the outer rims where one comes across newly built houses, mostly in marble, whose modern architecture harmonizes with Arab tradition and craftsmanship. Nothing was ostentatious, nothing gaudy, just a hint of wealth; a sharp contrast from Baghdad and Damascus. I spent a few days visiting the Royal Scientific Society and called on a few friends at the University of Jordan. Then, I decided to call on Baqa, the Palestinian refugee camp.

The Baqa refugee camp was located about ten kilometres to the north-west of Amman. The drive from the centre of Amman, along the narrow, winding road, up and down the seven hills on which the modern city with very ancient roots is situated, does not prepare one for the sight. As you approach Baqa, the huge dish aerial of a radio telescope first catches your eye. From a distance, amongst row after row of nurseries protected with semicircular cellophane structures, the dish looks like a giant saucer catching eternal manna pouring from the heavens. Turn and look to the other side of the road, and adjacent to a wonder of modern technology is one of the most ancient sights of humanity: a makeshift squatter settlement, a monument to squalor and wretchedness, a sudden transition from placid elegance to harsh misery. Misery, though it is evident everywhere, is not the impression the camp leaves in one's mind. That is determination. Determination is written on every face. On the rugged faces of old refugees, on the reflective faces of young women, in the innocent faces of young children who seem to be playing everywhere one turns. Outside a school, I saw a group of young boys kicking a football. Although their uniforms were torn, they were clean; the children themselves were all well groomed. The boys gathered around me. One held my hand and took me inside his school. He seemed to take pride in showing me around.

I followed a woman clutching a child firmly against her breast into a surgery. Inside the waiting room a number of patients sat determined and patient on old wooden chairs. Dr Nabil Harish came out of the surgery to greet me. He asked to be excused to attend to the woman and her child. A few moments later he emerged from the partition, which was his consulting area, and began to speak in truncated Urdu.

'*Kiya hal hay?*' (How are you?)

'*Alhumdulillah*, I am fine,' I replied, trying not to laugh at his accent.

Nabil determinedly continued, with a smile, to explain that he was born in Haifa but studied medicine at King Edward College, Lahore, Pakistan, where he learned to speak Urdu. We walked out of the surgery on to the main street of the camp. On one side the street was lined with small grocery and dress shops, along with many enclaves offering repairs of all varieties that appeared to be doing good business. I noticed a small foundry making iron beds. On the other side, just in front of an open sewer flowing gently downwards, stalls assembled from pieces of wood proffered fresh vegetables and dairy products. In between the stalls sat women, and in front of each woman there were little bundles of mint, or a small pile of shoes, or an equally small pile of undergarments. We passed a small building with a large pole flying a UN flag. A board on the front wall declared: 'Baqa Emergency Camp. 7390 shelters in this camp have been constructed with funds from the Federal Republic of Germany.' The Mercedes standing in front of the gate looked conspicuously absurd.

'This camp was established in 1968, after the Arab–Israeli war when Israel annexed the West Bank,' Nabil explained in his determined Urdu. 'Around 400,000 Palestinians fled from the West Bank after the Israeli occupation. There are 70,000 refugees in this camp. Originally, they lived in makeshift tents; now most of the dwellings have brick walls. It's become a small city with its own economy, its own clinics and schools. We have between 18,000 and 20,000 students in our schools; and over eighty per cent literacy. It was supposed to be a temporary camp but we've been here for almost two decades. We think of nothing else but going back home.' He paused for a moment. 'Even in this hell, we have tried to make life as normal as possible. But paradise for us lies in returning to Palestine. And return we certainly will.' The determination resounded in his voice and shone from his eyes.

We turned into a side alley. It had an open sewer running in the middle. The houses on either side consisted of four whitewashed brick walls with a thin sheet of tin pretending to be a roof. Most residents had placed large stones on the edges of the tin sheets to ensure the roof stayed in place. After a few minutes' walk we arrived at the Youth Centre, which was being cleaned and decorated by girls from the Jordan Community College. A group of girls were putting whitewash on the walls of the playground. Another group were painting the markings of a football pitch. Yet another seemed to be cataloguing books in the library. I walked to the other end of the football pitch and, through an opening in the wall, came out somewhere on the main street and found myself in the midst of a group of infants leaving their school.

A small boy stopped right in front of me, looked up, and smiled, revealing gaps in his teeth. I knelt down to his height and gently tapped him on his chin. 'Do you like going to school, young man?' I asked.

'Yes. I like school very much,' he replied without hesitation.

'And what do you want to do when you grow up?'

'I want to fight for my homeland,' he shot back without a moment's thought. He held my gaze, looking me straight in the eye to ensure that I saw the determination was within him, not just in his words. It was a sight to behold; and a warning of things to come.

I moved on to Dubai from where I intended to fly back to London. Dubai wasn't so much a city, or a city-state, as a building site. The oil revenues were being used to rebuild the city from scratch. The city was being resurrected as an exotic shopping mall where all life was fetishized as pure consumerism. There was an absence of spirit; an absence I saw and experienced as a metaphysical death. Not surprisingly, there wasn't much in terms of science and technology I could look at; so I decided to call on a minister ostensibly responsible for science policy. I happened to arrive at his palace at the same moment as an old Asian labourer, in search of work, was entering his gate. He in his dhoti and vest, me in my jeans, T-shirt and flip-flops, we looked like two of a kind.

The gatekeeper saw both of us approach.

'We don't want the likes of you here,' he shouted from his pillbox. 'Get lost!' I tried to explain I was expected, that I was here for an interview, but even before I could explain myself he closed the electronically controlled gates.

'It's becoming harder and harder to find work nowadays,' the labourer commented by way of commiseration. 'It's got something to do with the oil glut. The price of oil, you see. It's not what it used to be.'

I was interested by this observation and turned my attention to the labourer, forgetting my interview with the minister.

'How long have you been looking for work?' I asked.

'Since last week,' he said. 'I managed to find three days' work last week. But since then, nothing.' He paused for a moment; and then smiled.

I was surprised a man facing such hardship could smile so generously. We walked together towards a roadside café.

'I am Lord Ahmad,' he said, extending his hand in friendship.

'Lord Ahmad?' I enquired, shaking his hand.

'Yes,' he replied. 'Lord Ahmad. My family owned lots of land in

India. We were big landlords. Once I was as rich as the Sheikh you were visiting. But then the colonial powers divided India into two and I had to migrate to Pakistan. So now, having left my land in India, I am simply a lord. Wandering here in Dubai looking for work. And what do you do?'

'Oh! I am a writer.'

'Writer, *han*,' he shook his head. 'You write books?'

'Well, I haven't actually written any yet. But I intend to.'

'What about?'

'About development, science and technology in Muslim countries, about the future.'

'What about people? Don't you want to write about people?'

'Yes,' I said. 'Yes, I do want to write about people.'

'People like me, or people like the Sheikh?'

'Both,' I replied.

'I bet,' he said, 'you only want to write about rich people. Because they're interesting. They've created a paradise for themselves, and you're naturally fascinated by their paradise. And you probably think that those of us who are excluded from their paradise are not very interesting.'

'No,' I said. 'No, I think poor people are interesting. In fact, I find ordinary people much more interesting than rich Sheikhs.'

'Tell me,' he said, changing the drift of the conversation, 'What do you see?'

'Well,' I mumbled, 'I see you. Lord Ahmad.'

'What am I wearing?'

'You are wearing a dhoti and a vest.'

'Ho! Ho!' He leaned forward and tapped me enthusiastically on the shoulder. 'How can you write about the poor when you have not even learned to see us? What looks like a dhoti, a loincloth, to you is much more than that to me. At night it becomes my duvet. When it is torn, I divide it into two small pieces of cloth, one I use as a towel, the other I carry on my shoulder to wipe my sweat. And when it is so torn that I cannot even use it as a towel, I tear it into small strips, which I roll into wicks, and use in my oil lamp. Finally, it returns to where it came from – mother earth.'

It took a few moments for me to absorb these revelations.

'What are you doing here? I mean, how did you manage to come to Dubai?'

'Well, life back home in the village was getting really hard. I had to do something. So I went to Karachi, but there wasn't much work there either. Eventually, I made my way to Dubai.' He leaned forward and whispered in my ear, 'I am illegal. I don't have residence visas or anything.'

'Don't you miss your children? Does your son or daughter ever visit you?'

'Yes,' he replied, reflecting for a moment. 'I miss them a lot. But what options do I have? I have to go wherever I can find work to feed my family.'

'So what are you going to do next?'

'Nothing,' he replied. 'Just carry on looking for work,' and after a moment's thought he added, 'and dodging the police.' He winked.

I smiled back.

'Are you going to write about me?'

Before I could reply he spotted a policeman approaching the café. 'Do remember to send me a clipping,' he said, clasping my hand. Then in the blink of an eye he was gone.

The following day, I dressed more formally and left my hotel early in the morning. This time the gatekeeper allowed me in without hesitation. The minister received me in the garden by the swimming pool. It soon transpired he was not interested in science and technology. His standard reply to every question I asked: 'Why bother about it when we can afford to buy it?' He kept gazing around, turning his eyes here and there, everywhere except in my direction. I tired of my questions and turned my attention to the pool, which was unusually large. 'Is it because you have a very large family?' I enquired.

'No, just an average family,' replied the minister. 'But I do like to swim a good length.'

I nodded to show I understood.

'Do you know that I have three swimming pools?' the minister volunteered. 'This one has cold water – it is kept just at the right temperature. Over there – you can see it if you stand up – is the pool I use in winter. It is heated to just the appropriate temperature.'

I stood up to admire the second pool. I couldn't help making the point: 'But in Dubai the temperature stays more or less the same all the year round.'

'Well, it can get chilly in the morning,' replied the minister. 'You can see the third pool from here.' He grabbed my hand and escorted me to a spot from where the third pool was clearly visible.

'But it's empty. It has no water,' I observed.

'Sometimes,' the minister, upset at my interventions, retorted sternly, 'sometimes I just do not want to swim.'

I covered a considerable distance during my travels in the Middle East. But it was nothing compared to the distance between the rulers and those who are ruled. The desire of ordinary Muslims to live in a state of justice and equity was always at odds with the elite vision of an ideal life. I knew my own quest would be shaped by this clash.

Chapter 7

SAVING MECCA

I had been to the source of civilization. It was a ruined dream. Yet, wherever I turned in the Muslim world, there appeared to be a new determination that from the mess of modernity a way had to be found to remake past glories. Civilization, people were insisting, was more than material accumulation or technical advance. The way forward was recovery of the inner core of ideals, the values and spiritual ethos that created the Golden Age of Islam. Everyone was beginning to see this hope, just over the horizon. All my Muslim friends talked incessantly about the coming 'Islamic resurgence'. Paradoxically, for in such discussion old conundrums always abounded, their confidence was inspired in large part by the new acquisition of material means. The formation of OPEC (Organization of Petroleum Exporting Countries) in 1960, and its subsequent emergence as a global force in the early 1970s, was seen as an indication of a 'renaissance' that was just around the corner. The oil revenues were going to transform the Middle East and propel Islam on a new trajectory. The Organization of the Islamic Conference (OIC), set up by various Muslim states in 1969 and spearheaded by King Faisal of Saudi Arabia, provided a concrete expression of 'Muslim unity'. Kings and heads of state as well as foreign ministers of Muslim countries were meeting regularly – now in Rabat, now in Jeddah, now in Islamabad – to discuss the struggle against oppression and injustice and find ways of cooperating together. And the first 'Islamic Revolution' in history was bubbling away, ready to erupt in Iran.

One afternoon, during the winter of 1975, just at the time of day when the present is bleak and only thoughts of coming light and warmth can fend off the gloom, I was sitting in our flat in London. I was slumped in a chair, trying to tune into the climate of general optimism. I was interrupted by the ringing of the doorbell. I opened the door and a fabulous vision greeted me warmly. 'Brother Zia,' it said, 'I have come to make you an offer you can't refuse.'

Why do they always come in twos, I wondered? There stood two men, but with only minimalist beards. Things might be looking up, after all. The vision stood in front, nonchalantly awaiting the invitation to enter. Sami Angawi, as I was to learn he was called, was an Orientalist painting in corporeal form: his honeyed complexion flawless; his long, flowing hair pulled into a ponytail; his dark eyes large, enticing. He was all western perceptions of the 'Sheikh', up to and including the aura and charisma of Rudolph Valentino, rolled into one. His companion was less prepossessing, as befits a protégé. He stood awkwardly in the background, juggling a variety of devices and peering into the flat, anxiously searching for somewhere to set his burden down.

I ushered in this new adventure and permitted Sami to introduce himself. He had just finished his Masters in architecture at the University of Austin, Texas, he explained. His companion was Bodo Rosh, a student of the German architect Frei Otto who rose to prominence largely because of his innovative tent architecture. Bodo was a recent convert to Islam. They had come on a matter of some urgency to recruit me for a rescue mission. I was asked to sit down and observe a presentation, courtesy of the slide projector they had brought along. There was an interlude of fumbling as the equipment was set up. It pleased me then to sit and observe.

The shaft of light trained on the living room wall clicked off momentarily and was replaced as quickly by an unmistakable image in vibrant colour. The Prophet's Mosque in Medina, resting place of the Beloved Prophet Muhammad, is a sight known to all Muslims. Medina, the ancient city of Yathrib, is the second holiest city of Islam. It is in Medina – which is also the generic term for 'the city' – that the civilization of Islam was born. As various views of Medina leaped across the wall a convenient commentary was provided by Sami. 'Despite the fact that Medina gave birth to one of the most dynamic and intellectually profound civilizations,' he began, 'the city itself has always been simple.' He went on to explain how the social and commercial life of the city focused around the Prophet's Mosque. The original mosque was built of sun-dried brick, the floor was of earth and the ceiling constructed of palm fronds covered with mud and supported by pillars of palm wood. This mosque has been rebuilt a number of times over the centuries, added to and made splendid by caliphs and kings. The Ottomans in particular paid a great deal of attention both to the Prophet's Mosque and to the city; Ottoman architecture reflected the beauty, grace and splendour of the holy site. Conveniently a slide showing the Salutation Gate, one of the main entrances to the mosque, clicked into view. It is embellished with beautiful ceramics given by Sultan Süleyman (known as the Magnificent) in the beginning of the sixteenth century.

My eyes were content to feast upon places that belonged to my heart, but which as yet I had never visited. But Angawi's voice took on a harder edge. 'Since the formation of the Kingdom of Saudi Arabia,' he said, 'the city has undergone two transformations.' In the time of King Abdul Aziz, it still retained its Ottoman flavour, he explained. At the entrance to the city, a splendid inner castle stood as a reminder of the medieval wall which once defended it. Streets were lined with stucco houses, ornamented with intricately worked wooden lattices. The Prophet's Mosque was rose red with Ottoman minarets and magnificent gates surmounted with gold inscriptions set there by Turkish calligraphers. All this he had shown me. But the parade of slides had come to a halt. There was only Sami's voice now, explaining that between 1948 and 1955, during the reigns of two successive Saudi Kings, the mosque was extended by one-third and entirely rebuilt in grey stone, in neo-Mamluke style. The two styles clashed somewhat but, during this period of transition, most of the old city was left untouched. Only a few large modern hotels overshadowed the old houses, and here and there occasional car parks appeared as eyesores.

There was a silence. 'In June 1973,' Angawi's voice was clipped with emotion, 'there came a second transformation. In a matter of days,' he said, commenting on slides of bulldozers demolishing ancient cultural property, 'the whole city was razed to the ground.' No one complained. Indeed, not many knew what had happened. 'Fourteen hundred years of history and tradition disappeared in a dust cloud, gone.' Sami sat silent. Rosh relentlessly kept working the projector. The slides of the 'modern city', with large multilane roads, gaudy and whimsical hotel buildings, hideous mosques standing in place of the old Ottoman ones, spoke for themselves.

Angawi said simply and quietly: 'They will do the same to Mecca. We have about five years to save Mecca.' Rosh intervened: 'We need you to work with us on this cause.' Simultaneously they made the offer that could not be refused: 'Join us at the Hajj Research Centre.'

How could I refuse? Was Mecca not the physical and metaphysical destination of every Muslim's journey? Perhaps Saudi Arabia, the only country to implement Islamic law in all its historic glory, was exactly the place to resolve the questions about transcending modernity in a new way. It was after all about to be the greatest beneficiary of the new oil wealth. It was the moving spirit behind the assertive doctrine of OPEC. Its urbane Oil Minister, Sheikh Yamani, had touched a powerful chord among many in the West with his cogent argument that profligate consumers in developed nations should pay a just price for finite natural resources. Certainly, his argument had touched a raw nerve in developing nations who all agreed that primary producers of basic raw materials had the right to a just return on these resources. Saudi Arabia, Yamani pointed out, had to raise the revenues needed to invest in alternative economic options against the time when the oil was gone. The oil price hike had been a wake-up call to ecological consciousness, a therapeutic indication of the limits to growth. Across the Third World it had provided demonstrable hope that the imbalance of power between producers and consumers in an inequitable world order might be realigned. It had stirred new debates, new ideas, a new search for alternatives in the West and the Third World. How were the consequences and potential going to be worked out? In particular, how were they going to influence the idealism of Islamic resurgence in the birthplace of Islam? If the objective was to conserve the resources that generated national wealth for genuine development, to assert self-confidence and pride in one's heritage, then it had to be possible to succeed in saving Mecca from the fate of Medina. The images that flickered across my wall had been a metaphor for all that defined the wrong kind of material development. If there was to be optimism and a new way forward for Islam, then Saudi Arabia had to be the best place to observe and participate in making this new route to paradise.

Angawi was not waiting for my rationale. As I uttered the words of agreement he rushed to embrace me, kissing me on my left cheek, then on my right. When he attempted to kiss my nose, I pushed him. Effusion has its limits, like growth, I thought. It was settled, my next adventure was secured, all that remained was details. We set about gathering up the projector and slides. 'There is one more thing,' Rosh said. 'I am looking for a wife and I am told you are about the best person to consult on these matters.'

In the deep of winter the first stirring of spring, how fitting a conclusion to the afternoon. It took me only a matter of weeks to arrange Rosh's wedding. A month or so later, I moved to Jeddah. Angawi's visit had been one of a series of such encounters. He gathered a hand-picked, interdisciplinary group of dedicated Muslim intellectuals. When they were assembled, the Hajj Research Centre came into existence. For us, the members of the team, it was that simple. Besides Rosh, there were three other 'returnees' to Islam: James Ismael Gibson, a British town planner; Peter Endene, a British transport engineer; and Jamil Brownson, an American sociologist. And beside myself – a physicist and information scientist – there were two other British Muslims: Zaffar Abbas Malik, an artist and designer; and Zaki Badawi, our Shariah expert. Then there was a certain 'Dr Dabash', an Egyptian veterinary surgeon who specialized in talking in gory details about scrapie, foot-and-mouth disease, and the plumbing of animal reproduction. Angawi, as befitted a man made in Valentino mould, used his considerable charm, his Meccan family connections, and the few contacts he had in the Saudi Royal Family to establish the Centre. 'Establish' is perhaps the wrong word. Angawi always managed to secure the relevant funding. Sack-loads of money would arrive mysteriously so we could buy the latest research technology, fly in absurdly overpaid consultants, and secure the specialized services of European and American firms.

I started working at the Hajj Research Centre with great relish. Mecca is the light that still remains with me, the shimmering, flawless light that illumines the still point to which all Muslims turn. It is what I remember most of my first visit to the Haramain, the sacred precincts at the heart of Mecca. Mecca, the birthplace of Muhammad, the site of the Holy Kaa'ba, is the prime focus of the Muslim world. The profound intensity of the moment burst upon me as I stepped out from the colonnaded mosque into the great open space surrounding the Kaa'ba. A little voice within me, overpowered and amazed, whispered 'I am here.' Before me was the great cube-shaped building, draped in black cloth edged with gold embroidered calligraphy: the Kaa'ba. No image more familiar, no location better known, no direction more sought-after exists for any Muslim anywhere at any time. I was here. The Kaa'ba stood silent and still. I could hardly breathe as I walked out into the pool of light and radiant heat; I felt as if every butterfly everywhere was flapping its wings and I was wafted along on the updraught. I moved, unconscious of my movement, to make the journey seven times around the Kaa'ba. In that heart of light I was enfolded in what it is to be me, what it is to be a Muslim. One can live with the awe of that moment far better than one can describe or communicate it.

The Kaa'ba is the pre-eminent symbol of Islam. It is a house of worship of The God, believed to have been built and dedicated for this purpose by Prophet Abraham. Events in the life of this Patriarch of Judaism, Christianity and Islam underpin and define the traditional rituals of being in Mecca. This fixed point provides Muslims with their sense of direction: five times a day, the faithful turn to face not only Mecca but the Kaa'ba within Mecca, when they pray. From every point on earth a Muslim seeks an orientation towards this central place, the starting point of dedication to The God and his guidance of values and ethics, to which they must constantly return on the daily journey through life. It is also the ultimate goal, the embodiment of the spiritual objective to hold a constant course through the vagaries of life's trials and tribulations. It is a definite, finite goal of spiritual endeavour since every Muslim, once in their lifetime, if they can afford it, is required to perform the Hajj, the pilgrimage to Mecca, when they will each take that walk seven times around the Kaa'ba, united in awe, humbled by the experience.

Of all the practical manifestations of Islam, the Hajj most potently captures the imagination. Muslims may save all their lives to accumulate the required means to embark on the great journey to the Holy Places. In history, and still in some parts of the world, people dispose of their capital, their source of livelihood, make over their worldly goods, leaving their affairs as if preparing for death, not just to find the necessary funds for the journey but genuinely to bring one part of their life to a culmination. Taking stock, auditing the achievements of their mundane existence, they liquefy the assets of their life to reinvest it in spiritual capital. Some still cover the journey to Mecca on foot. The endeavour can take years to accomplish, demonstrating an unparalleled devotion and spiritual yearning. All pilgrims come not in search of belief but to express, confirm, rededicate and redouble their belief. Quite simply, the Hajj is the apex of Muslim spiritual experience. Literally, the word *hajj* signifies an exertion. The Hajj is an effort, the great Effort. It is the concentration of all the dimensions of meaningful existence at a moment in space and time. It is this assimilation, this drawing together of all the dimensions, that generates the spiritual significance of Hajj; and it is the effort, physical as well as mental, that brings the pilgrim to a new level of understanding, a higher spiritual state. When they return to their homes the pilgrims will be known by the honorific of Hajji (male) or Hajjah (female) in recognition of their engagement with and experience of the completeness of a life of faith. The sacred nature, the living history, the spiritual dynamics – all this makes Mecca much more than a geographical location. It is a Sanctuary. A frame of mind. A profound experience. It is the Beginning, the Present and Forever.

Overpowering and humbly humdrum: a walk here, a walk there, a stop here, a stop there: these are the simple mechanics of the most complex experience in the life of a Muslim. To research it our Centre was building a computer model of Mecca and the Hajj. Simulations have a voracious appetite for data; and a great deal of our time was spent gathering data. Data of every kind: from the ecology and physical geography of the city to traffic flows, locations and extent of cultural property, population movements and growth, the social and cultural habits of Meccans, varieties of business, public expenditure, imports, demand for skilled labour, goods and services to the rate of increase of hotels – it all went into the computer. But it was during the Hajj season that our data-gathering activities reached fever pitch.

During Dhu al-Hijjah, the twelfth month of the Islamic calendar when the Hajj takes place, the population of Mecca increases fourfold. Half a million local inhabitants play host to two million pilgrims from every corner of the Muslim world. The Hajj falls on the ninth, tenth, eleventh and twelfth days of this month and follows a routine established by Prophet Muhammad himself. The pilgrims are required to move from ritual point to ritual point by specified routes at specific times. In each of the five years I worked at the Centre I would target a group of pilgrims – Pakistanis one year, Nigerians the next – and follow them throughout the entire Hajj, observing their behaviour and noting any problems they might encounter. I would watch as they, on entering the holy areas, prepared their minds for the transition from worldly thought and desires, a spiritual transformation accompanied by changing their everyday clothes for the pilgrim garb, *ihram* – two white, unsewn sheets of cloth – and acquired a state of grace. I would follow them to the Sacred Mosque, where they would perform the *tawaf* – walking seven times anticlockwise around the Kaa'ba, circumambulating in reality the fixed point that had always given meaning and direction to their lives. In this exultant moment men walked with their right shoulders bared to demonstrate their humility. Men and women walking alongside each other, no segregation, not in separate lines, mutually engaged in common activity, a quest and objective that was the same for everyone no matter who or what they were. After *tawaf* comes *sa'y*. In remembrance of the plight of Hagar, wife of Prophet Abraham, the pilgrims run seven times between the hills of Safa and Marwah, just as she ran desperately seeking water in the desert before God showed her the well of Zamzam. Then, it is out of Mecca and to the hill town of Muna.

The following day is the Day of Arafat, the supreme moment of the Hajj. The pilgrims leave early to cover the eight kilometres that separate

Muna from the Plain of Arafat, arriving before midday. When the sun passes the meridian, the ritual of *wquf*, or standing, begins. At the mosque of Al-Namira, before Mount Arafat, the congregation of over two million prays as a single entity. Nothing in the world can match this spectacle; or surpass this experience. Already in the preceding days the pilgrims have experienced a brotherhood and humility the like of which they have never known. In ritual and reality they experience humanity as diverse, interconnected and united. Rich and poor, different races, different languages, male and female, the distinctions irrelevant in the commonality of endeavour, the shared effort and mutual support in which they come together for a higher purpose. Here in this valley, the Magnificent, the Beneficent, the Merciful, will send down His forgiveness on those whom He will – and they will feel His presence. In this enormous mass of indistinguishable humanity, the pilgrim knows unity and the most profound moment of individuality and personal identity they can ever hope to experience. This is the simple profundity of the Hajj, of Islam, of religion or indeed any form of human philosophy. In all of this crowd it is I, and my Lord; and the noblest hours of my life. Each says simply '*Labaik*', here I am, in the knowledge that each is individually heard, individually known, individually valuable, distinct and particular.

Immediately after sunset, on the ninth of Dhu al-Hijjah begins the *nafrah*: the mass exodus of pilgrims from the valley of Arafat, towards Muzdalifah. Muzdalifah is an open plain sheltered by parched hills with sparse growth of thorn bushes. The pilgrims spend a night under the open sky of the Roofless Mosque, the Sacred Grove, *Al Mush'ar al-Haram*. On the morning of the tenth, the pilgrims return to spend three days in Muna. During this second stay in Muna, an animal is sacrificed and the ritual of 'Stoning the Devil' takes place. Three small pebbles are thrown at each of the three masonry pillars marking the different spots where the Devil tried to tempt Prophet Abraham; a gesture that symbolizes the pilgrims' intention to cast out the 'evil within'. Once these rites are performed the pilgrims conclude their Hajj by removing their *ihram* and cutting their hair.

Our team at the Centre recorded the Hajj in every conceivable way. We measured the influx of pilgrims to the Sacred Mosque, recorded the pressure on an individual pilgrim when over 100,000 of them tried to go round the Kaa'ba in unison, and noted how long it took them to go from one ritual point to another. We carried out extensive surveys of the traffic in the holy areas and measured the output of exhaust fume pollution. We studied the accommodation problems of the pilgrims, examined their health and hygiene issues, and identified the hazards and the accident black-spots. We took aerial photographs, made time-lapse films, and captured images of the Hajj from every conceivable angle. And we studied the past, the present and the future of Hajj. Everything went into the computer model; and it was already telling us a few important things.

The dynamics of Hajj and the intricacies of Mecca were more complex than we realized. There was a web of interconnections that maintained the city and the entire Hajj system in a delicate balance. The hills and the mountains, the valleys and the plains, the geology and the ecology of the holy areas gave the 'barren valley', as the Qur'an describes it, a pluralistic, multi-dimensional feel. The entire Hajj environment was structured in such a way that pilgrims moved through it like water flowing in a gentle stream. Groups of pilgrims moved from ritual point to ritual point at their own pace, negotiating their way around mountains and valleys, bushes and sparse land, resting under shaded areas, arriving at designated places at different times – but always on time to perform the necessary ritual. Such a sophisticated system would not submit either to simple analysis or to simplistic, one-dimensional technological solutions. The physical changes brought about by modern technology were throwing the whole system rapidly out of sync. From a sublime spiritual experience, the Hajj was moving towards a nightmare obstacle course generating hazards in which the very survival of the pilgrims was at stake.

Angawi spared no effort in communicating what we had discovered. Princes, ministers, and influential businessmen would arrive at the Centre at all hours of day and night. They would sit spellbound watching the time-lapse sequences that showed pilgrims behaving like drops of water, the documentaries that focused on potential and actual disasters such as fires, structural collapse at ritual points and mass choking on exhaust fumes, and the simulation that showed what could happen to the entire Hajj environment if one variable, such as traffic, should experience manifold increase. All these meetings ended in exactly the same way. The visitors showed awe and appreciation, expressed through physical gestures. One common gesture involved a loud hissing sound, accompanied by a movement of the hand away from the lips, with the thumb and the tip of the forefinger pressed together, and the other three fingers fanned out upwards. They were all impressed by our technology and what it could do, but not with our results. When the influential visitors looked at our simulation, they would, almost by instinct, draw a downward line with their index fingers on their cheeks below the eye signalling the expression: 'Isn't it pretty'. Outside the Centre, they would make similar gestures in front of their brand-new, shining Mercedes.

The Saudis approached technology as though it was theology. And in both, complexity and plurality was shunned. God is one, the Prophet is one, the *ummah* – the international Muslim community – is one. Just as plurality of opinions within Islam had led to discord and weakened the *ummah*, so different perspectives on Mecca, and diverse solutions to different problems of the Hajj, would complicate matters and lead to disasters. All problems of Hajj had a single solution: modern technology. If two-lane roads out of Mecca cause congestion, then they should be increased to four, or six or eight – as many as necessary to relieve the congestion. The fact that more lanes produced more congestion was not part of the equation. Moreover, if Truth was monolithic, then the holy areas should reflect the monolithic nature of Truth. So, everything had to be at the same level. There was no place in Mecca for history or tradition or culture, the human wellsprings of diversity, even if these are, according to the Qur'an, Divinely created, purposeful endowments of human nature and human society. I remember the fateful day when the old Ottoman library was demolished and the land cleared flat. Traditional houses, the ancient mosques, and the magnetic contours of the holy areas – hills, valleys and mountains – followed into the oblivion of dust. Everything was rendered flat and monolithic.

At the Centre we raised wails of protest and mounted phalanxes of arguments against the tide of events. In consequence we had many enemies but none as formidable as the Bin Laden Group. Originally from Hadramawt in Southern Yemen, the Bin Laden family had developed a special relationship with the Royal Family. The family business, established by the patriarch Mohammad bin Laden in the 1930s, focused largely on building palaces and grand residential properties for the Saudi monarchs. So pleased were the Royals with their efforts that they were given the sole contract not just to renovate the Sacred Mosque in Mecca but to all construction of a religious nature in the Kingdom. And the Bin Laden Group was as zealous in its development work as it was in its religious outlook. The more we issued calls to 'suspend all demolition and construction projects for reconsideration in view of their far-reaching and irrevocable character', the more they demolished.

In 1979, I performed the last of my five Hajjs. During the 1977 pilgrimage, my father joined me. My mother, being much more adventurous, had already done her Hajj even before I had met Sami Angawi. I got married towards the end of 1977 and my wife joined me for the 1978 Hajj. I say 'joined' but in fact she performed her Hajj independently. For in 1978 I made my Hajj on foot in the company of my friend and Hajj Research Centre colleague Zafar Malik and a donkey, walking the seventy kilometres from Jeddah to Mecca, over the mountains and across the desert. Taking the time, the pace constrained and determined by the heat, to feel the landscape, its colours and textures, its response to light, shade and darkness. As I walked my mind and spirit prepared for the timeless observance of the Hajj. I found myself sensing the ground beneath my feet, conscious of each footstep, but not mine only, also of all the generations before me who had passed this way. When I arrived in Mecca I walked everywhere to perform each of the ritual stages of the Hajj. The purpose of the exercise, a reconnection with tradition, was to show that walking was not only more humane and ecologically sound, it was also safer, and a more direct route to the fulfilment of the spiritual objective that is the Hajj.

But this year I became an ordinary present-day pilgrim. I took a pilgrim bus. I sat in the bus for around eleven hours in the burning sun and unbearable heat as it negotiated the few kilometres from Mecca to Muna through a web of multi-lane roads and spaghetti junctions, one gridlock after another. I saw the innumerable vehicles, the Mercedes and the like, that took VIPs, the rich and powerful, in insulated, air-conditioned, cocooned luxury from place to place. In the area where the Devils are stoned, which has been converted on the unmistakable model of a multi-level car park, I was nearly crushed to death as a wave of pilgrims came toppling down, cascading over the edge of the top level, propelled over this precipice by the weight of humanity behind them anxious for their opportunity to cast out evil. Throughout my journey to Muna, Arafat and Muzdalifah, I was coughing and choking on exhaust fumes – all eighty tons of it produced on a daily basis seemed to be coming directly at me, assailing every pore of my being. Every now and then I would be drenched with DDT from one of numerous helicopters that constantly hover over the heads of the pilgrims. While going round the Kaa'ba, I was constantly harassed, shooed and beaten with a long stick by the religious police inside the Sacred Mosque. As I sat in the Sacred Mosque, reconstructed to resemble an underground station complete with escalators, I looked up beyond the Kaa'ba. In the glare of innumerable arc lamps the entire area beyond the Sacred Mosque was also bathed in night-banishing light. I could see where a brand-new palace, overshadowing the Kaa'ba, was about to be completed.

Something profound happened at that instant. A transcendent moment of profound revulsion stirred me to definite conviction. I had made Hajj and now, here, this moment was anti-Hajj. When matter and antimatter collide, nothing is left. How could I endure any longer the moment of everything being rendered to nothingness? What I witnessed was not merely a physical assault on cultural tradition. It was an ideological onslaught on its spiritual and philosophical richness, as delicate and intricate as all the *mashrabiah*, the tracery of lattice windows, so rapidly disappearing along with all that was old, that had endured and spoke of the creativity and potential of tradition. I observed subtle complexity disappearing from the mental environment at a commensurate rate. The brash concrete and asphalt embrace of modernity retained and then bounced back the oppressive, overbearing, searing heat with increased power. The updraughts of hot air were turning the wits, broiling the brains of everyone around me. Enervated by the convection currents the hot air was making them fit only for the pathologically reductive brand of Islam that alone could flourish in this arid man-made landscape with its unyielding straight lines and propensity to see the world in simple black and white terms. What was happening to Mecca was about to happen to me. How could it be otherwise? Mecca is the microcosm of the world of Islam. After five years there, I knew that I had to leave Saudi Arabia.

Chapter 8

LEAVING SAUDI ARABIA

As soon as the Hajj was over I submitted an application for an exit visa to the *idara*, the administration of King Abdul Aziz University. The mechanics of departure cannot be accomplished with dispatch. In a moment a decision is made. Many, and I mean many, moments are needed to make the dream a reality. Disengagement is a procedure as complicated and delicate as arranging an engagement for star-crossed lovers from contending houses, and potentially as deadly. One exit visa is the culmination of a plethora of forms and signatures, each of which takes a determined act of will to elicit. I spent several weeks going from office to office collecting signatures. In all, I collected eighteen. Each testified to some important fact such as, for example, that I was not walking off with the property of my employers, the University. Others witnessed that I was not leaving the country with a library book, that I had collected my last salary and the University did not owe me anything, another that I had fulfilled all the requirements of my contract. There were signatures to prove I had not offended anyone during my five-year stay in the country and that I was not leaving behind large arrears of rent. Now, all that was wanting was the final signature from the head of the administration.

I presented myself to Abdul Aziz Al-Turki, the *mudir* or director of the administration. He was a lean man with a falcon-like face who sat behind a huge desk. 'Would you sign my application?' I asked. He looked at me, smiled, and said: '*Inshallah*.' I smiled back. Our smiles were different. His casual, glibly courteous expression, barely hovering within the rubric of a smile, announced indifference. The set civility of my forced facial exertion, the conscripted memory of what a smile might be, said: I don't really believe you.

He repeated the litany: '*Inshallah*.' A single word, the essence of a worldview founded on the proposition of the omniscient omnipotence of One God, yet so capable of expressing an infinity of mood and circumstance that one must always think of the particular significance born by each utterance of the words. 'If God so wills', 'If God is willing', 'God willing it to be so' – the subtle implications of how the affairs of man stand in relation to the enormous complexity of divine creation in even the simplest of undertakings. The phrase covers all permutations from positive affirmation of the duty of humans to act to the spirit-crushing evasion of any duty to perform any act of human volition. In the end the phrase merely implies that everything takes time because everything bears such an immense philosophical burden, too much almost for humankind to manage. 'God willing,' Al-Turki repeated himself, 'I will sort your papers out in a few hours and you can be on your way by tomorrow. No problem, *Inshallah*. Why don't you sit down and have some tea?' Like most Saudis, Al-Turki was more polite than frank. Not to accept the invitation to tea might offend, and that was the last thing I wanted.

A *farash* (personal attendant) came in, holding a set of miniature cups in his left hand and a traditional brass kettle in his right. Everyone in the room was presented, in a matter-of-fact way, with a cup full of sweet *chai*. As soon as the cup is empty, it is refilled; unless the visitor indicates he has had enough by tipping the mouth of the cup towards his chest, away from the *farash*. Seeking any decision is a strain on the kidneys, a matter of concentrated bladder control. I sat there stubbornly in front of Al-Turki, drinking endless cups of tea. Eventually, Al-Turki looked at me and made a common facial gesture. He raised his chin upwards, and flicked his right hand in a dismissive manner. For emphasis, he made an accompanying derisive sucking dental click. I knew this was a sign of displeasure. '*Inshallah, bukra!*' (God willing, tomorrow), he said in a matter-of-fact voice, a definite statement of indeterminacy. Today God most definitely would not will any action on or for my behalf, tomorrow was another day and who could tell, foretelling being heresy, what that day might bring. There was nothing further my attempt at menacing presence could achieve. The logic of circumstance led inevitably to my only option, to leave this office: I was not going to collect my final signature today.

As I returned day after day in search of the final signature on my file, *bukra*, tomorrow, proved again and again the old adage as subsequent days began to stretch into weeks without the arrival of the momentous tomorrow. Realizing my file could lie on Al-Turki's desk for months, I decided to intervene in the cyclic recurrence of the constant indeterminacy of his permutation of '*Inshallah, bukra*' by exercise of an alternative Islamic premise: I would pray and tie my camel. *Inshallah* carries the semantic possibilities of a fervent prayer for the blessing of the Almighty on any human action. To get the blessing, as the Prophet so clearly pointed out, one must take decisive action: to prevent an animal straying one must both pray and hobble the beast. To permit a bird to fly one must both pray and acquire innumerable signatures, especially the one final scribble that releases the pinions on its wings.

One morning I arrived at Al-Turki's office before sunrise. I parked myself, as was usual, on the sofa, selecting a central position directly in front of his desk, and amused myself by reading. He arrived a few minutes later and was surprised to see me so early in the morning. As no one else was in his office, he was forced to direct the ritualistic greetings towards me.

'*Ahlan. Ahlaaaan. Ahlan wa sahlan*' (welcome), he said.

'*Ahlan*' (welcome), I replied.

'*Kayfa-l Haal?*' (how are you?) he asked.

'*Kayfa-l Haal?*' I replied.

'*Alhamdulillah. Allah yubaarikfi. Allah yubaarikfi*' (Allah be Praised. May Allah bless you. May Allah bless you).

'*Alhamdulillah. Allah yubaarikfi. Allah yubaarikfi. Allah yubaarikfi.*'

He paused as he made himself comfortable in his executive chair and noticed that I had not lifted my face from the book.

'*Kayfa sihhat?*' (How is your health?)

'*Kayfa sihhat?*'

'*Alhamdulillah. Allah yubaarikfi. Allah yubaarikfi.*'

'*Alhamdulillah. Allah yubaarikfi. Allah yubaarikfi.*'

I carried on reading without looking at him.

'*Esh akhbar?*' (What is the news?) he said.

'*Esh akhbar?*'

'*Alhamdulillah. Allah yubaarikfi. Allah yubaarikfi.*'

'*Alhamdulillah. Alhamdulillah. Allah yubaarikfi. Allah yubaarikfi.*'

He couldn't control himself. He leaned forward in an attempt to discern what I was reading. I maintained my motionless attitude, poised in a way that kept the cover and contents shielded from his view, thus forcing him to the last expedient:

'What are you reading?' he asked.

'It's *Ibn al-Marzuban's Book of the Superiority of Dogs Over Many of Those Who Wear Clothes*,' I said without looking at him.

'Oh!' He was unsure whether to look surprised or smile.

'You know the book?' I continued. 'It is a collection of stories and poetry inspired by a conversation in tenth-century Baghdad between Ibn al-Marzuban and a friend. They contemplate the decline of moral standards and sense of responsibility amongst the Arabs, sigh with nostalgia for the days when things were done punctually and efficiently, and praise the fine qualities displayed by man's best friend, the dog.' I paused, and then repeated, 'The dog, his consistency, intelligence, quick reactions and his guarding instinct.

'Let me read a little for you,' I said, taking a side-glance at his reaction.

'No, no,' he said, 'no need.'

But I read anyway. And I read aloud:

You (O Arabs) have acquired qualities that are inferior to the dog's.
The dog is fashioned to provide help and defence.
He is faithful and keeps to what you would expect him to do,
protecting the whole neighbourhood.
He gives voluntarily, not by compulsion.
He cures you of your anger and rescues you from distress.
If you were like him you would not be like a burning oven on my
   heart.

Al-Turki chuckled. 'I like Ibn al-Marzuban's ambiguous use of the word "many" in the title of his book,' he said. 'At least he concedes not everyone has acquired qualities which are inferior to the dog's.'

I raised my hand and described a squiggle in the air in visual imitation of a signature. Al-Turki raised his hand and made inviting gestures with his palms. I moved to a small chair next to him. He placed his right arm over my shoulders and whispered in my ear, 'Tell me, brother, in strictest confidence, how much money you are taking with you.'

'Fifty thousand pounds, cash,' I replied without hesitation. 'This is what I have saved during my five-year stint at the Centre.'

Al-Turki roared with laughter. 'That's all! Now, let me see, where is your file?'

A Kasparov could never have been more exultant. It was an elegant ploy that succeeded beautifully. Al-Turki began rummaging through mounds of paperwork. He shuffled a few pieces, removed a few files from one end of his desk and placed them at the other. 'It must be here, somewhere,' he muttered. He moved more files from his desk. Minutes later, he threw his hands in the air. 'I can't find your file. It's lost!'

He read the undisguised anger and frustration on my face. '*Malish!*' he said. '*Malish* – never mind. Stay here for a few more years. Imagine how much more you can save. *Malish.*'

It was, of course, checkmate. From an unassailable position, suddenly I had been defeated by the ultimate defensive strategy: IBM, the intercontinental ballistic missile by which the Muslim world nukes itself: *Inshallah, bukra, malish*. I must have moaned the mantra aloud in my misery.

'IBM?' He leaned forward on his chair.

'Yes,' I said. 'IBM. The transnational infectious disease that's taken the whole Arab world to the dogs.'

The process of collecting signatures would have to start all over again. Unable to face that prospect, I decided to take a drastic step. I went straight to Abdullah Naseef, my friend from the FOSIS days, who was now the President of the University. It was Naseef who had directed Sami Angawi towards my house. And it was Naseef's influence and skill that ensured the survival of the Hajj Research Centre. A slim, elegant figure, he had returned from Britain, after obtaining his doctorate, to become the Secretary-General of the University; and had risen rapidly through the ranks. He was both my mentor and my best friend. And now I really needed him.

Naseef read on my face that something was wrong. 'I want to leave,' I said. He smiled knowingly. I was ready to launch into an explanation but he ushered me towards his office in a seamless movement that demonstrated he understood instinctively. I sat on a chair next to him. 'I tried to follow the normal procedure, but . . .' He stopped me before I could finish my sentence. 'I know,' he said. 'I know everything.' He made a telephone call, talked animatedly for several minutes, and then looked at me with his broad, generous smile that always rose to shine and twinkle through his eyes. 'I think I have found a way to get you an exit visa today,' he said. He asked his *farash* to call Shaikh Abdullah.

A few moments later Shaikh Abdullah entered the room and stood with respect and reverence in a corner. I knew Shaikh Abdullah well. A short stubby man in his early sixties, he sported a handsome white beard and had responsibility for arranging exit and entrance visas for the employees of the University. It was a job Shaikh Abdullah relished: it gave him a lavish sense of importance and power. Every single employee of the University had to pay his respects to the Shaikh at least twice a year. One visit to get an exit and entrance visa; and one simply to show appreciation, to acknowledge his doing what he ought to be doing anyway. Shaikh Abdullah never took less than three weeks to get anyone an exit visa despite his numerous assistants who were always kept busy. Naseef gave him a letter. 'Take this to the *jawazat*,' and pointing towards me, 'make sure you get him an exit visa *today*.'

Shaikh Abdullah looked dazed, as though he had suddenly walked into a wall. 'It cannot be done. It cannot be done,' he murmured. 'I have used every single trick I know to get this man exit visas. It just cannot be done in less than three days.' He looked sheepish.

'It can be done in a day. I will speak to the director of the *jawazat* myself.'

'But . . .'

Naseef raised his index finger and pointed it in the direction of Shaikh Abdullah. That was a direct command. 'Go now. Straight to the *jawazat*.'

Shaikh Abdullah responded with the 'ready to comply' signal. He pointed to the tip of his nose and then the right eye with his right index finger. The verbal equivalent is, literally, your command is on my head and in my eye.

Naseef looked at me and smiled. 'You go with him and stay with him till he gets the job done.'

I followed Shaikh Abdullah out of Naseef's office.

Shaikh Abdullah sported a perpetual grin. Now, he looked more serious than I had ever seen him. I decided an effort at polite chat was not indicated and merely followed him in silence. He went to his office, placed Naseef's letter and my passport in a file and informed his assistant he was going to the passport office on a special assignment and would be there for the rest of the day. We drove in Shaikh Abdullah's old pickup truck to the Ministry of Interior, off the old Airport Street.

At the *jawazat*, the visa section of the Ministry of the Interior, we walked straight into the office of the Director of the Visa Department. Shaikh Abdullah placed the letter, clipped inside the file, in front of him. The Director read the letter carefully, wrote something on it and asked Shaikh Abdullah to take it to a particular window outside the building. The window was actually a small opening in a very large wall. It was about eighty by fifty centimetres, protected with five iron bars some ten centimetres apart. Through them about a dozen individuals were simultaneously trying to pass files and talk to the man inside. My heart sank at the spectacle: forget the visa, I thought; we won't even get near the window.

Shaikh Abdullah sensed my thought and gently tapped me on the shoulder. 'I know my job,' he said with some confidence. 'Now, stay back and watch.'

He counted off a number of paces from the crowd surrounding the visa window like a fast bowler preparing his run-up. At about twenty metres from the crowd he stopped, turned and shouted for two or three people standing between him and the crowd at the window to move out of the way. He then pulled up the bottom half of his *toupe*, his long white outer garment, and tied it around his waist. Finally, he looked at me and grinned, revealing the gold tooth at the bottom corner of his mouth.

Suddenly Shaikh Abdullah yelled, '*Ya Allah*,' in a dreadful voice and charged the crowd with the look of an Afghan Mujahid running into battle. The people gathered at the window turned in horror, unable to believe what was about to hit them. Shaikh Abdullah jumped on top of the crowd, walked at lightning speed on their heads and shoulders and placed his file right into the hands of the man behind the window before descending elegantly in an effortless dismount. Calmly and nonchalantly he walked back to stand beside me.

'Never fails,' he said triumphantly.

'I can't believe a man of your age has so much energy and dexterity,' I said in genuine amazement and admiration.

'That's exactly what my wife says,' he replied, grinning, allowing the sun to glint off his gold tooth.

'When performing this incredible manoeuvre, have you ever hit one of those iron bars?'

'Never.'

'What now?'

'*Choia*.' He joined the fingers and the thumb of his right hand and raised them to the level of the chest: '*Choia*' (We wait).

After about half an hour the window was closed. The crowd dispersed. A few people remained, loitering and waiting. Some sought shade elsewhere. Shaikh Abdullah and I squatted under a tree.

The Saudis have developed waiting into an art form. *Choia* is undoubtedly the most common word, and gesture, in the Saudi idiom. It has something to do with the Bedouin notion of time. Throughout their history, it is said, the Bedouins had nothing and owned nothing; but they had plenty of time. They enjoyed hanging around, waiting, not rushing to do anything in particular. So, waiting has become an essential ingredient of all Saudi life. In its most dramatic sense, the Saudi notion of time is revealed in the conflict that often arises between a western technician who counts the minutes and seconds in performing a certain task and his Saudi counterpart who looks at life in terms of seasons and years. Saudis never give a precise time for anything. When someone says that *Inshallah, bukra*, he will visit you, he could possibly mean tomorrow, the day after, in a few days or sometime in the near future, or any time before eternity. Similarly, rendezvous times are never given in relation to hours or their divisions but in relation to prayer times, the five daily prayers describing arcs of time between and after. *Bad Zuhr*, after the midday prayer, could mean any time after midday and before sunset. Time when calibrated in hours always occurs in round numbers: it is five o'clock, when it could be twenty minutes before or after five.

In a strangely perverted sense, this notion of time has become integral to Wahhabism, the revivalist movement founded by Muhammad ibn Abd al-Wahhab, that has become the state creed of Saudi Arabia. Abd al-Wahhab was born in 1703 in a small town in Najd, the northern part of the Kingdom, and brought up in the Hanbali sect, the most severe of the four Schools of Islamic thought. Abd al-Wahhab advocated 'the return to Qur'an and Sunnah' (the practice of the Prophet). His call was for a return to the purity and simple profundity of the origin of Islam. He rejected practices that had accreted and become permitted in traditional Islam such as celebrating the birthday of the Prophet Muhammad or visiting the graves and shrines of saints and divines. He firmly set himself against all popular superstition by which humankind attempts to fathom the Divine and then ends up seeking to appropriate and manipulate this Power, seeing it as an adjunct of special individuals or particular adepts or those who undergo special preparation. Rather like the Reformation thinkers in European Christianity, Abd al-Wahhab set himself against the abuses by which religion pandered to the gullible masses rather than educated or ministered to them. His reforming zeal sent many back to the elegant purity of Islam as a Message of humility, unity, morality and ethics motivated by equality and justice. If one needed a parallel one could think of the elegant refinement and simplicity of Shaker furniture. And think of the Nonconformist sects whose influence in European thought, as a consequence of their religious philosophy, has been enormous. The entirety of Whig history, the growth of the liberal tradition of representative democracy, civil and human rights takes its inception from the firm conviction of men and women, who, knowing they stood equal without need of mediators before their God, could not condone nor accept that they should stand unequal or disadvantaged before the might of other men, be they kings or bishops. It is the outlook known in European history as Puritan. It is, of course, an outlook that in Europe eventually generated Ian Paisley.

The contemporary Saudi creed owes as much, or possibly as little, to Abd al-Wahhab as it does to the thirteenth-century Muslim political scientist Ibn Taymiyya, who belongs to a long and heroic tradition of intellectual zealots. Ibn Taymiyya was concerned, almost exclusively, with the strength and survival of the Muslim community at a time when Islam, recovering from the onslaught of the Crusades, was under siege from the Mongols. He saw dissension amongst Muslims as their main weakness and sought to ban plurality of interpretations. Everything had to be found in the Qur'an and the Sunnah; and even theology and philosophy, Ibn Taymiyya asserted boldly, had no place in Islam. The Qur'an had to be interpreted literally. When the Qur'an, for example, says God sits on His throne, He sits on His throne, period. No discussion can be entertained on the nature of the throne or its purpose. Nothing can be read metaphorically or symbolically.

I learned a great deal about modern Wahhabism from students at Medina University. During the Hajj season, we would hire these students by the hundred to help us with our surveys and studies. A few of them were Saudis, but most were from other parts of the Muslim world. Without exception, they were on scholarship and were guaranteed badly paid employment by the Saudi treasury on finishing their course. All were being trained to be *dias* – preachers, who would, on graduation, go out to Asia and Africa, as well as Europe and America, to do *dawa*: run mosques, *madrasahs* and Islamic centres, to teach and preach. What did they learn? And what were they going to preach? From the *dias*, I discovered that in modern Wahhabism, there is only the constant present. There is no real past and there is no real notion of an alternative, different future. Their perpetual present exists in the ontological shadow of the past – or rather, a specific, constructed period of early Islamic history, the days of the Prophet Muhammad. The history and culture of Muslim civilization, in all its greatness, complexity and plurality, is totally irrelevant; indeed, it is rejected as deviancy and degeneration. Hardly surprising then that Saudis had no feelings for the cultural property and sacred topology of Mecca.

The students from Medina University were fiercely loyal both to their Saudi mentors and their particular school of thought. The Wahhabism they learned was manufactured on the basis of tribal loyalty – but the place of traditional tribal allegiance was now taken by Islam. Everyone outside this territory was, by definition, a hostile dweller in the domain of unbelief. Those who stood outside their domain were not limited to non-Muslims; they included all those Muslims who have not given allegiance to Wahhabism. The ranks of unbelief were swollen by the Shias, the Sufis, and followers of other Islamic schools of thought. In the minds of these *dias*, and in Saudi society itself, the demarcation between the interior and the exterior, with us or against us, insider or outsider, orthodox or heretic, is almost total. The students would often tell me that any alliance with the unbelievers was itself unbelief; that one should not just refrain from associating or making friends with them, but should also shun their employment, advice, emulation, and try to avoid conviviality and affability towards them.

In Saudi Arabia, the expatriates are treated in this fashion, confined to their specific quarters according to their status. The maintenance of rigid, sharp division is evident also in the treatment of women. It is not just that women are totally marginalized in society as a whole. The distinctive difference of women's position has to be emphasized at every juncture. All men in the Kingdom are dressed in white – crisply ironed *toupes* and *jallabiyahs*. White is the natural colour for such an extreme climate: it reflects the sun and absorbs very little heat. Women have to be covered, from head to toe, by law, in black shrouds that absorb all the sun and all the heat. Women wear their shrouds ninja fashion, observing not traditional female Muslim dress, *hijab*, but the more extensive *niqab*, the head-covering that leaves only a narrow slit where the eyes are visible. The only place in Saudi Arabia where this refinement of dress is not seen is within the precincts of the Sacred Mosque itself where the conventional Islamic precepts of female garb include the requirement for the face to be uncovered.

Initially, I dismissed the confessions of students from Medina as the ranting of over-zealous young men. I also suspected my own observations of Saudi society. As someone brought up and educated in Britain, I thought, I was looking at the Saudis from a biased perspective.

And what about people like Angawi and Naseef? I had not, and still have not, met more rounded, humane, compassionate or refined individuals. In the hands of Naseef, the simple profundity of Islam that Wahhabism sought to recapture soars beyond any simplistics that could be termed fundamentalist. Both in his own lifestyle, and the way he related to others, Naseef was a sublime minimalist. He oozed culture in a society that was totally devoid of any art or culture; he radiated subtlety and finesse while being surrounded by clumsiness and ugliness. He operated unfailingly with a gentle, peaceful tolerance while all around him a harsh, brutalizing incivility and disdain were becoming the normal routine of Saudi life. This is why he was so universally loved. It dawned on me there was a significant difference between the Najdis, those, like the Royal Family, who are from the northern province of the Kingdom, and the Hijazis from the region where Jeddah and Mecca are located. The term 'Hijaz' means the barrier by which two things are separated. The Hijazis mark the difference between deathly literalism and a life-enhancing approach to an eternal text.

When the old King Abdul-Aziz, the founder of Saudi Arabia, first entered Jeddah as a triumphant conqueror, most of the families of the Hijaz came out to greet him. The Bughshans, the Bin Ladens, the Al-Turkis and Al-Shaikhs all came; with the sole exception of the Naseefs. The Naseefs were a scholarly family, proud of their cultural inheritance. The old patriarch, Muhammad Naseef, born in 1884, was a celebrated scholar and editor. And his house, at the centre of the souk overlooking the entire city, contained an impressive library, with thousands of priceless manuscripts, rare books and collections of old newspapers from 1924 onwards. He entertained visiting scholars from as far away as Morocco and Sudan, Syria and Iran, India and Malaysia. But he was not favourably inclined to the Najdi King; and the family paid for this by being marginalized. Much of Old Jeddah has gone the way of Mecca. But the Naseef House, in all its renovated magnificence, with its delicately crafted *rawshin* bay windows, intricate panels, cornices, eaves and shutters, is still there. The Naseefs fought tooth and nail to preserve it. In the hot Jeddah summers, when the temperature reaches beyond forty degrees Celsius, it is the coolest place in town. Whenever there was a power cut – in those days this was an almost daily occurrence – and the air conditioners came to a grinding halt, I used to walk down to the old town and sit under that rare tree in front of the Naseef house. It was the best place to smoke a *sheesha* – the Saudi version of the 'water pipe'.

The true import of Saudi Wahhabism was brought home to me in November 1979. During that fateful month, a group of zealots occupied the Sacred Mosque in Mecca. Under a pale scimitar moon, and amongst thousands of worshippers circling the Kaa'ba, a group of Bedouins brought out sub-machine guns, rifles and revolvers concealed beneath their robes and fired into the air. They allowed most of the worshippers to leave the Sacred Mosque, then they bolted all thirty-nine doors to the mosque from inside. Their twenty-seven-year-old leader, Mohammad Abdullah al-Khatani, proclaimed himself 'the Mehdi' (redeemer) who had come to purify Islam. The insurgents came largely from the Oteiba tribe, which had actually helped King Abdul Aziz to seize control of the Arabian Peninsula in 1902, and included many European and American converts to Islam. They belonged to the Al-Moshtarin sect and believed that a man had to buy his place in paradise by devoting all his goods and his life to religion. They accused the Saudi state of cooperating with Christians, confirming the heresies of the Shias, promoting dissension by permitting more than one interpretation of Islam, introducing television and film in the Kingdom, and instituting the fetish of money. Mecca was cut off from the rest of the world and the mosque was surrounded by both the army and the National Guard, whose main function is to guard the Royal Family. But before the rebels could be (literally) flushed out of the mosque, they had to be formally sentenced to death. The task fell to Sheikh 'Abd al-'Aziz bin Baz, the chief scholar and the Mufti of the Kingdom.

Bin Baz was blind and I used to see him often in the Sacred Mosque, performing the circumambulation around the Kaa'ba. The spectacle was always the same. A young student, holding him by his left shoulder, would lead him around the Kaa'ba, while hordes of admirers and devotees would try to kiss his right hand. Bin Baz would allow them to hold his hand, but the moment they tried to bring their lips to his wrist, he would pull his hand away. The accusations of the rebels against the

Saudi state were read out to Bin Baz. He agreed totally with the thesis of the rebels. Yes, he said, a true Wahhabi state should not associate with the unbelievers. Yes, the heresies of the Shias cannot go unchallenged. Yes, more than one interpretation of Islam should not be allowed under any circumstances. Yes, images of all kind were forbidden in Islam, including television and film. And, yes, money should not be fetishized. The only thing Bin Baz actually disagreed with was that these things actually happen in the Saudi Kingdom. So the Sacred Mosque was flooded and the messianic rebels were drowned. It seemed to me that the puritan rebels were at least honest, truer representatives of Wahhabism; unlike the dishonest Wahhabite State.

By radically denying the complexity and diversity of Islamic history, over time and vast areas of the world, and rejecting diverse, pluralistic interpretations of Islam, Wahhabism has stripped Islam of all its ethical and moral content and reduced it to an arid list of dos and don'ts. To insist that anything that cannot be found in a literal reading of the sources and lore of early Muslims is *kufr* – outside the domain of Islam – and to enforce this comprehensive vision with brute force and severe social pressure for complete conformity spells totalitarianism.

At around two o'clock, when it was time for offices to close, the *jawazat* window opened. A hand holding a file materialized through the window and flung the file in the air. A man waiting patiently in the shade jumped up, caught the file, opened it to take a brief look and walked briskly out of the compound with a satisfied look. A few moments later the hand emerged again, another file was flung in the air. Another man caught it and walked out. The process continued for several minutes. Finally, the hand appeared once more and Shaikh Abdullah jumped up from a squatting position and caught the file.

He opened the file and glanced at it. I looked at him anxiously. 'Have I got the exit visa?'

'Well, not quite,' Shaikh Abdullah replied. 'You haven't got the visa but the letter from Doktur Naseef has been honoured.'

'What does that mean?' I asked.

'I don't know. I have never faced this situation before. But I think you can leave the country tomorrow.'

'As long as I can leave the country. That's all I want.'

I took the file from Shaikh Abdullah. There was an official-looking letter attached to my passport. Shaikh Abdullah pointed at the letter and said: 'I think it is an emergency visa. Read it to me.'

'You read it,' I passed the letter to him. 'My Arabic is not good enough.'

'That's what my wife always says to me.' He handed the letter back to me.

At that moment I had a strange thought. 'Considering all files look the same, and the man behind the window did not indicate anyone or anything, how did you know which file to jump and catch?'

'Are you in charge of the passport section of the University or am I?' Shaikh Abdullah was irritated with the question. 'I can't tell you everything. Now if you take this letter to the airport, you will find they will allow you to leave the country.

'*Khalas*,' he said, stroking his palms and fingers as though he was dusting his hands. '*Khalas*,' he repeated: 'It's over.'

Without waiting for a reply Shaikh Abdullah jumped in his pickup truck and drove off.

The following day was the first day of Ramadan. During this blessed month a whole new inverted lifestyle emerges. The city, indeed all of Saudi Arabia, stays up all night. Day becomes night. Once the cannon is fired (actually there are twelve cannons fired in unison) to mark the end of *suhur*, the time for taking a last light meal before the beginning of the fast, just before dawn, the city goes to sleep. The streets are deserted; offices, shops and business establishments are closed, opening for only a few hours between ten and one. The city begins to show signs of life just before sunset. By the time the cannons have been fired again, now to announce the *iftar*, the light meal that marks the end of the fast, the city becomes vibrant with excitement. The skyline is illuminated with a riot of colour, roads become jammed with bumper-to-bumper traffic, and streets and alleyways are crowded with people shopping for the following day. The offices and shops open again at around ten at night and will close only after two o'clock in the morning. Some restaurants and shops will still be doing brisk business right up to dawn.

It is truly astonishing how easily and speedily the Saudis adjust to change, to living by night and sleeping by day. The previous Ramadan, after the siege of Mecca, I had started thinking about permanence and change in Islam. I had begun writing *The Future of Muslim Civilisation*. It was an attempt to articulate my own vision of what an Islamic society should and could be. Nothing remains 'contemporary' forever, I argued. Islam has to be rearticulated, understood afresh, from epoch to epoch, according to the needs, requirements, the specific demands of geographical location and the circumstances of the time. What changes is our understanding of the constants. And as our understanding develops, Islam of one particular epoch may not bear much resemblance – except in devotional matters – to Islam of another epoch. Wahhabism, I had concluded, had been employed to introduce two metaphysical catastrophes in Islam.

First, by closing the interpretations of our 'absolute frame of reference' – the Qur'an and the life of Prophet Muhammad – it had removed agency from believers. One could only have an interpretative relationship with a living, eternal text. Without that relationship of constant struggling to understand the text and find new meanings, Muslim societies were doomed to exist in suspended animation. If everything was *a priori* given, nothing new could really be accommodated. The intellect, human intelligence, became an irrelevant encumbrance since everything could be reduced to a simple comply/not comply formula derived from the thought of dead bearded men.

Second, by assuming that ethics and morality reached their apex, indeed an end point, with the Companions of the Prophet, Wahhabism, which became the basis of what later came to be known as 'Islamism', negated the very idea of evolution in human thought and morality. Indeed, it set Muslim civilization on a fixed course to perpetual decline. Instead, I suggested that it is not only possible but necessary both for individuals and societies, now and in the future, to rise to higher levels in understanding and realization of Islamic values than those achieved by the Companions of the Prophet or their society. Indeed, the challenge of our time, I argued, was to work out values and norms that were clearly and distinctively better than those worked out by the Companions of the Prophet.

From the perspective of Wahhabism, these were heretical thoughts. And I kept them mostly to myself. But now the manuscript was finished. I spent the night checking and making final changes. I typed a false title page and placed the real manuscript between some mundane writing on Hajj – just in case they checked at the airport. A small suitcase, containing mostly rare books and manuscripts I had rescued and scavenged, was already packed. A friend had agreed to take my furniture, stereo, and my beloved hammock – I used to lie on it, swinging in the middle of my living room, listening alternately to the recitation of the Qur'an and Tangerine Dream – and other belongings I had gathered during my sojourn in Jeddah. I placed the manuscript of my book, and the £50,000 I had saved, in a Saudia Airlines shoulder bag, and headed for the airport.

I was at the airport by seven, hoping to catch the eleven o'clock Saudia flight out of Jeddah. Unlike the new King Abdul Aziz Airport, which is some thirty kilometres outside the city, the old Jeddah airport was only a few minutes' drive from Sharafia, where I lived. It couldn't be more different from the tent-like structure and technological efficiency of its modern counterpart. It was little more, it seemed to me, than a loosely linked collection of pre-fabricated sheds. I got there before everyone else; but I had no booking. So I gave the Palestinian man behind the check-in counter a long sob story. My grandmother had died. My uncle had died. Half of my relations over the age of fifty had died. But he wasn't convinced.

'Who else do you want me to kill?'

He looked slightly bemused. 'OK,' he said, 'it's Ramadan and I believe you.' The blessed month has an unfailing hold on Muslim consciousness. In forgoing food and drink during the hours of daylight, breaking the normal habits of daily life, everyone focuses on the need for human understanding, compassion and peaceable sociability. Life isn't easy under the requirements of this self-discipline; this object lesson propels people to accept the necessity to be kind and accommodating in confident expectation that other people will respond likewise. 'But even in Ramadan we have to eat,' he added. Underneath the desk, I could see that he was rubbing the thumb of his right hand across the tips of his fingers. *Falus*, said his gesture. Money. I slipped

500 riyals surreptitiously into his hands. 'Normally, you would have to go on the waiting list, but considering that your grandmother has died . . .' He paused for a moment. 'I'll take the risk and give you a seat.'

I thanked the man and handed him my passport.

The clerk flicked through the pages of the passport. 'You don't seem to have an exit visa.' He looked puzzled.

'I do,' I said. 'I have an emergency exit visa. It's that piece of paper in the passport.'

The clerk looked at the piece of paper, turned it over to examine the official passport office stamp and nodded. 'No one has ever left this country on an emergency visa,' he said. 'But still, it's Ramadan.'

While I was digesting the clerk's words, I noticed the porter was putting the wrong labels on my suitcase.

'London, London,' I shouted. 'Not Rome. London. London.'

'Don't shout,' said the porter. 'It's Ramadan.' And he carried on putting the wrong labels on my suitcase and then placed it on the conveyor belt.

'Forget the luggage, worry about your exit visa,' said the clerk as he handed me my passport, ticket and boarding pass.

At passport control, two officers sat at two separate desks casually stamping passports and collecting exit cards. After filling an exit card, I pushed through the crowd. I handed my passport and the sheet of official paper, which gave me clearance from the blacklist, to one of the officers. He looked closely at the paper, taking his time. Eventually he spoke: 'Sorry, I'm not qualified to give exit visas. You'll have to see the *mudir*.'

'Where's his office?' I asked.

The man pointed in an arbitrary direction. 'Over there,' he said.

I came out of the crush and found my way to the passport section of the airport. Three men were sitting inside chatting. I placed my passport and clearance sheet on the table. 'Please,' I said, 'I have an emergency exit visa. I need the director to sign it.'

One officer forced himself to get up. He looked at the clearance visa closely. Then he walked to a desk virtually covered with a very large register. He turned a few pages of the register and checked my name against it. After a few minutes' examination, he closed the register. He initialled the paper and pointed me towards another office.

There, a very small man sat behind a very large desk. I pushed my piece of paper in front of him. He took several minutes to examine it and then signed it at the bottom.

'You will get your final clearance at the Immigration Office in Arrivals,' he told me.

'Arrivals?' I was losing my cool. The flight was now being called. 'Arrivals? I want an exit visa not an entrance visa.'

'Don't shout,' said the official. 'It's Ramadan. I know what you want. But you have to follow the procedure. You have to go to Arrivals. *Khalas.*' Without a word I took the paper from his hand and ran out. I could hear the last call for my flight. I ran from the Departure Lounge and out of Terminal One, almost knocking over a Nigerian pilgrim carrying a basket on her head. I ran along the old airport road and turned into Arrivals.

A Bedouin soldier at the gate of the Arrivals Lounge stopped me, almost assaulting me in the process. But I did not wait to argue with him; I ran straight ahead into the first office I could see. Inside, a rather old, full-bearded man sat, quite aloof, on a very large chair. '*As salamu 'alaykum,*' I said, and without waiting for an answer I grabbed the man's beard. I pulled it gently and kissed it wildly. I kissed it on the left side, and then on the right side. I kissed it from the front and under his chin.

The old officer was completely transformed. He looked both embarrassed and concerned.

'Tell me, O Brother, what can I do for you?' he said.

I explained the situation.

'Don't worry,' he said. 'Your paper needs several signatures and I will go with you to collect them. After all, today is the first day of Ramadan.'

We went from office to office collecting signatures. After completing the procedure, the old officer took me back to the Departure Lounge. We ran towards a group of Saudia ground staff.

'Flight SV 172. Flight SV 172.'

'Quick,' said one of them, 'get in the coach.'

I jumped in the coach. I was the sole passenger. The driver closed the door and made for the plane. I sat anxiously. Halfway through the journey, the coach was stopped.

'Turn back, turn back,' somebody shouted.

From the window of the coach I could see the plane still standing on the tarmac. A very long limousine with a Saudi flag whizzed past the coach. A few moments later, a princely-looking Saudi was boarding the plane with his entourage.

'There goes your seat,' said the Filipino coach driver. 'None of the princes stay in the country this time of year. It's Ramadan, you know.'

'Yes,' I said. 'I know. It's Ramadan.'

I looked at the plane as it took off and made a gesture of universal validity. Holding my index and adjacent finger in the reverse manner to the victory sign, I thrust my hand vigorously skyward.

Chapter 9

THE HEAVENLY REVOLUTION

I am convinced it was not Rolls-Royce engines that powered my flight back to London on the second day of Ramadan but my own emotional energy. Overnight, I amassed an enormous surfeit as I roamed Jeddah fretting over my prospects of taking wing. The entire city, caught in the night-for-day reversal of the fasting month, mirrored my restlessness. As the hours passed I became so hyper I felt I might levitate on emotional thrusters alone, my trusty Saudia airline bag serving as my magic carpet to get me out of here. The more I fretted, the more I reflected, the more I fuelled my turmoil. We Muslims live among the wreckage of our heritage, we lop off its sophistication, lose precious works of subtle minds that once strove to pursue inventiveness within our own dynamic framework. When I returned to the airport no one dared to deny me. It was as if my emotional state was visible. I was whisked through the system and put on the first available flight. Forget *Inshallah, bukra, malish,* they seemed to say – this is another kind of IBM altogether, get it out of here, let it explode somewhere else. So I departed, struggling through all the pains of what we have become. I departed; but actually I had not left Saudi Arabia. Anti-paradise is not a place, it is a state of mind. The only way to leave is to find an alternative route to paradise, a different state of being.

After my return from Saudi Arabia, I became even more determined to work for a genuine Islamic revival. By now I had acquired a small reputation as a writer and journalist. The publication of my books provided me with ready access to Muslim intellectual circles. I was a regular presence at conferences, seminars and symposiums, where everyone, including myself, pinned their hope on Iran. But apart from Iran, we had another, broader, concern: we wanted to build an 'intellectual foundation' for the revival of Muslim civilization, develop a general theory of Islamic resurgence of which Iran would provide a practical example. Indeed, various groups of Muslim intellectuals in Britain and the USA, India and Pakistan, Malaysia and Indonesia and Egypt and Turkey had started to seriously think and work along these lines by the mid-1970s. I was an active member of a group of British Muslim intellectuals who had established an Institute in London with the specific objective of developing 'theories and plans' to rebuild the Muslim civilization of the future. The group was led by Kalim Siddiqui, a charismatic political scientist; and it was to Siddiqui I turned next both for inspiration and to work on specific intellectual projects.

I first met Siddiqui, a stylish, compelling man with a full neat beard, in 1972. He was working for the *Guardian*. I was President of the London Islamic Circle and invited him to give a talk to our group, mostly comprised of students and those who had recently graduated, on 'The future of Muslim Youth in Britain'. The following year, in the summer of 1973, Siddiqui was invited to Tripoli, Libya, to attend 'The International Islamic Youth Conference'. The Conference was to serve as a platform for unveiling the 'Third International Theory', invented and propagated by Colonel Muammar Muhammad al-Qaddafi, the new ruler of Libya. The theory was based on three concepts: religion, nationalism and socialism – 'the three forces that have moved history'. Qaddafi, who claimed to have worked on the theory since the early 1950s, argued that Islam needed the 'scientific context' of nationalism and socialism. The function of the Conference was to 'learn' the theory and approve it. The consensus of the Conference would serve as the basis to export the theory to the rest of the Muslim world. The Conference overwhelmingly rejected the Third International Theory. This consensus made a great impact on Siddiqui. He was taken aback by the passion and the intellectual candour of these young Muslims. They rejected the Islamized Nationalist and Socialist paradise Qaddafi offered, but in the process of rejecting what was on offer the Muslim youth of the world clearly indicated the direction in which they believed their destiny lay.' And it was not in the direction of the West. 'At this precise moment in history,' Siddiqui declared, 'Muslim intellectuals make their stand against the West.'

Soon afterwards, Siddiqui suffered a heart attack. He claimed he had 'actually died' for a few minutes on the operating table: a 'death' that led him to question his Marxist sympathies, his Trotskyite leanings, and his entire life. As a result, he gave up his job at the *Guardian* and decided to work full-time with Muslim youth on 'shaping a new destiny for Islam'. In his case he did not turn up on my doorstep to whisk me off on a rescue mission as others had done. It merely became evident over a series of meetings that I was one of 'the youth' he identified and targeted for recruitment to his cause.

I was impressed by Kalim Siddiqui: his eloquence, analytical skills and passion were quite overwhelming. Indeed, so influenced was I by his sophistication, graceful general demeanour and the elegance with which he handled himself that I began to copy him unconsciously. He called his wife 'Begum' – My Lady – so I started to call my wife 'Begum' too. He spoke not just with his mouth but also with his arms and body; I let my natural inclination for demonstrative gesticulation have free rein. I even began to think I was going to have a heart attack and 'die'.

Besides me, the group around Siddiqui included my old FOSIS friend Ghayasuddin Siddiqui, who had finished a doctorate in production engineering at Sheffield University, and Ajmal Ahmad, whose sense of confusion prevented him from finishing his doctorate in Political Science at London University. Ajmal and I would often go to Slough to meet Kalim Sahib, as he was popularly known; sometimes we were joined by Ghayasuddin Sahib. Kalim Sahib's wife would prepare a lavish meal: fragrant biryani with white and yellow rice, koftas (meat balls) in curry, and dal – the gastronomic array I invariably associate with intellectual exertion. And there was always *metasse*: a sweet dish. Kalim Sahib loved *metasse* and no meal was complete without it. There was only one problem. After his heart attack, he was not allowed to eat such fatty fare. We would eat the biryani and the kofta and take particular care to linger over our *metasse* – usually mouth-watering carrot halwa – while poor Kalim Sahib would have to make do with dal and plain rice.

After the food, the talk. The conversation always began with Kalim Sahib asking: 'What is to be done?'

This was my cue. 'I do not think,' I would reply routinely, 'it is possible to repair or restore the social order in Muslim societies. From what I've seen, many Muslim societies are beyond repair. We need to conceive and create alternative social and political orders, fundamentally different from the existing ones.' In our talks we came to the conclusion that our knowledge of Islam prevented us from generating viable alternatives.

'Our real problem,' Kalim Sahib said in a deeply reflective mood one day, 'is that we have two types of knowledge. Let us call them operational knowledge and non-operational knowledge. Our operational knowledge is one of western sciences – social, physical and technological – acquired either in the West or in western-type educational establishments. This western knowledge makes sense to us because the social and economic orders in which we live are the product of western civilization. For example, the economic theory we read is part of our daily experience and we can see it at work.' He paused. Kalim Sahib liked to play with his glasses: repositioning them on his nose; removing and replacing them with diverse flourishes and sweeps; turning them in his hands; examining the angles formed by manipulating the side pieces and the flexibility of the hinges. He took off his spectacles, placed them carefully on the table. 'As Muslims,' he continued, 'we also have knowledge of Islam. This is our non-operational knowledge. Either Islam is non-operational in our lives, or Islam's operational forms with which we are familiar are confined to prayer, fasting and the rituals at birth, marriage and death. No operational and functional social order of Islam either exists in its entirety today or has existed in recent history. The model social, economic and political orders of Islam in fact existed so long ago, during the time of the Prophet Muhammad and maybe during the Abbasid period, that, for minds immersed in western disciplines, it is difficult to comprehend how social, economic and political problems of today can be solved along Islamic lines.'

'Yet,' Ajmal Sahib intervened, 'as committed Muslims we feel the need to assert our identity and free our personality from the stranglehold the West has on us.'

'Precisely,' Kalim Sahib shot back. 'We do this by asserting the supremacy of Islam. We declare that Islam is superior, but do not know why. We declare that Islam can solve all our individual and collective problems, but do not know how. When we try to solve our problems we end up with something resembling either the capitalist and democratic model or the socialist, Marxist model, or a variant of both. We then proceed to "Islamize" the model of our choice by calling it "Islamic".'

'What we need to do is to discover how we can put our Islamic knowledge into practice,' I said, stating the obvious conclusion.

'And how do we do that?' Kalim Sahib asked.

'By drawing detailed conceptual maps and operational plans of a Muslim civilization of the future,' I replied, not exactly sure I understood precisely what this confident pronouncement meant.

'Yes,' Kalim Sahib replied. 'We need a bagful of new conceptual tools to examine why the recent revivalist movements have failed and to prepare the blueprint of a post-nation-state era that would usher in a new dynamic, thriving future civilization of Islam.'

'And where do we start?' Ajmal Sahib asked.

'We need to start by developing various academic disciplines such as economics and sociology, alternative operational models of political systems, and concrete policies for advancing science and technology,' I said.

'Every civilization needs its own political science,' added Kalim Sahib, the political scientist. 'Yet we have managed to do without one for over a thousand years.' He paused for thought. 'I think this is because Muslims could not conceive of Islam or themselves outside the framework of a political system. But now that we have realized that the idea of State in Islam is fundamentally different from the idea of the modern nation-state, it has become essential for us to develop our own political science.'

'But how can we do this all on our own?' Ajmal Sahib cried. 'We don't have to,' Kalim Sahib said. We all looked at each other; and allowed Kalim Sahib to articulate what we hoped might be done. 'Let us establish an Institute, with a core of young intellectuals, to undertake the project.'

Thus, in the living room of Kalim Sahib, fortified and emboldened by his wife's brilliant biryani, koftas and carrot halwa, was born the Muslim Institute for Research and Planning. Siddiqui turned the discussions we had in his house, along with his experiences and observations at 'The International Islamic Youth Conference', into a small booklet. We made him the Director, his living room was turned into an office, and we established a small publishing house – The Open Press – to publish our manifesto, *Towards A New Destiny*. A few months later, we published *The Draft Prospectus of the Muslim Institute for Research and Planning*, containing our basic assumptions and objectives, written by me, and an outline of our 'strategy for change' written by Siddiqui.

We had big ideas; but no funding. Our first major project, an innovative two-volume biography of the Prophet Muhammad, was entitled *The Road to Medina*. It involved excavating the life of the Prophet to unearth information on the principles and practice by which the first Muslim community forged its social and political systems. Just as Mecca is the eternal focus of all Muslims' spiritual quest, so Medina, the living city of the Prophet, is the eternal reference point for the ideals of Muslim community. It sets the objectives as well as the moral and ethical framework; the can, ought and should of living together in the real world. Yet, as we realized with some astonishment, Muslims write, talk and think less about the mechanics, the operational principles of how this community lived and dealt with the challenge of its times than how it prayed or struggled to survive. Without such information we lacked the ability to ask the right questions: what targets should we set and what means ought we to employ to tackle the problems of today's Muslim societies and bring them nearer to Islam? Our project was designed to fill the information gap, to make it possible to 'develop a rationally convincing programme to reshape and rebuild the entire socio-economic and political structures of Muslim societies'.

While I was working for the Hajj Research Centre in Jeddah, I moonlighted on behalf of the Muslim Institute. A great deal of my free time was spent raising funds for the Institute, to acquire the cash to secure the future of Muslim society. Kalim Siddiqui would visit me regularly, often staying with me, and together we would wander around Jeddah calling on potential supporters. We met and befriended Sheikh Ahmad Salah Jamjoom, a devout but simple man, who made a fortune importing Peugeot cars. Our visits to the Peugeot showroom on Mecca Road in Jeddah became more and more frequent. Eventually, we persuaded Sheikh Jamjoom to talk the Ministry of Higher Education into backing the *Road to Medina* project. We asked for half a million pounds for the five-year study that was to be conducted largely by Kalim Siddiqui himself. The Ministry agreed to pay £300,000 in three instalments, and insisted the project should be completed within three years.

By the time I returned from Saudi Arabia, Kalim Siddiqui had still not begun work on the project. Every year, Siddiqui produced a new excuse for the delay; but every year, Sheikh Jamjoom made sure the cheque arrived on time. The Muslim Institute bought a number of properties with the funds; and leased an office building in Endleigh Street, near Euston Station, in London. Naturally, I was concerned; and suggested that I should start working on the project so we would have something to show – not least to keep the Saudi Ministry of Higher Education, which was demanding its funding back and threatening legal action, at bay. Siddiqui rejected the proposal – his mind was elsewhere: on the developments in Iran.

Towards the end of the 1970s, demonstrations and strikes against the regime of Mohammad Reza Shah had become widespread. The demonstrators were protesting not just against political repression but also against widespread corruption, rising economic inequality, and the influence of American multinational companies. The demonstrations were led by the students, but they were backed and supported by the clergy and, more importantly, by the bazaaris, the well-organized traditional, urban businessmen. The Shah's modernization policies, based on Japanese and South Korean forms of highly concentrated capitalism, benefited the relatively small elite of oligarchic capitalists and non-Iranian multinational companies. These favoured firms dominated the domestic markets, kept wages at a bare minimum and received generous support from public funds. For the bazaaris, the Shah's brand of capitalism represented nothing short of full-blown 'western imperialism'. They became his most militant critics and generously financed the agitation against him.

Each demonstration brought a customary response from the Shah: brutal suppression and more violence against the agitators, perpetrated particularly by SAVAK, the vicious secret police. The demonstration that set the revolution in motion was held in Qum on 9 January 1978. The students were objecting to a visit by US President Jimmy Carter and demanded that Ayatollah Khomeini, in exile in Iraq, be allowed to return to Iran. The police opened fire, killing seventy students. I recall Kalim Siddiqui declaring, 'We have now reached the point of no return.' Forty days later, in accordance with Shia tradition, protesters throughout Iran took to the streets to commemorate the massacre at Qum. This time, the police shot and killed over a hundred people in Tabriz. Less than two weeks later, over a hundred demonstrators were killed in Yazd. Both the protests and the killings continued. On 8 September, which came to be known as 'Black Friday', Iranian troops fired on a demonstration in Tehran, killing several hundred people. The following day, the Shah arrested all opposition leaders and declared martial law.

The revolutionaries now changed tactics and switched to strikes. The long series of strikes during October, including bazaaris and oil workers, had a devastating effect on Iran. The Shah reacted by persuading Iraq to expel Ayatollah Khomeini, who was forced to move to Paris. The move proved fatal for the Shah. In Paris, Ayatollah Khomeini acquired an international audience and became more directly involved in shaping the revolution. The Shah now tried a more conciliatory route. He asked the Ayatollah to return to Iran. Khomeini refused: he declared the Shah's government illegitimate and that he would never set foot in Iran as long as the Shah was in power.

The Islamic month of Muharram began on 2 December. It is the month when the Shia community commemorates the martyrdom of Imam Hussain, the grandson of the Prophet Muhammad. Hussain, and his small band of followers, were massacred in the battle of Kerbala in 679. The event marks the emergence of the Shia as a distinct community and is highly charged with religious passion. This was the month of martyrdom and the demonstrations throughout Iran during Muharram were truly awesome. Millions upon millions came out on the streets, seized government buildings, attacked police stations and, clad in the white dress of martyrs, tried to provoke the army to fire on them. When the army too joined the demonstrators, the fate of the monarchy was sealed.

The Shah left Iran for good on 16 January 1979. On 1 February, Ayatollah Khomeini returned triumphant to Tehran where he was greeted by a crowd of several million people. The revolution was over; and Iran became a new 'Islamic Republic'.

The Iranian Revolution was undoubtedly the event that crystallized the zeitgeist. It had a profound effect on all of us. It was more than the academic clarion call we hoped our project would provide. It was the beginning of wrestling for real with the questions we envisaged. It seemed natural for me and my friends to support the revolution. I understood the deep emotional roots from which it sprang, and the aspirations it aimed to fulfil. At the outset, it made dreamers of us all. It also introduced the world to Islamic fundamentalism. Once discovered, fundamentalism became the buzz word, the one-stop explanation for everything. And like a demented wasp that will not cease buzzing around you the word soon drove me mad, because from my perspective it explained nothing while making understanding anything a lot harder. But the word made lots of work for an eager freelance to pitch. By now the arrival of a daughter and a son had added to my family responsibilities.

So I persuaded *Nature*, the British science journal, to send me to Iran; I visited the country a few months after the revolution. And, despite political turmoil, I found potential for optimism. In my attempt to examine the 'scientific thinking behind Khomeini', I spoke to scientists, engineers, lecturers and philosophers and found them all eager to build a new Islamic Iran on the basis of equity and justice. I even found my old friend Reza, still unemployed, but hoping for a university job. Through revolutionary transformation, and through the dedication of young men like Reza, Ayatollah Khomeini, I thought, might take us to the Promised Land. There was something in the slogan they were shouting in the streets: *Azaadi, Esteglaal,*

Jomhouriyeh Islaami (Freedom, Independence, Islamic Republic). Like Muslims everywhere, weaned on the desolation of our civilizational heritage and the depressing moral bankruptcy of our governments, I hoped Iran was a watershed. Here, it seemed, was a nation ready to opt for a moral agenda, rather than the unending realpolitik of expediency, a nation with the confidence to declare it could find the answers we all needed in the things we proclaimed to believe and that gave our lives meaning: Islam. After so many failures, setbacks and false starts, Muslims looked towards Iran as their first potential success story. A bloody revolution might have been necessary to overthrow the Shah, but here Muslims would attempt to build their first modern paradise. Nevertheless, I had concerns. The overemphasis on the Shia nature of the revolution troubled me. Everyone I spoke to insisted that the revolution was not only 'Islamic' but Shia: a well-structured and organized clergy with the ability to lead a revolution could be found only in Shia Islam. Sunnis, therefore, could not produce such a revolution. As Reza asked me sarcastically: 'Where is your Sunni Ayatollah Khomeini?' There was a logical corollary of this assumption: that this specific model of revolution had to be exported to the rest of the Muslim world.

Kalim Siddiqui, however, had no concerns. The revolution transformed him totally. In all my dealings with him over the preceding years it had been evident he had authoritarian tendencies, hidden just beneath a charismatic personality. He manipulated his glasses much as he sought to manipulate and dominate a meeting, direct a discussion, emphasize his pre-eminence in a gathering. The revolution turned him into a full-blown Trotsky, physically he even reminded me of grainy old archive films of Trotsky haranguing mass gatherings. When I suggested, during our discussions at his home, that our need was to produce alternative visions of a Muslim civilization of the future, in my mind the accent was on pluralism. I was arguing for diverse, numerous possible alternative Muslim futures, each of which could be advocated, debated, even contested. Not for the first time, I discovered, the images in my mind did not correspond to those in the minds of others. Many and diverse were not words that described the images forming in Kalim Sahib's mind's eye. What he was arguing for was *the* Muslim blueprint of the future: a single all-embracing utopian vision that everybody else was obliged to follow. For him, the Iranian revolution provided just such a vision. Having found the model and location of his ideal, he set about developing a theory to justify why and how it should be imposed on the rest of the Muslim world. He shelved the *Road to Medina* project and severed all connections with Sheikh Jamjoom. Indeed, the Muslim Institute abandoned all pretensions of being a research organization. He became a frequent visitor to Tehran, where, by all accounts, every true revolutionary, every follower of 'the line of the Imam', knew him well. Soon, a new avenue of lucrative funding from Iran was opened; and the Muslim Institute became an extension of the Iranian Embassy in London. Kalim Siddiqui declared himself to be *the* most influential theoretician of the 'Islamic revolution'; indeed, he was actually guiding the course of the revolution from London!

I began to have serious doubts about the revolution when Iranian students occupied the American Embassy in Tehran – 'the den of spies' as they called it – and took most of its staff hostage. 'Taking hostages is both foolish and an un-Islamic thing to do,' I said to Kalim Siddiqui over dinner one day at his house in Slough. He was eating his usual dal and plain rice with his hands. He pushed his plate aside, picked up his glasses, placed them on the tip of his nose, and peeked at me, straining his eyes.

'We must not be weak-kneed about it being un-Islamic to hold hostages,' he said firmly.

'But the means through which an Islamic revolution is carried out are just as important as the ends. We can't let the ends justify the means,' I replied.

'To challenge and defeat the existing system we must use all available means,' he shot back. He noticed the displeasure on my face. 'Look,' he said in a reconciling mood, still looking at me above his glasses, 'revolution is the only viable approach to Islamic revival. Islam cannot be brought about in any country following the democratic method. And revolution has its own dynamics. You have to accept that.'

'But . . .' Before I could say anything, Siddiqui intervened.

'The Islamic revolution in Iran is the model of Muslim political behaviour that Muslims everywhere *must* accept. Iran provides a reality to which we can relate our ideals, to which we can relate our history, to which we can relate the development of the *ummah* as a whole. We must be patient; and we *must* allow the revolution to take its full course.'

Kalim Siddiqui produced elaborate theoretical justification for every twist and turn of the revolution. Since theory always followed actions, and in many cases actions were haphazard or disingenuous, so were the theories Siddiqui produced to justify them. A Sunni himself, he became obsessed with Shia political thought. He declared the Shia to have 'an extra sharp edge which the Sunni political behaviour has been lacking'; and that therefore the Sunnis should be required to adopt the political norms and values of Shiism. When Iran declared that Ayatollah Khomeini was *Vilayayt-I-Faqih*, the earthly shadow of the Twelfth Shia Imam who was in occultation, he produced an elaborate, convoluted theory to justify 'Imam Khomeini' as not just the absolute leader of the revolution, but the undisputed leader of the entire Muslim world. Islam, he suggested, is incomplete without an Islamic State; and all Islamic movements in the world were duty bound to establish Islamic States on the lines of Iran. Once Islamic States have been established in other Muslim countries, these states should come together under a single leader – Imam Khomeini. All those who were against the Iranian Revolution, within and without, were declared by Siddiqui to be counter-revolutionaries. When he coolly asked for the 'eradication' of 'liberals' and 'counter-revolutionaries', and suggested that Bani Sadr, the first elected president of revolutionary Iran, and Mehdi Bazargan, the liberal leader of the opposition, should be 'eliminated', I became incensed with rage. These were the intellectuals whose debate and search had inspired not just me but the spirits of countless Muslims everywhere. They, and many more like them, were now being swept aside. If people like this, so committed to their faith as a way of life and thought, were expendable what hope could we have? Siddiqui's pronouncement was just too much for a liberal like me to take. So I went to the Muslim Institute to confront the arch-theoretician for the last time.

Siddiqui was sitting in his office, expecting me. As soon as I walked in, he lowered the frame of his glasses until they were sitting just on the tip of his nose. He looked at me over the top. 'You don't seem to be your normal self,' he said.

'What is this talk of eliminating Bani Sadr?' I shot back.

'The revolution must take its course. I have already told you.'

'Where does it end? When does the killing stop? You will be describing me as a counter-revolutionary next!'

'Next?' shouted Siddiqui. 'You are a counter-revolutionary. Unless you change your ways.'

'So anyone who disagrees with you is a counter-revolutionary?'

'Not me,' Siddiqui screeched. 'The Islamic revolution.' He pushed his glasses back to the bridge of his nose and in the same movement leaned back in his chair. 'You must understand the significance of the Islamic revolution. It is a unique event in history. The Islamic revolution is that state of a society in which all the Muslims of an area become mobilized to the point where their collective will and effort becomes irresistible and undefeatable. The Muslim society acquires a leadership positively committed to the civilizational goals of Islam and has no class or other interests of its own. Moreover, the energies thus released are capable of restructuring the society at all levels internally; and the social order acquires the confidence and the ability to deal with the external world on its own terms. When you grasp this dynamic you too will see the Islamic revolution as the only way forward.'

'There is nothing Islamic about the Iranian revolution,' I replied calmly. 'Even if I accept that the revolution in Iran is Islamic, it cannot be a prototype for all other Muslim countries. Those who insist *their* approach is the only *correct* one and that all other Muslims, if they are genuine believers, must give them unconditional support and must adopt their approach, are either making the fatal mistake of treating Islam and the Muslim world as a monolithic whole, or, worse still, claiming divine rights for themselves. People like you, people who theorize justifications for turning Islamic revival into a single, all-purpose, uncompromising ideology are worse than Stalin.' There, it was said!

'Get out of here!' Siddiqui screamed. 'You are not welcome here any more.'

'This Institute is a product of my efforts as much as yours. Without the Saudi funds I helped secure, you wouldn't be sitting in this office.'

We were shouting at each other across the desk. Siddiqui had turned red with rage. He was holding his chest and breathing erratically. I was incandescent as I let my hidden fears express themselves for the first time.

'I will leave when I have said what I want to say.' I took a deep breath; and tried not to think about Siddiqui's heart condition. Now my mental images, the blueprint I cherished, had to be stated. Now the arch-theoretician had to learn that other theories must and would contend. They could not be allowed to go silent into the dark night of revolutionary harangues. 'The Iranian revolution is just *one* of many possible approaches to Islamic revival. In other situations other processes, say a carefully nurtured democratic process – as in Pakistan or Turkey or Malaysia – might better meet the conditions of an Islamic revival: democracy *can* be used to mobilize the collective will of a Muslim society; it *can* produce a leadership committed to the civilizational goals of Islam and it *can* lead to a restructuring of society – although I grant you that it will be a slow and painful process – the transformation thus produced *will* acquire confidence and ability to deal with the external world on its own terms. Why is it inconceivable that Islamic movements can bring about Islamic revival by democratic and accountable means? The fact that various movements have not succeeded so far may reveal more about these movements than the process of democracy. Your declarations are going to create a Stalinist State.'

'Go and preach democracy to the Iranians if you want,' Siddiqui said, gasping for breath. 'But if you come here again, I will have your legs broken.'

I took his advice. I had to see Iran as more than Kalim Siddiqui and his theorizing and justifications. I decided to visit Iran once again in a last-ditch effort to convince myself Siddiqui was totally wrong. I had to undertake the journey, mix and mingle with the people and have my own understanding expanded by the experience. I could not judge an entire nation and a historical revolution on the bitter taste of soured relations with one man.

I landed at Tehran's Mehrabad Airport early on the morning of 4 May 1980. The only problem was that I arrived without a visa. After entering the terminal building I joined the usual parade of people forming a queue for passport control. A number of revolutionary guards, sporting unruly beards and brandishing guns, some with photographs of Ayatollah Khomeini tied around their shoulders, came running in and demanded to see our passports. One approached me, even though I was right at the back of the queue, and snatched my passport from my hands. He flipped through its pages.

'Where is your visa?' he inquired in a withering, angry voice.

'Well, you see . . .' Without waiting for more he pushed me out of the queue.

'Over there,' he shouted. I could see his anger turning into rage. '*Voisata aanja*. Stand over there.' He called out to another guard who came running. The second guard took my passport and flipped through it.

'What is this? You are here without a visa?'

'Yes,' I croaked, trying to swallow the lump that had materialized in my throat. 'You see, I was supposed to collect the visa yesterday – but the Iranian Embassy in London was under siege.'

'You are British?'

'Yes.'

'You are here without a visa. You are a spy.'

'Hang on.' I was unimpressed by the logic. 'Just a minute. I'm British – but that doesn't make me a spy. Do I look like a spy?'

'Yes,' he said emphatically.

'But if I was a spy I'd hardly draw attention to myself by coming here without a visa.'

'Do not argue with me.' Unheeding, I continued the habit of a lifetime, trying desperately to modulate my tone to the circumstances.

'Look! I couldn't get a visa because your embassy was under siege,' I shouted back.

More revolutionary guards came running and clustered around me. 'You are a spy sent by the Queen,' said one. 'While the Britishers have taken over our Embassy they have sent you to spy on us.'

'It's not the British who've taken over your Embassy,' I yelled back. 'It's dissident Iranians from Khuzestan. The British have nothing to do with it. They call themselves the Democratic Revolutionary Front for Arabistan. They're protesting against the Ayatollah Khomeini, and demanding the release of ninety-one of their comrades who've been imprisoned here.'

As I spoke a revolutionary guard stepped forward. His face was so close to mine I could smell the aromatic bitterness of sumac, the herb that is the ubiquitous accompaniment to Iranian food, on his breath. His eyes bored into me with unflinching intensity as he declared: 'We are ready to die.'

'But I am not,' I said instinctively.

'You will die too,' he howled, and head-butted me. I staggered, holding my head, and felt the solid force of a boot impact with the soft centre of my stomach. I fell to the ground. Two revolutionary guards grabbed me by the shoulders and dragged me into a small room.

'Wait in here,' they instructed my crumpled form.

It was a small room, with no furniture, and glass walls. Through these I could see what was going on outside – revolutionary guards checking people's passports, shouting at them to come here and go there, looking at everyone with suspicion and contempt. Inside, I sat on the floor nursing my head and stomach. I felt as though I was in a prison.

My mind caught the word and could not let it go. I came for hope, for a way forward. My mind took me back to the days when we were establishing the Muslim Institute and the words of Kalim Siddiqui. 'We feel like we are in a prison,' he had said. 'The world around us does not reflect our hopes, values and aspirations. That is because we, the Muslims, have hardly played any part in shaping it. We must accept the reality that we live in a prison and endeavour to define the scale and model of this prison. We must map the social, economic and political dimension of this prison in every detail. To plan and ultimately execute an escape from this all-encompassing "open" prison, we may for a while have to behave like model prisoners and mix among our tormentors in a way that does not arouse suspicion. To some extent it might even be possible to take the "guards" into our confidence. They might even cooperate with us so long as we do not become a threat to their positions and leadership roles in the short run. When we are fully prepared, we will make our daring escape. That will be a revolution to behold.'

Imprisoned in walls of glass I watched the guards. I observed the behaviour of the inmates in the prison yard beyond my cell for about two hours. Then, the revolutionary guards returned and marched me to another building, away from the Terminal block. I was pushed inside another small room. It had no windows and was badly lit. It revealed its detail slowly and tortuously to eyes struggling to acclimatize. There was a small desk and two chairs. Time passed of its own volition, but how much time and what that time meant was hard to comprehend. After an interval of this strange timeless time a small, middle-aged man in khaki trousers and short-sleeved white shirt, his face encrusted with several days' stubble by way of a beard, was shown into the room. He looked as though he had just woken from deep sleep and was sweating profusely. He took a handkerchief from his pocket, wiped his forehead and asked me to sit down.

'In your passport it says that you are an information scientist. What is an information scientist?' he asked in a matter-of-fact way.

'An information scientist is someone who handles, processes, stores and retrieves information. He is a sort of glorified librarian who knows how to use computers,' I replied calmly.

'You mean information scientists gather information.'

'Yes, they also gather information.'

'Just like spies?'

'No. No,' I said. 'Information scientists are not spies. They are nothing more than technical librarians; they gather information just like librarians.'

'So you are here to gather information on Iran? Technical information?' It was as if I had wandered into a sub Le Carré scenario, one rapidly spiralling out of control.

'Look,' I said, 'if I were a spy, I would hardly declare it on my passport. Would I?' The line had failed to convince already, but my interrogator was no George Smiley. I was getting nervous, floundering, looking for something to say to make a connection, to establish my credentials. 'I'm a Muslim like you. Would the British send a Muslim to spy for them?' I prattled.

'Yes,' he replied calmly. 'They would. If you have not come here to spy, what have you come here to do?'

'I've come here to find out about the revolution. I supported your revolution. I want to see how it is progressing, where it is going, what social and political changes it has introduced in the society.'

'Who invited you here?'

'I was invited by Dr Ali Berzagar, the Deputy Minister of Higher Education. He is a friend of mine.' At last a potential glimmer of sanity.

The mention of Dr Berzagar's name produced a noticeable change in the expression of the interrogator. 'How long have you known him?'

Hoping I had found my stride, I could not wait to respond. 'About a year,' I said. 'I met him last year in Vienna, at the United Nations Conference on Science and Technology for Development.'

'Have you met him since?'

'Yes, when I was here last October.'

'What did you talk about?'

'We talked about Iranian science and technology.'

My interrogator leaned forward, placed his elbows on the table, rested his unshaven chin on his clasped palms, and looked at me directly. 'I want you to tell me everything he said to you.'

Eye contact! This was more like it. 'We talked about industrial policy under the Shah,' I told him. 'He said the American and European multinationals plundered Iran with their joint ventures. Most of the contracts signed with the multinationals by the Shah were ruthlessly one-sided. He told me about the Iranian Ball-bearing Company which was established in 1969 as a 9-million-dollar joint venture with the Swedish firm SKF. Even when the Iranian plant began production, SKF continued to import ball-bearings into Iran. As the local product lacked quality, the Iranian Ball-bearing Company suffered tremendous losses and had to reduce its capital by half.'

'Good,' he said. 'Tell me what else he said.'

'He told me about the Shah's nuclear programme. The Shah wanted to build a network of twenty-three reactors throughout Iran. Before the revolution, work on four nuclear plants had started and a further nineteen were being negotiated. He said the contracts signed for the four nuclear plants, two to be built by the German company Siemens and two by the French company Framatome, were remarkably one-sided. He claimed the Iranian Atomic Energy Authority was warned not to interfere with the work of the foreign companies. And he said the prices charged for these plants were ridiculously inflated. He said . . .'

The interrogator thumped the table with his fist. 'Look,' he said angrily, 'I am not interested in ball-bearings or nuclear power plants.

What did he tell you about the revolution? What did he say about the students following the line of the Imam?'

'We didn't talk about the Imam,' I replied hesitantly. 'He said the revolution would change everything. He said it would infuse human values and the principles of Islam into Iranian science and technology policy. He said Iran is no longer interested in big, conspicuous projects with grandiose goals. Instead, the focus would be on small, more humble and humane projects that do not get out of control and that utilize Iranian abilities and resources and develop local capability. He said Iran wants to pursue science and technology to meet its basic needs, that Iran does not want to create a consumer society, or chase excessive profits, but concentrate on creating quality.'

'And you wrote about all this?' He seemed to have calmed down.

'Yes,' I replied. 'I wrote an article in the British science journal *Nature* based on my conversations with Dr Berzagar and other policy-makers and scientists.'

There was a momentary silence. 'Can I ring him?' I asked. 'I have his home number.'

'If you wish,' he replied. 'Come with me.'

He took me to another room where there was a telephone. I dialled the number and waited. The phone rang, and rang, and rang. 'He is probably sleeping,' I said anxiously, 'can I try after an hour or so?'

'If you wish,' the interrogator replied, 'But I doubt if he will be there.' There was certainty in his tone.

'Can I ring some of my other friends?' I asked.

'Go ahead,' replied the interrogator, waving his hands. 'Ring as many people as you want.'

I dialled Reza's number. There was no reply. I rang several other friends but no one seemed to be at home. The interrogator led me back to the windowless room.

'Do you know why none of your friends are at home?' he asked as he pulled over a chair, turned it around, and sat on it.

'No.'

'Because they are all counter-revolutionaries. Ali Berzagar is not a minister any more. He has been charged with counter-revolutionary activities. He questioned the line of the Imam followed by the students and revolutionary guards. All your friends are trying to undermine our revolution. We will teach all of them a good lesson.' He paused to look at me. I tried to avoid his eyes. But he could read the fear on my face. 'Do you know what this makes me think?'

I stayed silent. There were no words for the terror that gripped me.

'I think, like your friends, you are a counter-revolutionary. You have come here to undermine our revolution. We will have to teach you the same lesson.' He pushed the table away from me in one swift move; and grabbed my chin, pushing my face upwards with his right wrist. 'What do you have to say in your defence?'

From the corners of my mouth as he compressed my face I mumbled, 'I am only here to observe the revolution,' trying to look away from him, trying not to see his eyes looking at me. 'I have supported the revolution right from its inception.'

The interrogator released my face; and returned to his chair. He sat there quietly for a while. Then he left without saying anything.

In the windowless room, in the gloom of the timeless time, I began to think about the 'Islamic revolution'. This revolution was not following the 'Road to Medina'. When the Prophet Muhammad returned to Mecca, after years of exile in Medina, he forgave all those who opposed his 'revolution'. In contrast, Ayatollah Khomeini went on a revenge spree. The Prophet and his followers overlooked the actions of individuals during pre-Islamic days and those who committed atrocities against them were absolved and absorbed into the Islamic community. But the Iranian revolutionaries were seeking out and eliminating all those who had stood in their path. In *this* revolution what had we done but Islamize the familiar model adapted from the history of revolutions both West and East? What had the unleashing of enthusiasm achieved? A profusion of thinking, debate and yearning for change had burst forth, breaching the restraints of despotism and tyranny. But it had created just the same rapids on which previous revolutions had been broken and the wreckage gathered into a Terror, Purges and Show Trials where those who created and served the cause of change invented their own denunciations for imaginary counter-revolutionary crime.

The interrogator returned. He was accompanied by another man in full religious uniform: long black coat, a white turban and full, well-kept beard. He was holding a file in his hands. The interrogator indicated the awaiting chair with both his hands and respectfully uttered the words: 'Hojjat-al-Islam.' I knew immediately the second man was a middle-ranking religious scholar: Hojjat-al-Islam serves as a title, literally meaning 'the proof of Islam'. Hojjat-al-Islam sat on the chair, silent and seraphic in air and demeanour. He handed his file to the interrogator who stood leaning against a wall.

'We know all about you,' the interrogator began. 'You are the man who writes on Iran for British newspapers and magazines. We get some of these magazines here.' He opened the file and took out a photocopy of an article. 'In this article,' he said, 'you say bad things about the Imam.'

I knew the article he was talking about. 'I did not say bad things about the Imam,' I replied. 'I merely pointed out that he returned to Tehran from Paris in a western aeroplane. So western technology played some part in the revolution. That's all.'

'You go on to say the Imam is demonizing the West.'

'I just don't think that anyone should be demonized.'

'So you know more than the Imam.'

I kept quiet. The interrogator turned a few pages. 'I see that you have not written about the students' takeover of the den of spies.'

'No,' I mumbled.

'Where did you stay when you were here last?'

'I stayed in a small hotel. When I checked in the hotel was on Takhat Jamshid; when I came out of the hotel the following morning, it was called Talegani Road.'

'So you were less than 500 metres from the American Embassy, yet you did not write anything about it. What kind of writer are you?'

'Listen!' I replied, noticing the note of pleading in my voice. 'Almost every journalist in the world was writing about the siege of the American Embassy. I was not interested in that. I wrote about other things.'

'What did you write about?'

'I travelled outside Tehran into rural areas. I joined a team of volunteers to look at the *jihad sa zindigi* (fight for reconstruction) project. I studied how the university volunteers were coordinated, how they assessed the needs of the rural communities, how they collected data and how they assigned particular scientists, engineers and doctors to individual villages. I examined how the teams of specialists taught basic skills to the villagers, how they built houses, schools and clinics, how they tackled agricultural problems with locally available resources, and how they worked to make the villages self-sufficient. This is what the revolution was all about for me. I wrote about that.'

The Hojjat-al-Islam leaned forward to whisper something in Farsi in the interrogator's ear.

'You have written a lot about Bani Sadr. Do you support him?'

'I think he is amply qualified to be the president of Iran. He is good for Iran and good for the Muslim people.'

'What have you written about him?'

'I've written that he is working to create an egalitarian society in Iran. He's argued that everything belongs to God – and no individual, class or group has any exclusive rights to anything. All natural resources, land and capital belong to the whole of society, and everyone should have an equal share in them and equal access to them. In my articles, I have presented his plans for the redistribution of Iran's wealth.'

'Do you like him?'

'I like his ideas.'

'But do you like *him*?' the interrogator shouted angrily. The Hojjat-al-Islam got off his chair, patted the man gently on his shoulders and then returned silently to his chair.

'What we need to know,' the interrogator said, drawing a deep breath, 'is whether you support Bani Sadr or the line of the Imam?'

'There is no difference,' I replied calmly. 'Bani Sadr is Imam Khomeini's student. He is following his teacher.'

'The revolution cannot be soft on anyone simply because they were the Imam's students,' the interrogator retorted. 'Bani Sadr's days are numbered. What I want you to tell me is whether you like and support our revolution.'

'It's not that I don't like your revolution,' I said, turning towards the Hojjat-al-Islam in the hope that he would understand, 'it's just that I suspect that bloody revolution is not the best way to generate an Islamic revival.'

'What has produced this suspicion?' the interrogator said in an enquiring, half-mocking tone.

For the first time, I noticed, there was a smile on the face of Hojjat-al-Islam. Perhaps he understood English a little. But the smile said something to me. There was a tinge of indulgence there. I decided to tell them what I really thought.

'Well,' I began, 'every revolution in history has led to the strengthening of the state. A small group is necessary to carry the revolution through; then the surrounding insecurity becomes so overwhelming that a small group has to consolidate its power to preserve the ideas of the revolution. Dictatorship thus emerges. All revolutions, I am afraid, end with dictatorship.'

'And you think this is what has happened in Iran? The Islamic Republic is a dictatorship?'

'Yes, I do,' I said calmly. My fear had now evaporated. 'The new constitution hands all religious and political power to the Leader or Leadership Council. The Executive power is totally subservient to the spiritual Leader. The Mullahs,' I said, looking away from the Hojjat-al-Islam, 'have consolidated all power in their hands. Iran has become a theocracy; and theocracies are dictatorships. The struggle between the revolutionary guards and the left-wing Mujahidin has turned into an all-out battle. Everyone and anyone who doesn't agree with the revolutionary guards is a counter-revolutionary. All this indicates that the revolution in Iran is following a well-trodden historical path. It's in the nature of revolutions.' I felt relieved: I was not making my report at arm's length, to a surrogate, tinpot, would-be theoretician and justifier of the revolution. I had come and made my visit. This was all I wanted to say. I scanned their faces for responses. The Hojjat-al-Islam was now smiling zealously. The interrogator had turned red with rage.

'If you have read our constitution,' he barked, 'you will see that we have elections. The President you love so much was elected. We have a Majlis, a Parliament. An independent Judiciary. But as Muslims, we also have the Imam to guide us.' He paused for breath. 'You don't like our Imam, do you?'

This was a killer question. The revolutionaries decided who was for or against them on the basis of whether they supported Imam Khomeini or not.

'No,' I finally told the interrogator what he wanted to hear. 'I do not like the Imam. I do not think he is following the example of the Prophet. I do not think that all spiritual and earthly power should be in the hands of a single person. I am not a supporter of the line of the Imam.'

That's it, I thought. I am not going to get out of here alive. But to my surprise the interrogator and the Hojjat-al-Islam looked rather relieved. The interrogator pulled the table away from me and sat on it, dangling his legs.

'Just one last thing,' he said in a sudden change of mood, 'do you think that the Shah would have given up power if the people of Iran had not risen against him under the leadership of the Imam?'

'Probably not,' I replied.

'Do you really believe that western-style democracy is the answer to the problem of the Muslim people?'

'Well,' I answered, 'I find democracy problematic too. Elections may produce some changes in leadership but there's no assurance they'll automatically lead to the emergence of an intelligent, incorruptible government capable of fulfilling the aspirations of the masses.' I paused for thought.

'So what is the answer?' he asked, gritting his teeth.

'I don't know.' Honesty breeds honesty, what was there to say except precisely what I thought, felt and believed? 'I'm looking for answers. Just over a year ago, I thought maybe the revolution in Iran could provide an answer. Now, I am not so sure.'

'You are just confused,' he said. 'And confused men are dangerous. Those who do not know what is right and what is wrong often end up doing wrong. You have strong counter-revolutionary tendencies. That's why we cannot allow you into the country. You will end up providing support for the counter-revolutionary forces. You have to return.'

He folded the file he was holding in his hand and passed it to the Hojjat-al-Islam. Then he took my passport and airline ticket out of his pockets and gave them to me.

'According to your ticket, your next port of call is Karachi. There is a PIA flight at 6.30. You will be put on the flight,' he said as he turned around to leave the room. The Hojjat-al-Islam stopped him from leaving and whispered something in his ear. The interrogator turned towards me. 'The Hojjat-al-Islam tells me that the siege of our Embassy in London is over. Your SAS stormed the Embassy and killed the gunmen. The Imam has thanked your government and the perseverance of your police force during this unjust event. The Imam has also declared the hostages who were killed martyrs.'

He opened the door and stood aside deferentially for the Hojjat-al-Islam to lead the way. But the Hojjat-al-Islam walked towards me. He was still smiling; and this time I detected warmth. He shook my hand and patted me gently on the back. 'May Allah guide you to the right path,' he said in broken English. '*As salamu 'alaykum*' – peace be upon you. Perhaps he saw me as a genuine seeker – someone who would eventually see the error of his ways.

The two men left me standing.

I had once come to Iran and refused to climb down a precipice to see the fabled garden of a failed and corrupt paradise and my friend had called me a coward. I wished I knew where that friend was now. It mattered that I had stated my case. Though it was not an act of courage, just a consequence wrung from me by the process of interrogation. Perhaps this time my friend would not have felt the need to set me down on a long, desolate road. I prayed that if my fears were true he had found a safer, gentler road that led up to paradise. I bowed my head and thought a prayer for all those who should get the chance to live in gardens of paradise here and now and received only the gardens of the hereafter. I had no prayers for those who seek to die and are ready to kill for paradise. A year or two later, I learned that many of my friends had been imprisoned as counter-revolutionaries in Tehran's notorious Evin prison. Their final fate still remains a mystery.

A short time later, two revolutionary guards came and marched me into the Terminal building. Back in the world of time I found I was totally exhausted, all energy spent, and could hardly keep my eyes open. 'You can sleep in the lounge,' said one of the revolutionary guards. With the exception of a few guards, the lounge was empty. I looked around for somewhere to lie down. As in airport lounges the world over the seats were designed to be as uncomfortable as possible to ensure they could not be used as beds. I found a secluded corner, cleaned it as best

I could, and stretched out on the floor. I covered myself with my jacket. Within a few moments I was asleep. Too tired to think, too tired to feel, too tired to consider the state of my being or any alternate state of being I could or should desire. Just sleep.

I could not have slept for more than a few hours. I clawed my way back from sleep at the insistent prodding of a boot bestirring itself in contact with my stomach. Slowly, I prised open my eyes from the inside and saw, towering over me, a full-bearded revolutionary guard, his armpits covered with sweat. He was holding a handgun, as though taking aim. Instinctively, I pushed it away with the back of my hand. The moment he saw my eyes open his gentle prodding became a vigorous kick. As I struggled to stand up, he pulled me by the shoulders and pressed the gun beneath my left earlobe. 'You, spy! Get on the plane.' I was too frightened to say anything. A plane! Where is the plane? I had no sense of direction. As if he heard my thought, the guard spun me around. He tightened his grip on my shoulder; when he was sure I was firmly in his grasp, he eased the gun gently away from my head. Then he pushed me forward. I started marching in front of him, moving like an automaton, briskly in the direction of his volition. I assumed, in fervent prayer, the PIA flight to Karachi had landed and I was being deported. We left the terminal and walked out onto the tarmac. Dawn could not have been more than a few minutes away, but it was still dark. I peered through the lack of light. I could make out little except that the tarmac was deserted, with the exception of a single aircraft. Either all the passengers on this flight were already on board; or I was the only passenger. The guard marched me right up to the plane and ordered me to board. Even when I was inside the plane, he stood there staring at me. The disgust on his face declared: you are not welcome in this paradise!

They seated me near the door. I sat there dazed. Never had I felt such relief, such a sudden rush of relaxation as all tension ebbed away. Dreamily, ready to drift into dreams, I offered a greeting to the passenger sitting next to me. As my eyes began to close, I asked this gentleman languidly:

'Could you please ask the stewardess not to wake me till we get to Karachi?'

He looked at me in utter amazement. 'Technology has truly achieved wonders,' he said. He pointed towards me, 'that part of the plane is going to Karachi;' he pointed to himself, 'while this part of the plane is going to Zurich!'

Chapter 10

THE *INQUIRY* YEARS

The plane might as well have been flying in different directions, it would
have been fitting. I was deported from Iran, but Iran could not be
expelled from me any more than Saudi Arabia could. We Muslims live
as composite identities: various interpretations of Islam, with their
various histories, cultural, regional, ethnic variations, and now national
divergences, are always part of our individual and collective
personalities. Iran and Saudi Arabia were part of the composite person
I was becoming, and not just because their rebuff had scarred me. Iran
and Saudi Arabia were and are part of me because they belong to me.
However much we are a patchwork, a crazy paving, a mosaic of intricate
form, pattern and colour, however much a filigree of glories and abject
failures, false starts and wrong departures, a composite is a whole. We
are the *ummah*: the international community of Muslims; the composite
of belonging from which one cannot resign. The *ummah*, as the Prophet
Muhammad said, is like a human body: when one part is ill, the whole
body suffers. My head throbbed, my stomach was sore, my limbs
ached. I needed rest and recuperation. Belonging to the *ummah* is a
religious injunction experienced as the embodiment of a personal faith.
Muslim I am in the inmost existence of self, yet that self is never alone
or singular but simultaneously part of the multiple and diverse body of
the whole Muslim community. The *ummah* is not an added extra, not
an aggregate after the fact of me. What point in seeking paradise if one

is alone, bereft of the community that is integral not only to the who, how and why I am but to my idea of paradise itself?

When I got back to London, by a circuitous route, I spent a lot of time nursing my bruises. This, I thought to myself quite often, would be exactly the right time for some bearded persons to appear at my door. However, it transpires there is a connection, so far overlooked by philosophers, between beards, buses and taxis: when you really need them they are nowhere to be found. What was it Masud Sahib had said so long ago on my first exploratory venture: 'Paradise, like buses and train, waits for no one.' It may very well be the case, but like buses it seems there is no regular timetable either. I began to wonder if I had confused the issue by moving house. Investing the nest egg accumulated in Saudi Arabia I moved my family to a modest semi in a quiet cul de sac in that swathe of North London where British Asian identity was taking root. If they could find me on the seventeenth floor of Seaton Point now what's their problem, I asked myself disconsolately? Here we are at ground level in precisely the locale one would expect, so where are they? Then, suddenly, on a freezing cold day in January 1984, the doorbell of the by now refurbished, modest Sardar mansion rang. I opened the door to discover the long-awaited two bearded men.

I surveyed them coolly. They had kept me waiting long enough, now they could stand a while and share the chill wind that had enveloped me. 'You took your time,' I sniffed. One of these belated visitors was my old FOSIS friend Muhammad Iqbal Asaria he would expect no less of me. His indulgent tut-tut as he walked past me into the warmth said as much. His short, round-faced companion was introduced as Dr Akbar Mohammedali.

'So what do the Maulvis want with me?' I demanded as we settled ourselves comfortably in the living room. 'You know I don't mix well with Maulvis,' I said. Dr Akbar, who ever after would be known as Maulvi Doctor, gave an infectious chuckle. Iqbal rolled his eyes, then fixed me with an old-fashioned look as he noted in his dry and languorous manner: 'There you go again. Demonizing all bearded men; painting all Maulvis with the same brush.'

I had known Iqbal for well over a decade. In all the time I had known him he always wore the same style of clothing: a simple, grey traditional suit. A long-sleeved shirt-cum-jacket with matching baggy trousers. It was made of *kadhdir*, a particular kind of rough cotton worn principally by the labouring classes in the Indian Subcontinent. The suit was associated with the *khaksari* – literally servants of the people – movement, which came to prominence in India and Pakistan during the 1940s and 1950s. The *khaksaris* were a group of devout men who had vowed to live frugally and spend their lives serving the poor and marginalized members of the community. Iqbal seemed to embody the spirit of that philosophy. He looked like a prototype traditional Indian Mullah – or Maulvi as they are called in the Subcontinent – despite the fact that he was neither Indian nor particularly traditional. He came to Britain from East Africa; and was one of the most liberal and open-minded persons I knew. He was also the only person I knew who incessantly scratched his beard.

'We have a proposal for you,' Iqbal began, subtly changing the angle of address he was practising on his beard. 'Like you, we have thought long and hard . . .'

'Yes, yes,' I said impatiently. 'The plight of the *ummah*, what is to be done, how to save our civilization from itself.'

One of the joys of baiting Iqbal was his ability to remain perennially unflappable, overriding all interjections with increasing amounts of studied calm. He feigned a scratch of his beard by way of ignoring my comment. 'The Iranian revolution has turned out to be a nightmare,' he continued. 'And the Islamization show will lead us into a new cul de sac. We need to think our way out of this mess. We are suggesting we publish an intellectual monthly magazine devoted to systematic, critical thinking about Islam and the plight of the *ummah*.'

'And we want you to edit this magazine,' Dr Akbar added.

So there it was. This time I would think my way to paradise.

'Maulvis,' I said, 'who is going to finance this intellectual endeavour?'

The Maulvis looked at each other. There was a pregnant pause. Far too long a pause. They murmured a word in answer, which reverberated like a sonic boom in my head: 'Iran.' I leapt into the air. I stood a while, flapping like a shirt hung out to dry in a stiff breeze. 'Iran!?' was all I could eventually splutter. Iqbal noticed the look of disgust on my face.

'Calm down,' he said with indecent, long-suffering calm. He resumed languidly scratching his beard. 'Just calm down. Listen to what we have to say.'

'Maulvi,' I said angrily, 'only a fool would put his hand in the snake pit twice.'

'In which case, you are just the kind of fool we are looking for,' said Maulvi Doctor, his infectious chuckle contorted to a nervous laugh designed to ease the tension.

'We are going to be supported by the liberal wing of the revolution; people who wish to see real reforms. Anyway, we will use Iranian funding to launch the magazine and then only till such time as we become self-sustaining. After that, we will be wholly independent,' said Iqbal.

'And till such time, the magazine is supposed to keep its mouth shut?' I enquired.

'We have assurances that we can say more or less what we want.'

'I'm sorry, Maulvi,' I said categorically, 'I don't want anything to do with Iran.'

'*Think* about it,' Iqbal insisted; it was not an invitation, more a command. 'We are at a critical juncture of Muslim history. We have to rise above our individual experiences and concerns. We have to work within and with the *ummah*. We have to use whatever resources we can muster. And we are not talking about any magazine. We are talking about a magazine that injects urgently needed new ideas into Muslim debate, a magazine that relates events to ideas, and generates ideas that will shape events in the Muslim world. The kind of magazine that will knock theocracy out of our heads, and take us beyond the one-dimensional prescriptions of Islamization. Think of it as your personal instrument for reform. Imagine what you can do with such an instrument.'

'The *ummah* needs you!' added Maulvi Doctor, grinning like the Cheshire cat.

To be a man on a mission and needed, nothing could be more enticing. And of course, Iqbal had a point. Ideas are the real building blocks of civilization; thinking and spreading informed debate is the only real construction process that builds a road to paradise. So it had been in the beginning of Muslim civilization, so it would have to be again if we were to extract ourselves from simplistic certainties of observance, from following without question the prescriptions of venerated leaders, if we were to wrestle with the real gamut of our contemporary problems. If we could gather a group of like-minded intellectuals, we could huddle together for warmth and mutual support. Instead of thinking, each in our own slough of despond, we might be able to generate a host of new ideas and the critical mass to heave the *ummah* into a better future. Perhaps, even, a new School of Thought. And a magazine, what better vehicle could there be for critiquing existing ideas and disseminating new ones?

'OK,' I said returning from my airy way-stations of the future. 'I will do it on two conditions.'

'And what would they be?' asked Maulvi Doctor with a smirk.

'Maulvi Doctor,' I replied, echoing his grin, 'I choose who writes for the magazine. And I will have nothing to do with the Iranians.'

'The kind of thinkers and writers we are looking for,' Iqbal said, moving into full ruminative mode amidst his beard, 'will not be easy to find. You will have to discover them on your own. In this you will have complete freedom. Leave me to worry about the money and deal with the Iranians. I promise you: you will have nothing to do with them.'

'There is one small problem,' chimed in the Doctor with his customary grin.

'And what would that be, Maulvi Doctor?'

'You can't be the editor.'

'What? You want me to do this by mirrors? You want me to edit the magazine but I can't be the editor!'

'Calm down!' Iqbal said, stroking his beard. 'It will be your baby. You will edit the magazine. But we have to be aware of your reputation.

'Our problem,' he continued, 'is whether you can control yourself till we achieve two critical masses. First, our circulation and advertising have to reach a certain level so we can become fully self-sufficient and self-sustaining. Then we can cut off our links with Iran. Second, we need a critical mass of thinkers and intellectuals who understand and imbibe our analysis. Then, even if the magazine folds, our ideas continue and are there to be taken forward by others.'

'Agreed,' I replied instinctively. 'How long do you think we need to acquire a critical mass on both fronts, Maulvi?'

'I would say about five years.' Iqbal stroked his beard. 'Can you,' he said, scratching his beard vigorously, 'be a bit less of yourself for that long?'

'How can I not be myself?' I enquired in tones of wounded innocence.

'You can. Just don't take pot shots at individuals or leaders of the revolution. Temper your criticism just enough not to upset too much the hand that's going to feed us. And remember that Kalim Sahib will be watching us like a hawk. He'll do everything he can to stop our funding. I'm pleading with you for a greater goal: for the good of the *ummah*.'

'Well, if you put it like that, Maulvi, I'll have to try,' I said.

We three looked at each other, surveyed the earnest expressions of pompous self-importance we were exchanging, reflected a moment and collapsed in laughter. Oh, this is going to be just the thing required, I thought to myself. We spent the rest of the evening chatting and giggling and enjoying each other's company like overexcited children. Whatever we have to do, I thought, at least we will be spared the joyless horror of taking ourselves too seriously.

The two Maulvis had hardly left my house when the phone rang. It was Abdullah Naseef, the friend, mentor, protector and escapologist in chief of my days in Saudi Arabia. You see, exactly like buses! 'Can you take the next flight to Jeddah?' he asked. After serving as President of King Abdul Aziz University in Jeddah, Naseef had been made Secretary-General of the World Muslim League, known in Arabic as Rabita Alam Islami. The Rabita was essentially an arm of the foreign ministry; but Naseef, egalitarian to his core, was determined to open it up, get more intellectuals involved in its work, and provide it with a new vision. 'Could you use your expertise in futures studies and planning skills to prepare a ten-year plan for the kind of work Rabita should be doing?' he asked. Suddenly, it transpired the *ummah* not only needed me but was expressing an interest in the kind of work I did. When buses come along men on missions have no right to refuse the journey. A few days later, I was back in Jeddah.

When I went to visit Naseef he was, as usual, surrounded by people. With his familiar grace he introduced me to a slim bespectacled man, with a moustache and a headful of youthful hair, standing at his side. One never knows whom one will meet on a visit to Naseef. My initial impression marked this man down as a salesman, the kind engaged in trying to unload sand, camels or air conditioners on the unsuspecting Desert Kingdom. 'This is Dr Wasiullah Khan, Chancellor of East-West University in Chicago,' Naseef interjected with impeccable timing. 'You two should be friends,' he added, conveying, as always, more than was said.

I surveyed the Chancellor again. He was wearing an ill-fitting suit and a tie worthy of an upwardly mobile bookkeeper; he seemed to move like a lizard across the dunes. Our first meeting lasted several hours. Indeed, I quickly realized it was not possible to have a short, focused discussion with this man. He treated me as though he was my long-lost friend: embracing me warmly, smiling generously. Within minutes, he had me listening attentively to his sole preoccupation. '*Alhumdulillah*, Brother, we have established a university in Chicago. It is the first university to be established by Muslims in America. And Dr Naseef has graciously agreed to be our Chairman of the Board of Trustees. The idea of the university was conceived on 1 November 1979, and the university was incorporated as a non-profitable corporation and on 6 May 1980, *Alhumdulillah*, the Illinois Board of Higher Education granted approval and operating authority to the university.' It was like listening to an old Communist apparatchik from Eastern Europe going on about the achievements of the State, whose meaning was contained in the string of statistics.

The following day, Naseef had invited us to Mecca. I was asked to visit the head office of the Rabita and observe its Governing Council (Majlis-e-Tasisi), consisting of a selection of the Good and the Great of the Muslim world, in action. Since Khan had hired a car, Naseef suggested we travel together. We set off early in the morning. Almost immediately, Khan started.

'The University was started on my kitchen table, Brother Zia. I persuaded most of my friends to dig into their own pockets and borrowed the rest of the money to pay the deposit for the building.'

This was a reprise of our previous conversation. I allowed the living archive of East-West University to waft over me while scrutinizing Khan himself.

Khan had a rather curious habit. As he spoke he fiddled with his moustache. His fingers rummaging through the hairs until they found a suitable candidate, the selected bristle once identified was destined for punishment. There would be a momentary pause for tactile examination of the suspect bristle then, pluck! with one sharp, decisive movement the offending tendril was extracted. Once disembodied it was subjected to microscopic examination, at great length.

'*Alhumdulillah*, the building alone is now worth over a million dollars.'

The more he talked, the more he plucked, and each time I felt an accompanying twang through my body. Finally, I could take it no more.

'Stop,' I shouted. 'Pull over.'

Khan changed lanes and parked the car on the side of the motorway, an ample thoroughfare of which we were the sole users.

'I am not going anywhere with you until you stop plucking your moustache.'

Khan turned to me with a look of astonished innocence.

'Look,' I said, 'You may be into self-mutilation; but I am no sadist. As it is you have only got a couple of dozen hairs left on your lip – and they seem to be in agony. In a few months you'll have plucked them all out.' This was true. What from a distance appeared to be a moustache, up close resembled a badly tended lawn, the kind where bare patches and mole hills are surrounded by a few straggling spikes of grass.

Khan thought for a moment. 'You want me to stop for your sake or mine?'

'Both,' I replied.

'OK. I will,' he said, with some determination.

And he did.

Khan was a regular visitor to Rabita, consequently he knew his way around Mecca rather well. However, when we arrived in the Holy City, we discovered that an entirely new spaghetti junction had been built right in the middle of the road that should have led straight to our destination. Indeed, this intertwining of vehicular arteries was so new the builders had not yet found time to install signposts. We took one exit, our path described a wide arabesque and we found ourselves on the road leading out of Mecca towards Muna. We backtracked, entering the nexus of connecting arteries from the reverse angle, and described what we hoped was a compensatory alternative arabesque. This time we found ourselves on the road to Taif. We backtracked, junctioned, arabesqued again and ended up heading who knows where.

'Do you get the feeling,' Khan enquired, 'that the modern world is conspiring against us simple Muslims?'

'Well, once it is an accident. Twice, it's a coincidence. Third time it certainly looks like a conspiracy,' I replied.

It was, in reality, not a conspiracy, merely a metaphor: acquiring all the trappings of modernity merely leaves the Muslim *ummah* going round in circles but getting nowhere. It just keeps on describing circles it claims as arabesques, in honour of its heritage, neglecting to notice that all the movement is solving none of its real problems either of travelling or arriving. It succeeds neither in copying western societies nor in creating a modernity of its own making according to its own principles. By the time we managed to navigate our way out of the nexus we were over two hours late. The meeting of the Governing Council of the World Muslim League was in full session.

We ran breathless into the meeting hall. There were gathered about forty very old men, most with their feet dangling in the grave, sitting in a circular formation trying to catch the eye of the Chair. It was a day for encountering metaphors. The meeting was presided over by Sheikh 'Abd al-'Aziz bin Baz, the blind religious scholar and Mufti of Saudi Arabia. While people gesticulated animatedly to catch the eye of one who could not see, other members of the Council were engaged in speaking animatedly at the same time on different subjects and taking no notice of each other.

'What are we going to do about Palestine?' said one, speaking inordinately slowly.

'But the problem of Afghanistan is much more urgent,' said the other, speaking even more slowly.

'Surely we should be discussing the problem of Kashmir,' said the third, speaking and raising his hand at the same time, tasks that seemed to cause him great difficulty and to be possible only in slow motion.

'Order, order,' shouted Sheikh bin Baz, raising his hand and pointing in a direction where no one was either speaking or trying to catch his attention.

Naseef was sitting next to Sheikh bin Baz. He took hold of the raised hand and gently swung it in the direction of one of the speakers.

Khan and I stood for a moment on the fringes of the circle that stretched into eternity, absorbing the surrealist spectacle. Then, in unison, we turned our gaze on Naseef. He was clearly making valiant efforts to suppress a smile; together we burst into very loud laughter. Naseef followed. All eyes, even those that could not see, turned on us.

After the meeting, an angry Naseef summoned us to his office. The moment we set eyes on each other, hysterics returned. 'Do you realize,' he said, still laughing, 'that I have sat through three meetings of the Governing Council and managed to maintain my calm and be serious at all of them? Till you jokers arrived.'

The next day, Khan unveiled a cunning plan. 'Why don't we,' he suggested, 'establish a Centre at the East-West University specifically for finding a way out of ossified tradition and a model of modernity that just does not suit our societies?'

I liked the idea. 'Let us call it Centre for Policy and Futures Studies,' I recommended. Khan accepted the suggestion and immediately offered me the post of Director. This business of being needed and useful was becoming overcrowded with new designations.

'There is one minor problem,' Khan said, as we sealed the agreement with a warm handshake. 'We can't pay you. You will have to raise money not just for the projects of the Centre but also for your own salary.'

A few hours later we were sitting in Abdullah Naseef's house. It was Friday morning, and, as was his custom, Naseef was entertaining visitors. Most of the visitors, who on the whole were total strangers, came with a specific problem – some needed jobs, some needed exit visas, some simply needed money. And no one, not in all the decades I had known him, had ever left Naseef's house empty-handed or with their problems intact. People would enter, greet him, shake his hand, and then take whatever seat was available normally at a respectable distance from him. When seats closer to Naseef became vacant, they would, step by step, move closer. Eventually, it would be their turn to take a seat beside Naseef and whisper their problem in his ear. Naseef would listen attentively, shaking his head in a manner expressive of empathy, understanding and reassurance. If he could solve the problem quickly, he would pick up the phone, talk animatedly to someone, write a note and hand it to the visitor. He commanded so much respect and reverence that when he spoke to someone about somebody, something was usually done. If the predicament of the visitor was more complicated, he would take notes and make a case file on which he would work diligently until a solution to the problem was found.

Most of the visitors had had their say by the time I moved closer to Naseef and sat right next to him. I took his hand in mine and with great gravitas whispered gently in his ear. 'Doctor,' I said, 'we need some money to save the *ummah*!' He chuckled. 'How much and for what?'

I explained the plan. Naseef listened carefully, occasionally asking a question or two.

'The first task of this Centre could be to prepare a plan for the future of the Muslim World League,' he said.

'Indeed,' I replied without hesitation.

He thought for a while, sipped some water from a glass, looked at me and smiled.

'Would 150,000 dollars do as seed money?' he said.

'That will do nicely,' said Khan.

The 1980s was the age of the Conference. During this decade conferences were being held on every conceivable subject – from economics and education to information science, technology transfer, youth, and New International Order – in every Muslim capital from Riyadh to Cairo, Islamabad, Decca, Kuala Lumpur, Jakarta, Dakkar and Rabat. Each conference, no matter what the subject, resolved itself into an amorphous plaint about the state and fate of the *ummah*. In my opinion, this characteristic behaviour of the Muslim world performed much the same function as the spaghetti junction at the entrance to Mecca. All conferences signally failed to produce practical programmes for solving the malaise of the *ummah*. No matter what the topic or location, these conferences were attended by the selfsame standard group I irreverently termed 'professional Muslims' – that is, Muslim scholars and intellectuals who had turned Islam into a profession, and for some conferring appeared to be their only discernible occupation. I too was a bona fide member of the 'conference set'.

What distinguished the 1980s Conferences was the capital C. They were big Conferences. They were lavishly accoutred with the appropriate modern paraphernalia: the bags, pens, note pads, the design concept logos, video of and publications from – in short an entire cottage industry. And they had a connecting buzz word: 'Islamization'. The revolution in Iran inspired and frightened people across the Muslim world in equal measure. But the idea that one nation could exercise the Islamic option was a new kind of stimulus. The Conferences were, in many ways, attempts to wrestle with that possibility while containing, directing and managing the wilder excesses Iran had unleashed. For Muslims the *ummah* was the focus and Islamization the programme. And like the social upheaval and ferment that produced the revolution in Iran, the Conferences, grand and lavish as they were, remained invisible to western observers. This was bad news for those in the West who wanted to get some idea of what was happening across the Islamic world, post Iran. But on the other hand it was good news in not publicizing how disorganized and inchoate the discussion could be.

Islamization as the compound sovereign specific for all ills, a remedy related to but distinct from events in Iran, was largely the work of one man. In contemporary times, no one has devoted more energy to defining and explaining the concept of the *ummah* than the American Palestinian scholar Ismail Raji al-Faruqi. A clean-shaven, heavily built man who wore large glasses, Al-Faruqi was a regular visitor to London; and I was a regular presence in the audience at his lectures. He spoke with passion and conviction and, whatever the topic of his lectures, always returned to his favourite theme: the plight of the *ummah*. In one lecture, he suggested that 'the *ummah* is a universal society whose membership includes the widest possible variety of ethnicities or communities but whose commitment to Islam binds them to a specific (Islamic) social order'. 'The term *ummah*,' he said, 'cannot be translated and must be used in its original form.' It is not synonymous with 'the people', or 'the nation', or 'the state' or any other expression which is determined by race, geography, language, history or any combination of these. 'The *ummah* is trans-local, trans-racial, trans-geographical.' And 'each constituent part of the *ummah*, that is each Muslim community, itself constitutes the *ummah* even though it may not fall under the sovereignty of a Muslim state'.

In another lecture, Al-Faruqi argued that the divisions within the *ummah*, particularly between Arab and other Muslim communities, were created by the West. There was no difference between 'Arabic' and 'Islamic' identities, he argued; and all Muslims from different ethnic backgrounds and political persuasions must unite to struggle against the decay and degeneration of the *ummah*. As a universal religion, he said, Islam is unequivocally against nationalism. 'There is nothing more damaging,' he declared, 'than the introduction by western enemies of Islam of a meaning to Arabism that is foreign to it – namely, the racist or nationalist meaning differentiating the Arab Muslim from his Muslim brothers belonging to other ethnicities. The so-called Arab "ethnocentrism" or "nationalism" is a new innovation designed only to split the *ummah* asunder and separate Arab from Berber, Turk, Persian, Kurd, Indian, Chinese or Malay, to alienate white from black, and to set the Muslim against his co-religionists in a fratricidal conflict and war. Nationalism was used by the enemies of Islam, first to seduce the idealistic youths of Turkey in search of progress and dignity, and then induced into Arabs to set them against the Ottoman Caliphate.' He blamed Christian Arabs such as Michel Aflaq, the founder of the Ba'ath Party, in particular for spreading the 'disease of Arab nationalism'. In other lectures, he emphasized the importance of dialogue between the 'Abrahamic faiths' of Judaism, Christianity and Islam. For Al-Faruqi, who was a renowned authority on comparative religion, Judaism represented a sister tradition to Islam of congenial religious temper.

During the 1970s and 1980s, Al-Faruqi was a towering presence on the Muslim intellectual scene. A former governor of Galilee, he migrated to the USA where he came to occupy the influential chair of Islamic Studies at Temple University in Philadelphia. As a young scholar, I admired him immensely; as did many others. Indeed, many up-and-coming Muslim scholars were his students. He supervised numerous doctorates and was directly responsible for producing a whole generation of young Muslim academics. What appealed to me most in his lectures and writings was the total absence of nostalgia, the obligatory cry to return to the glorious past of Islam. He was certainly aware that things were different before, that Muslims were once the masters of their destiny and that their culture was more 'authentic and harmonious', but there was no apotheosis of the past, no incapacitating sentiment of loss. Instead, Al-Faruqi was concerned with the present and future: how are we going to rescue the *ummah* from its 'malaise' and chart a course towards a new destiny.

I really got to know and understand Ismail al-Faruqi at a conference in Mecca in 1977. The First Conference on Muslim Education, organized by King Abdul Aziz University when I was still working for the Hajj Research Centre, was aimed at nothing less than 'rebuilding Islam'. I was responsible for producing a special insert on the conference for the *Times Higher Educational Supplement*.

A number of scholars at the conference argued that the essence of the conflict between Islam and the West was not merely historical and political but also metaphysical and spiritual. The Muslim educational system had been destroyed by western secular education during the colonial period and by emerging Muslim states anxious to import the trappings of modernity. In the liberal West, all branches of knowledge are controlled and directed by ideas and concepts which are entirely against the spirit of Islam. Natural sciences are conceived as antithetical to nature, which can be twisted and tortured in the name of progress. Islam, on the other hand, does not encourage confrontation between man and nature. It teaches man to be 'natural' and thus work in harmony with nature. Similarly, social sciences have grown in the West as disciplines which demand that man should not believe in any predetermined code for a society but accept the principle that society is a continually evolving and changing phenomenon. There is nothing permanent or unchanging about human nature. Thus, values too go on changing. Islam teaches that moral values do not change; hence Truth, Goodness, Righteousness, Mercy are constant factors. A society may be 'primitive', 'traditional' or 'underdeveloped' in relation to the modern world, but could have a highly developed sense of values. So every sphere of secular knowledge is in conflict with Islamic assumptions and ideas.

Al-Faruqi used the conference to present his theory of salvation. The Muslim conflict, he argued, was not with western civilization per se but with the kind of personality and 'mind' it represents. The secularist mind and personality are found not just in the West but also in the *ummah*. There could be no hope of a genuine revival of the *ummah* unless the educational system was revamped and its faults corrected. Indeed, what is needed is for the system to be formed anew. The present dualism in Muslim education, its bifurcation into an Islamic and secular system, must be removed and abolished once and for all. The two systems must be united and integrated; and the emergent system must be infused with the spirit of Islam and function as an integral part of its ideological programme. Al-Faruqi suggested, rather boldly, that secularism should be weeded out of the entire corpus of human knowledge – only then can knowledge serve the goals of Islam. 'The task before us,' he thundered, 'is to recast the whole legacy of human knowledge from the standpoint of Islam. In concrete terms, we must Islamize the disciplines, or better, produce university level textbooks, recasting some twenty disciplines in accordance with the Islamic vision.' His message found a resonance at the conference. He strode across the Mecca Intercontinental Hotel, always surrounded by a group of adoring students, like a newly crowned king.

One evening I was sitting in the restaurant ready to give my full attention to the superb tabbouleh the hotel served with a plentiful accompaniment of warm, delicate thin bread. I tore a piece of bread, held it spread among my fingers like a scoop and used it to manoeuvre a mound of tomatoes, cucumber, onions, cracked wheat and masses of scented parsley steeped in oil and lemon juice to a corner of the plate. Then, again using the bread, I massaged the mound into a regular formation which, with delicate movements of my fingers, I gently enveloped in the bread, forming the whole into a perfect mouth-sized parcel. Like an artisan satisfied with his craft I lifted the fruits of my labour to my mouth. I saw Al-Faruqi saunter into the room and walk towards me with a look on his face that set my senses on alert. I suspected he was aware that I was the only one at the conference making snide remarks about the new Messiah and his theory of Islamization of knowledge. All that popped into my mind was one of those scenes from innumerable cinema westerns. It was High Noon and the train from Yuma had just pulled in, or was it Wyatt Earp striding down Main Street to keep an appointment with the Clantons at the OK Corral?

'Your baby was stillborn,' I fired my opening salvo without hesitation as Al-Faruqi settled himself in a seat opposite me.

'How so?' he shot back.

'You are arguing that knowledge is divided into secular and Islamic segments. Such a dualistic perception of knowledge implies a recognition – and, to some extent, even acceptance – of the kind of secularism that it seeks ultimately to eradicate.'

'It's a contradiction we will live with,' he answered.

'But you must at least acknowledge Truth and Knowledge are not the same thing.'

Al-Faruqi was adamant that from the Islamic viewpoint, there was no distinction between Truth and Knowledge. If God is Truth, then Truth cannot be many. Islamic Knowledge is thus Truth. I suggested that equating Knowledge with Truth was problematic because those who defined Knowledge end up defining Truth, and thus playing God. Furthermore, there will always be some amongst us who would hasten to suppress those Truths that, according to their view, do not serve the *ummah* well. And that will lead to suppression of Knowledge and to censorship.

Al-Faruqi was irritated by my arguments.

'Let us stop this philosophical juggling,' he shrieked. 'The important thing is that we must Islamize the disciplines. Economics, sociology, anthropology, psychology, political science, the whole lot of them, must be recast within the Islamic framework. The whole objective of the Islamization of knowledge project is to establish the specific relevance of Islam to each area of modern knowledge.'

I suggested it was not Islam that had to be made relevant to modern knowledge, but modern knowledge that had to be made relevant to Islam. This agitated him even more. So I tried to be conciliatory.

'Say for the sake of the argument,' I said, 'I accept your proposition. How do you propose to Islamize the disciplines?'

'We must,' replied Al-Faruqi, feeling more relaxed as he was now on more secure territory, 'master the modern disciplines, master the Islamic legacy, establish the specific relevance of Islam to each area of modern knowledge and then seek ways of creative synthesis between the legacy and modern knowledge. In this way, we will launch Islamic thought on a new trajectory which will lead to the Divine mission of the *ummah*.' He went on to argue that the task of Islamizing knowledge is one of the most formidable challenges the *ummah* has ever faced. The reformers of past centuries, unaware of the conflict between western knowledge and the vision of Islam, were content to acquire the knowledge and power of the West. Our generation was the first to realize the conflicts as we lived them in our own intellectual lives.

Then, Al-Faruqi picked up the knife and fork lying in front of him on the dinner table. 'Consider this knife and fork,' he said, waving the cutlery in front of me. 'Think of them as a discipline, say sociology or anthropology. Now, in the West, the fork is held in the left hand and the knife is held in the right. People eat with their left hands. But we Muslims eat with our right hands. So all we have to do is to switch: we must hold the fork with our right hands. Certain disciplines would require that kind of transformation in order to be Islamized. Others will need much more effort.'

I was dumbfounded. I couldn't believe that I was sitting in front of one of the greatest teachers and contemporary minds of the Muslim *ummah*. It took me a little while to recover from Al-Faruqi's naivety.

'But Muslims, on the whole, do not eat with knife and fork at all! Most of us eat with our hands. Forks and knives emerged out of a particular context. They were designed essentially to be used at the dinner table. They are part and parcel of a certain etiquette of eating. Where people sit on the floor they eat with their hands. Indeed, it is extremely difficult to eat with knives and forks if you are sitting crossed-legged on a carpet. Knives and forks also require a certain amount of energy to produce. So, in still other contexts, where cheap energy does not exist in abundance, chopsticks provide a better, widely available and cheaper alternative.' I continued, 'To a very large extent, the problem lies with the very notion of a discipline. Disciplines are not, as you seem to think, made in heaven, they are not a priori given. Neither nature nor human activities are divided into watertight compartments marked "sociology", "psychology" and "anthropology". Disciplines are born within the matrix of a particular worldview and are always hierarchically subordinated to that worldview.'

I went on to explain that the division of knowledge into the various disciplines that we find today is a particular manifestation of how the western worldview perceives reality and how western civilization sees its problems. Anthropology, for example, developed specifically with the purpose of studying the Other, non-western, societies in order to manage and control them. It has no real meaning for non-western cultures. Muslims do not need to Islamize disciplines, whatever that means; but to develop their own disciplines based on their own cultural context and geared to solving their own problems.

A Malaysian student of Al-Faruqi had accompanied him to the table. The trusty sidekick always walks behind the hero down the dusty Main Street to the climactic denouement. 'Producing different classifications of knowledge is an integral part of Islamic legacy. Through classifying knowledge in their specific ways, Muslim scholars generated new disciplines such as those of Hadith criticism, civilization studies and study of dreams. Maybe if we start with a contemporary Islamic classification of knowledge we will generate new Islamic disciplines. Brother Zia has already published an entirely new, conceptual classification of Islam.' He was referring to my book *Islam: Outline of A Classification Scheme.*

Al-Faruqi turned towards the student and stared at him for a few seconds. The student, looking ashamed, refocused his attention on his dinner, moulding rice into a moist ball with meat and vegetables. The manipulation seemed to take place at the base of his fingers almost into the palm of his hands in the distinctive way Malaysians use to make a neat round ball that is propelled from plate to mouth in the blink of an eye. Al-Faruqi turned his glare towards me. 'You want us to reinvent the wheel?' he asked sarcastically.

'On the contrary,' I replied. 'I am only pointing out that different vehicles need different kinds of wheels. You can't land a plane on bicycle wheels. And a bullock cart won't function properly with tractor wheels. Civilizations are like vehicles. They need appropriate wheels – their own disciplines – to move forward. Islamizing disciplines already infused with a materialistic metaphysics and western, secularist ethics is tantamount to a cosmetic epistemological face-lift and nothing more. At best, it would perpetuate the dichotomy of secular and Islamic knowledge that you are so keen to transcend.'

Al-Faruqi neatly placed his knife and fork on his dinner plate, wiped his lips with his napkin, and jumped to his feet. 'You go your way; we will go our way,' he said. He might as well have used the classic line: 'This town isn't big enough for both of us.' As in all the best westerns the townsfolk, our fellow conferees, lurk behind their doors and windows watching and listening to the fracas in the main street. As we talked I had been conscious of eyes and ears straining to catch the mood and spirit as well as the content of our exchange. When Al-Faruqi turned to leave, heads all around the room darted back to their dinner, hands once again became immersed in moulding activity of various types. I knew this showdown had done a great deal to cement my reputation as a troublemaker.

Two years later, Al-Faruqi brought a group of largely Arab scholars and businessmen together in Lugano, Switzerland. After two weeks of deliberation, the gathering declared that 'the evil in the system is located in the new universities of the Muslim world which have been adopted after the western model'. This 'evil' can only be eradicated by undertaking a project for 'reshaping all the disciplines of modernity from an Islamic point of view'. The project required the creation of an institute exclusively dedicated to the task. A number of Saudi businessmen came forward with a 25-million-dollar endowment to establish the International Institute of Islamic Thought (IIIT), which was to be based in Washington, DC. The following year, in 1982, Ismail al-Faruqi published his manifesto: *Islamization of Knowledge: General Principles and Workplan.* Suddenly, everyone in the Muslim world was talking about Islamization.

Islamization of Knowledge was, as I expected, a pretty mediocre work. It begins on a highly charged and emotional note:

The world-*ummah* of Islam stands presently at the lowest rung of the ladder of nations. In this century, no other nation has been subjected to comparable defeat or humiliation. Muslims were defeated, massacred, robbed of their land and wealth, of their life and hope. They were double-crossed, colonized and exploited; proselytised and forcefully or bribefully converted to other faiths. And they were secularised, westernized and de-Islamized by internal and external agents of their enemies. All this happened in practically every country and corner of the Muslim world. Victims of injustice and aggression on every count, the Muslims were nonetheless vilified and denigrated in the representations of all nations. They enjoy the worst possible 'image' in the world today. In the mass media of the world, the 'Muslim' is stereotyped as aggressive, destructive, lawless, terrorist, uncivilized, fanatic, fundamentalist, archaic and anachronistic. He is the object of hatred and contempt on the part of all non-Muslims, whether developed or underdeveloped, capitalist or Marxist, Eastern or Western, civilized or savage. The Muslim world itself is known only for its inner strife and division, its turbulence and self-contradictions, its wars and threat to world peace, its excessive wealth and excessive poverty, its famine and cholera epidemics. In the minds of people everywhere the Muslim world is the 'sick man' of the world; and the whole world is led to think that at the root of all these evils stands the religion of Islam. The fact that the *ummah* counts over a billion, that its territories are the vastest and the richest, that its potential in human, material and geo-political resources is the greatest, and finally that its faith – Islam – is an integral, beneficial, world-affirming and realistic religion, makes the defeat, the humiliation and the misrepresentation of Muslims all the more intolerable.

So, Al-Faruqi had the malaise part of the equation pretty well sorted. He then turns to the other part of the equation, the remedy: Islamization. He offers a twelve-step route to the revival of the *ummah*. In step one, the Muslim scholars are required to master the modern disciplines, in step two they have to survey their disciplines, in step three Islamic legacy has to be mastered, and so on to step ten where creative synthesis is achieved, step eleven where disciplines are recast in an Islamic framework and, finally, step twelve where Islamized knowledge is disseminated to the public at large. Al-Faruqi seemed to be stuck on the 'first principle' of his methodology and this consisted of nothing more than pious statements of belief: God is One, all creation is subservient to Him, Islam is a comprehensive way of life, there is Unity of Truth and Knowledge, and so forth. For me, the whole project conjured the image of a slot machine: put in this or that coin, turn the handle, utter your pieties, and hey presto collect your Islamized winnings! But the project set the whole Muslim world on fire. In Pakistan, it received the blessings of the country's military dictator, President Zia-ul-Haq. The newly established Islamic University in Islamabad was put at the disposal of Al-Faruqi and IIIT. The Institute opened its branches in a number of cities across the world and started recruiting young Muslim scholars to work on the project. Every Muslim scholar worth his intellectual salt was working on 'Islamization'.

After the stand-off at the Mecca Intercontinental I found my invitations to the conference circuit began to dry up. I and the small group of close friends around me were the only vocal critics of Islamization. When IIIT organized a number of conferences on various aspects of Islamization of knowledge, we were the kind of piquant condiment not required to spice the feast. I had not exactly determined on retiring from the *ummah* as I nursed my bruises and disillusion. But I was shunned by most of my 'Islamic movement' friends and given a wide berth by many of my mates from FOSIS days.

I spent the next three years commuting between London, Chicago and Jeddah. It took six months of preparatory work to launch the new magazine, *Inquiry*. Each issue was devoted to a single theme – such as 'Islamization', 'the Future of Islam', 'History', 'Books', 'Utopias', 'Media', 'Alternative Economics', 'Pakistan' and 'Turkey' – which was critiqued and examined from a number of different perspectives. The whole magazine had a probing and defiant but also confident and accommodating outlook. And I had managed to gather a motley crew of truly original writers. It was the bequest of a life spent on the conference circuits that I had from time to time encountered a number of round pegs who slipped through square holes. One walked past them sitting quietly on the fringes or looking disconsolate at some particularly bizarre utterance or giving vent to unpopular views that chimed with my own. Now I had a place to gather in these oddballs and set their talents to work. The *ummah* needed them too.

Inquiry needed an 'editor'– a front man – and I knew just the person, Parvez Manzoor. I first met him in June 1981 in Stockholm, at a seminar where Muslim and western scholars debated the issues of science and values with the aim of producing some kind of creative synthesis. Parvez struck me as a person with not an iota of dress sense; every garment on his body looked too large and out of place. He sported a ridiculously large moustache, reminiscent of Groucho Marx. In keeping with his bulky, uncoordinated appearance he spoke and laughed boisterously.

After observing him a while I walked over and asked: 'Are you the man who has written a thesis on the Beauty of the Intellect?'

'No,' he replied. 'I am the man who is writing a thesis on the Beauty of Intellection.'

'Either way,' I replied, 'you are a very ugly man.'

We became instant friends. I had never met a man who was so widely read. Parvez read everything. The problem was he read faster than he could think. So he was always in the process of digesting what he had read. Moreover, as a linguist and etymologist, he was eternally analysing words. So a conversation with Parvez was a real test of patience and comprehension. Unable to understand what he was saying, someone at the Seminar innocently asked him to speak more clearly. 'The act of "speaking",' he replied, 'is always arbitrary, irrecallable and involuntary. It was the tragedy of the Greeks that, for all their vision, they could not discover and speak to the God of the Prophets. The word *speaking* has an interesting etymological lineage. Speak the same language, to have the same sort of upbringing and therefore the same general idea. Speaker of the House of Common, does not normally speak but presides. Not to be confused with Spes, Roman goddess personifying hope. Speaking is also to make known, opinion and also truth. Wittgenstein. Language games. Muslim thinker Ibn Rushd ...' Unfortunately, he wrote the way he spoke. So no one really understood what he said or wrote; but no one would actually say so for fear of revealing their own ignorance. So he had to be the ideal front man for our magazine! Soon, Parvez acquired the nickname of 'Maulvi Etymology', later shortened to 'Maulvi ET'.

In contrast to Manzoor, Gulzar Haider was an exceptionally well-dressed and elegant man. He was Professor of Architecture at Carleton University, Ottawa, where I first met him during a short visit in 1980. A soft-spoken man with a modish moustache, he had built a string of small but exceptionally beautiful mosques and temples across North America, including the Islamic Centre in Plainfields, Indiana, which became the headquarters of the Muslim Students Association in the United States. Gulzar simply oozed grace; and produced prose that was just as thoughtful and graceful. But he was also a deeply melancholy man with an impossible notion of beauty. If one were to ask him, 'How are you?' he would reply, 'Last night in my dreams I saw snow crystals of such beauty that they will haunt me for the rest of my life.' Everywhere he looked he saw ugliness, wherever he went he met people he hoped he would never see again. I once offhandedly asked if he had had a good week.

'Good week?' he replied. 'I haven't had a good moment for most of my adult life.'

Gulzar, who spent considerable time lighting lone candles of hope and placing them on his window ledge, was deeply troubled by the state of the *ummah*. Events in post-revolutionary Iran had made him despondent. The Iran–Iraq war had depressed him even further. He found the antics of President Zia-ul-Haq in Pakistan disheartening. 'I am caught between a dreamlike past and a nightmare present,' he would say. 'Is there no way out of this grand drama of deception?' His presence was guaranteed to bring unbridled melancholy to every meeting, every discussion. He had a particular dislike of Maulvi ET's boisterousness. 'If you but knew, you would laugh less and cry more,' he would declare. 'Relax,' someone would inevitably say, 'you are amongst friends.'

'I really have no friends,' Gulzar would reply. 'My body is a squatter colony of dichotomous spirits. No wonder I cannot sleep well.' No wonder we all dubbed him 'Maulvi Depression'.

Haider and Manzoor were offset on the magazine by Merryl Wyn Davies, a jolly, insightful person, very proud of her Welsh ancestry. A genuine fire-breathing dragon lady: Merryl chain-smoked and enjoyed asking questions that could seldom be answered, read almost as much as Parvez, but was articulate and refined. She wrote just as brilliantly and gracefully as Gulzar, but had a much more cheerful disposition. Trained as an anthropologist she had taken to journalism, which she called anthropology with pay, and ended up working for the BBC on programmes like *Everyman, Heart of the Matter* and *Global Report*. On the day I was supposed to collect my visa for Iran at the London Embassy now under siege, I stopped in at Regent's Park Mosque. In a crisis it was a good place to pick up on the gossip and snippets of news. Merryl was there filming a segment for *Heart of the Matter* and I was roped in to join an unwieldy and unproductive round table discussion that thankfully ended on the cutting-room floor.

We kept in touch and a few months later Merryl rang to use me as a sounding board for a decision she was contemplating: converting to Islam. As a Muslim, it is my duty to encourage people to convert. But my experiences with English and American converts to Sufism had given me a particular aversion to converts. Most of the converts I knew tended to be more Muslim than the Muslims themselves; each one seemed to have a strong puritanical and decidedly unsavoury trait. This clever and quick-witted woman, I thought, will turn into a boring, stiff religious nut. So I advised her to think again; and abandon the whole idea if at all possible. But Davies was seldom to prove scrupulous in adhering to my best advice. Unbeknownst to me, she persisted. A few weeks later, she took the *Shahadah* – the act of bearing witness that 'There is no god but God, and Muhammad is His Messenger' – and embraced Islam. We lost touch for a year or two as she made her own peregrination through the byways of the British Muslim community. Occasionally, I heard reports of her speaking at some obscure meeting. Our paths recrossed at one such gathering where I overheard the first clear sign that Merryl was a different sort of convert. 'Sister, why haven't you chosen an Islamic name for yourself yet?' she was asked. 'My name is already Islamic enough, thank you,' she responded. Then she broke into an explanation, clearly well worn with repetition: the first Muslims were all converts but only one had been asked by the Prophet to select a new name, since just as Abdullah means slave of God, so this individual's name meant allegiance to pagan deity. 'My name is Welsh, it means something white from the sea, and there's nothing objectionable in that. Besides, I've converted to Islam to find out who I am in the midst of my Welsh identity, culture and history with my personality, as I am.' The brain was clearly still intact. Davies wrote a trenchant regular 'Opinion' column for *Inquiry*.

Why did Merryl become a Muslim? When I insisted on an answer, she replied: 'Islam offers a coherent and intellectually satisfying framework in which to ask and seek answers for all the pertinent questions about the purpose of life. I have discovered what faith means.' It wasn't the kind of answer I was expecting; I was still trying to work out what faith meant to me. Muslims love converts, and actively seek to make them; it confirms their own convictions and soothes their lurking insecurities. And Merryl was a prize catch – much to her embarrassment. She was fêted and sought after and soon became a popular speaker in Muslim circles.

I loved editing *Inquiry*. Bringing all the different elements of the magazine together, persuading writers with different talents and peculiar character traits to focus on the theme of each issue, working with a network of stringers around the world, making everyone's copy readable, while writing my own 'Idea' pieces, gave me more enjoyment than anyone was legitimately entitled to have. From the first issue, which appeared in June 1984 declaring that any notion of 'Islamic resurgence' based on Arab money and the Iranian revolution was pure delusion, it captured the imagination of the Muslim intelligentsia. Within months, we were selling 30,000 copies worldwide – escalating towards 50,000. I spent ten days a month editing the magazine, ten days travelling around the Muslim world attending conferences and seminars, and ten days at the Centre for Policy and Futures Studies at East-West University in Chicago. The Centre was more of a network than a solid institution; it moved with me, and functioned wherever I happened to be. Our network kept on growing as other thinkers and writers identified themselves and climbed aboard: Munawar Ahmad Anees, a Pakistani-American biologist and bibliophile; Ibrahim Sulaiman, a Nigerian scholar of West African history and Islamic Law; and Anwar Naseem, a Pakistani-Canadian scientist who specialized in genetics.

Whenever we could gather in London there would be an all-night session, usually at my house, sometimes at the home of Gulzar Haider's sister who lived in deepest South London. It would commence with the aromatic flavours of biryani, kofta and carrot halwa for the sake of tradition. It would be full of laughter, good jokes and endless debate as ideas we could discuss with no one else came flooding forth. For each of us it was like winter ice bursting in a spring thaw. We'd get increasingly excited and loud as we fought to get a word in, conscious of the novelty of addressing others who would understand. And on occasion we would take this travelling roadshow to seminars. On a flight to Chicago, en route to one such seminar on the 'Contemporary relevance of Islam', someone suggested we should officially incorporate ourselves, rather than just being a 'boisterous group of roving intellectuals'. 'We will need an appropriate name,' I observed. Parvez ran through his etymological memory tapes and came up with the name *Ijmal*. And, for the first, and I think the last, time, Gulzar agreed with him: the root word *jml* conveys the idea of beauty on the one hand and wholeness on the other.

So, in Essex Inn on Chicago's South Michigan Avenue, adjacent to East-West University, in a rather tacky room, which drove Gulzar to despair and was so copiously air-conditioned we were all visibly shivering, we fabricated an inaugural ceremony and Ijmal was born. The Ijmalis were a beardless lot. But there had to be an exception. Two members of Ijmal shared the same surname: Ayyub Malik and Zaffar Malik. Ayyub was a clean-shaven, tall and suave architect, responsible for some award-winning buildings and shopping complexes in and around London. His passion was poverty eradication and 'the plight of the average man and woman' about which he talked incessantly. Zaffar, my colleague at the Hajj Research Centre and on my fourth Hajj, was a graphic designer with real flair, a brilliant sense of design: a sensitive, humble soul who nurtured a deliberately understated sense of humour played out in elaborate scenarios where he feigned total innocence until the pith of the joke sank into the densest skull and all dissolved in laughter. He was reminiscent of Karl Marx, his beard did not betoken religious significance; it was an accoutrement of his superb aesthetic sense. We dubbed them 'Malik With' and 'Malik Without'.

What the Ijmalis lacked in facial architecture, they made up for with their passionate commitment to liberating Islam from a fossilized tradition and religious obscurantism. We thought a lot, argued all the time, discussed everything, criticized everyone (particularly each other) and wrote as though everything depended on what we had to say. And, my God, we wrote as though tomorrow was Judgement Day. Initially, we saw ourselves as critics. We considered it our responsibility to critique contemporary Islamic thought and expose its hollowness mercilessly. We threw scorn at the pious and their pieties. Almost every issue of *Inquiry* systematically 'deconstructed' certain cherished notions of modern and traditional Islam. A group of rowdy Ijmali thinkers, who took little for granted, was a frightening and formidable sight at any Muslim conference. But soon, running out of things to critique, and receiving complaints from many quarters that we were more concerned with 'demolition' than construction, we moved to the second component of our name. We sought synthesis, to generate new thought as true to the spirit of Islam as it was to the contemporary needs and aspirations of the *ummah*.

The Ijmalis emphasized ethical aspects of Islam and insisted on using Islamic concepts to dissect contemporary problems. While we were a heterogeneous group, with different disciplinary backgrounds, we were united by a methodology of conceptual analysis that we learned together and hammered out in all-night sessions. Rather than 'Islamize' already existing disciplines, we argued for new discourses, rooted in Islamic concepts, through which the external expression of Muslim civilization – science and technology, politics and international relations, social structures and economic activity, rural and urban development – can be studied and developed in relation to contemporary needs and reality.

Islam, we Ijmalis were agreed, emphasizes diverse ways of knowing as well as the interconnectedness of all things. All forms of knowledge are interconnected and organically related by the ever-present spirit of Qur'anic revelation. Thus, Islam does not only make the pursuit of knowledge obligatory but also connects it with the unique Islamic notion of worship: *ilm*, the term for knowledge, is a form of *ibadah* (worship). So the pursuit of scientific knowledge, social sciences and humanities are also forms of worship – and should be just as important for any Muslim society as daily prayer and fasting during the month of Ramadan. Indeed, without due emphasis to all varieties of knowledge, worship remains incomplete. But knowledge is not just connected to worship, it is also connected to every other Qur'anic value such as *khalifah* (the idea that people are trustees and stewards of this earth), *adl* (social justice), and *istislah* (public interest). While the connection between knowledge and worship means that knowledge cannot be pursued in open transgression of Islamic ethics, the connection between knowledge and stewardship transforms nature into the realm of the sacred. Men and women as the trustees of God are the custodians of His gift, and cannot pursue knowledge at the expense of nature. On the contrary, as the guardian of nature, we seek to understand nature, the cosmos and all it contains, not to dominate but to appreciate the 'signs' of God. The study of nature, therefore, leads to two outcomes: an understanding of the material world as well as reflection of spiritual realities. The interconnection of knowledge with social justice and public interest ensures that knowledge is pursued to promote equality, integrity and values that enhance the well-being of Muslim society and culture.

The first new discourse that Ijmalis produced was that of Islamic science. The Ijmali notion of Islamic science used the basic concepts of the Qur'an – such as *tawheed* (the unity of God), stewardship, knowledge – to delineate and shape a science policy that was ethically worthy of being labelled 'Islamic'. We argued, for example, that it was unethical for Muslim societies to build weapons of mass destruction, or for Muslim biologists to use vivisection, or to pursue fashionable fields of research, such as theoretical physics, without paying attention to the needs of society. Muslims had to develop an alternative way to undertake biological research and test drugs, and concentrate their efforts on problems such as diarrhoea, river blindness and malnourishment which were plaguing their societies. Merryl developed a similar conceptual framework for the study of human societies. Islamic anthropology, she argued, cannot just be the study of Muslim societies – as was suggested by the Islamization brigade. It had to be comparative, cross-cultural and historical and concerned with all types of human, cultural and social organization of whatever scale or density of social relations. Similarly, Munawar Anees looked at gender and technology from the ethical and conceptual perspective of Islam. During the later part of the 1980s, the Ijmalis published over a dozen books, which, we hoped, would lay the foundation of a humane, dynamic, thriving future civilization of Islam.

But the Islamization brigade, which now consisted of a huge network of scholars across the Muslim world, went out of its way to ignore or sidestep our critique – and they seemed to have little comprehension of the alternatives we were suggesting. *Inquiry* was a different matter. It became the main vehicle through which the Ijmali message was filtered to the Muslim intellectual community. Every other month, when we had published something contentious, Maulvi Iqbal, who was billed as 'Editor-in-Chief', would regale us with tales of how Kalim Siddiqui had tried to subvert our operation, how this or that group in Iran manoeuvred to cut off the funding. But despite Parvez's frequent and quite insightful swipes at Shia thought and history, our regular attacks on the excesses of the Iranian revolution, and our non-partisan criticism evenly spread among all sections of the Good and the Great of the Islamic movement, we managed to survive.

But I increasingly felt as though I was simultaneously courting two equally authoritarian and seductive mistresses. The relationship between Iran and Saudi Arabia had degenerated into open hostility. During the Hajj season, it had become a ritual for the Iranian pilgrims to shout anti-Saudi slogans. Ayatollah Khomeini had openly suggested that the Saudi monarchy was not a suitable guardian of the holy cities of Mecca and Medina. Saudi Arabia had warned Iran 'not to export its revolution' to areas of Saudi influence. Would my Iranian mistress get suspicious first, leading to the closure of *Inquiry*? Or would the Saudi organizations and philanthropists who supported the activities of the Centre for Policy and Futures Studies through the good offices of Abdullah Naseef, and provided us with so much freedom to think, write, travel, criticize, and organize conferences, seminars and meetings, get wise, and pull their purse strings leading to a collapse of the Ijmali enterprise?

Then, towards the end of May 1986, the intellectual community of the Muslim world was stunned by some shocking news. It was the month of Ramadan. At around 2.30 in the morning of 27 May, an assailant, in combat gear with a black scarf across the lower half of his face ninja style, and carrying a forty-centimetre 'Rambo type' survival knife, entered the residence of Ismail al-Faruqi in Wyncote, Pennsylvania. He used a screwdriver to force open the kitchen window. Al-Faruqi's wife, Lamya Faruqi, a renowned art critic who was working on developing a new theory of Islamic art, was in the kitchen preparing *suhur*, the morning meal which precedes the fast. The assailant attacked her, stabbing her twice in the chest, and left her bleeding to death on the kitchen floor. Lamya's scream woke Anmar az-Zain, Al-Faruqi's married daughter, pregnant with her second child. She came down from her room to be confronted by the killer and ran back to phone the police. The man chased her, caught her, and stabbed her several times. Wounded and bleeding profusely, Anmar still managed to phone the police. At 2.34 the police knew an intruder was in the Al-Faruqi household. Meanwhile, the assailant, who seemed to know the house reasonably well, moved to Ismail al-Faruqi's bedroom. He found Al-Faruqi up and ready to defend himself. In the struggle that followed, Ismail al-Faruqi was stabbed five times in the chest and arms. The assailant left Al-Faruqi fatally wounded and returned his attention to Anmar. He stabbed her a few more times, before making a hasty exist. When the police arrived moments later, they found Anmar sitting in a pool of blood on the kitchen floor. Lamya al-Faruqi was lying face down in a second-floor den at the front of the house. Both Anmar's parents were dead. The Al-Faruqis' second daughter, Tayma, who was also in the house, escaped the assailant's attention by hiding along with Anmar's child, in a closet. The deadly knife was on the scene of the crime. The screwdriver used to break into the house and the leather sheath for the knife were found in a dustbin two houses away from Al-Faruqi's home.

Who could have committed such a heinous crime? Muslim intellectual circles were rife with speculation. Was Al-Faruqi singled out for assassination because of his efforts to revive Muslim thought and resurrect Islam as a viable challenge to western civilization? Three months before the assassination of the Al-Faruqis, their second son had died under mysterious circumstances. He had joined the US army and was studying in a military academy in New Mexico. The parents only learned of his death a full week after his body had been buried. The College claimed that he had died of food poisoning. The Al-Faruqis' had openly rejected this explanation. Was the American government behind their son's assassination? Were the CIA or FBI involved? Or perhaps Al-Faruqi's outspoken defence of Palestinian rights had led a Zionist extremist belonging to the Jewish Defence League to brutally assassinate him? Maybe it was a group of Muslim extremists who took exception to his views on Islam? Had the Islamization of knowledge project died with Al-Faruqi?

We devoted a whole July 1986 issue of *Inquiry* to 'the legacy of Al-Faruqi'. His assassin turned out to be an Afro-American convert with a personal grudge – further strengthening my conviction that converts tend to have extremist tendencies. But his brutal murder, far from decreasing his influence, actually increased it. He became an icon. Islamization now assumed the proportions of an uncontrollable forest fire that consumed everything in its path. Wherever I went in the Muslim world – in Nigeria, in Pakistan, in Malaysia, in Egypt, in Bangladesh – committed Muslim thinkers and intellectuals talked of nothing else besides Islamization. Our critique was completely brushed aside.

Just over a year later, on a warm late summer day, I had finished editing an issue of *Inquiry* on Malaysia when Maulvi Iqbal ushered me into his office.

'We have lost the race,' he said, trying not to look at me.

'Don't tell me, Maulvi, they've cut our funding,' I shot back.

'That would be *my* failure. Our failure is that I could not restrain you and you could not control yourself. They have asked me to sack you.'

'Not another offending editorial?'

'No. It's not something you wrote in *Inquiry*. It's that review you did of *The Holy Qur'an and the Sciences of Nature* for the *Muslim World Book Review*.'

I recalled the piece. It was an examination of a book by the Iranian philosopher of science Mehdi Golshani. On the whole, it was a complimentary review, although I did point out that Golshani had not followed recent developments in the history and philosophy of science, and appeared to be oblivious of the debate on Islamic science outside Iran.

'But, Maulvi,' I said, 'I bent backwards to praise Golshani in that review.'

'It's not what you said about Golshani that has upset the Mullahs in Tehran,' Iqbal replied. 'It's what you said about Imam Ja'far as-Sadiq.'

Ja'far as-Sadiq, the sixth of the twelve Imams of the Shia, was martyred in 765 through the intrigue of the (Sunni) Abbasid Caliph Al-Mansur. He became Imam by Divine Command and the decree of those who came before him. He is credited with collecting more sayings of the Prophet Muhammad than all the other eleven Imams combined. I picked up the copy of the *Muslim World Book Review* lying on Iqbal's desk, turned to the appropriate page, and started reading aloud. 'All his quotations and supporting arguments come from Shia scholars as though Sunni scholars were non-existent. A discerning reader may legitimately ask: how many quotations from Imam Ja'far as-Sadiq is one supposed to swallow?'

'Surely you know by now that there are no discerning readers amongst the Mullahs in Tehran!' Iqbal observed, trying to suppress his smile.

It transpired that Kalim Siddiqui had faxed a copy of the review – with offending passage suitably highlighted – to his contacts in the higher echelons of the revolutionary guards, pointing out that this was a major act of sacrilege against the Fifth Imam, and urging them to take urgent action. They did.

'Do you want to negotiate a suitable departing package?' Maulvi Iqbal asked.

I did. And I cleared my office the same day.

I recollect walking out of the *Inquiry* office in Banner Street, central London that last time and noticing a group of passers-by. What struck me was that they were all wearing a chic version of Maulvi Iqbal's *khaksari kadhdir* suits. What began in the back streets of India and Pakistan out of altruism and to emphasize frugality was now the height of expensive fashion, featured on the catwalks of Europe, avidly copied by celebrities, a designer statement of fine tailoring. I remember thinking: Is nothing sacred? An interesting thought to dwell upon, under the circumstances. A number of people followed me in short order, decamping from *Inquiry* in solidarity although, surprisingly, Parvez Manzoor did not. Less than a year later, our valiant experiment folded.

Inquiry was dead. The Ijmalis, however, survived as a group of friends. We continued to huddle together for warmth, the kind that comes from striking sparks off each other. We realized that our agenda for changing Islam required long-term effort and commitment – there were no short cuts, certainly those which required funding by a Muslim government were doomed to failure. And we consoled ourselves by declaring that true reformists and thinkers always go against the grain – so our isolation from the mainstream of Muslim intellectual and academic circles could actually be a blessing.

Chapter 11

THE LAWS OF HEAVEN

The loss of *Inquiry* was a blow felt by all Ijmalis. While it existed we had the comfort of knowing we were making contact with a wider world, both Muslim and non-Muslim, not just talking among ourselves. Without that regular conduit to the wider world we were all haunted by frustration. And the wider world simply would not leave us in peace to resolve all issues in the best possible way. On the global level, the vapid consumer culture of the Reagan–Thatcher era was lulling the senses of all and sundry: a social conscience was for wimps, and we were all fully paid up, non-sectarian super-wimps. And, on the level of the *ummah*, we were deeply concerned that across the Muslim world all future prospects were increasingly summed up in a single all-embracing ready-made off-the-shelf answer: Shariah.

The word *Shariah* literally means 'the path or the road leading to water'. In its religious use, it is the path that leads to God and thus to paradise. God, in His Infinite Mercy, has shown this path in the Qur'an and through the Traditions of the Prophet. The Muslims are thus required to give concrete shape to their religious values by following this path, by using it as a general and legal framework for family relations, crime and punishment, inheritance, trade and commerce, and relations between communities and states. It is through the Shariah, commonly translated as 'Islamic Law', that Islam is expressed in Muslim societies.

The global demand for Shariah was a distinguishing feature of the 1980s. Ruling authorities in Malaysia, Pakistan, Egypt, Nigeria and the Sudan repeatedly faced hostile criticism from student groups and Islamic movements, parties and scholars – all demanding that Shariah should become the law of the land. Even Muslim minorities in such places as India wanted to be judged by the Shariah in matters of family and personal law. Thus, it was simply not possible for any self-respecting Muslim intellectual not to engage with the issues of the Shariah. The Ijmalis were no exception: we too were obsessed with it. It seemed natural to us that one of the most cherished goals of any Muslim community should be to establish the rule of the Shariah. But the sense in which the term has come to be understood both perplexed and worried us. For there is a great deal in the Shariah that the Ijmalis rejected – such as its oppressive treatment of women and minorities, its emphasis on extreme punishments, and its fixation with ossified jurisprudence. Moreover, we were concerned that Shariah had come to signify Islam per se. If Islam is submission to the Will of God, then Shariah is the path by which submission is enacted, the actual route map of religion as a way of life. Hence, for many Muslims, Islam is the Shariah and the Shariah is Islam.

This neatness, this exact fit by which one term means and comprehends the other, perverts the basic principles of Islam. Not surprisingly, it also leads Muslims to perceive the Shariah as a panacea, the one-stage process for delivering Muslim society from the era of neocolonialism to the paradise of Islam. For us, the Shariah as it exists today, and the spirit of Islam, were two quite distinct things. The monolithic construction of the Shariah also undermined the diversity of Islamic thought which we valued enormously. To ask a Muslim to be against the Shariah is like asking someone to vote for sin. But we opted for sin: and started questioning the Shariah. How was it constructed and evolved in Muslim civilization, why did it have such an inherently medieval flavour? At Ijmali 'think-ins', we repeatedly asked: what exactly do we mean by the Shariah?

On a freezing day in the winter of 1985 the telephone rang and Abdullah Naseef made me an offer I could not refuse. Would I like to join him as an adviser on a World Muslim League mission to Pakistan and China? I knew Naseef was going on an errand for the Saudi King; but the offer presented prospects I could not overlook. 'Very big, China,' as Noel Coward so pithily noted, and I'd never been there before. The Prophet said one should search for knowledge, even to China. How could a seeker after knowledge refuse? And the journey would provide an opportunity to explore what the Shariah meant to ordinary Muslims and their leaders. I flew to Jeddah and discovered that Wasiullah Khan, the living archive of East-West University, he of the threadbare moustache, was to join us.

We would be travelling with Sheikh Salah Kamel, the founder of Bank al-Brakah, one of the first Islamic banks to open a branch in London and many other cities around the world. Also in our party would be Abdo Yamani, the former Saudi Minister of Information, who now worked for Sheikh Kamel and headed his charitable foundation, the Iqra Trust. We flew in Sheikh Kamel's private jet to Islamabad.

In Islamabad, we were received with all the fanfare of a diplomatic mission. It was after all a very 1980s sort of thing: travel like glitterati and you get treated as glitterati. We were put up at a government guest house – so this was what the Raj was like, I thought to myself. I exulted on behalf of my forebears who would have been confined to guarding the exterior or labouring in the servants' quarters. The first item on our agenda was a meeting with President Mohammad Zia-ul-Haq, the military ruler of Pakistan. The President kept us waiting for a couple of days, as presidents are wont to do. Naseef and I whiled away our time listening endlessly to Khan's monologues about the achievements of East-West University. Naseef seemed to relish Khan's company and shamelessly encouraged him to repeat his recycled jokes ad nauseam. I began to suspect he drew even more amusement from studying my reactions and vain attempts to remain convivial under extreme duress. Sheikh Kamel, a tall well-built man with impressive features, spent most of his time being measured for suits. We learned he had fallen in love with a noted Egyptian film actress and took every opportunity to dress in ways that would impress. Finally, the call came and we were summoned to an audience with the President.

President Zia-ul-Haq was in a jolly mood. He greeted the entourage in the Presidential House with considerable warmth, hugging everyone as Naseef introduced us individually. When I was introduced, he shook my hand enthusiastically, thought for a moment, and said: 'I recall reading something by you recently.' He did not recall exactly what he had read and we were ushered on to a reception room. When we were all seated on large sofas the President started to speak. 'Thanks to your help, and our friends in the USA and Britain,' he began, 'the Russians have almost been defeated in Afghanistan. Everywhere they are in retreat.' The Afghan Jihad, he said, had received a tremendous boost from a young Saudi by the name of Osama bin Laden, who only the other day had led a daring raid on Kabul. He wished to thank His Majesty, the King of Saudi Arabia, for this gift. 'But we mustn't forget,' the President said, 'the help we have received from all over the Muslim world.' Over 30,000 Mujahidin – freedom fighters – from forty-three different Muslim countries had joined the Afghan Jihad. Thousands were studying in the *madrasahs* – religious schools – in Northern Pakistan, and being prepared for the jihad. He thanked both Saudi Arabia and the USA for their support in this 'recruitment plan'. We were all listening to the President in total silence. 'Our main concern,' the President said, 'is what happens after the Soviet withdrawal. There is a danger of civil war which we must work to avoid.' The gathering nodded vigorously in agreement.

Then the President changed gear and started talking of how he was introducing the Shariah in Pakistan. 'It is the demand of the people,' he said. 'And I must bow to their wishes. Islam is a total system and it must be imposed on society in its totality.' He described in great detail how law-breakers would be lashed, thieves have their hands cut off 'humanely' and adulterers be stoned. Khan turned his saucer eyes towards me, I tried very hard to suppress any external sign of my own rising horror. When the recitation concluded Khan and I were whisked off to the guest house to permit the Saudis to exchange some private words with the President. I departed with a profound sense of relief.

In the evening, the President hosted a dinner in our honour. I was asked to sit at his table. During the first course – lentil soup – he again chatted with everyone about his passion for the Shariah. When the main course – biryani, lamb korma, and mixed vegetables – arrived, he suddenly turned towards me.

'Do I look like a deranged dictator to you?' he demanded. The whole table was stunned and immediately everyone seemed to find their food fascinating. I was conscious of turmoil in my inner self. Diplomacy is not my strong suit; tact, caution and a prudential turn of phrase have long been strangers to my nature. My instant reaction was to shout out: 'YES!' I wrestled spontaneity to a draw and merely sat still and quiet. There is a famous Latin epithet to the effect that silence is assent; this would have to do.

President Zia-ul-Haq did not look angry. He seemed amused. 'In your book *Islamic Futures*,' he said, beaming, 'you describe me as a deranged dictator.' He signalled to an aide to come forward. The aide, in full military uniform, came running with a copy of the book, already opened at the relevant page.

The President read:

No wonder that the average Muslim cringes with fear at the mention of 'Islamic rule'. And every time an attempt is made to turn a country into an 'Islamic state', as in Pakistan, Libya, or in the Sudan, their worst fears are realized. The picture is always the same: a deranged dictator sits on the throne charged with the belief that he has a divine mandate to impose Islam on the masses. His first actions are to introduce 'Islamic punishments' – as if Islam begins and ends with them – and various public floggings take place to convey the message that he means business. Various groups of ulema – religious scholars – and Islamic parties seek appointments in his government and applaud his actions. He declares women to be non-entities, establishes a 'Council of Islamic Ideology' and various 'Shariah courts' where summary justice is seen to be done. Can there be a better invitation to Islam than this?

He closed the book; and chuckled. Everyone at the table joined in the laughter, with a tinny edge of nervousness. But I wasn't sure whether they were laughing at me or the President. The conversation moved on to other topics.

When the dinner ended Zia-ul-Haq – meaning light of the Truth, as distinct from my plain Zia, meaning light, who claims only to be a searcher after the paradise of knowledge – stood at the main door of the

Presidential House, while the guests filed past. He shook everyone's hand, uttering pleasantries. When I shook his hand, he held my right hand and placed his left over it. 'I hope we will meet again,' he said. 'If we do not meet in this life, I will see you in paradise.' An aide came forward and presented me with a gift. A table lamp made of solid green marble, packed in a wooden case, covered with red velvet. It was enormously heavy. Wasiullah Khan received an identical present. I passed mine to him: 'Take it with my compliments,' I said. 'He gave it to you,' Khan replied, returning the weighty box, 'you carry it. Think of it as the burden of the Shariah!'

The following day we flew in a Pakistani air force helicopter to Peshawar, the capital and largest city of Pakistan's North-West Frontier Province, located near the Khyber Pass. A meeting of leaders of various Mujahidin groups fighting in Afghanistan was being held. The Afghan Tajik leader Burhanuddin Rabbani, who was tipped to be the first President of 'liberated Afghanistan', chaired the meeting. I spotted Ahmad Shah Masood, Rabbani's right-hand man; the Pushtun leader of Hizbe Islami fighters, Gulbuddin Hekmatyar; and a number of leaders from Pakistani religious parties. A tall, thin Saudi, with a turban and a wispy beard, known as Osama bin Laden, stood out from amongst the gathering. He was obvious not only for his height but his manner, he carried himself with a certain majesty and decorum. Almost everyone at the meeting seemed to adore him. The debate under way concerned the nature of the coming 'Islamic state' in Afghanistan. Everyone wanted to establish the Shariah in the new state but there was a dispute between Rabbani's Shia interpretation and the Wahhabi variant favoured by Hekmatyar, Pakistani religious scholars and the Saudi delegation. It soon transpired that the difference was political rather than religious, as Rabbani simply wanted to have total control of the reins of power at the expense of other groups. The most frequently used word during the negotiations seemed to be 'impossible'.

After a day or so, I got bored with the meeting; and decided to put to good use the official car at our disposal. I would visit Akora Khattak, halfway down the road from Peshawar to Islamabad. It was then home of the *madrasahs* training the Mujahidin, the ones President Zia-ul-Haq spoke of so glowingly and was supporting so enthusiastically. I particularly wanted to see Dar-ul-Uloom Haqqania, founded in 1947 and thus one of the oldest Deobandi seminaries in Pakistan. The principal of Haqqania was Maulana Sami-ul-Haq, a large, jovial man with a henna-dyed beard. The traditional herb henna, when applied to black hair, produces rich auburn highlights. Liberal application of the same herb to greying hair turns the mop in question to the colour of a good carrot halwa before gradually fading to a mottled gingery hue. In Pakistan, hirsute people of bright orange hue are typical of the Northern Provinces and one such was Sami-ul-Haq. What made him distinctive therefore was not the colour of his beard but his militancy and demand for Shariah Law in Pakistan. Indeed, many considered him an architect of General Zia's Islamization programme.

I arrived at the sprawling complex of classrooms, dormitories and public auditoriums that make up the Haqqania seminary on a cold day in December. There was an unabashed medieval air about the place. The whole institution was full of beards: every teacher, every student, even the teenage boys, were sporting facial furniture in a bewildering range of reds. Many had long hair, shaved upper lips, unruly flowing beards, and eyes lined with *surma* – kohl. Maulana Sami-ul-Haq was not in residence. But a teacher was more than happy to show me around. He started by explaining that most of the students were receiving free tuition. Indeed, some of the 1,500 students were even getting a small stipend. For many poor Pakistanis, the *madrasah* was the only viable way of acquiring an education. He described the Haqqania as 'a seat of learning' where the *talibans* – the students – pursue an eight-year course in Islamic studies. Many graduates of the Seminary, I was told, held important positions in the government, the judiciary, the military and the bureaucracy. Students from abroad were increasing too. 'They come here to learn a pure vision of Islam,' he said. But how pure was pure, I asked, as we wandered from one building to another, from class to class. 'Our curriculum,' he said, 'focuses on the Qur'an and the Shariah. We teach an undiluted, chaste version of the Shariah.' This turned out to be based mostly on rote learning, memorizing the Qur'an, memorizing a select collection of the Traditions of the Prophet Muhammad, and memorizing the legal opinions and rulings of eighth-century, classical jurists.

I asked if they followed the classical curriculum, the sort of things I was taught by Sheikh Jaffar Idris, including philosophy, logic and rhetoric as well as diverse commentaries on the Qur'an. The teacher recoiled in horror at the mention of philosophy. 'We teach pure Shariah here,' he emphasized. 'But the curriculum does include mathematics and astronomy.' What about Sufi thought, I dared to ask. The teacher was visibly upset. 'I keep telling you,' he replied, 'we teach a pure version of Islam. Sufism has nothing to do with it.' Further conversation revealed that the Seminary also regarded Shia thought as a deviation from the true path of Islam and looked at Shias in general with contempt. Indeed, the teacher came close to advocating that the Shias should be 'persuaded' to accept the Sunni way. Eventually, the teacher excused himself and went off to teach a class.

One student, a rather slim Pakistani in his twenties, had been keenly listening to our conversation. He came forward to introduce himself when the teacher had left.

'Are you a Shia?' he asked after the standard salutation.

'No,' I replied.

'Shias are not Muslim,' he said without hesitation. 'They do not belong in a truly Islamic republic. We should have a pure leader – an *Amir* – who imposes the total Shariah of God on Pakistan.'

I did not reply; but looked at him passively.

'Are you a good Muslim?' he asked.

'I am a Muslim,' I replied, 'I am not sure about the good bit.'

'If you are a Muslim why don't you have a beard?'

'Because it is not necessary to have a beard to be a Muslim.'

'It is the Sunnah (the tradition derived from the customary practice) of the Prophet. A man who does not follow the Sunnah of the Prophet is not a Muslim.'

'So why aren't you riding a camel?'

He was startled at my reply. 'What do you mean?'

'It's Sunnah to ride a camel. The Prophet spent a great deal of his life on the back of a camel.'

'But today we have cars and buses.'

'Well,' I answered, 'if blades had been available in his time, I am sure the Prophet would have used them.'

I looked at him to see if I could detect the hint of a smile. He lowered his gaze and kept quiet.

'I notice that you are wearing *surma*,' I said.

'Yes. It is Sunnah.'

'But do you know that it contains lead? It could damage your eyes and poison you.'

He kept quiet.

'Many things the Prophet did were a product of his times. I do not regard them as an essential part of the Sunnah. I think the Sunnah is largely located in the spirit he promoted. His spirit of generosity, love and tolerance, his insistence on forgiving those who had persecuted and oppressed him, the respect and devotion he showed to the elderly, the children and marginalized in society, his concern for justice, equity and fair play, his dedication to inquiry, knowledge and criticism – that is the tradition we ought to be following.'

'Who are you,' the student shouted angrily, 'to say what is and what is not the Sunnah? You don't even have a beard.'

On my way back to Peshawar, I remember shivering with apprehension. Has the great legacy of Islamic thought and learning come down to this? A fetish with the Prophet's physical appearance. An exclusivist notion of purity. A medieval perception of Divine Law. Far from being 'a seat of learning', *madrasah* Haqqania was a hatchery of hate. It was producing not men of education and learning, but narrow-minded bigots absolutely certain their way was the only right way. How long before they reach critical mass and start fighting with all who disagree with them, I recall thinking. How long before they declare war on the Shia? How long before they turn Pakistan into their hellish version of paradise? The total lack of humour, the conspicuous absence of the joy of life so evident in the *madrasah*, convinced me the students had to be taken seriously.

By the time I returned to Peshawar, the Mujahidin meeting had broken up in discord and resentment. 'These people know nothing but how to fight,' Naseef said on our return journey in the helicopter to Islamabad. 'They will be killing each other after the Russians leave Afghanistan.' 'It won't just be the Mujahidin,' I added. 'The *talibans* in the Deobandi *madrasah* will no doubt follow suit.'

From Islamabad, we had to take a PIA flight to Beijing. But the flight had been cancelled, forcing us to hang around Islamabad for a few days. I decided to leave the government guest house, the official transport, and my companions behind and venture out on my own. Islamabad is a relatively new city built adjacent to the more historic city of Rawalpindi. A short road, only a few kilometres long, connects the two. The most popular way to travel between them is a rapid transit system known locally as 'wagon'. The 'wagon' is basically a Ford Transit van designed for a maximum of twenty people. But between Islamabad and Rawalpindi, a wagon can easily accommodate twice as many. I hailed a passing wagon as it sped by. It slowed down, a hand came out and pulled me inside. 'Why don't you Conductors look before you pull people up?' someone said angrily. I tried to turn around and see who was complaining. But my face was trapped between two other faces and I could not move. Bus drivers and conductors in this part of the world are experts at shaping and adjusting a human body to fit the minimum space; this skill goes beyond yoga into the realms of pure body contortion. I had no option but to remain still till I reached my destination.

I managed to disentangle myself from the wagon just before it entered Rawalpindi. The contrast with Islamabad could not have been greater. Islamabad, a modern capital with wide roads arranged on a grid pattern, and huge rectangular government buildings, offers hardly any street life. It is a planned city; a shining example of how not to plan cities. It has turned one of the most beautiful and breathtaking pieces of scenery into a confined, autocratic eyesore. Rawalpindi, in contrast, is bursting with activity, people, congested roads and an incredible amount of dust. It is an unplanned organic city with a strong Pathan – who must be amongst the most rugged and militant people on earth – character. In almost every part of the city, *thalawallas* – street vendors – sell a variety of cooked and uncooked foodstuffs and a galaxy of fruit juices. From a distance, their stalls appear a delicately controlled riot of colour and smell. The sheer visual and aromatic excitement of walking around these streets makes one hungry while the dust stimulates thirst. To make myself one with the scene I bought a cold glass of heavy, greyish, sugar-cane juice. Its colour and consistency always remind me of Kipling's recurrent phrase in the *Just So Stories*: 'the grey-green greasy Limpopo'. Since Kipling spent far more of his life in the Indian Subcontinent than in Southern Africa I always wonder if the description owes more to memory of sugar-cane juice than actual riverine observation. Was it the waterfalls of juice cascading from the contraption so reminiscent of a mangle in which the raw sugar cane is crushed that he had in mind when seeking words to summon up a sluggish mighty river of life? This beverage was not only very sweet but contained the entire life of the street – the dust, the sweat, the exhaust fumes, the smoke; all human life, as they say, was there in that glass! But it is also impeccably thirst-quenching.

Replenished and revitalized I moved on to an overcrowded kebab stall. The stallholder was simultaneously performing four different tasks: mixing pieces of meat in pinkish yogurt gravy, putting the meat on the skewer, thence straight onto an open coal fire, and removing the cooked finished product. He then pulled the piping hot tikkas from the skewer with his bare hands at incredible speed. The entire operation was a highly choreographed performance with a strong rhythmic cadence matched to his breathing. I ate a plateful of kebabs. As I finished the man from the next stall offered me some carrot halwa. 'I'll have some,' I said, 'but only if you pour off all that excess ghee (fat).' I washed my kebabs and halwa down with a glass of pomegranate juice.

As I ate, I became aware of being watched by a barber across the street. He was sitting by the roadside inviting passers-by to sample his expertise. My meal concluded, he waved towards me and asked me to come over. For reasons beyond my conscious mind, automatically, I responded to his call.

'Come and sit down right here, Sahib,' said the barber, cleaning a chair knocked together from a few odd pieces of wood. 'After a meal like that you deserve a relaxing shave.' Uneasily I sat on the chair, it creaked alarmingly as it accepted my weight. He tied a towel, which had already served several customers that morning, round my neck.

'They call me Rustom,' he said, 'after the great Persian wrestler who defeated all his opponents.' He poured some hot water from his kettle into a soup can. He then dipped a brush possessing few remnant hairs into the boiling water and splashed it all over my face. He rubbed his brush as vigorously as its condition permitted on a bar of soap and proceeded to paint my face with the resultant lather. His movements were quick, yet just as with the kebab seller, there was an element of choreographed ritual in everything he did. Once he had generated a profuse lather on my face, he installed a blade in his razor. Actually, from the corner of my eye I noted it was only half a blade; the other half was safely tucked away for later use. Once his implement was armed and ready, Rustom gripped my head with his large, left palm and with his right hand set about attacking my stubble.

Rustom gave individual attention to every single hair. If the razor did not remove the hair at the first go, which was frequently the case, he did not hesitate to try again. Often four or five determined efforts were required before he succeeded. At each successive attempt he approached his task with renewed vigour, each effort removing another layer of my skin. When I could endure no longer, 'Ouch,' I exclaimed and weakly enquired, 'Do you shave everyone like this?'

'I am taking particular care because I want the Sahib to come back,' said Rustom. 'But there are a few customers . . .' he paused for a grin, 'I don't want them to come back. My special treatment is reserved for them.'

'And who might these customers be?'

'Mostly they're soldiers. We have no way of telling them how we feel about their government. You know this is the third time they've grabbed power, and now that they have a taste for power, God knows how we will get back to civilian rule. But you'd be surprised at what they'll put up with once they are underneath my razor. It's my only chance to hit back. So they get a special treatment. It is a very satisfying experience for me.'

'So you don't like President Zia-ul-Haq?' I asked innocently.

The moment the words 'Zia-ul-Haq' issued from my mouth, Rustom jerked, and instinctively pressed the blade against my cheek.

'I am so sorry,' Rustom was apologetic. 'But don't worry, Sahib. I have some *phitcurry*. It's very good for cuts. Stops bleeding instantly.'

And before I could say anything, Rustom was holding a small, irregular opaque crystal in his hand. He rubbed it on a few particularly bad cuts, giving his attention to the biggest and freshest. It felt as if he had set fire to my face. I yelled in agony. And the more I yelled the more *phitcurry* he put on my face. But the bleeding continued.

'Ah,' Rustom exclaimed. 'I forgot. You are not from this part of the world, are you? Traditional remedies don't have effect on people who have left Pakistan to live in the West. I have a modern solution. It will stop the bleeding in no time.'

He then produced a box of Johnson's Baby Powder and smothered my face with it.

'There,' he said, proudly placing a broken mirror in front of me, 'It's stopped.' I looked into the mirror and surveyed a strange face. Just so must people feel as they emerge from their swathes of bandages to examine the results of plastic surgery. Underneath the extensive layer of dusty lunar white powder numerous bright red blood clots were clearly visible. Rustom read the look of horror in my expression.

'Do not worry, Sahib. Do not worry. When I have finished shaving you will look like a newborn child.'

He pushed me back on his wobbly chair, wiped my face with a wet towel, smothered it with foam again, and continued as if nothing had happened.

'Sahib,' he said, 'do you live in America?'

'No,' I replied, 'I live in London.'

'Ah!' he retorted, lingering and extending the 'h' for several seconds. He proceeded to regale me with his thoughts on the Queen, the Mother of All Parliaments, and Mrs Thatcher, 'the mother of all mothers', as he put it.

Would he, I asked just to change the conversation, like Shariah Law to be established in Pakistan?

The word 'Shariah' generated the same effect as the words 'Zia-ul-Haq'. Rustom jerked, his hand slipped, and my face recorded a new cut. 'What's the matter with you?' I shouted as I jumped off his chair. 'Sahib, Sahib, I am so very, very sorry. But you do keep mentioning all those special subjects that deserve special attention.'

'What do you mean?' I enquired naively.

'Think about it,' Rustom said. 'What would I, a barber, do if the bearded ones become the masters of our society? What I want is a decent living, proper education for my children, a proper roof over my head. What their Shariah will give me is public floggings, beheadings, compulsory beards and lock my poor long-suffering wife and daughter behind *purdah*.'

'So you are against the Shariah?'

'No, Sahib, I am not against the Shariah. I am against the Shariah of the bearded ones. For their Shariah knows nothing of justice and mercy, forgiveness and generosity. In the name of the Shariah, they want to ban everything. Cinema. Music. Television. It is this joyless Shariah that promotes fear and hatred that I am against. And I am against all those, particularly the military and bearded types, who want to impose it on us.'

I reinserted myself unsteadily in his unsteady chair.

'I agree with you,' I said. 'I too am against the military and bearded types and their brand of the Shariah.'

Rustom looked very pleased. 'Why didn't you say so?' he said, tapping me on my shoulders. 'We are brothers. I thought you were one of those England-returns who think the Shariah is a bar of soap and the only way to apply it is to force people to scrub themselves silly with it.'

Rustom's whole manner now changed, as did his shaving style. He worked with exceptional gentleness. When he finished shaving, he splashed some Old Spice aftershave in his hands, and proceeded to apply it generously to my face. The moment the aftershave made contact with my skin, I performed an ejection manoeuvre from Rustom's rickety chair. 'How much do I owe you?' I asked, eager to make a hasty exit.

'For Sahib only one rupee. After all Sahib is my brother. And I hope to see you tomorrow.'

Involuntarily I cringed at the thought. 'Here's a hundred rupees.' I slipped a crisp note into his hand. 'It will save you shaving me for the next ninety-nine days.'

'Sahib,' Rustom said, accepting the note and looking remorseful, 'please forgive me for the special close shave I gave you. I did not know.'

'Never mind,' I replied, nursing my face, 'I'll know better next time.' Just so.

'By the way,' Rustom shouted, as I was walking away, 'if you are going to Islamabad don't bother looking for a taxi. I'd take the wagon if I were you.'

A wagon was cruising nearby. I ran towards it without answering, my waving arm serving as a signal to the conductor and my farewell to Rustom. The wagon slowed a little. I increased my pace and managed to get a foothold, unaware of another man, just behind me, desperately trying to do the same. Having secured my place I turned my head, anxious to offer Rustom a departing greeting. What I saw was the lunging would-be passenger. When it seemed he would be left behind, the conductor, hanging from the bar on the side next to the entrance, swooped down to give this man a hand. He grabbed him by his dhoti – the loose piece of cloth guarding his loins – and just managed to find a spot for him on the outer rims of the entrance. I turned my attention to insinuating myself in the available space. Behind me I overheard the panting passenger angrily observe: 'You should look before you pull people up!' 'And why do you passengers have to wear dhotis? Why can't you wear trousers like the Sahib before you?' the conductor snapped back.

I managed to turn around and see what was happening. Gasping for breath the man was holding on to the conductor with both hands, clinging closely not only to secure his place but to shield his modesty. He was wearing a badly fitting shirt but was naked from the waist downwards. Behind us a long streamer of cloth waved forlornly to the departing wagon as it hurried down the highway to Islamabad.

The following day we flew to Beijing. At the Kunlun Hotel, by the bank of Liangma River in the opulent Chaoyang District, where we were staying, Muslims from all over China had gathered for a conference. Ostensibly, we were discussing the problems of Muslims in China. But it transpired Muslims in China had no real problems. Or at least such was the view of representatives of the China Islamic Association. The days of the Cultural Revolution, when Muslims and other religious communities bore the brunt of attacks by the Red Guard who turned on mosques, religious ceremonies and Islamic beliefs, were over. Tolerance was the new watchword. This meant Chinese Muslims could maintain and manage their mosques, even build new ones, and freely participate in religious ceremonies, and that a large number could go on Hajj, the annual pilgrimage to Mecca, without any bother. The official view asserted that as long as Islam in China did not conflict with the interests of the State, it was in the interest of the State to encourage it.

But all was not harmony. Conflict existed within and between various groups of Chinese Muslims and between the State and the Muslims, and it centred on the Shariah. Whenever one spoke privately to people attending the conference they invariably expressed their strong desire for the Shariah, in whispered tones. I spent the first day of the conference, destined to last a week, listening to official presentations. The next day I broke away from the main event to talk to various groups I had identified as dissidents. I soon discovered the mainstream Muslims in China call themselves *gedimu*, which is a literal translation of the Arabic word *al qadim*, 'the ancient'. The oldest and most established tradition of Islam in China is of Sunnis belonging to the Hanafi School of Law. So the *gedimu*, followers of the 'Old Teaching', are, by and large, orthodox Muslims for whom, like orthodox Muslims everywhere, the Shariah is of paramount importance. Without the Shariah they felt incomplete as Muslims. 'An essential part of our identity,' I was told, 'is missing.' But at the conference there were a number of groups representing 'New Teachings' and 'New New Teachings'. These were Sufi orders or brotherhoods, largely from the north-west of China. They referred to themselves as *menhuan*, a Chinese term that corresponds to the Arabic word *silsila*, meaning the chain of hereditary Sufi masters who trace their lineage and authority right back to the Prophet Muhammad himself. The *menhuan* claimed – I think rightly – that they were largely responsible for preserving Chinese Islam during the Cultural Revolution. And it is not the Shariah – the way of the Islamic Law – that completed the identity of Chinese Muslims but the *tariqa* – the way of the Sufi mystic. Most astonishing, the majority of Muslims I met in China, both young and old, spoke fluent Arabic.

The conference, in the style of grand conferences, was punctuated with various cultural events. Lavish dinners, visits to the Forbidden City, the Great Wall of China, and a string of mosques. On Friday, we were taken en masse for the congregational prayer by Imam Sulaiman Gong Qinzhi, deputy Secretary-General of the China Islamic Association. Through a translator, Imam Sulaiman furnished us with some background material. It was a cumbersome process, but most of us managed to get the gist of what he was saying. Muslims first came to China in the hundred years after the advent of Islam. Evidence for this is provided by Muslim tombstones discovered in Quanzhou City,

Fujian Province, which date back to Teng Dynasty in the seventh century. For at least 300 years, throughout the Song (960–1279) and Yuan (1279–1368) dynasties, wave upon wave of Muslim merchants, scholars and travellers came to China and settled in the country. In the seventh century Muslims learned the art of papermaking from the Chinese and imported the paper industry to Samarkand, Baghdad, Fez and Cordova. One of the most noted travellers to China was none other than the Moroccan globe-trotter, Ibn Battuta, who visited the country in the thirteenth century. Most Muslims in China are of Hui nationality; many are descendants of the merchants and scholars who first came from Arabia and Persia during the ninth and tenth centuries. The men tend to be tall and handsome; women slim and elegant. The oldest mosque in China is the Huaisheng Mosque in Guangzhou which was built in the early seventh century. It is known locally as the Light Pagoda because its lighted minaret once served as a navigation guide.

Imam Sulaiman knew his facts. But doesn't everyone have an obsession with facts and statistics in China? He changed gear, and came down from the broad sweep of history to more recent times and to Beijing. Some 60 million Muslims now live in China, he informed us. In Beijing alone there are over fifty mosques, numerous halal restaurants, and certain neighbourhoods where almost everyone is a Muslim. Indeed, Wung Fu Xing, one of the most famous streets in the city, has a high-rise building which is inhabited totally by Muslim families. Al-Hajj Abdul Rahim Horuni was the first to establish a school in Beijing. That was in 1609. After that Jamal Uddin, an astronomer, established an observatory which is still in use. During the Cultural Revolution (1966–76), Muslims were harshly suppressed; and the Association of Chinese Muslims, formed in 1951, was itself banned. But the open door policy, after 'the elimination of the Gang of Four', ushered in a new era of Islamic revivalism. The magnificent new Islamic Centre and the head office of the Association were recently completed – built with the help of Saudi Arabia. An Islamic museum was under construction. The Faud Library, donated by King Faud of Egypt, had been reopened. An Islamic Institute was established at Beijing University in 1982. All eight universities in Beijing now have active departments of Arabic; and Arabic is also being taught at a number of foreign language institutes. 'You should not be surprised to discover' – as I had discovered already – 'that most of our young people speak fluent Arabic,' Imam Sulaiman said in matter-of-fact style.

We arrived at the Niujie Street Mosque to discover that the sermon for the Friday prayer had already started. Imam Sulaiman had told us that it was built in 996 and has two rectangular double-eaved minarets, a hexagonal tower in the middle of the spacious courtyard and a number of ancillary buildings. The mosque was crowded to saturation point. I managed to find a foothold near the entrance of the magnificent prayer hall. From the outside, the Niujie Street Mosque looked less like a mosque than a pagoda; in fact, a number of pagodas. But once inside the single-eaved prayer hall, it was difficult to tell this was a mosque in China; unless, of course, one looked for a dome! The ceiling had an intricate design of intertwining plants and the walls combined calligraphy with lotus flowers.

After the prayer, I joined a discussion group of adolescent Muslims. All of them were students of Arabic, some had come from other parts of China to study at the Arabic Departments of various Foreign Language Institutes. 'Why are you so keen on Arabic?' I asked them collectively.

'It is the language of the Qur'an,' answered a young man with a beard consisting of at most three hairs. 'Without Arabic we would not have direct access to the Qur'an. And without understanding the Qur'an how are we going to implement the Shariah in our lives?'

A girl, unusually tall by Chinese standards, joined in. 'Everyone now recognizes the mass character of Islam. People in Yinchuan in Ningxia Hui Autonomous Region, where I come from, now appreciate that Islam is not spiritual opium or the same as ignorance and superstition but a kind of ethics able to help promote society's moral and economic development. Party members are now asked to respect religious activities and they are forbidden to preach atheism and Communism in the mosques. Since 1978 we have been building new mosques and there are 2,200 mosques in the Region, one in each village of over 1,000 Muslims. All these mosques need qualified Imams who speak and understand Arabic, can teach the Qur'an and explain the finer points of the Shariah.'

'When you say you want to implement the Shariah what do you mean?' I enquired.

'We want our lives to be governed by the Shariah. We want our family relations and communal affairs to be decided on the basis of the Islamic personal law. We want Islamic criminal law and prescribed punishments to operate on the level of society,' replied the tall girl.

'Do you want to end up looking like Saudi Arabia?'

The students looked at each other. They were clearly surprised by my questions. 'We want to look like any other Islamic society,' they replied in unison. The tall girl added: 'We want Islam in its totality. Not just the few bits that the officials choose to give us.'

We were joined by two Pakistanis who, I learned later, held senior positions at the Pakistani Embassy. Afterwards, over dinner, Saleem and Iqbal Sahibs suggested I should spend some time in a Muslim village. 'It will be a good opportunity for you to experience village life at close quarters and you will be able to get a different perspective on Islam in China,' said Iqbal Sahib, who held the rank of First Secretary. And, what's more, given a few days, they would be able to organize an official visit for me through the good offices of the Embassy! I could hardly believe my good fortune.

When the conference finished, I said farewell to my friends and the luxurious Kunlun Hotel and moved into a modest guest house. During the conference, I had become quite friendly with a lecturer in English at the Department of Foreign Languages at Beijing's Northern Jiatong University. Aisha Ling Feng, a beautiful petite woman in her late twenties, described herself as a Hui. Unlike other Muslim groups, such as Uyghur or Kazakh, who are located in specific regions and have their own Turkic languages, the Hui are spread all over China – they can be found in every province and every city – and speak the regional form of Chinese that prevails where they live. Aisha was a bit depressed as her fiancé had abruptly broken off their engagement. 'Would you mind terribly,' she said one day during a heavy-handed session on the history of Islam in China, 'if I became your friend?' 'Not at all,' I replied, 'I have an affinity for depressed people.' From then on, she stayed by my side and became my personal translator. She would collect me from the guest house every morning and take me for a guided tour of the Muslim districts of Beijing. We visited a number of local *madrasahs, qingzhensi* (which literary means 'temple of pure truth', the most commonly used term for a mosque in China) and even joined in a *zikr* – remembrance of Allah – session with a *menhuan* Sufi order. One morning Aisha declared that she was fed up ushering me around the Beijing Muslim community. 'Wouldn't you like to do something different?' she said. 'Would you like to visit the Forbidden City again? Or, perhaps, the Great Wall Sheraton Hotel?'

'Not really,' I replied.

'Would you like to play golf? Beijing now has a new eighteen-hole, seventy-two-par International Golf Club. It opened last year. It's very good, the Japanese are helping us to manage it.'

'Any other options?'

'We can go to the North China International Shooting Academy. It's world renowned. You can fire all sort of rifles, sub-machine guns, anti-aircraft guns, and even anti-tank rocket launchers.'

'How about something a little less combative?'

'I know,' Aisha exclaimed, 'let's go to the stock exchange. I went there a few months ago with my fiancé. It's great fun; totally mad.'

'Somewhere a little more sane, perhaps?'

Aisha was racking her brains. I noticed a commotion at one end of the lobby of the guest house. 'Ah! There is a fashion show at the International Hotel. We will go there,' she announced with a sense of joy.

'Let's go and find out what the fuss over there is all about, first,' I said. We walked to the crowd. An exceptionally old and lean Chinese man was giving free demonstrations of the ancient art of qigong. A younger man was explaining the performance in an immaculate American accent to the gathering, consisting largely of foreign visitors. 'Today qigong has gained a new meaning in China,' he said. 'It has once again won attention and been put through strict and scientific tests. Millions of people have felt certain effects in the course of qigong experiences, which differ from traditional western religious experiences and modern-day superstition. Qigong is not so much a belief as a successful practice. It has received support from more and more intellectuals and scientists. It constitutes a decisive breakthrough opening exciting possibilities for direct interaction between thought and matter.' We learned that the old man giving the demonstration was a distinguished qigong master. There were six main schools of qigong: Taoist, Buddhist, Confucian, medical, wushu (martial arts) and anonymous. 'The theory and technique of qigong,' the young man with an American accent went on to say, 'is now being taught in thirty-seven Chinese universities; and over 50 million people follow its routines on a daily basis. Qigong can help people in all sorts of ways from improving health to curing inoperable cancers. It can also improve personal talents. Concentration and memory, and consequently grades, have gone up in ordinary schools where qigong is used. Masters of the technique have achieved a wide range of success by releasing *waiqi* [outside breath] into sick people.' A long queue had formed. I joined the queue.

'You don't have to stand in the queue,' Aisha said, pulling my hand. 'I will do *waiqi* on you. What are friends for?'

I liked the idea. 'Sure,' I mumbled. And let her have her way with me.

I was made to sit comfortably on a chair in a quiet corner of the lobby. She covered my face with the palms of her hands and began to move her hands, very slowly, towards my chest and then lower parts of my body. Her hands never actually touched me, they were always a centimetre or two above the surface. She asked me to close my eyes and continued the process for over forty minutes, moving to my legs, and up again, to my back and down to the toes. When she finished I had a tingling feeling throughout my body. I felt refreshed and warm. And hungry.

'Thanks so much,' I said to Aisha. 'Whenever I need a *waiqi* session I will come to you. Which school of qigong do you subscribe to?'

'Anonymous,' she replied. And we both laughed.

'Let's go for dinner,' I said.

'Good idea,' Aisha replied. 'I am going to take you out for a special meal.'

I followed her to a limousine masquerading as a taxi outside the guest house. We pulled up at the south-west corner of Tiananmen Square. Aisha jumped out of the taxi and pointed to the restaurant, announcing triumphantly: 'This is the biggest Kentucky Fried Chicken Restaurant in the world. It opened only this week.' We walked in and Aisha read off various statistics on a placard inside the restaurant. 'Its three floors cover 1,080 square metres and it can seat 500 people. The automatic cookers turn out 2,300 pieces an hour and they can fry 1,300 chickens every day. The most any other Kentucky Fried Chicken Restaurant can fry is 1,000. On an average day the restaurant serves over 1,000 people an hour. On weekends, this number can reach 1,800 to 2,000. More than 100,000 people pass by the restaurant every day . . .'

The following morning Aisha arrived early. 'Today,' she said enthusiastically, 'I want you to come with me for a video recording.'

'Video recording? What kind of video recording?' I was intrigued.

'A couple of kilometres from the University, there is a woman who runs a service,' Aisha explained. 'She charges three yuan for women and thirteen yuan for men.'

'What kind of service?'

'You know. We speak into a colour video camera. She shows them to her other clients. This creates more and better chances for men and women to get acquainted with each other by means of modern communication technology.'

'Ah. I see,' I said, decoding the local patois into the more familiar terminology of a computer dating agency with refinements. 'But why would we need such a service?' I asked.

'The service also tells people if they are compatible,' Aisha said, looking a little shy.

I realized what was happening. 'Aisha,' I said, 'I am already married.'

She held my hand lovingly. 'But the Shariah allows Muslim men to take more than one wife,' she replied. Then she put her arms around me, rested her head on my chest, and whispered: 'I can be your second wife.'

'Oh!' I exclaimed, taken aback and retreating hastily from this sudden turn of events. 'I don't actually believe that part of the Shariah.'

Aisha looked shocked. She released me from her grip and took a few steps back. 'Are you telling me you are not a true Muslim? Why have you been visiting all those mosques and joining in all those prayers, then?'

'Well,' I said, trying to explain myself simply, 'one can be a Muslim without believing every bit of the Shariah as it exists nowadays.'

She looked puzzled; and a little dejected at my response. Then she pulled herself up to her full height and delivered what was obviously intended to be a defiant put-down. 'The Arab brothers,' she said, 'are always looking for a second or a third wife. But you choose to believe in only those bits of the Shariah that serve your purpose.'

The Pakistani Embassy officials arrived as I was explaining my view of the Shariah to Aisha. Most Muslims consider the Shariah to be divine. But there is nothing divine about the Shariah, I explained. The only thing that can legitimately be described as divine in Islam is the Qur'an. The Shariah is a human construction; an attempt to understand the divine will in a particular context – and that context happens to be eighth-century Muslim society. We need to understand the Shariah in our own context; and reconstruct it from first principles. The Pakistanis urged me to hurry up. If I was interested in visiting Muslim villages, I had to accompany them straight away. What to do? I left Aisha looking rather sad, and drove with them to Quanju and Chen Yen, twin villages about thirty-five kilometres from Beijing. The wide, multi-laned roads of Beijing quickly gave way to a single, overcrowded, dusty road that led to Quanju. The splendours of Beijing were replaced by abject poverty. It took us three hours to cover just over twenty kilometres once we had left the motorway. Quanju and Chen Yen are less than a kilometre apart, but both boasted active mosques. The mosque at Quanju, a historic monument, was being renovated by the villagers. The Chen Yen mosque had been built by the inhabitants of the village, after the Cultural Revolution. It was not quite finished. At Quanju, we were greeted by Musa Hui, Imam of the mosque. He showed us around with undiluted pride. The mosque looked like a pagoda surrounded by a rectangular room. The wooden roof nestled on brick walls. Inside, the walls were decorated with richly coloured Chinese flowers and calligraphic patterns. Occasionally, the heating pipes, carrying hot steam, protruded from the walls or came down from the ceiling making it difficult for a visitor to fully appreciate the calligraphy. Musa Hui informed us the mosque was built in the early fifteenth century and was almost destroyed during the Cultural Revolution. The government was now providing the villagers with a small grant to renovate it; he also received his salary of a few hundred yuan from the State. We joined the congregation, made up of a large proportion of the 6,000 residents of the village, for evening prayers. Afterwards, we were ushered into the Imam's study, which also served as a library, for tea and Chinese fare.

The focus of Musa Hui's study, like most rooms in a Chinese house, was an iron stove. The fuel consisted of pellets made from coal dust, with numerous holes that increased the surface area. Every few minutes the Imam would pick up a pellet or two and shove them inside the stove. The smoke produced passed through a roughly made tin pipe which touched the ceiling, turned, and made its serpentine way to an outlet on the far wall. The heat generated provided just about adequate warmth for the room – the tin pipes acted as radiators – and was also used for cooking and making tea. We sat round the stove, drinking tea and leafing through the collection of ancient manuscripts, some clearly even older than the mosque itself. I spent some time looking through a history of Muslims in China written in Arabic, while Saleem Sahib admired an illuminated fifteenth-century book of Chinese medicine. As we were looking through the manuscripts, the assistant Imam, Haji Noorudin, invited us to his house. I was going to be his guest, I was told, during my stay in the village.

Haji Noorudin lived with his wife and four-year-old daughter, Afia, in a two-room house about five minutes' walk from the mosque. All three spoke fluent Arabic. The rooms were very small (around three by two metres), but, I learned, were normal by Chinese standards. Each room had a single entrance. The bedroom had a double bed, the inevitable coal-pellet black stove, and a huge pile of cabbages that the Haji and his wife had saved for winter. In the living room was a washbasin adjacent to a gas cooker, a table, and in one corner a half-sized wardrobe on top of which rested a Sony colour TV. A mattress was laid out in front of the TV as my bed. Saleem and Iqbal Sahib left me with the Noorudin family, promising to return after a week to take me back to Beijing.

The following morning, after a simple breakfast of noodles and tea, I asked if I could visit the toilet. The Haji asked me to follow him; we walked some fifty metres from the house. He pointed towards a low-roofed brick building inside which a series of cubicles containing squat type toilets were plainly visible. Each cubicle had a small door, but the entire arrangement was obviously made to serve Lilliputians. It was like being ushered to the toilets of a primary school. Any normal-sized adult who squatted within their individual cubicle would remain clearly visible to the occupants of all other cubicles and would be able to conduct a diverting conversation. I noticed all the current occupants had an open book they were diligently trying to read. It was a relief, but I could find nothing else relieving about the experience. I stood inside the communal toilet building – but couldn't quite get myself to enter a cubicle.

Throughout my stay, the residents of both villages took great pride in entertaining me. Every evening I was invited for dinner – mostly cabbage and noodles – at a different house. And wherever I went, I was always accompanied by Imam Hui and Haji Noorudin. The conversations always started with hardships of the Cultural Revolution, moved to the death of Maoism and Marxism, meandered towards the open door policy and democracy and concluded with the importance of Islam for the villagers. It soon became evident that the most cherished and passionate desire of the inhabitants of the twin villages of Quanju and Chen Yen was for the Shariah. More than democracy, more than wealth, they wanted their daily lives to be regulated by Islamic Law. As the days passed I realized their emotional and spiritual yearning was not altogether different from my own immediate and physical desire. Each morning I would go to the communal toilet and try to muster enough courage to enter a cubicle. Each day, I would return after abject failure. So by day four, totally overloaded with cabbages, I was simultaneously constipated and bursting to go. Was this, I wondered, an apt metaphor for the general Muslim condition?

By the time the Pakistani Councillors returned to collect me, I was in bad shape. They were extremely generous and gracious. Not only did they arrange for me to visit a toilet I could actually use, they also found a seat for me on the next available PIA flight back to Islamabad. While waiting for the flight, I thought about the intractable hold the Shariah had on the Muslim consciousness. Even the Chinese Muslim community, so isolated and cut off from the mainstream of the Muslim world, had an unbridled passion for the Shariah. It was the main vehicle of their Muslim identity; it is precisely what makes them – the Chinese

Muslims as well as Muslims all over the world – different from all others. But, I asked myself repeatedly, is it necessary for this difference to be expressed solely in terms of medieval formulae, through the opinions and analysis of ancient religious scholars? By constantly falling back on a historical construction of the Shariah, Muslim communities had become passive receivers rather than active seekers of truth. The notion that centuries-old social constructions could solve all their contemporary problems served as a psychological balm. Nostalgia and certainty may turn out to be a potent mixture. Still, as I had discovered, not everyone who desired the Shariah lives in the past: I thought of Aisha, so deeply attached to the Shariah yet so 'modern' in her behaviour.

I returned to Islamabad in the middle of a scandal. At the centre of the outrage was a shy, severely myopic, twenty-year-old woman called Sofia Bibi. She had given birth to a child out of wedlock. After the birth Sofia's father lodged a complaint charging his daughter with *zina*, the technical term for sex-related crimes in the Shariah. Sofia accused a man, Maqsood Ahmed, of raping her nine months earlier and being responsible for her pregnancy. The police registered a case against both Sofia and Maqsood. The court ruled there was insufficient evidence against Maqsood; they declared Sofia's testimony to be inadmissible. She was thus sentenced under the *zina* ordinance to three years' imprisonment, fifteen lashes, and a fine. The case, one of the first to be tried under President Zia's 'Islamization Programme', became a cause célèbre. It was covered extensively in Pakistani newspapers and magazines, as well as the international press. As it turned out, the appeal court declared that 'if an unmarried woman delivering a child pleads that the birth was a result of a commission of rape upon her, she cannot be punished', and Sofia was set free. But the Sofia Bibi affair raised some important questions about the Shariah's treatment of women.

'Just what is the Shariah's problem with women?' I asked my friend Asma Barlas. Asma was one of the first women to join Pakistan's Foreign Service. But the promising career of this elegant diplomat was cut short by President Zia-ul-Haq who took exception to her criticism of his military regime and fired her. When I met her she was working as assistant editor of *The Muslim*, a reputable opposition paper. Asma had acquired a fierce reputation as an outspoken feminist scholar of Islam, particularly concerned with the politics of meaning and construction of religious knowledge in Islam. She had all the learned trappings of a Mullah – or as they called her in Pakistan, a *Maulani* – and all the passion of a fighter for women's rights. Indeed, as she admitted to me one day, she seemed to have an innate need to rescue, much like Don Quixote, any woman in trouble.

'It really is a shame,' Asma began, 'that what passes as Islamic law does not do an adequate job of reflecting the general ethos or even the specific teachings of Islam's own scripture.' The Shariah, she explained, was formulated by jurists, all of them male, during the Abbasid period (749–1258), a time in history well known for its sexism and misogyny. This male bias is evident in the way the Shariah treats women and men unequally, particularly when it comes to criminal justice. An obvious example relates to testimonies where we have the notorious 'two-for-one formula'. 'Equating the testimony of two women with that of one man,' said Asma, 'naturally leads to a view of the woman being half a man.' But, explained Asma, the Qur'an discusses at least five cases which involve the giving of evidence, and in only one case does it suggest taking two women as witnesses in place of one man. In the far more crucial case of adultery, the Qur'an privileges the testimony of the wife over that of the husband. So, for example, if a husband charges his wife with adultery and cannot produce four male witnesses to the act of penetration, he cannot serve as his own witness. In such instances, the Qur'an allows the wife to testify on her own behalf and if she swears her innocence, it does not give her husband any further legal recourse against her. 'Now, the classical jurists did not take this to mean that men should testify in fours or that the woman's word outranks that of the man's!'

The Shariah also fails to distinguish between different types of extramarital sex, Asma said. For example, it does not differentiate between adultery, fornication and rape. As a result, women who are victims of rape and sexual abuse can find themselves – and have found themselves, not just in Pakistan but also other Muslim countries like Nigeria and the Sudan – being charged with a crime and sentenced to be stoned to death. 'Stoning to death,' Asma emphasized, 'is another aberrant law since the Qur'an does not sanction stoning to death for *any* crime whatsoever.'

'Perhaps,' I said, 'the classical jurists could not do better for they were a product of their own time. And knowledge cannot be produced in a vacuum.'

'But we can and should,' Asma replied with an emphatic tone. 'We are able to do better given that we have so many centuries of experience with the law and know that its stance on sexual equality is wrong and not at all in accordance with the teachings of the Qur'an.'

'So why don't we?'

'Because to call for reforming the Shariah is equated with an attack on Islam,' Asma replied with hesitation. The Mullahs have been particularly clever in equating religion with law. By conflating law with religion, an effort to reform the law is made to look like an attempt to change the religion. To change the Shariah we have to stand up to powerfully entrenched clerics and interpretive communities who will put up a deafening roar against such an exercise on the grounds that it is un-Islamic or even anti-Islamic. And in this way they continue to underwrite their own monopoly on religious knowledge. 'Another irony for a people whose religion does not sanction a class of professional interpreters of religious knowledge in the form of a clergy.'

'Why are we Muslims so attached to this unjust notion of the Shariah?' I asked, thinking about all those Chinese villagers and ordinary Pakistanis who held so fervently to a romanticized notion of the Shariah.

'The Shariah and veiling for women have become the quintessential symbols of Islam. As we know, the veneration of symbols can keep people from thinking about what the symbols actually symbolize.' She thought for a moment. 'I guess it's like the irrational flag-worship we see in such places as the USA in times of crisis or war. The more Muslims have felt ideologically attacked and threatened by western secularism and, prior to that, colonialism, the more deeply wedded they've become to an unthinking veneration of certain symbols they associate with their religion. It all adds up to a totalistic notion of Islam.'

A few months after our conversation, Asma was hounded out of Pakistan and forced to seek political asylum in the USA. Back in

London, when I heard the news, I could not get our conversation out of my mind. How much more could she have done? How much more could Muslim society everywhere be if it liberated the efforts of all the believers, female and male? I kept thinking about that word: 'totalistic'. President Zia-ul-Haq wished to impose Islam in its 'totality'. The students I had met at Madrasah Haqqania desired nothing less than 'total Shariah'. The Afghan leaders talked constantly of 'Islam as a totalistic way of life'. Even the Chinese villagers and students wanted their lives to be governed by 'Islam in its totality'.

I started rereading the literature on Islamization, the topic that had been the focus of Ijmali attention. Soon, I discovered that 'totalistic' was a favourite word for one of its main architects, Ismail al-Faruqi. 'The Islamic state is totalistic,' he states categorically in *The Cultural Atlas of Islam*, which he wrote with his wife, Lamya, 'insofar as the imperatives of God are not only morally binding on all humans but are also relevant to every human activity.' What made an Islamic state Islamic was the Shariah, whose application, Al-Faruqi asserted, 'is the *raison d'être* of the state'. The Shariah, he insists, 'is comprehensive, covering every field and every action'. 'The Islamic social order,' he explained further in his *Tawhid: Its Implications for Thought and Life*, 'is *totalist*' (his emphasis): 'the totalism of the Islamic social order does not only pertain to present human activities and their objectives. It includes all activities in all times and places, as well as all the humans who are the subjects of these activities'; all Muslims are 'conscripts in its programs and projects'. I found this view of the Shariah and Islamic social order rather frightening; and became very depressed.

Ever since *Inquiry* had folded, Parvez Manzoor too had become very depressed. He would ring me frequently, talk endlessly about the sorry state of the *ummah*, and would only give up when both of us were firmly mired in the slough of despond up to our armpits. When he rang me after my visit to Pakistan and China and discovered that I was already depressed he was taken aback. 'Come and stay with me for a few days,' he suggested. 'We can be depressed together and try to console each other.' It should have reminded me of that line in Marlowe's *Dr Faustus*, the explanation of hell that runs something along the lines of 'misery loves company'. On previous experience the prospect of being consoled by ET was dim to nonexistent but I accepted his offer. He had started writing under the pseudonym Abu Laila Sulani, in which guise he was surprisingly coherent. We spent a few days in his house in Salantuna, one of the most monotonous parts of the remarkably boring city of Stockholm, watching Indian films and listening to Urdu poetry together. Parvez had an insatiable appetite for old Indian film songs. He had gathered a huge collection of song videos acquired over decades from his numerous visits to London and Karachi. He would play his favourite songs again and again and again. But any sane mind can only take so much. To distract him from slipping yet another video in the player, I asked him to explain the significance of the term Shariah.

'Ayatollah!' he began pontificating in his usual way. 'Muslim consciousness conceives of the Shariah in three complementary ways: as truth, method and history.' He went on to explain that Shariah perceives the world as *history* rather than *cosmos*, morality as an *event* rather than an *idea*, and faith as *acting* the Will of God rather than *knowing* His Essence. The best way of describing the Shariah, he suggested, would be as 'the ethics of action'. The moral perspective of the Shariah, for instance, demands 'doing right' rather than 'being good'. Thus, to call the Shariah 'Law' is to do violence to its multiple meanings.

'So, in essence, the Shariah is morality and ethics rather than law,' I said.

'Precisely,' Parvez shot back, looking rather pleased with himself. 'But the Muslim mind does not distinguish between ethics and law.'

'What if law becomes unethical? And truth becomes equated with method?'

'Ah,' said Parvez, 'this is precisely what happened in Islamic history.'

I was now led on a historical detour. There was no Shariah at the time of Prophet Muhammad, Parvez explained. For almost 150 years after the death of the Prophet, the accumulated ensemble of the exercise of 'learning' and 'understanding', which was the religious knowledge of Islam, was not called the Shariah. This knowledge was largely personal, free and somewhat subjective. The first act of objectification and reification occurred during the early Abbasid period when this accumulated knowledge was confused with history. From this period onwards, the exercise of learning was no longer seen as the history-making enterprise of Islam but as a product of Muslim history itself. Thus, history became a substitute for religious inquiry and learning. Learning was seen not as the process of reasoning and understanding but as the historically frozen corpus of juristic rulings. The Will of God, which was previously discovered through intellectual methods, was now seen as being expressed in injunctions and prohibitions. 'It was this reification that came to be known as the Shariah,' Parvez declared.

From the second Islamic century onwards there emerged a set of mechanisms, or disciplines, for understanding the Word of God. Towards the end of the Abbasid period, that is around the thirteenth century, this mechanism, known collectively as *fiqh*, came to constitute 'the jurisprudence of Islam'. It entirely determined the form and content of the Shariah. 'The "method" of the Shariah became indistinguishable from the "truth" of Islam itself,' Parvez explained.

'So, in fact, the Shariah, as understood by Muslims today, has nothing really to do with the truth of Islam. It is in fact largely *fiqh*, a body of historically frozen judicial thought and rulings?'

'Indeed,' replied Parvez. 'It is a theoretically founded mechanism for traditional authoritarianism. Small wonder that Islamic theology and law have developed little since then.'

We both concurred that the method of the Shariah does not encourage bold, innovative and speculative thought. Its preoccupation with existentially concrete 'dos' and 'don'ts' stifles creative imagination, and as a consequence, makes Shariah-minded individuals and cultures conservative and backward-looking in their general outlook on life. Far from being an enterprise of liberation, it had become a tool of oppression.

Parvez got up to change the cassette in his video player. 'What is the connection between the Shariah and Islamic fundamentalism, Maulvi?' I asked.

He returned to his armchair. 'It has to be understood,' he began, 'that Islamic fundamentalism is a modern heresy. It has no historical precedent; it is not based on a classical religious narrative or Muslim tradition. It is a recently concocted dogma. And what makes it modern is the notion of the State. There is no notion of a nation-state, based on geographical boundaries, in classical Islam as such. Traditionally, we have been concerned largely with community and empire. Islamic fundamentalism combines a constructed, romantic and puritan past with the modernist ideal of a nation confined in a territorial nation-state to generate a wholly new religious and political outlook.'

'So what is so special about this outlook?'

'Well, what is special about Islamic fundamentalism, and what distinguishes it from traditional Islam, is the fact that the idea of "state" is "fundamental" to its vision of Islam and represents a paramount fact of its consciousness.' This is why all Islamic fundamentalists zealously pursue the ideal of an Islamic state – for them, Islam is simply not complete without a state ruled by Islamic Law, the Shariah, Parvez explained. From a God-centred way of life and thought, of knowledge and action, Islam is thus transformed into a totalistic, totalitarian, theocratic world order that submits every human situation to the arbitration of the state. So society and state become one and politics disappears. Cultural and social spaces are totally homogenized, everything is bulldozed into monotonous uniformity, and that's why the end product so often mirrors fascism. 'The Shariah as truth thus becomes indispensable to their cause. Indeed, it serves as an instrument for creating the totalitarian order. That's why dictators and tyrants all over the Muslim world love the Shariah so much!'

'And that's why no matter how modern certain Muslim leaders say they are, they are always ready to cut off people's hands and stone innocent women to death,' I added.

Parvez jumped from his armchair. 'Enough of this despondency,' he said, 'Let's listen to some more songs.'

Despite its melancholy overtones, my visit to Parvez had a joyful outcome. I had finally reached a firm conclusion: without reforming the Shariah, which actually amounts to reformulating Islam itself, a humane earthly paradise will always elude Muslim societies. The journey towards paradise required socially constructed laws of heaven to be rethought and reframed. In other words, Muslim individuals and communities had to reclaim agency: the right to reinterpret their religious texts according to their own time and context. In reality, the

Shariah is nothing more than a set of principles, a framework of values that provides Muslim societies with guidance. But these sets of principles and values are not a static or indeed a priori given, but are dynamically derived within changing contexts. And the duty to reinterpret the basic sources of Islam belongs not to revered men long dead, or to obscurantist Mullahs who exercise power over Muslim communities in the name of these classical scholars, but to each individual Muslim. The believers cannot simply be blind imitators; they have to be knowledgeable interpreters who exert themselves constantly and continuously to gain a fresh understanding of Islam. The hurdles obstructing the path to a new watering hole come, as they always have, from deeply entrenched religious and political power structures. I resolved to work even harder to remove these hurdles.

Chapter 12

THE DELIGHTS OF SECULARISM

I would work harder to remove the hurdles impeding the reform of Islam. It was a fine ambition, but what did it mean? An answer sounding markedly similar regularly made the rounds among western experts: Islam was ripe for its Reformation. I was never sure I understood exactly what they meant by this statement. Their Reformation had a capital R and referred to something akin to the experience of Europe in the fifteenth and sixteenth centuries. It was undeniable that the European Reformation had prompted an intense burst of theological and intellectual inquiry; an opening of debate and questioning was exactly the antidote we needed to the forces so anxious to prevent any thought whatsoever in Muslim circles. But whenever the subject of commending this sort of Reformation was raised in Ijmali discussions, it was pooh-poohed by Merryl Davies, who regarded herself as our resident expert and special adviser on matters of Christianity and European history. Her basic objection was that arguments for an Islamic Reformation were based on a crude historic parallel: Islam was now in its fifteenth century, and this was exactly the point in Christianity's history when it underwent its Reformation. QED: Islam was due to be reformed.

But were there not some pertinent points inviting more careful examination? The European Reformation led to a radical shift on all the most basic questions arising from faith. It pioneered a new way of seeking answers to the origin and purposes of the world, largely because of a pendulum shift in the balance between faith and reason. Modernity begins with the European Reformation, everything from capitalism to modern science is seen as its legacies. The biggest change in the one generation that separated Columbus's voyage and Magellan's first circumnavigation of the globe – from 1492 to 1526 – was that reason became central to understanding everything. Europe needed reason to be liberated; but Islam had no such need. As far as Islam is concerned, reason has always been the equal and necessary partner of faith. Even the most fundamentalist Mullah or simplest village Imam would be only too delighted to discourse at length about the emphasis placed on reason in the Qur'an, the Prophet's insistence on objective knowledge, and the intellectual glories of Islamic civilization. They are inordinately proud of what their sacred sources say about reason, how the use of reason was central once upon a time to Muslim society, and, without a hint of irony, take all this as proof of the superiority of Islam. Our problem was not stressing the importance of reason but exercising it, rekindling the educational system on which this vast sphere of achievement in Muslim history had depended.

No, the knot I had to unravel was something else. It had to do with the problem of the saeculum, the Latin term for 'the present world', the here and now of material existence. The European Reformation resulted in the transfer of authority for the governance of this world from the Church to the State, from Popes to princes. It was the origin of the process known as secularization. This began with the theological struggle for reform of religion, and it culminated in the secular state being seen as the only authority that could guarantee liberty of conscience and diversity of religious belief. The Reformation was the process by which the quest for liberty of conscience, the freedom to believe as personal faith and reason dictated, became the bedrock of all civil liberties. It began with Martin Luther's 'Here I stand. I can do no other,' and culminated with Thomas Jefferson's resounding conclusion that the State can never settle matters of conscience for the citizen, too much blood having been squandered in the attempt, so Church and State must be forever sundered. Secularization once begun remained a continuing and expanding transfer of power.

It was easy to see how this issue of authority had become entangled with the intellectual search to explore, unconstrained by theology, the origins and purpose of the world, how liberty of conscience and freedom of thought and inquiry had become companion projects. When both aspects were complicated by religious wars and the propaganda activities of the protagonists, religion itself had earned a very bad name. There was another deeper point. The potential lurking beneath the freedom of conscience the Reformation unleashed was the construction of a totalitarian secular state as the successor of the religiously based one it replaced. The first modern totalitarian state was conceived by the French Revolution in its most radical secular period. The incredible power of the modern state was certainly everyone's problem. It stems from a definition of modernity that is based on the antagonistic legacy of Church and State in Europe. In this definition, everything placed in the arena of 'Church' is seen as irrational, unscientific and therefore inferior. Was it not possible to think beyond the ideological battle lines and see faith and reason as two ways of understanding reality? When I stopped to think about it, I realized such a debate had taken place before; it had preoccupied the great minds of Muslim history. What was called secularism had its own Muslim antecedents. By going back to the future the secular route might indeed hold answers for resolving our contemporary problems.

What do you get when you separate Shariah from the State, religion from politics? The question haunted Muslim scholars and thinkers from the early days of Islam. Given the fact that law, morality and politics are so interconnected in Islam, it seems almost a contradiction to speak of Islamic secularism. But secularism has a strong presence in Islamic history even though it was not articulated as a clear and distinct separation of religion and political power. The Umayyad Empire, which emerged just fifty years after the death of the Prophet Muhammad, and the Abbasid Empire, which is conventionally seen as the 'Golden Age', were religious only in a symbolic sense. The Caliphs had no spiritual power; that rested largely with the religious scholars. With the sole exception of the Fatimid Empire, which was based on Ismaili theology, the states that followed were even more secularized.

Early Muslim thinkers also had little problem separating religion from politics. One of the foremost Muslim thinkers to give serious thought to this issue was the philosopher Al-Farabi, who is known reverentially as the 'Second Master' (after Aristotle). Born in Transoxiana, Al-Farabi invented a musical instrument called the Quanan and liked to wander about tenth-century Central Asia in disguise playing music and engaging those in authority in philosophical dialogues. Before he retired to spend his last days working as a gardener, he wrote *On the Perfect State*, the first serious attempt in Islam to harmonize Greek political thought with Islamic ideals. Al-Farabi considered 'the Philosopher, Supreme Ruler, Prince, Legislator and Imam' to be a single idea and perceived his perfect state as a universal, secular state. The main goal of any state, he argued, was 'the attainment of happiness' which could only be ushered in by the 'virtuous regime' of the philosophers.

Al-Farabi belonged to a group of thinkers who were collectively known as the Mutazilites, literally the Separatists. The group consisted largely of philosophers, but also included scientists, poets, administrators and even Caliphs – all denounced strict, Shariah-based faith and worked to transform Islam into a more humanistic religion. The Mutazilites argued that with reason alone one could know how to act morally; and by corollary, there was no necessity to combine religion and statecraft. Some historians consider the ninth-century philosopher Al-Kindi, popularly known as 'The First Philosopher of the Arabs', to be the founder of the Mutazilite school. But the school has a much older history; and its origins can be traced back to two lesser-known philosophers, Wasil bin Ata and Amr ibn Ubayad, both of whom were born in 699. As the story goes, the two young thinkers were attending a lecture by the Sufi mystic, ascetic Hasan al-Basri. After the lecture, Al-Basri was confronted by two men with conflicting views on the state of a believer who had committed a great sin. The first man argued that the perpetrator of a grave sin should be considered as a Muslim but labelled as an unbeliever, and that his case should be left with God. The second man put forward the argument that the committer of a mortal sin had *ipso facto* deviated from the path of Islam and could not possibly be considered a believer. Before Hasan al-Basri could reply, his young students intervened to present a third option: such a person, they suggested, was neither a believer nor an unbeliever. Hasan al-Basri was not amused and asked the young philosophers to leave the study circle. So Wasil and Ubayad broke away from the circle of the master, went to another corner of the mosque and began teaching their views. The Mutazilites, who are largely seen as freethinkers and aggressively independent, included amongst their ranks such philosophers of distinction as Ibn Sina, the eleventh-century polymath and physician, and Ibn Rushd, the twelfth-century rationalist.

The Mutazilites were pitted against the Asharites who categorically rejected the idea that human reason alone can discern morality and argued that it was beyond human capability to understand the unique nature and characteristics of God. The Asharite school was established by Abu Hasan al-Ashari who was born in 874 in Basra. The young Al-Ashari was a devout freethinker and the favourite pupil and intimate friend of Al-Jubbai, the head of the Mutazilite party at the time. One day, according to the biographer Ibn Khallikun, who flourished in the thirteenth century:

Ashari proposed to Jubbai the case of three brothers, one of whom was a true believer, virtuous and pious; the second an infidel, a debauchee and a reprobate; and the third an infant: they all died, and Ashari wished to know what had become of them. To this Jubbai answered: 'The virtuous brother holds a high station in paradise; the infidel is in the depths of hell; and the child amongst those who have obtained salvation.' 'Suppose now,' Ashari said, 'that the child should wish to ascend to the place occupied by his virtuous brother, would he be allowed to do so?' 'No,' replied Jubbai, 'it would be said to him: "Thy brother arrived at this place through his numerous works of obedience towards God, and thou hast no such works to set forward."' 'Suppose then,' said Ashari, 'that the child says: "That is not my fault; you did not let me live long enough, neither did you give me the means of proving my obedience."' 'In that case,' answered Jubbai, 'the Almighty would say: "I knew that if I had allowed thee to live, thou wouldst have been disobedient and incurred the severe punishment [of Hell]; I therefore acted for thy advantage."' 'Well,' said

Ashari, 'and suppose the infidel brother were to say: "O God of the universe! since you knew what awaited him, you must have known what awaited me; why then did you act for his advantage and not for mine?"' Jubbai had not a word to offer in reply.

On a Friday, while sitting in the chair from which he taught in the great mosque in Basra, Ashari made a public announcement at the top of his voice:

> They who know me know who I am: as for those who do not know me I will tell them. I am Ali b. Ismail al-Ashari, and I used to hold that the Qur'an was created, that the eyes of men shall not see God, and that we ourselves are the authors of evil deeds. Now I have returned to the truth; I renounce these opinions, and I undertake to refute the Mutazilites and expose their infamy and turpitude.

The Asharites were supported by giants like Al-Ghazali, the theologian and author of *The Revival of the Religious Sciences in Islam*, who directly challenged the might of the Rationalists; his contemporary the mathematician and physicist Fakhr al-Din Razi, and the great fourteenth-century historian and sociologist Ibn Khaldun, fought bitterly with the Mutazilites. Indeed, to a very large extent, the history of Islam during the classical period, from the seventh to the fourteenth century, can be seen as one gigantic struggle between the Mutazilites and the Asharites. It was the clear-cut victory of the Asharites that sealed the fate of secular humanism in Islam; and hurled Muslim civilization on its present trajectory.

If the debates already existed and had their own antecedents and context in Muslim thought, did this mean that secularism, a shift in the pendulum between Asharites and Mutazilites, was the corrective manoeuvre we not only needed but could take as an authentic path to reform? It was a legitimate question; one requiring some personal reflection. During my twenties and thirties, the days of FOSIS and the Iranian revolution, I was a firm supporter of the Asharite position. A copy of Al-Ghazali's *Book of Knowledge* and Ibn Khaldun's *Introduction to History* were always present on my bedside table. I read them frequently; and quoted them generously. The Asharites appealed to me not just for their learning and intellectual acumen, but also for their more holistic perspective on Islam. What I needed was a serious discussion with someone convinced by the secular dispensation. And I knew just the man.

Iftikar Malik is an old friend and distant relation of our Ijmali Malik With (Zafar of the beard, that is). An exceptionally tall man with bushy hair, he is entirely clean-shaven, as befits a genuine secularist. It would be quite like old times to invite Iftikar to dinner and then settle back for an intense discussion. And I had my question well prepared. It ran: 'What can secularism offer Islamic societies? Those who long for a secular paradise understand neither religion nor politics. Muhammad Iqbal was right when he said: "If religion is separated from politics you are left with the terror of Genghis Khan."'

'Both Iqbal and you are wrong,' Iftikar shot back when I made my opening statement. There is no better way to disconcert a Pakistani, especially one such as Iftikar whose speciality is the political history of Pakistan, than presenting a quote from the greatly loved and venerated poet-philosopher Iqbal with whom they have to disagree. The gambit took us straight to the heart of the matter.

'Secularism is the only antidote to the vicious literalism, supported by a spiritless and meaningless ritualism that's taken hold of the Muslim mind,' he asserted. Iftikar was not about to suggest that secularism, like any ideology, did not have its problems. His position was that just as we consider fundamentalist Muslims an aberration so we should see dogmatic secularists like the Ba'athists in Syria and Iraq, or the authoritarian secularist parties – the National Liberation Front in Algeria and the Constitutional Party in Tunisia, for example – as deviations from liberal secularism.

So secularism was also a form of religion. It too produced a true path – the path of liberal secularism – and various misinterpretations. It had its essential belief system – separation of State and religion, absolute right to freedom of expression and so on. And Iftikar was ready to concede that secularists can be just as doctrinaire as religious persons. But in his view secularism provided an umbrella for pluralism to flower, for dissent to be tolerated, for democracy to flourish in Muslim societies. 'Religious feuds and violence have now reached such a level that it is necessary for Muslims to separate *huqooq Allah* [the rights of God] from *huqooqal ibad* [the rights of people],' he declared. In the Muslim context, secularism was not so much the opposite of the sacred as the antithesis of chauvinism, exclusivism, ethnocentrism, and fanaticism. 'A Muslim secularist would not be disrespectful towards religion but equally respectful to all religions.'

I had several problems with this, I had to admit. The very function of religion in general, and Islam in particular, is to produce balanced individuals who can integrate the two – the rights of God and the rights of people. By divorcing them would you not inevitably undermine the very purpose of religion? Second, the opposite of religious fanaticism and chauvinism is not secularism but religious tolerance and pluralism which we need to promote in our societies. Third, secularism in Muslim societies has been a force for exclusion not inclusion. It's inclusive only for those in the modern sector. Those outside modernity, the vast majority of traditional Muslims, who are regarded as superstitious and inferior by the modern sector, can only play a marginal role. With secularism, traditional Islam is reduced to servant status, there to be manipulated by those who hold the vast majority and their religion in utter contempt, often demonizing tradition, traditional people and their religion. Moreover, this doesn't keep religion out of politics; it only ensures religion enters through a more surreptitious – even reactionary and violent – route.

'You've missed my point,' Iftikar insisted. 'Our experience with secularism notwithstanding, I'm arguing for secularism not at the expense of religion but as a method for reinterpreting and revisiting religion itself.'

'But how can you separate the idea of secularism from its European history?' I asked. Wasn't the problem that secularism as we conceive of it today not only remains a product of Europe but retains its Eurocentricism: their ideas of liberty and freedom become the only basis for the future of other cultures and civilizations, because they are the only universal standard by which liberty and freedom are assessed and understood?

Iftikar allowed this was a difficulty but simply asked why there could be only one interpretation of secularism. There had been secularism in Muslim history and it existed in a context quite different from that of European history with significantly different outcomes in the society it helped to generate. There had been secularism in Indian history too. The Subcontinent had always been heterodox and heterogeneous and had found distinctive ways to accommodate this reality in personal, social and political life. Even the modern conception of India as a secular state had not entirely eradicated loyalty to these older conceptions of plurality. They had their trenchant defenders among Indian writers, activists and thinkers precisely because the old dispensation was coming under such pressure from both religious and secular fundamentalists. It was a striking thought. What we were dealing with was a failure of imagination, a failure to think beyond the dominant solutions on offer, and that was not just our problem but one we shared with the West.

'The logic of too many people's analysis is that we can't accept any solution to our problems simply because it comes from the West,' Iftikar observed.

'And the western world has great difficulty admitting there are any problems at all in its idea of secularism. It cannot see the need for more than one version. Making an alternative form of secularism a lived reality would be good for everyone. It would help everyone to think beyond the impasses of European history,' I replied.

We could agree that the problems associated with reforming Islam could not be divorced from Islam's problem with the West and vice versa. This only left the problem of whether there were any hopeful stirrings of Muslim secularism for us to identify with.

'I see signs of hope in Turkey,' Iftikar offered tentatively. 'Despite all its problems, Muslim secularism in Turkey has to be the wave of the future.'

I recalled his words some months later as I stared into the dark cylindrical recesses of a guardian of Turkey's secular republic. I was looking down the barrel of an enormous gun mounted on a tank. After a morning spent wandering at leisure round Istanbul, breathing in the sights of two continents, watching boats and ships of all kinds ply the waters of the Bosphorus, I had decided to visit a friend at the Istanbul

Technical University, a professor of political science. I wanted to get beyond the picture postcard views of this glorious city, and to continue my exploration of the possibilities of the secular route. I knew my friend, a specialist on secularism in Turkey, was the man to talk to. And that's when I encountered this bastion of the army guarding the university campus.

I was caught in what I can only describe as my very own Tiananmen moment. As the centurion of secularism lumbered forward a soldier popped his head out of the turret and yelled, 'What do you want?'

Behind the tank a huge statue of Atatürk (Mustafa Kemal), father of Turkish secularism, grimly cast upon me its unseeing gaze of disdain. Its uplifted hand bid me to be gone. But I could not move. The soldier clearly understood I was not a local; presumably they needed no encouragement to move off. He spoke in English. 'What do you want?' he repeated.

'I just want to get inside the university,' I croaked in a pathetic plaint. 'I've come to see a friend, a professor in the political science department.'

The tank manoeuvred the barrel of its huge proboscis up and then down, as if acknowledging my words. Then the entire machine lurched closer. I flinched as the great gun ended a couple of metres from my chest.

'No visitors are allowed. Go away,' said the soldier.

'The professor is expecting me,' I said, summoning a modicum of determination.

The soldier leaped out of the tank and walked towards me. 'Don't you understand English?' He pushed me with both hands. 'No visitors allowed.'

'Look,' I tried to reason with him. 'I'm British!' How readily the argument from authority comes to the lips of even a scion of the wrong end of the Raj. 'I just want to go inside the University to see a friend.' I handed him my passport in an 'Enough of this nonsense, my dear chap' gesture. He looked at it carefully, threw it on the ground, and stamped on it. '*No visitors allowed,*' he shouted.

'This is precisely the kind of behaviour that's a major impediment to Turkey joining the European Economic Community,' I said in befitting dudgeon; Tunbridge Wells would be proud of me! I gathered up my passport and walked away. The soldier punched the air in response; and climbed back into his tank.

I called my friend Feruh Alptekin and explained my predicament. Actually, Feruh was not so much my friend as a friend of my brother, Jamal. Both were followers of Sheikh Nazim and constant companions in search of mystical ecstasy. The next morning he turned up early. 'No problem, boss,' he said, handing me a few books, 'just pretend to be a student.' We returned to the University. As we got closer I found myself being secreted among a large group of students. We moved in unison, dodging tanks and soldiers, till we reached the main door. A soldier standing at the door searched everyone before allowing us in. Once inside, a small group stayed with me till they found my friend. We were searched again outside his department before I was finally standing in front of him.

'You're lucky to find me here,' he said. 'The powers that be aren't very happy with my politics. I suspect I will soon be back in prison.'

I was aware that he had just been released from prison after serving several months for 'attacking the secular principles of the State'. His offence, as I understood it, consisted of making a speech suggesting female students who wanted to wear the scarf – for religious or other reasons – should be allowed to do so. Why would women wearing a headscarf threaten the roots of Turkish secularism? The question was not limited to Turkey. It had significance for Europe as well. In France and Germany, Muslim girls in headscarves are often seen as a threat to secular civilization and banned from attending school. But non-Muslim (white) women wearing scarves are seen as chic and fashionable. Why this dichotomy?

'Very simple,' he answered with determination in his eyes. 'The scarf has symbolic power.' In a secular society, he explained, freedom is subject to secular principles – just as in a religious state, it is restricted by religious notions. A secular society does not provide its citizens with absolute freedom but confines it within the boundaries of its own absolutes. The scarf represents a symbolic violation of these absolutes.

'Turkey,' he continued, 'has been hijacked in the name of secularism by generals and westernized elites. I simply want it to be handed back to the people and let them stamp their personality and culture on our politics and national affairs. It's not too much to ask!'

And it certainly sounded innocent enough in the mouth of this heavily built man in his forties who spoke English with an accent that was a legacy of his postgraduate studies in Germany. We'd first met in 1981 at a conference on Atatürk held at the Bosphorus University. 'What's your main problem with Turkish secularism?' I asked, getting to the point of my visit.

'Quite simply,' he replied, 'it is a product of our inferiority complex. Turkish secularism wasn't invented by Atatürk as most people tend to think. Its roots are in the days of the Ottoman Empire.' He explained that the inferiority complex towards the West evolved after military defeats at the hands of European powers in 1699 and 1718. One can sense this in the diaries of Yirmisekiz Mehmed Celebi, the first Ottoman envoy to Europe, who became convinced of the intellectual superiority of western civilization after visiting Paris and Vienna. From then on the feeling of admiration for western culture and worldview grew radically, displacing all confidence in indigenous ideas and ideals. The vast majority of Turkey's religious scholars lacked the intellectual acumen and ability to generate new indigenous knowledge or creatively synthesize western science and technology. They reacted by becoming even more dogmatic and narrow – and thus increased admiration for the West.

Westernization in Turkey began in the Ottoman Palaces. The intellectual justification for the whole exercise was provided by the Young Ottomans, a group of Turkish intellectuals (allegedly, there were only six) who came to prominence towards the end of the period. They were the first Turks to embrace the ideas of the Enlightenment and seek a synthesis with Islam. The Young Ottomans – Sinasi, Ali Suavi, Faud Pasa, Mustafa Rasid, Ziya Pasa and Namik Kema – were by no means outstanding philosophers or thinkers. But the religious scholars, who were largely responsible for the decay and despotism of the Ottoman Empire, just couldn't compete and didn't possess their skills at manipulating the media to voice extremely articulate criticism of the government and the Empire. Of course, that's not to say all religious scholars were incompetent: there were formidable exceptions. Ahmet

Cevdet Pasa, for example, argued that the educational structure of Ottoman Turkey, the *madrasah* system, was incapable of producing the type of scholar the future needed. Turkey should begin 'preparation for the future without the destruction of the past', he argued. But such scholars were few. The majority were happy with issuing fatwas (religious rulings) justifying the rule of despotic Sultans. Once an empire, however mighty, produces scholars who act as surrogates of the rulers or sell their minds to another civilization, physical and intellectual subjugation follows as a matter of course. Atatürk was the logical conclusion of what the Sultans themselves started. If Mustafa Kemal hadn't appeared he'd have to be invented. He was a necessity for Turkey and a natural outcome of more than a hundred years of decay and degeneration.

'Atatürk presented secularism as a theology of salvation. Coming to terms with the "European miracle" required embracing every component of Europe's ideology: being modern meant being exactly like Europeans. Imitation was duplicated in minute detail, up to and including how one dressed and behaved. He replaced Ottoman history based on religious community with a "national history" he hoped would replicate the history of the West. In a real sense, Kemalism internalized how the West conventionally represented Islam: as the darker, degenerate opposite of the Christian and secular West. He represented Islam as "the Orient" of the West suffused with all the ills conventionally ascribed to it, from being ignorant and stupid to inferior, ugly and fanatic, my friend explained.'

I asked how the course of Atatürk's revolution differed from other revolutions in history.

'It is important to understand,' he replied, 'that the Kemalist secular revolution isn't different. It doesn't differ, say, from the course of the "Islamic Revolution" in Iran. It's the standard pattern: a charismatic leader heads the initial movement; once his regime is established, demands for greater radicalism and purism culminate in a reign of terror and virtue where the leader is transformed into a demigod and becomes sole arbitrator of what's "revolutionary" and what "counter-revolutionary". That's what happened in Turkey. Mustafa Kemal played the role of demigod admirably: "I am Turkey," he declared, "to destroy me is to destroy Turkey." The ideology of the old system was the enemy: Islam, its religious scholars, and its rituals and mentality were preventing Turkey from becoming a prosperous nation, a modern state respected by other countries. He set out to destroy the old system with the same zeal the Mullahs used to dismantle the Shah's state. The period of terror and reform in a revolution is followed by what we political scientists call the "Thermidor" – the period when revolutionary reforms are solidified and turned into permanent fixtures.'

The 'Thermidor' in Turkey occurred between the years 1924 and 1949, when Islamic activity and thought were banned. The generation reared in this period is almost totally divorced from the tradition and Islamic past of Turkey. Some Turkish historians even refer to it as the 'Age of Ignorance'. It had a devastating effect on Turkish intellectual life. Post-revolutionary intellectuals tend to be ideologues faithfully reproducing, without adding or subtracting, the thoughts of the father of the revolution. Turkey produced only dogmatic Kemalists, poor clones of western scholars. Even worse, the westernized intellectuals of the late-Ottoman period had said most of what could be said in the Turkish context about imitation and adoption of western philosophy and outlook on life. All the ideas had been discussed by the preceding generation. The Kemalists had little to add except to echo their sentiments.

This generation, because of state support and its vast numbers, still dominates the Turkish intellectual scene. But numbers and grants are no substitute for thought and analysis, even if these mediocrities receive welcome and patronage from the United States and Europe. Western historians describe Atatürk's revolution as 'perfect', and the treaty of Lausanne, where his secular Republic was recognized, as one of 'the great political miracles of the twentieth century' and Mustafa Kemal himself as a Fabian socialist! 'Such nonsense only increases the resolve of our secular modernists to suppress popular sentiment even more ruthlessly', my friend noted ruefully.

The age of ignorance ended in one respect in 1949. In post-revolution days most religious schools were closed and replaced by the 'laic' (lay or secular) education system. Turkish secularism, like its European counterpart, didn't allow Muslim institutions to function independently of the government. However, after the Second World

War, when Turkey entered the 'democratic phase', many politicians adopted the cause of religious education and succeeded in establishing special middle and secondary schools known as 'Imam Hatib' schools. For the first time in over thirty years, the teaching of the Qur'an and its commentaries, the life and traditions of the Prophet Muhammad, Islamic law, history and philosophy in conjunction with modern science and ideas became common. These schools found an enthusiastic welcome among the people, not as institutions of professional training but as an alternative to the secular schools. In 1975, a reform act transformed and reorganized the Imam Hatib schools and Lycées, giving them a full teaching curriculum, including of course Arabic and Islamic studies. After the 1980 military coup, graduates of Imam Hatib schools were given permission to enter universities for higher education.

'I suspect the future of Turkey will be determined by graduates from these schools,' he said.

'I don't have much faith in *madrasahs*,' I replied. 'The ones I've seen in Pakistan and other Muslim countries only produce dogmatic fundamentalists. Why would you think Imam Hatib graduates are so different?'

'Don't confuse them with *madrasahs*. We in Turkey know only too well the limitations of traditional *madrasahs*. Graduates of the Imam Hatibs are taught not traditional but rather classical Islam . . .'

They are well versed, he went on to explain, in modern critical thought, ideas, science and humanities. They don't wear their Islam on their sleeves – like products of the *madrasahs*. They're at ease with the modern world. But there's another reason Imam Hatib graduates are important. The first generation of Republican intellectuals had a major handicap: they had no access to the historic sources of their own society, thanks to Atatürk's adoption of the Roman alphabet as the script for modern Turkish. Almost overnight, this destroyed the historical and cultural roots of Turkish society. Those who couldn't read or understand the basic works of Turkish history and culture had to turn to secondary sources. They ended up learning about their own history and thought from the flawed and prejudiced works of western Orientalists. Turkish intellectual life became a rootless tree unable to bear fruit.

He tapped my arm with good humour, 'Imam Hatib graduates read

Turkish sources in the original, they can connect the past to the present and both to the future. That's why I think they'll shape the future.'

'How can you teach in this atmosphere of tension, with soldiers and tanks on the campus?' I asked, connecting my experience outside the university to the calm atmosphere within.

'Oh, we press on,' he sighed. 'In Turkey, the army is very quick to send tanks onto the streets. Every time they feel that secularism is under threat, or the Islamic party will come into power, they move quickly and decisively to defend the principles of Atatürk. They tackle the issue of headscarves by surrounding the university with tanks. We've come to accept that Turkey is like the Bosphorus.'

'Really! How?' I was intrigued.

'Well, the Bosphorus has a two-tier current system. The upper layer flows from the Black Sea to the Sea of Marmara which is lower. But the lower layer flows in the opposite direction because there's a difference in the density of the two seas: the Sea of Marmara has a higher salt content and therefore a higher density. Now, Turkey has this external shell of a doctrinaire secular state, but internally we're a Muslim nation. So like the waters of the Bosphorus, rulers and the ruled always go in opposite directions.'

'You hope the Imam Hatib graduates will square this circle?' I asked, concerned that my friend might find the tension pulling him off to the prison again.

'I hope so,' he said reflectively, as if he caught my drift. 'Of course,' he added, trying to reassure me with a smile, 'we can learn a great deal from the Ottomans. They knew a thing or two about the Bosphorus and made it work to their advantage. They developed a highly sophisticated sewage network . . .'

I laughed.

'No, it's true,' he chuckled, 'all of Istanbul's refuse was discharged into the lower layer, taking it out to the Black Sea. Clean water they took from the upper layer and used it for utilities like public baths. If only we could develop a political system to cart away the secular refuse and bring in some fresh ideas . . .'

He looked directly at me. 'Wonderful things, Turkish baths, nothing like them for cleansing every cell in your body.'

'I intend to have one,' I replied emphatically.

Istanbul in high summer gets hot and sticky. And nothing fires and drains you like a solid burst of education. By the time I left the university the afternoon heat was well established and I could think of nothing better than luxuriating, soaking, wallowing and relaxing. 'Can you find me a Turkish bath?' I asked Feruh. 'No problem, boss,' he replied. 'Follow me.'

We walked for what seemed like miles, each step getting sweatier and steamier. When we finally came to a halt I looked at my watch and was surprised to find barely an hour had passed. Feruh pointed exultantly to an eighteenth-century public bath in an acute state of disrepair. It was not at all what I'd anticipated. 'It hasn't been used for a few years,' Feruh said, as if sharing the best joke possible. We went inside to find a cavernous space which, thanks to its thick walls, at least had the advantage of being cooler than the street. The cavern was divided into three segments. Feruh explained, dwelling too gleefully I thought on the words 'when in use', one area would be for disrobing, one to sweat, and one to take a cold dip. We entered the domed disrobing room, which would have had a central fountain and an alcove 'to make coffee'. A low door led into the cool room where clothes were laundered and preparation made for the hot room with its marble slab for massage under a dome, basins for washing and a corner closet for privacy. With irrepressible amusement Feruh expatiated on the ingenuity of the water system. A stone cased in a niche on the wall of the water reservoir, called *maslak*, distributed cold water to the fountains of the *sogukluk* and toilets of the *iliklik* and to the reservoir via a network of terracotta pipes. I began to fantasize about sweating in the hot room after a long and relaxing massage and then taking a cold bath with fresh, clean fountain water. But alas! I was a couple of hundred years too late.

I came out as sweaty and grimy as I came in. Feruh, probably detecting that my sense of humour was as tired and emotional as the rest of me, found it politic to take his leave. It should be no trouble to get back to my hotel in Taqsim Square, driven by my desire for a much needed shower. I hailed a *dulmos*, only to find it steaming with more people than its official maximum load. I turned away as a bus pulled up nearby. A sudden tidal wave of humanity materialized and surged towards the bus. Before I realized what was happening, I was drowning in a sea of people, finding myself ensconced in the bus, unable to see where we were going. By the time I managed to get to the exit, I was in Bebek, several kilometres in the opposite direction to my intended destination. Now I was not only sweaty, grimy, tired and emotional, buffeted and angry, I was also very hungry. I needed the kind of nourishment only a decent fish restaurant could provide.

The veranda of the restaurant overlooked the Bosphorus and caught the first breath of the evening breeze. I stood drinking in one of the most intoxicating skylines the world has to offer, glittering and shimmering in the westering sun. I paced the veranda shifting my head from side to side like some expectant bird coming to land. I perched on the railing, craning my neck in all available directions. Each vantage point offered a slightly different perspective on hills rising from the waters adorned with graceful minarets, impressive monuments and houses nestling in subtle curvatures embedded among trees and shrubs. How could one ever get enough of looking at this resplendent city! Clearly it was possible. As I pulled back from the railing and made for the other corner of the veranda I caught a glimpse of what struck me as the most incongruous sight: an old man sitting alone totally preoccupied, absorbed in the pages of a book. Intrigued I moved closer. I peeked over his shoulder: it was a stamp album. He seemed to be examining one particular stamp with the aid of a magnifying glass. The words 'Turkish miniature' popped into my head and brought a smile to my face. As if by extrasensory perception the old man stiffened, realizing he was being observed. He looked up, lifted his glass to take a sip of raki and replaced it with a sweeping gesture of invitation. I took my seat in front of him.

'That's a very impressive stamp album,' I commented nodding to the large leather bound volume that looked as if it should house an illuminated manuscript, which in a way it did.

'I started collecting stamps at an early age,' he replied. 'I have almost all Turkish stamps from the very first Ottoman one issued in 1863. They're like a blow-by-blow account of Turkish history and they're my memory. I look at stamps and see my own history, recall personal incidents, the life I've lived.'

I leaned forward for a closer look. It's not often you are invited to peruse the intimate details of a life. Obligingly, the old man turned the pages of his life before me. Many simply carried portraits of Atatürk. One large 100 kurus stamp bore an image of the Father of the Republic overlaid with a long text in minuscule letters. 'What does it say?' I asked.

'Oh, it's Atatürk's address to Turkish youth,' he replied gratified by his receptive audience. 'Do you want me to translate it for you?' Without waiting he picked up his magnifying glass, and started to declaim. 'Turkish youth! Your first duty is to protect and preserve Turkish independence and the Turkish Republic forever. This is the very foundation of your existence and your future. This foundation is your most precious treasure. In the future, too, there may be malevolent people at home and abroad who wish to deprive you of this treasure. If some day you are compelled to defend your independence and your Republic, you must not tarry to weigh the possibilities and circumstances of the situation before taking up your duty. These possibilities and circumstances may turn out to be extremely unfavourable. The enemies conspiring against your independence and your Republic may have behind them a victory unprecedented in the annals of the world. By violence and ruse, all the fortresses of your beloved fatherland may be captured, all its shipyards occupied, all its armies dispersed and every part of the country invaded. And sadder and graver than these circumstances, those who hold power within the country may be in error, misguided, and may even be traitors. Furthermore, they may identify their personal interests with the political designs of the invaders. The country may be impoverished, ruined and exhausted.' He paused and looked at me. I was already aware he'd ceased to read and was reciting with fervour words known by heart that clearly moved him deeply, now he wound himself up for the ringing climax. 'You, the youth of Turkey's future, even in such circumstances, it is your duty to save Turkish independence and the Republic. The strength you need is in your noble blood and within your veins.'

On that crescendo he ordered more raki with gusto. I took out a cigar from my pocket and ordered my grilled fish. We sat there for hours eating, smoking, talking, and looking at stamps. Each stamp set him off on a different trajectory, revealing fragments of his biography, invoking reminiscences of Turkish history, thoughts of Kemalist triumphs. Bayan Muhib, my chance acquaintance, was ninety-four and a dedicated Kemalist. Age had not withered his handsome stature. His classical Anatolian nose supported a pair of thick glasses, which he constantly adjusted. 'I was born in 1894 in Midilli, a beautiful island in the Aegean,' he told me. 'In those days Midilli was part of the Ottoman Empire and its inhabitants were farmers, mostly growing olives. My father was the director of the Lycée. He was a pretty religious man who commanded respect in the locality. We lived among a large extended family. My mother's house, my mother's sister's house, my grandmother's house were all in one row. I used their back gardens like one large park – running from garden to garden with my many cousins.'

'What is your most vivid memory of childhood?' I asked.

'The most vivid? The new Constitution,' he replied without much hesitation. 'In 1908, the Young Turks forced Sultan Abdul Hamid to change the Constitution. My father told me now we had much more freedom. Before that I never heard anyone mention freedom at all. "What is freedom?" I remember asking my father.'

Bayan talked and talked. When, way past midnight, I suggested it was time for me to leave he was noticeably upset. 'Don't go,' he said. 'Come and stay with me.' I didn't even think of refusing; we walked up the hill to his spacious house, tastefully furnished with antique Ottoman artefacts. The living room extended onto a balcony overlooking the Bosphorus. The lights of two continents glittered and twinkled alluringly at each other. With a view like this, I remember thinking, how could one possibly sleep! There was only one other person in the house, Bayan's grand-daughter Zahra. A recent graduate of Istanbul University, she was working as a conference organizer. 'I like to spend time with my grandchildren,' Bayan said wistfully. 'But, with the exception of Zahra, they live in Ankara and I don't get to see them as often as I'd like.' Zahra scuttled off to make us Turkish coffee while Bayan turned my attention back to his stamp collection.

I ended up spending several days at Bayan's house. When he'd exhausted his stamp collection, he moved to albums of family photographs. I was enthralled by one taken at the turn of the century, of his entire family gathered around the grandmother. Bayan, no more than eight or nine years old, stands behind the matriarch with his cousins. All the boys and men are wearing the fez. The women and the girls have their heads covered. A studio portrait had Bayan, wearing a fez, a long black coat and well-worn boots, sitting while his elder and younger sisters stand beside him. Both photographs carried the Islamic dates: 'Midilli, 1339'.

'This photograph,' Bayan said one evening, 'was taken in 1911, after I'd finished the Lycée and was about to go to the University of Liège in Belgium to study mine engineering.' Bayan stood stiffly, his hand resting on a wooden chair, wearing an ill-fitting but clearly modish suit with a conspicuous fez on his head. 'I used to walk around Liège wearing a fez. It was a very odd feeling; I stood out like a sore thumb. There were only a handful of Turkish students there and we all tended to stay together. Most of us were studying technical subjects. After a few weeks, we all changed our fez for a hat and a tie.' Bayan pushed a couple of photographs towards me. The first was a portrait of Bayan who stood, his arms folded, wearing an elegant suit and tie, his short hair parted in the middle and neatly arranged. The second was a group photograph of the Ottoman students in Liège. They all wore smart suits; and everyone had their hair parted in the middle. The date on the photograph written in Ottoman script was: 'Liège, 27 February 1911'.

As I examined the pictures Bayan explained how his studies were interrupted when the First World War broke out. Liège, he recalled, was swiftly occupied by German forces; but the Germans treated Turkish students with considerable respect and politeness. They were given a special train carriage to return to Turkey. When he returned to finish his education after the war, Liège had changed. 'Turkey was an enemy country and its citizens were treated badly. We weren't allowed to resume our courses; technical subjects were out of bounds for Turkish students. I was forced to study commerce and had to start again from the first year.' He returned home after the 1923 Lausanne Armistice was signed. 'I remember,' he said, 'thinking the Turkish delegation at Lausanne sat at the conference table almost as though they were victors. Quite a contrast to how Germany had to deal with the Allies.' He settled in Ayvalik and was elected the town's Mayor in 1938. 'It was during this time I really got to know Kemal Atatürk.' As always when Bayan mentioned Atatürk his eyes lit up. 'He was a frequent visitor to the town and often stayed with us. He was a very charismatic man, a strong presence. From the time of Gallipoli, when Atatürk held together the Turkish Army and then decisively defeated the Europeans, I'd admired him. Now I got to appreciate his thoughts and ideas. I became a strong follower of his reforms; the change of alphabet, the hat revolution, the banning of the veil. But these were only outward signs of what Atatürk wanted to do. He wanted to change the thinking and outlook of Turkish people. He wanted to turn Turkey into a real nation, to join the rest of the world on an equal footing.'

In all his stories of Atatürk I was struck by how closely Bayan's veneration mirrored that most Muslims have towards the Prophet Muhammad. 'I've modelled my life on Atatürk,' he would say frequently. 'Since my days as the Mayor of Ayvalik I've worked to promote the goals of Kemalism. I opened a private school in Ayvalik, with the help of a few friends; we taught French and mathematics. Even after I retired as General Manager of the Union of Cooperatives, I've continued to promote and defend Kemalism. Without Kemalism Turkey would not be Turkey. It would perish.'

I loved Bayan's company. He was a warm and generous host, a kind and indulgent companion, a humane man with a wealth of experience gained in working to make life better for his people. Yet he had clearly lived a life in two parts, before and after the coming of Kemalism, the dark followed by the light. He insisted he was a secular Muslim – 'I read the Qur'an often' – but he could not disguise how much he had internalized a negative Orientalist notion of Islam. At the end of the day, for Bayan Islam was the opposite of the civilization of the West. One could hardly disagree with him when he said 'many crimes have been committed in the name of Islam'. But, to my mind, that's not the same thing as concluding contemporary Islam has little to offer the modern world. For Bayan one thing was certain, all that was good stemmed from Atatürk, all that was Ottoman was degenerate and inhumane.

In the late 1980s I became a frequent visitor to Istanbul. Or more precisely to the International Research Centre for Islamic History, Art and Culture (IRCICA), a body established in 1982 by the Organization of Islamic

Conference (OIC), which functions as a Muslim United Nations. The invitations were issued by Ekmeleddin Ihsanoglu, the Director of IRCICA. An elegant, well-dressed man, the epitome of the suave international diplomat, Ihsanoglu established the headquarters of IRCICA in the historic Yaldiz Palace complex, renovating the site with great love and care. The Yaldiz had a chequered history: it had been a theatre, a museum, a foundry and a sawmill, and had a zoo and an aviary around its artificial lake and palace gardens. Thanks largely to the efforts of Ekmeleddin, IRCICA became one of the most successful institutions of the OIC. There was always some sort of conference going on; and I was always welcomed. Over the course of my visits Ekmeleddin became my image of the finest kind of Ottoman Pasha. Not only a perfect diplomat, he also occupied the professorial chair in the history of science at Istanbul University. He was working on a massive multi-volume study on 'scientific literature in the Ottoman period'; and an equally monumental and ambitious two-volume study, 'History of the Ottoman State, Society and Civilization'. Here was the dark of Bayan's reminiscences seen in a new light.

The Ottoman dynasty held power for 600 years, an extraordinary achievement in a region where states and empires emerged and then disappeared in a few generations. Throughout the Ottomans history the extent of their wealth and power changed enormously. In the early thirteenth century the Ottomans held power only in a small area of Anatolia. By the end of the fifteenth century they had become an important regional power, ruling most of modern Turkey and a large part of the Balkan peninsula. During the sixteenth century they became masters of a vast, multinational empire, stretching from Slovakia to Nubia and from Algiers to the Caucasus, significant not only for its military prowess but also for its substantial contribution to cultural, artistic and scientific life. They were successful in integrating communities of various ethnicities, religions, cultures and languages on three continents within one framework. They emphasized local identities and respect for ethnic and religious diversity. The use of force against their people was never an Ottoman strategy. They never forcefully converted or Turkified people in the conquered lands. And it would be totally wrong to say naked imperialism or linguistic, cultural or religious assimilation was ever their policy.

Where Bayan was content to denounce the Ottomans, Ekmeleddin bridled at the way their achievements have been demonized, both by the West and by Muslims. According to European perception, the Ottoman state was always an enemy at the gates or, as Francis Bacon dubbed it, the 'present terror of the world' – to be subverted and disparaged, its accomplishments marginalized and rendered invisible. It is re-imagined as The Sick Man of Europe – the classic precursor of the basket-case Third World power. The Muslim mind associates the Ottomans with the 'decline' of Muslim civilization. The conventional view has it that the Ottoman Empire reached its peak around 1600 and spent the next 300 years dwindling while science and learning disappeared and Ottoman civil society degenerated. Ekmeleddin and his associates saw things differently. Two decades of extensive research led them to turn this standard view on its head. Far from disappearing, science and learning were very much alive in the Ottoman Empire right up to the end of the eighteenth century, when it shifted towards learning and assimilating European thought through translation and adaptations. The decline of the Ottoman Empire was part of the general decline, and subsequent colonization, of the Muslim world itself.

Of course, the Ottomans had their faults, as Ekmeleddin frequently acknowledged. But he and his fellow historians were now representing them as a human community. 'If we can relate to them in human terms then we can have more confidence in our history and tradition,' he said. By dehumanizing the Ottomans, the Kemalists also dehumanized Turkey. And they divided the nation between pro- and anti-Kemalist secularist sentiment. They also divorced Islam and the West from each other. 'You cannot separate the one from the other,' Ekmeleddin once told me. 'There would have been no "West" as we know it today without Islam. Where did the European Enlightenment come from? Did it emerge ready-made from the minds of the *philosophes*, the intellectuals who supposedly perfected it? No. Its foundations were laid by Islam. Islam taught Europe virtually all it knew about science, philosophy and education. Starting with the basics, Islam taught Europe how to reason, how to differentiate between civilization and barbarism, and to understand the basic features of a civil society. Islam trained Europe in scholastic and philosophic method, and bequeathed it its characteristic institutional forum of learning: the university. Europe acquired wholesale the organization, structure and even the terminology of the Muslim educational system. Not only did Islam introduce Europe to the experimental method and demonstrate the importance of empirical research, it even had the foresight to work out most of the mathematical theory necessary for Copernicus to launch "his" revolution! Islam showed Europe the distinction between medicine and magic, drilled it in making surgical instruments and explained how to establish and run hospitals. And the Ottomans played an important part in all this.'

Indeed, liberal humanism, of which Europe is so proud, and which Kemalists wished to imitate in every respect, is itself Islam's gift. 'Liberal humanism, the hallmark of post-Renaissance Europe,' Ekmeleddin explained, 'has its origins in the *adab* movement of Islam, which was concerned with the etiquette of being human.' Islam developed a sophisticated system of teaching law and humanism that involved not just institutions such as the university, with its faculties of law, theology, medicine and natural philosophy, but also an elaborate method of instruction including work-study courses, a curriculum including grammar, rhetoric, poetry, history, medicine and moral philosophy, and mechanisms for the formation of a humanist culture such as academic associations, literary circles, clubs and other coteries that sustain intellectuals and literati. Europe adopted this system in totality, including the textbooks, the institutions, even dress and modes of behaviour. So there is little to distinguish between European and Islamic humanism. The conclusion? If Kemalists were really interested in liberal humanism they should look into their own history rather than imitating an imitation.

Over the course of my regular visits, as I learned more from the friends I made, I began to detect signs that Turkey was striving to transcend the facile divisions of Kemalism. I met numerous intellectuals, including Ali Bulac, a publisher who wrote a regular column in a local newspaper. A bulky chap with a thick moustache, he didn't speak a single word of English; but somehow we always managed to communicate, there was always someone in his ever-present entourage of young intellectuals ready to translate. 'Are you for or against Kemalism?' I once asked.

'Not for or against,' he replied without hesitation. 'That doesn't concern me or my group. We're much more concerned with the dehumanization aspect of both secularism and religion. We're concerned with the social and economic betterment of the vast majority of the people, the provision of social justice, the spread of equality, the ecological and environmental problems of Turkey, the epistemological basis of our civilization, the reconstruction of a critical Islamic tradition, the flowering of our art and culture, poetry and fiction. We seek Islamic alternatives to answer these issues. And it's precisely these issues which concern university students and young academics, Muslim and non-Muslim, throughout Turkey.'

It was becoming obvious that the influence of Muslim intellectuals like Bulac could be translated into votes when necessary. The initial beneficiary was the Milli Selamet Party which led to the brief, flawed but encouraging political career of Najmuddin Erbakan, a mechanical engineer and son of an Ottoman-era religious court judge, as Minister of State and Deputy Prime Minister during the early 1970s. There were a host of young politicians, many of whom became mayors of their cities and towns, in the new mould who suggested Islam was going to play a major, and positive, role in Turkish politics.

Each time I arrived in Turkey it rekindled the *idée fixe* acquired on my first visit. I wanted a Turkish bath! Regularly Feruh would turn up early in the morning and ask me to follow him. One day he took me to the Sultan Hammam where coloured glass skylights created a mystical atmosphere. The architect had achieved an effect of uniformly diffused light by creating a series of loopholes high in the walls. The light bounced across marbled floors and walls decorated with ornamental titles.

'Do you know, boss,' Feruh said, 'Istanbul had steam baths long before Versailles had a single toilet.'

'I can imagine,' I replied.

'During the reign of Sultan Süleyman the Magnificent (1520 to 1566), Istanbul had hundreds of public baths. Sultan Süleyman himself commissioned the famous Turkish architect Sinan to enlarge the Sultan Hammam and fit it with true Ottoman splendour. By the beginning of the eighteenth century there were over 14,500 bathing establishments in Istanbul. Some 150 of them were large, public steam baths.'

Feruh was determined to show me all of them. We walked everywhere. The Cagaloglu Hammami, one of the largest Turkish baths in Istanbul, had an incredible, picturesque interior. Outside the entrance hall there was an elegant marble fountain. The main cupola in the bathing room was supported by eight columns, which looked more like the handiwork of a lace-maker than a stonemason. The Galatasaray Hammami was the most luxurious of the historic baths. According to Feruh it was built in 1481 by order of Sultan Bayazid II, and sited next to his castle. It had been lavishly decorated; during our visit it served as the set for a Turkish film. I concluded there were as many public baths in Istanbul as mosques, their lead-covered cupolas competing with the domes in the city's skyline. Yet Feruh was determined to keep me away from one that was actually operational!

The gleanings of my many visits, as well as my frustrations at the lack of a Turkish bath, were shared with my Ijmali friends. The perplexity of the secular route became one of our regular topics of discussion. 'How should we relate to secularism as Muslims? How are we to avoid the tendency, common enough in Islamic circles, of painting secularism in the colours of evil?' I asked Parvez Manzoor on one of his regular visits to my house.

'Look, Maulvi,' Parvez replied, 'I've been thinking a lot about this. We Muslims cannot relate or not relate to secularism. We cannot accept or reject it. What we need to do is examine it. We need to look at it from the perspective of our own category – *zulm*.'

Here was an entirely new insight, something I had not considered before. I insisted Parvez expound his thoughts, as simply as possible. *Zulm*, the Islamic concept of injustice, is a complex term. It has, as Parvez explained it, at least four layers of meaning. It can simply mean to do wrong, to treat wrongfully, or to deal unjustly. But it also means withholding what is rightfully due to someone or something; to commit *zulm* against persons or things, even against truth and trust, is not to accord them what is their due. So, by extension, it also covers such things as tyranny, perversion, distortion and ignorance. Finally, it refers to the wrong the Self commits against itself. Being an Islamic concept none of these layers of meaning are separate and isolated; they are interconnected. In which case, looking at secularism from the perspective of *zulm* would have specific ramifications for Muslim societies.

'What we ultimately seek,' Parvez said, 'is liberation from the tyranny of the West and such western notions as modernity and secularism. But this tyranny is deeply connected, promoted by and implicated in the tyranny we perpetuate on ourselves: the tyranny of the romanticized past, the tyranny of an ossified and historically frozen Shariah, and the tyranny practised by our rulers, who are often maintained in power by the West. On the one hand we must excavate the layers of *zulm* we, by our own thought and deeds, are visiting on our people. And on the other hand, we must examine the West as the historical agent of oppression, as the perpetuator of colonialism, and the injustices it has perpetrated by imposing its structures and institutions on our societies.'

'Both the West and the non-West need liberation from all kinds of *zulm*. And the liberation of one is tied up with the liberation of the other. So what we should do is use the notion of *zulm* to develop a discourse of liberation simultaneously Islamic and universal,' I declared with aplomb. Then, I caught myself and added more diffidently, 'My initial concern is that we somehow have to ensure we do not end up demonizing the West as the West has demonized Islam and Muslims.'

'Maulvi,' Parvez replied with some relish, 'it is precisely to get away from such reasoning that I'm suggesting we focus on the notion of *zulm*. The West needs to stop seeing Islam as its opposite: the evil of Islam as opposed to the goodness of secularism. And vice versa: Muslims mustn't see the West as the evil binary opposite of Islam. There is no solution to evil: evil can only be eradicated. And efforts to eradicate evil are always fruitless. Human communities can't relate to each other on the basis of evil, in terms of our light and their darkness.' Parvez explained that giving proper importance to the idea of 'not according anyone their due', implicit in *zulm*, is eminently suited to the evaluation of our dealings with other humans. What we Muslims had to do was to expose the *zulm* intrinsic in the concept of secularism, and not treat it as though it were inherently evil.

There was one more thing we had to appreciate, Parvez suggested. 'We must acquire a clearer perception of the relationship between ideas and the vessels that carry them. The idea of secularism, for example, cannot be separated from the vessel of modernity. Secularism and modernity go hand in hand. Muslim aversion to secularism is based, at least in part, on the fact it is embedded in modernity – so an acceptance of secularism leads inevitably and only to the embrace of modernity. And modernity, as we have learned from recent postmodern thought, comes complete with its privileging of the history of the West, its suppression and marginalization of tradition, and its specifically western definitions of science, development, progress and freedom. We must make it possible to see secularism as something distinct from the construction we are currently offered as the proper and only true meaning of modernity.

'If we desire separation of religion and politics,' Parvez said, 'we have to forge a different vessel, perhaps one with its roots in Islamic thought, without the mechanisms of *zulm* – a modernity that is defined by our own categories and shaped by our own history and tradition.'

'You realize, Maulvi,' I said, burying my head in my palms, 'this places an intolerable burden on us poor sods. Muslim thinkers have to behave like Janus, the Roman god with two faces. We have to look towards *zulm* in our own tradition; and we must face the *zulm* of western ideas, institutions and mechanisms. We have to accept and reject secularism at the same time as distilling it of its institutional injustices. We have to shape our own modernity. And we have to exist simultaneously on three planes, conscious of the impact of history on the present, and the consequences of the present on the future.'

'Who said being a Muslim is easy?' Parvez replied, as he lumbered towards my shelf in search of a suitable song and dance routine to ease his burden.

I decided to take a more conciliatory approach to secularism. But little did I realize at the time that I was heading straight for an appointment with the *zulm* of history. On this projected secular route to paradise, ambiguous as it was, undertaken with considerable doubt on my part, just like every other I had travelled, a denouement awaited. It arrived with a vengeance.

Chapter 13

THE SATANIC VERSES

Towards the end of 1988, I was returning from a conference in Kuala Lumpur. It would take more than twenty hours of pressurized incarceration to be conveyed home. To while away the purgatory I buried myself in Salman Rushdie's new novel, *The Satanic Verses*. I had respect for Rushdie as a spokesperson for the oppressed; I'd enjoyed the exuberance of his 1981 Booker Prize-winning novel, *Midnight's Children*. I found his next novel, *Shame*, mediocre: all the mechanics of his magical realism showed through a threadbare scenario, which spoilt the trick; and it seemed overly full of irrational hate for Pakistan. So I approached *The Satanic Verses* with mixed feelings.

A long and convoluted novel, *The Satanic Verses* begins with a mid-air explosion of a hijacked plane. The two main characters, Gibreel Farishta and Saladin Chamcha, are thrown out and miraculously survive their fall, landing on the English coast. Farishta is a Bollywood movie star who suffers from strange and terrible dreams which feature his own namesake, the archangel. Chamcha is an actor too; but in England, he is forced to eke out a living doing voice-overs for television commercials. On terra firma, Saladin grows horns and Farishta a halo. We follow Saladin's exploits in London; while Farishta pursues his career as an archangel that ends in disaster. Farishta moves in and out of dreams which constitute the narrative of the novel itself, with themes and characters that are meant to echo the birth of Islam and the life of

Prophet Muhammad. Finally, the two actors return separately to Bombay to engage in a concluding dialectic of good and evil.

As I turned the pages of the novel, I began to feel my anger rise, what I read gave me a nagging sense of being put upon. Halfway through all became clear. It felt as though Rushdie had plundered everything I hold dear and despoiled the inner sanctum of my identity. Every word was directed at me and I took everything personally. This is how, I remember thinking, it must feel to be raped. By the time I arrived back home, I was transfixed with anger, fear and hatred. No sooner was I in the house than Merryl Davies rang to say 'Welcome back'. A barely audible 'hello' issued from my mouth. 'Rushdie,' I managed after several tries. 'Rushdie? The novelist?' a bemused Davies enquired, 'what about him?' '*The Satanic Verses*,' I stammered, 'I've just read it.'

What was it about *The Satanic Verses* that upset me so much? I had no objection to Rushdie interrogating and severely criticizing Islam, even in fiction. Indeed, I had been doing just that most of my own life. What I, and most Muslims, took exception to was Rushdie's deliberate attempt to rewrite the life of Prophet Muhammad in an exceptionally abusive and obscene way. Frankly, I would not have cared too much if he had taken an odd fact or two from the life of the Prophet Muhammad, an occasional verse from the Qur'an, and constructed a narrative to suit his purposes. But Rushdie had plundered the life of the Prophet, the paradigm of Muslim behaviour and identity, in its entirety, systematically piling up fact after fact of his established biography. The conceit that it all happened in a dream sequence only added insult to injury – particularly when, in the novel, Rushdie goes out of his way to show that he is really dealing with facts.

In the novel, Rushdie uses the abusive term 'Mahound', coined in the Middle Ages in Christendom to describe the Prophet as a devil, to reframe the biography of Muhammad. Mahound, we are told at the outset, is engaged in founding one of the world's great religions, 'the religion of submission', the literal translation of the word 'Islam'. Mahound is described as 'broad in the shoulders', 'average height', with a 'high forehead'; a 'lightfooted man' who takes large strides – the description that classical scholars have given of the Prophet Muhammad. Lest anyone still think that Mahound is a fictional character, Rushdie tells us that his real name 'pronounced correctly [it] means he-for-whom-thanks-should-be-given' – in other words, Muhammad. When Mahound has a revelation, these are not imaginary constructions but *real* verses of the Qur'an. And, in an attempt to be too clever by half, Rushdie is not content to quote the Qur'an directly – but actually tells us in subsequent references that these verses are from 'the true recitation, al-quran'.

Mahound lives in Jahilia which is Mecca and is described as such. In Islamic parlance, *Jahilia* is the term applied to pre-Islamic Mecca. In Mecca, the main features of the biography of Prophet Muhammad – the prophetic mission in Mecca, the migration to Medina (Rushdie uses the old name of Medina, Yathrib), the conquest of Mecca, the death of the Prophet – are described in exact detail interpolated with appropriate ideological fiction. So names are changed to keep the pretence of fiction going. The Cave of Hira, where Muhammad received his first revelation, becomes Cone Mountain; and Abu Sufyan, the leading figure of Mecca who fought against the Prophet, becomes the Grandee Karim Abu Simbel; but Hind, his wife, remains Hind. Also retained in the dream narrative are the names of most of the Prophet's associates, such as the first Persian to convert to Islam, Salam Farsi, and the noted general Khalid bin Walid.

The passages of *The Satanic Verses* that caused most offence to Muslims relate to the wives of the Prophet Muhammad. In the episode of the Curtain, a prostitutes' den, Rushdie explicitly gives each prostitute the name of one of the wives. The name 'Curtain', the author tells us, refers to the *hijab*, the chador, or any veil that a Muslim woman uses; thus it suggests that a prostitute is not simply someone who offers her body for sexual intercourse for payment, but also someone who offers her body for religious rite. The clear inference is that women who veil themselves are prostitutes, that the 'harem' of the Prophet in the mosque in Medina was little more than a brothel. Inside the Curtain, the author tells us that Ayesha, who was fifteen, was the most popular of the whores; that the eldest and fattest of the whores was Sawdah who had married Mahound the same day as Ayesha; that Hafsah was hot-tempered; that Umm Salamah and Ramlah were haughty. He names Zainab bint Jahsh, Juwairiyah, Rehana the Jew, Safia, Maimunah, Zainab bint Khuzaimah, and the most erotic, Mary the Copt. No one is spared. The ages, the dates, the physical descriptions are precise; and the factual parallels are impossible to miss.

So, where is fiction actually located in *The Satanic Verses*? Rushdie is not really making anything up; he is taking all the substance of his narrative from the established sacred texts of Islam. To anyone with knowledge of Islam, and particularly to a believing Muslim, three things seem clear: that Rushdie is writing about the Prophet Muhammad and the events of his life; that his writing is a deliberate exercise, that he knows exactly what he is doing and has planned with care the use of historical sources and word-game references; and that the purpose of the exercise is not simply to present the biography of the Prophet Muhammad in a distorted and fictionalized form, but to abuse, mock, malign, throw contempt and score ideological points. The blasphemies in the novel were not accidental; they were the essential reason that the novel was written.

The life of the Prophet Muhammad is the source of Muslim identity. Muslims do not merely emulate his character and personality and follow his sayings and actions: it is the Prophet Muhammad who provides them with the ultimate reason for being a Muslim. The Prophet and his personality define Islam; and every Muslim relates to him directly and personally. That's why I felt that every word, every jibe, every obscenity in *The Satanic Verses* was directed at me – personally. There was no way, I knew, this would or could go unchallenged. Just as people threatened with physical genocide react to defend themselves, Muslims en masse would protest against this attempted annihilation of their cultural identity. It could not be otherwise. Not surprisingly, immediately after the publication of the novel, pandemonium broke out in Muslim circles.

But what could we do? The phone rang constantly. Every conversation was a personal onslaught, the counterblasts to the personal onslaught of the book itself. 'What are *you* going to do?' friends and acquaintances wanted to know. 'You should be out there defending the Muslims,' I was told repeatedly. I felt more and more harassed until I identified completely with the fox in the chase: in the last extreme, when caught at bay like a fox I was too paralysed to do anything. I wandered aimlessly around the house, I traipsed listlessly to various public meetings organized to discuss a collective Muslim response. I was in a perpetual state of stupor, largely because I could not see a way out. Some Muslims wanted the novel withdrawn; others insisted some sort of 'health' warning should be pasted in the book. Still others wanted to prosecute the author for blasphemy. Ijmali friends sought an intellectual response: 'as Muslim intellectuals, it is our responsibility to confront Rushdie and deconstruct his pestiferous book', Parvez kept saying ad nauseam.

Then came 14 February 1989. The day is etched in my memory not for its association with love but its connection with death. Ayatollah Khomeini's fatwa not only declared a death sentence for Rushdie, it made me redundant as an intellectual. Implicit in the fatwa is the proposition that Muslim thinkers are too feeble to defend their own beliefs. The mayhem that followed echoed an old Malay proverb: when two elephants fight it's the grass between that gets trampled. I was the grass. It was me they were fighting over. I felt every hefty footfall. And they just could not stop rampaging, coming at me from all directions, leaving nothing unbruised. Rushdie and the Ayatollah were fighting over the territory that was the last refuge of my humanity – for somewhere between these two extremes was the humanistic interpretation of Islam, so evident in the life of the Prophet Muhammad, that I worked endlessly to construct for modern times. Both appealed to absolutes – Rushdie to the secular absolute of freedom of expression, the Ayatollah to the absolutes of Islamic Law. And it was not as if the damage was confined to them alone. The avalanche of bile and hatred, abuse, undiluted racism and bogus parallels coming from the press and television in the wake of the fatwa was unrelentingly sweeping the entire Muslim community into an isolated, terrified, siege mentality. It was straightforward guilt by association, group culpability. We were the bad guys – nor were women exempted, especially if they walked around wearing *hijab*. The Ijmalis were mortified. Parvez was almost suicidal with depression. Gulzar Haider was lying on a sofa watching television at home in Ottawa when news of the fatwa broke. So catastrophic was the effect he couldn't move, it was as though his body had been struck by a disease. He was sofa bound for almost a year. And Merryl Davies bellowed like a fiery dragon goaded by a million arrows, writhing by turns with sorrow and rage.

We were powerless and reminded daily of our powerlessness. We were diminished, made abject, but there was a precise moment we reached our nadir. The worst point of each successive humiliation was the daily ordeal of watching the news. It was pure masochism, but we couldn't keep away from it. I had no idea it could get worse. One evening we had endured Channel 4 News, my affliction of choice. Everyone in the room, including Merryl who had delayed her departure to suffer in company, was sitting silently internalizing their own personal grief of the day. No one had energy to switch off or change channel, so we were powerless to resist the power of telecommunication that brought us a programme called 'Opinion', and the access to power that gave voice to the feminist novelist, and friend of Rushdie, Fay Weldon. Uninterrupted she spoke straight to camera, in a self-mocking tone, delivering words that were like hot knives driven directly into us. Versions of her address were later published in the *Listener, New Statesman and Society*, the *Observer*, and, in a more developed reincarnation, as a Chatto Counterblast pamphlet under the title *Sacred Cows*. In the latter, she described Islam as 'This revelation from Allah in the sixth century, this set of rigid rules for living, perceiving and thinking'. And she argues that 'The penalties for doubt and disobedience' it lays down are 'the fires of Gehenna' which 'wait and burn fiercely and painfully for anyone who dares to argue, or say "hold on a moment, are you sure?" Chastisement for non-belief is plentiful and extreme. Just open it and read, and your peace of mind has gone.' The Koran, she declared, is abusive of non-belief. Its 'prayer is kill, kill, kill'. 'The Bible', on the other hand, 'in its entirety, is at least food for thought. The Koran is food for no-thought. It is not a poem on which a society can be safely or sensibly based. It forbids change, interpretation, self-knowledge or even art, for fear of treading on Allah's creative toes. My novels don't sell in Muslim countries.' 'Maybe because they are crap,' shouted Merryl; it's the Welsh in her that keeps her energetic, I thought.

From the television screen, Weldon continued to hold forth: 'my particular parables, my alternative realities, don't suit. How could they, being the work of an unclean female unbeliever. Though if we are to trust the Koran, women (believers, that is) do get to heaven. They do have souls. That's something. But since heaven is a place where men delight themselves with virgin houris, with glasses of wine beneath the bough, it's hard to see what the grown women do there. Fetch the wine and wash the glasses, I expect.' Merryl and I looked at each other in utter disbelief. This was ignorance on a monumental scale. Weldon continued. 'Muslims?' she asked in fake irony. 'Their hearts are in the right place – it's just they're a bit primitive. Well, Arabs, Pakis. Muslim. All the same. They live in this advanced and intelligent society of ours.' We were now down to pure racism. 'They insist on their religious right in this multicultural, multi-religious, benighted society' to Islamic schools. 'And almost convince us, so great is our guilt. Of course they're not right. You cannot, should not, teach a primitive, fear-ridden religion.

'I think it a pity,' Weldon went on, 'when they attach themselves to the Koran, because I see it as a limited and limiting text when it comes to the comprehension of what I define as God. Look, you can build a decent society around the Bible: if you value the Gaia notions that pervade the Old Testament, puzzle over the parables of Jesus . . . But the Koran? No. It doesn't acknowledge the concept. Heaven (or hell) is for the hereafter: forget now.' Once she was through with the Qur'an, Weldon moved on to the Prophet. 'To be good, in terms of the Prophet's instructions,' she thundered, 'is too often the exact opposite of being good in ordinary terms. To be good according to Muhammad is to chastise your wife and children when they're rebellious – and you take the hand of the unbeliever when he offers it to you, but when his back is turned the advice is to slay him. "You have my full authority," says the Prophet . . .'

I became conscious of another sound accompanying Weldon's voice. I looked around and there was Merryl with great fat tears rolling down her cheeks, sobbing uncontrollably from her heart's core. The house was in uproar. My children were panicked, flying to fuss around the godmother they relied on to make them laugh in any crisis. My wife joined the comforting brigade. 'Oh, how could they? How could anyone allow this?' Merryl gasped in utter misery. I put my arms around her and recalled that Al-Ghazali, who, unlike Weldon, knew a thing or two about doubt, said deep ignorance comes out of the mouth of people who think they know when in fact they know not. 'These are the most tyrannical people in the world,' I said, not having to strive for venomous effect. Weldon had committed a gross act of *zulm*.

Merryl cried for two days. 'I can't get it out of my head,' she kept explaining through the tears. 'It's just hate-speak,' she'd say before breaking down again. 'I am going to complain,' she said one day. Not that complaining made much difference. At last I was stung into activity. I replaced the word Muslim in the Chatto Counterblast pamphlet with the word 'Jew' and took it to a lawyer friend. 'If the word Jew was really there,' he told me, 'she'd be in the dock at the Old Bailey before you could say the word "racist".' Then, I replaced Muslim with 'homosexual', and showed it to a gay friend from my days at London Weekend Television. 'If she'd really said that she wouldn't be able to walk the streets of Hampstead,' he told me. I got a similar response when I replaced 'Muslims' with 'blacks'. It seemed Weldon could fabricate whatever she wished and produce a prejudiced diatribe simply because Muslims were fair game. I rang Stuart Weir, editor of *New Statesman and Society*. We first met in my student days, when he was working for *The Times* and we were both members of Hackney Citizens' Rights. 'Would you publish a response from me to the Weldon essay?' I asked. 'I know you'll write a powerful response,' he said. 'But what it says is so self-evidently true.' So, the absolutes of secularism were beyond question. I rang the *Observer*, the *Independent*, *The Times*. No one wanted to hear my point of view. It was clear some people had a damn sight more freedom of expression than others. The *zulm* of history had me in its grip.

Of course, Weldon was not an isolated incident. Every defence of Rushdie, every attack on Islam and Muslims, every racist article in the press hit home – hit me personally as if I was its singular target. And it was the same for everyone I knew. It would have been more than too much without having to cope with what some Muslims were up to. The double offensive seemed unendurable. I was equally enraged by those who chose to burn the book in Bradford. Did they not know the history of book burning in Britain and in Europe? And I was more than usually outraged when Kalim Siddiqui began encouraging young Muslims to answer the call of the fatwa. I was being brutalized from both sides. I was being overrun by the combined forces of the liberal inquisition and Muslim fanaticism. I felt my humanity seeping out of me.

'What are we going to do?' Merryl kept asking when the days of tears abated. 'We will do what Muslims have always done,' I replied. 'We'll fight the *zulm* of this wretched book with a book.' We were both due to leave for Malaysia in a few days to start work on a series for Malaysian television. It was our lifeline to financial security, but it felt like plotting a desertion. I think the prospect of leaving confirmed the commitment we knew we had to make. 'We'd never forgive ourselves if we didn't do this no matter what,' we kept telling each other.

We had come to the unavoidable, unvarnished truth of our condition. And in our last extreme we grasped hold of our tradition and submitted to what its ethos and reflexes demanded of us. In Islam, there is a rich and well-established tradition of books fighting books; the most celebrated example being the war of the books between philosophers and their critics. Al-Ghazali opened the attack in the early eleventh century with his monumental *The Incoherence of the Philosophers*. Immediately afterwards, Ibn Rushd, the doyen of rationalist philosophers, replied with *The Incoherence of the Incoherence*. The battle raged for centuries leading to 'The Incoherence of the Incoherence of the Incoherence' to the nth degree – ending when the victory was finally conceded to Al-Ghazali on the basis of his arguments. It was by no means an isolated case. In their history Muslims became 'people of the book' in all senses of the term. The connection between reading the Qur'an and reading in general exemplified the pervasive meaning attached to pursuit of knowledge as a form of worship, that knowledge and worship are two faces of the same coin. We were going to be true to our history: we were going to answer a book with a book. *Khalas!* It was settled.

During March 1989, Merryl and I sat down to write *Distorted Imagination: Lessons from the Rushdie Affair*. Our position was established quickly, it needed little debate. We were not interested in banning the book; as liberal Muslims we were against censorship and as sentient people we knew it would simply push *The Satanic Verses* underground, making it even more of a cult. Neither were we interested in the notion of blasphemy as understood in British law, for which we could find no counterpart in Islam – indeed, *The Satanic Verses* can be credited with introducing the very idea of blasphemy for the first time to Muslims. Anyway, the powerful never need blasphemy laws – they command sufficient levers of influence to stop a play, a film, a book that violates their sacred territory even before it gets in front of an audience. We had three specific goals. We wanted to examine *The Satanic Verses*. It was evident virtually all non-Muslims had no idea of the precise 'problem' with its content. It required knowledge of Islam to decode the text. And even if people had the required knowledge, the decoding would only be possible by those who actually got around to reading the book! We wanted to examine Rushdie's oeuvre and locate it in Orientalist lore, and we wanted to explore the (il)legitimacy of the Ayatollah's fatwa.

My conversations with Muslim youth in Bradford, Manchester and East London made me realize the fatwa had become a source of pride for them. For the first time in their lives the fatwa gave them a perverse and real sense of power and identity. They could not fail to notice that when the late Patriarch of Qom, a master of panic politics who knew the value of power, issued his fatwa those who but a moment before were throwing scorn on uncouth literalist Muslims stood up and listened. Their contempt, no doubt, doubled, but they *listened*. When power is met with equally brute power, publishers begin to put profits aside, the very authors who mocked and ridiculed the powerless suddenly begin to apologize, freedom of expression turns into fried egg, sunny side up, spread all over their faces.

We wanted to show Muslim youth that this sense of power was nothing but a mirage. The Ayatollah's version of Islam does not draw its sustenance from the real world: it is based on a mountain of obscurantist jurisprudence fossilized in history and totally divorced from the world of today. The exponents of this jurisprudence are so sure of themselves that they allow no room for dynamic change or complexity. They are so sure of the compassion of their religion that they never have to practise it. They are so convinced of their own righteousness that it is impossible for them to understand that other people can also have a just cause. This variety of Islam – based less on the Qur'an and the Prophetic paradigm and more on the logic of

Muslim imperialism – can only generate momentary power. We wanted to provide Muslims with a different sense of power: the power of their intellectual tradition and its contemporary relevance. And finally, we were interested in re-establishing the integrity of our culture and religious history. This process, we argued, will necessitate a change in western perception, and will naturally lead to a genuine shared understanding that a real offence has been committed. Only then could we discuss how the offence could or should be treated.

We spent just over a year working on *Distorted Imagination*. Now we had a way to deal with the continuing onslaught. We could even deal with the playground taunts and questions my oldest children brought home from school. 'Islam doesn't mean that, does it, Daddy?' 'Muslims don't think that, do they, Merryl?' For most of the year, I hardly went out; days, weeks would pass without a shave. I began to resemble those bearded Mullahs I so dreaded. Every morning I'd ring Merryl. In the course of the conversation she would pose the pertinent question of the day, and I would spend most of the day trying to answer it. Our stance was solid and unified, our analysis was another matter, hammered out in the heated arguments characteristic of our working method.

'What about the fact that *The Satanic Verses* is a work of fiction?' Merryl asked one morning.

'I think this is rather important,' I argued. 'Muslims, of all people, as their history demonstrates so vividly, are aware of the power of ideas.' Faith may or may not move mountains; but ideas certainly do, particularly when transformed into literature or technology. For then they can be turned into ideologies, bulldozers, tools of suppression, physical and psychological torture and used to justify the eradication of entire cultures and histories. There is no vehicle more powerful for a direct onslaught on a people's cultural and religious identity than a work of fiction. It gives no recourse to the victims to shoot it down. But we were also interested in demonstrating how much of Rushdie's 'fiction' was in fact grounded in what Muslims regard as established fact. We noted that the dream sequences in *The Satanic Verses*, particularly the chapter on Mahound, read like paraphrases of passages from a well-known contemporary biography of the Prophet: Martin Lings's

Muhammad: His Life Based on the Earliest Sources. Here, for example, is Rushdie's description of the destruction of the idols in Mecca.

When the guardian of the temple . . . saw the approach of Khalid with a great host of warriors, he . . . went to the idol of the goddess . . . he hung his sword about her neck, saying, 'If thou be truly a goddess, Uzza, defend thyself and thy servant against the coming of Mahound.' Then Khalid entered the temple, and when the goddess did not move the guardian said, 'Now verily do I know that the God of Mahound is the true God, and this stone but a stone.' Then Khalid broke the temple and the idol and returned to Mahound in his tent. And the Prophet asked: 'What didst thou see?' Khalid spread his arms. 'Nothing,' said he. 'Then thou hast not destroyed her,' the Prophet cried. 'Go again, and complete thy work.' So Khalid returned to the fallen temple, and there an enormous woman, all black but for her long scarlet tongue, came running at him, naked from head to foot, her black hair flowing to her ankles from her head. Nearing him, she halted, and recited in her terrible voice of sulphur and hellfire: 'Have you heard of Lat, and Manat, and Uzza, the Third, the Other? They are the Exalted Birds . . .' But Khalid interrupted her, saying, 'Uzza, those are the Devil's verses, and you the Devil's daughter, a creature not to be worshipped, but denied.' So he drew his sword and cut her down.

And here's how Lings describes it:

The nearest to Mecca of the three most eminent shrines of paganism was the temple of al-Uzza at Nakhlah. The Prophet now sent Khalid to destroy this centre of idolatry. At the news of his approach the warden of the temple hung his sword on the statue of the goddess and called upon her to defend himself and slay Khalid or to become a monotheist. Khalid demolished the temple and its idols, and returned to Mecca. 'Didst thou see nothing?' said the Prophet. 'Nothing,' said Khalid. 'Then thou hast not destroyed her,' said the Prophet. 'Return and destroy her.' So Khalid went again to Nakhlah, and out of the ruins of the temple there came a black woman, entirely naked, with long and wildly flowing hair. 'My spine was seized with shivering,' said Khalid afterwards. But he shouted, 'Uzza, denial is for thee, not worship,' and drawing his sword he cut her down.

'What about the fact that he's a postmodern author?' Davies imperiously set the question of another day.

'Highly relevant,' I replied. Postmodernism is a reaction against modernity but like modernity it is grounded in secularism. While postmodernists claim to be relativists, there is nothing relative when it comes to such absolutes of secularism as total freedom of expression. With its stress on the purity of art and the autonomy of culture as a whole, postmodernism has turned secular humanism into a sacred theology. Here the God-centred religiosity of traditional religions is replaced by literature which occupies the conventional place of God. While all religions recognize the value and importance of literature – both the Bible and the Qur'an are seen by their adherents as great literature – the postmodernists do not even have the courtesy to acknowledge the fact that religion may be as important, meaningful and necessary a part of the human condition as fiction. Their quest is for perpetual, continuous and meaningless (since there are no truths to be discovered) doubt, which is the basic foundation of the postmodern creed. Such a quest has frightening implications for personal identity; it can only produce more and more personal anxiety and insecurity.

'In this regard,' I suggested, 'both Rushdie and the Ayatollah are on the same ground.' When one's ideology becomes the yardstick by which reality is measured, one exists in a totally insulated space that permits no counter-reality. In this insulated space it's not possible to see the objectivity of others with any objectivity, or to see one's own infantile emotions in similar terms. The world is divided into black and white. Or to use Rushdie's own words, 'the light of secularism and the darkness of religion'. It is not possible to understand the position of others, let alone comprehend their arguments, when one's own value is *the* fundamental value to which all other values must defer.

'Are we going to forgive Rushdie?' Merryl asked as we reached the end of *Distorted Imagination*.

'We must argue that no physical harm should come to Rushdie,' I replied. 'But equally we're not going to forgive him.' We would be fools to do so, on two accounts. If we don't defend our cultural and historic territory we can't hope to survive the future without losing our religious identity. The fact that *The Satanic Verses* is a work of fiction does not mean it is not real or cannot be condemned. There are many things which are not real and yet have caused immense suffering. The myth of manifest destiny is pure fiction; yet there is nothing benign about this fiction as Native Americans and people from Africa and Asia will testify. Much of the literary fiction of the eighteenth, nineteenth and even twentieth centuries used this myth to shovel out the manure about the exotic Orient, the beastly savages, and the noble white men taking up their burdens in tropical hellholes and getting no thanks for their pains. *Mein Kampf* is as much a work of fiction: a work of imagination. How many educated Europeans scoffed and said it was too silly to take notice of, only a book after all, we should be able to rise above it? Oppressive thought, ideas and malign imagination find their expression first and foremost through words, and the potency of fiction often serves as its main vehicle of transmission. That's why we cannot turn a blind eye and forgive Rushdie, I said. Moreover, we shouldn't forgive because, as Rushdie says in *The Satanic Verses* itself, our 'forgiveness [would] make possible the deepest and sweetest corruption of all, namely the idea that he [has done] nothing wrong'. 'Oh, nice one, *chappou*,' Merryl shot back using the label she had recently accorded me, 'quoting Rushdie back to himself.'

'He obviously knows a thing or two about identity and corruption,' I observed with a grin.

Writing a book is one thing; getting it published quite another. Power orders what passes for freedom of expression. I was hoping *Distorted Imagination* would be published by Cassell, my usual publishers. They, regretfully, declined. The mass paperback house Headline accepted the manuscript, then changed their minds. We touted the manuscript from one publisher to another; all of them praised its contents but refused to publish it. Then, something extraordinary happened.

My publisher at Cassell resigned in disgust at its refusal to publish *Distorted Imagination*. John Duncan, an American long settled in Britain, was of Native American ancestry and rejoiced in his Indian name of Little Red Cloud. I met him in the early 1980s, during *Inquiry* days. He was the director of Mansell, an independent publishing house with a highly respected Middle East and Islamic list. Mansell had published over a dozen of my books before it was taken over by Cassell. I followed John to the new imprint. He was a deeply humane, totally secular person; and we became close friends. 'I don't understand what the fuss over *The Satanic Verses* is all about,' he said. 'But I hear your screams. I can see being a Muslim nowadays is much like being a Native American: to live perpetually on the edge, to be constantly bruised by an existence at the margins.' He quit Cassell, cashed in his pension, and set up on his own as an independent publisher. Grey Seal, his new imprint, took its name from the Red Indian designation of his elder daughter. *Distorted Imagination* became Grey Seal's first book. It received some glowing reviews; but was solemnly ignored by most of the liberal establishment. Later, it acquired a cult status in Muslim circles, particularly amongst students.

For us, freedom of expression turned out to be a one-way street. We fought a book with a book but our book remained silent, marginalized. In the world of western secularism, freedom of expression belongs to those with secular power, or access and opportunity within the secular structures of power. That's the problem with secularism. As the pre-eminent truth and doctrine of the West, it renders insignificant and makes invisible all that is outside its purview, all the possibilities and potentials outside its framework of power. Secularism masks the will to power; and like all authoritarian ideologies, it nurtures homicidal tendencies.

After *Distorted Imagination* was published, I didn't feel like staying in Britain. The atmosphere was foul with bitterness and acrimony. While I contemplated getting as far away as possible, I recalled I still had unfinished business in Turkey. And, as usual, Ekmeleddin Ihsanoglu obliged with an invitation to yet another conference. As usual, once the official business was over, Feruh Alptekin ushered me around Istanbul. 'This time, Feruh,' I told him in a determined voice, 'no more jokes: I really do want a Turkish bath.' 'No problem, boss,' he replied, 'I know just where to take you.' We went to Cemberlitas Hammami, also known as the 'rose bath' because the big stone in the centre of the bathing room was encrusted with marble roses. The writing on the stone declared: 'this hammam is of a beauty unique in the world'. The bath was crowded; but I decided to join the patrons anyway. A *tellak* – a bath attendant – accompanied me through a procedure lasting well over two hours. One is not allowed, he told me, to be naked in the hammam – not even for a second. Remembering the incident of the bus in Rawalpindi, I repeatedly made sure my loincloth was firmly in place. He scrubbed me with a *kesse*, a goatskin glove, until my skin began to peel and I could not contain the pain, shades of the shave in Rawalpindi. Then I was lathered with huge masses of soap and washed with boiling hot water, followed by a vigorous massage. Finally, I took a plunge in excruciatingly cold water. I emerged from the process resembling a well-boiled lobster. But I was refreshed, exhilarated. My friend was right. It cleanses every cell in your body. I lit a fresh Havana cigar, took a few puffs, and felt prepared to take on all the *zulm* history could hurl in my direction.

Chapter 14

MULTICULTURALISM, THEN AND NOW

However ready one may be it is still possible to be taken unawares. It was a cold February morning, and as is my wont, I was luxuriating over the Sunday papers. Quite a few pieces were dedicated to yet another approaching anniversary of the fatwa. Little had changed. Nowhere in the western media could I detect any appreciation of the profound impact the Rushdie affair had produced among Muslims. It had generated a hasty abandonment of the secular road as the route to reform of Islam. I kept running into more and more British Muslims beating a retreat from the comfortable enclaves they had made for themselves in what they regarded hopefully as adaptive secular assimilation. All were disgusted, affronted to the core of their being by the tirades of intolerance, prejudice and ignorance that had overwhelmed them. They found unceasing vitriol in the outpourings of the press and the liberal establishment, from the likes of Harold Pinter, Freddy Forsyth, Anthony Burgess, the luminaries of Charter 88, to Robert Kilroy-Silk. The fatwa mentality was generally and readily accepted as the entirety of what Islam meant and was about, leaving no space for any other kind of Muslim identity or outlook. All those Muslims who had been evicted by the secular fundamentalists were appalled at the simplistic choice presented to them. Faced with the dichotomy of Islam bad, Rushdie paragon of all secular virtues, these

Muslims were required to choose the latter without question or caveat. And one by one in the inner recesses of their consciousness each had revolted. It was not the kind of either/or the West was supposed to represent, not the liberty and freedom they expected or conceived a multicultural society should mean. Shell shocked, they were making a journey back to Islam, seeking a refuge of sanity in their original identity. I even knew a Bangladeshi Maoist, a true political animal, now submitting himself to a personal course of re-education in Islam. It meant only one thing: there was much work to be done. Life rafts had to be made for these ideological refugees. And just possibly, maybe, the exercise would enliven the process of reform for the entire *ummah*.

The doorbell rang. 'Not Jehovah's Witnesses again?' I murmured. Reluctant to break my train of thought, I grudgingly bestirred myself. I opened the door to be greeted by two exceptionally short men. The golden brown features of neither sported a beard. Destiny too moves on. Before I could say 'Yes?' one darted forward with the speed and agility of a gecko to embrace me with unbridled enthusiasm. It was Nasiruddin, an old friend from Malaysia. A 160-centimetre matchstick of perpetual motion, arrived as the emissary of my new adventure. He was accompanied by an official from the Malaysian Embassy, a solemn person accoutred in the de rigueur style of the upwardly mobile: a Dunhill suit, a conspicuous Dunhill watch, a Dunhill briefcase held firmly in his hand suggesting it might contain a large amount of cash and an immaculate pair of what I deduced were Dunhill shoes. It was obvious he was not going to say much.

'How long since we last met?' Nasiruddin asked as he prowled past me into the house; I trotted behind to keep pace.

Well, it must have been quite some time. We'd met during my student days in FOSIS. Nasiruddin, or Nasir for short since he really was, was active in the Malaysian Islamic Study Group, one of the constituents of FOSIS. For a small man he was a large presence. He spoke with the rapidity characteristic of all his activity: the speed of light. None of his perpetual motion went to waste and he acquired an awesome reputation for getting things done. However impossible Nasiruddin could do it; and do it in record time. But I was in Sunday morning fallible human mode; when I caught up with him I bent down, pulled his chin up with my index finger, looked him straight in the eyes, and stated categorically: 'Nasir, whatever it is, I don't want to do it!'

'Relax! Brother Zia,' he replied. 'I'm only a messenger,' he said, walking off for three rounds of the living room pausing momentarily to look out of the window. I noticed the Mercedes parked in front of the house. 'Have you brought your family with you?' I asked.

'Yes.'

'Well, ask them to come in.'

In came Nasir's charming and nimble wife. She was even shorter than Nasir. There followed, in single file, six tiny kids in decreasing order of size. The eldest, a boy of twelve, was less than two feet tall. He walked, talked and behaved just like his father. Indeed, all his children looked like perfect cloned miniature Nasirs.

'I see you've been rather busy,' I said with a congratulatory smile, patting Nasir on the back.

'You know I'm private secretary to Brother Anwar now?' Nasir asked, taking my compliment in his stride which took him twice more round the room before I could reply.

'I've heard the rumour.'

'I'm here to tell you Boss wants to meet the Ijmalis.'

Brother Anwar was Anwar Ibrahim, now the Minister of Education of Malaysia. We went back a long way. When I was the general secretary of FOSIS, Anwar led the Muslim Youth Movement of Malaysia (ABIM). We met whenever he visited London. When, in 1974, he led mass demonstrations in Kuala Lumpur against peasant poverty and hunger, we organized rallies in London in his support. When, in the aftermath of the demonstrations, he was arrested under the Internal Security Act and spent twenty-two months in jail, we agitated for his release. During my first visit to Malaysia he drove me around Kuala Lumpur; and persuaded me to address a gathering of his youthful followers. In 1982, Anwar was brought into mainstream Malaysian politics by the then Deputy Prime Minister, Mahathir Muhammad. When Mahathir became Prime Minister, he accelerated Anwar's rise within the ruling party, the United Malay National Organization or UMNO. In swift succession Anwar became Minister of Youth and Sports, Minister of Agriculture, and within a few years, occupied the influential Ministry of Education. While Mahathir was undoubtedly responsible for the meteoric rise of his young protégé, there could be no doubt Anwar himself was a shrewd politician with a brilliant knack of mobilizing the masses. In particular, Anwar was an amazing public speaker. To hear him was to witness a tour de force of unparalleled linguistic dexterity, he could leave audiences spellbound. During the 1980s, Anwar used his oratorical skills to reciprocate Mahathir's patronage and rally the Malays behind their leader during a string of political crises: the 1983 Constitutional crisis, the 1987 split of UMNO, and the 1988 dispute with the Judiciary. To Malaysians, it seemed Anwar was Mahathir's heir apparent. Mahathir, popularly known as the 'Old Man', actively encouraged the idea.

Besides being an astute politician, Anwar was also an intellectual. Poverty, illiteracy, environment, science policy, economic development – he was concerned about all these, alive to all the contemporary debates and critiques and in search of sustainable solutions. What made him distinctive was seeking solutions within the worldview of Islam. But his passion, above all else, was pluralism. Anwar was not only at ease with his Muslim identity, which defined his approach to all matters. He was just as much at home with the philosophy of Buddha, Confucius and the ancient Indian sages as with the great thinkers of Islamic civilization. Unlike other Muslim intellectuals, he appreciated and acknowledged the truths and values of other faiths, cultures and civilizations without ever feeling this impinged on his own identity or fearing the loss of his own faith. For him, tolerance was a practical virtue, one that emerged from his own lived experience of pluralism. As he never failed to remind people, he came from that wondrous crossroads and meeting place of human history and cultures, the island of Penang, Pearl of the Orient. In sum, it made Anwar not only exceptional; but someone on the same wavelength as the Ijmalis.

'We lack thinkers and intellectuals.' Those were Anwar's first words when we met in the Awana Club, on the outskirts of Kuala Lumpur. The entire extended Ijmali clan had been brought together for the occasion; though, ostensibly, we were there to attend a conference. We sat in the spacious living room that came as standard with each of the

Awana Club's suites. The door to the balcony was open, giving spectacular views over the golf course, Awana's *raison d'être*, and the encircling mountains clad in thick equatorial rainforest. Fortunately, the room looked away from the tallest mountain peak where the gambling casinos of Las-Vegas-like Genting Highlands perched like an ungainly concrete eagle's nest on the summit. Anwar, as always, was attired in an elegant suit and chic tie. He was a commanding presence; and enjoyed being the centre of attention. He was also an inveterate tease with a sharp sense of humour. 'It is sheer undiluted pleasure to be amongst such an illustrious gathering of luminaries,' he said, the look on his face reflecting the fact that his tongue was firmly implanted in his cheek. 'But there just aren't enough of you to go around. We lack a critical mass of intellectuals. Somehow, we must produce a plethora of serious thinkers and intellectuals. The trick will be to recapture the conditions of our time in Andalusia.'

A waiter brought coffee; and the conversation stopped momentarily. Anwar liked Nescafé which came in a plastic sachet, accompanied by equally plastic dry milk. Most of us had Malaysian coffee: a black viscous liquid, with an over-abundance of sugar to which was added gooey condensed milk poured from a tin.

'Spanish historians of today speak of experiments in *"convivencia"* – live and let live, a harmonious and enriching way of living together which lasted around eight hundred years – as the main characteristic of Muslim Spain,' Anwar resumed as we imbibed our local coffee.

But he was quick to caution against jumping to the conclusion that *convivencia*, because it lasted so long, was totally harmonious. There were hostilities on all sides. In his view, what made *convivencia* such a dazzling success, and propelled it for so long, was the intellectual climate it generated and sustained. 'Do you think we can generate such an intellectual climate in Malaysia?' he asked.

We all looked at each other. Everyone realized Anwar had thrown down a challenge.

Anwar sketched out his view of Malaysia and the task ahead. In Malaysia, he argued, Islamic society has to be inclusive. Authoritarianism and jingoism could not be permitted to dominate society. Cultural jingoism, in the guise of puritan Islam, while understandable as a reaction to western dominance, could not redeem or liberate – it would simply mean a change of personnel, with Malays now assuming the top slot, only to replay the old history of oppression and injustice. The essence of Malaysia was being a multicultural society. To be a just, pluralistic, civil society, Anwar asserted, it must bring in perspectives from Islamic and Confucian, Indian and western thought to generate a dynamic moral and economic order. The consequences would not be confined to Malaysia: for the West it would mean seeing Islam, Confucianism, Hinduism and the former colonies in a new perspective, appreciating the pluralism and humanism of Asia, acknowledging that democracy can be embraced without losing one's spiritual tradition – that secularism is not an evolutionary necessity. Anwar liked to quote; and quoted extensively from Muslim, Chinese and western scholars in his speeches. For our benefit on this occasion he cited the Indian philosopher Muhammad Iqbal, the Bengali novelist Rabindranath Tagore, and the Filipino writer Jose Rizal.

'There are today in Asia,' he said, 'progressive trends and retrogressive counter-currents. Reactionary elements have their horns locked with ardent advocates of democracy and civil society. We need thinkers who can argue with conviction for pluralism and open society from the perspective of Islam. We need these people to lay the foundation for an intellectual *convivencia*.'

Anwar liked to be called 'Brother'; or, more appropriately, by the Malay equivalent, 'Sudara'. He refused to play the appellation game typical of Malaysian politics. The rise of Malaysian politicians along with worthies of every stripe could be tracked by the addition of a string of titles and their accompanying initials before and after their names. The titles were honours handed out by the monarch. Since Malaysia had seven monarchs and each took a turn at being the elected Agong, king of Malaysia, there was an abundance of titles to go round. Anwar remained just Anwar. Ijmalis, however, chose to call him by his official Parliamentary accolade: 'The Right Honourable', which in Malay reads 'Yang Behormat', or YB for short. We pronounced it 'Why Be': why be a politician of integrity and moral acumen with intellectual concerns in an intellectual desert of a country knee deep in political corruption and authoritarianism? Why be an Anwar?

The sun disappeared over the horizon as Anwar left. In the tropics day turns into night almost instantaneously. The Ijmalis sat ruminating in the gloom. Then Anwar Nasim, an occasional member of our group, jumped up exclaiming 'Eureka!' A tall, lean man, prone to dramatic outbursts, this Anwar acquired an international reputation as a geneticist in Canada before returning to work in his native Pakistan. He spoke as though the world were a theatre, and he a Shakespearean actor. 'I've got it,' he announced, elaborately miming his emergence from a bathtub for the benefit of the classically challenged. 'All we have to do is to clone Anwar. Every Muslim country should have one. With Muslim societies awash with cloned YBs, sanity will return and we can all hang our intellectual hats on the hook behind the door.' We clapped and cheered the performance. If only it was that simple! The 'Mini Me thesis' of Muslim reform – what a shortcut that would be on the road to paradise.

Since Anwar Nasim made no immediate move to develop the necessary cloning technology we had no option but to prepare for the long haul. Two Ijmalis – Merryl and Munawar Anees – moved to become our contingent in residence in Kuala Lumpur. Despite Anwar's insistence, I chose to keep my roots firmly in London. I commuted between Kuala Lumpur and London four or five times a year. School summer holidays meant the whole family could accompany me, descending on Merryl's tropical residence for the duration and becoming eager enthusiasts for all things Malaysian. The Ijmalis' work began with 'intellectual discourses': specialized seminars on contemporary thought and philosophy for small, selected groups of professionals, bureaucrats and academics. We were to be the catalyst in discussions of the relevance – or otherwise – of Islam to modern problems. Our goal, as specified by Anwar, was to force the group to think creatively, to think in terms of ethics rather than ready-made Shariah injunctions, to think about the future rather than the past and to probe and critique all varieties of established thought. Most of all, our task was to challenge any and all forms of complacency. We ran dozens of 'intellectual discourses' during a year, and became involved with a whole range of Malaysian institutions. Eventually, the closed seminars became larger, more open conferences and workshops. On one occasion

Merryl even found herself addressing a roomful of obscurantist religious scholars, all trained at Al-Azhar University in Egypt, on the sophisticated challenge posed by the scientific worldview. It was hard to ascertain whose complacency got the biggest jolt as a result.

The traffic of ideas certainly wasn't one-way. We were in Malaysia to learn as much as to teach. And we found *one* man, a true scholar of classical proportions, who had much to teach. Syed Muhammad Naguib al-Attas commanded great respect and reverence throughout the archipelago for the sheer virtuosity of his intellect as well as his outspoken views. He was the first holder of the Chair of Malay Language and Literature and the first Director of the Institute of Malay Language, Literature and Culture, which he founded in 1973, at the University of Malaya. He cut his intellectual teeth by resolving the controversy of the dating of the Terengganu Stone, an unprepossessing granite tombstone on which hinged the academic puzzle of when Islam arrived in Malaya. Through an ingenious variety of logical, mathematical, linguistic, cultural, philosophical and mystical arguments, and by reconstructing the lost part of the stone, the Professor overturned the conventional Orientalist dating and produced '*The Correct Date of The Terengganu Inscription: Friday, 4th Rajab, 702 A.H./Friday 22nd February, 1303 A.C.*', as he snappily entitled his paper. He went on to discover '*The Oldest Known Malay Manuscript: A Sixteenth Century Malay Translation of the Aqaid of al-Nasafi*'. He topped his accomplishments by writing two monumental commentaries on the mysticism of Hamzah Fansuri and Nur al-din al-Raniri, the grandfathers of all South-east Asian mystics. The tomes were worthy of a Nobel Prize for the footnotes alone! By virtue of his position he taught everyone who was anyone in Malaysia, including Anwar. Throughout the land he was known simply as 'The Professor'. 'He's the shining light that's guided us all,' Anwar used to say, 'though at times he becomes dazed and confused with his own luminosity.' The Professor had no doubt he was a towering intellect in a land of midgets and made sure everyone appreciated the fact. 'I am surrounded by fools and imbeciles,' he told anyone willing to listen. 'They come and ask me questions,' he was fond of saying, 'but a stupid question makes a fool of anyone who deigns to answer, so I send them away.'

I first encountered the Professor at FOSIS summer conferences in my student days. But I really came to know him while making 'Encounters with Islam', a series of interviews I did for BBC TV in 1985. The Professor was one of the interviewees and after the recording he stayed on for a few days as my house guest. We discovered a shared passion for Havana cigars and deep cerebral explorations. In person, the Professor loomed as large as his reputation. His bulky frame was solidly fleshed; he sported a well-kept white beard and a head of speckled white and grey curly hair which betrayed his Yemeni ancestry. The Al-Attases originate from the Hadramaut in Yemen where they are a hereditary clan of saints. The trade routes of the Indian Ocean brought them to South-east Asia where his ancestors were influential in the spread of Islam. The Professor was a Syed, meaning he claimed direct descent from the Prophet Muhammad. He wore this distinction with a military bearing, a legacy of being educated at Sandhurst and a high-ranking army officer before switching to the life of an academic. Together these elements added up to a simple fact: the Professor insisted on formality, decorum, protocol and proper etiquette. Or as he always termed it, *adab*, the classical Islamic term for proper behaviour.

When in Malaysia we made a habit of visiting the Professor in pairs at least once a month. On rare and special occasions, when the Professor was willing to entertain a large group, we all went together. The ritual was always the same. We arrived at his house in Petaling Jaya about eleven o'clock at night. It was a beautiful house, designed and built by the Professor himself. Walking in was like entering twelfth-century Andalusia. The rooms were arranged in a rectangle overlooking an inner courtyard, with covered walks supported by pillars. The courtyard was surrounded by lobbies and balconies. A set of stairs led to the private rooms overlooking the courtyard on the upper storey. It was perfect in every imitative detail, the Professor even had titles, doors, windows, sculpture, decorative armour and other paraphernalia imported from Spain. We would sit in the flower-filled patio. Turkish coffee and Malaysian sweets would arrive. And the Professor would begin by offering me a freshly cut cigar and lighting one for himself. 'Justice,' he once told me, 'is putting a thing in its proper place.' Justice always demanded our discussions be conducted with proper *adab*.

'What is the question of the day?' he would ask. There was only one question, a question the Professor had struggled with all his life: what is knowledge? And we asked it every time we met, with only slight variation – what is the *problem* of knowledge, how do we *define* knowledge, what is *true* knowledge? The Professor was slightly deaf and wore a hearing aid. Once the question was put, the hearing aid was switched off to prevent the distraction of supplementary enquiries. We would settle back and listen. Not hearing did nothing to blunt the Professor's awareness. If he detected any wavering in the reverential attention of his listener, he would drop his original topic and start explaining why swine are incapable of recognizing the value of pearls and donkeys can never appreciate gourmet meals. As we became accepted novices we were occasionally allowed a few supplementary questions to clarify matters – provided we asked with due etiquette and respect. When the Professor reached an appropriate conclusion, the meeting would end, by which time the early hours of the morning were creeping towards dawn.

We delighted in the atmosphere of this beautiful land, excitedly exploring its potential parallels with the circumstances that generated the glorious era of Muslim Spain. Secretly, in Ijmali circles, we began to hope concentrated efforts to address the shortcomings of Malaysian society might recreate that intellectual ferment and pluralism. Granada might live again! Muslim Spain could be made to flower once more in an equatorial hothouse, a new Islamic paradise, a shining example to all.

Muslims first landed near a little island on the southern tip of Spain in 711. The island is named for their commanding general, the Rock of Tariq after Tariq Bin Ziad: *Jabl al-Tariq*, more familiarly known as Gibraltar. Their advance was swift; within decades virtually the whole Iberian Peninsula was a part of the *ummah*. Once their rule was established Muslims demonstrated a tolerance towards the Christian and Jewish population unmatched in history. The Qur'an describes Christians and Jews as 'the people of the Book': Islam considers itself a continuation of Judaism and Christianity, the Abrahamic religions. It was part of the mindset of early Islam to regard Christian and Jewish communities as fellow, if slightly misguided, religious travellers. Nowhere was the meaning of this outlook given greater effect than in

Muslim Spain. A text survives of the agreement signed by the Arab commander Abd al-Aziz and Theodomir, Visigoth Prince of Murcia, in 713. The Christians were allowed to keep their churches and monasteries; and the Jews their synagogues. Members of both communities retained their personal possessions and regulated their life according to their own laws. The Visigoth system of taxes, with its manifold burdens, was replaced by a single tax in lieu of having to perform military service. Moreover, this tax was on a sliding scale according to the ability to pay and professional status; and women, children, monks, invalids, the sick and slaves were exempt. For the most part, slaves were set free. Many sources indicate that living conditions actually improved for the bulk of the population. Muslims held sway in Spain for almost 800 years. The last sultanate, Granada, fell in 1492 and in short order the commanders of the *Reconquista* (the Spanish Crusades to expel Muslims from Spain) expelled all Jews from their territory. Within a dozen years, all Muslims were banished. Multiculturalism and the intellectual excitement it made possible were expunged in favour of purity of the blood and monolithic orthodoxy of worship.

Ah, for the gardens of Granada, where once coexistence was more than a dream. Moorish Spain was a heterogeneous and heterodox land. Malaysia too over the centuries developed a rich multicultural patchwork under the auspices of Islam. From ancient times the archipelago had been a fulcrum of trade. Malay peoples developed innovative shipbuilding skills and sailed and settled as far as Madagascar by the first century AD. Around this time, the archipelago enters history as part of the Indianized world of South-east Asia, with connections to the Arabian Peninsula, India and China. By the early fifteenth century Malacca, a city on the west coast of Malaysia, had become the pre-eminent trading centre of the region. Its Baba Nonya Chinese community, still there after all this time, are an indication of how pluralism worked in the old indigenous system so redolent of Muslim Spain. The Baba and Nonya (Baba designating a male, like Mr, while Nonya indicates the female), live in their own quarter of Malacca, the city once dubbed 'the Emporium of all the world'. Their houses are typically Chinese but their occupants speak Malay, adopted a distinctive variant of Malay dress and developed a rich fusion cuisine while retaining their original Confucian ideals and religious practices.

Indian traders, especially a group known as Chettiers who specialized in financial services, also formed a distinctive community. In one of the main streets of Malacca's Chinatown a dozen paces will take you past the oldest Chinese temple, a typical mosque in the local Malay style and a Hindu temple. But the tidal waves of 1492 and all that engulfed Malaya. Columbus's plan was to reach the spice islands of the Indies, outflanking and overturning Muslim dominance of the economic life of Europe and replacing it with a European monopoly of possession. Malacca, the greatest centre of the global spice trade, was the prize. It was conquered first by the Portuguese in 1511; the Dutch displaced them in the 1640s and were then displaced by the British early in the nineteenth century. The modern nation of Malaysia and its contemporary multicultural mix bears the legacy of European colonialism. New waves of Chinese were imported by the British to run the tin mines and became the commercial class serving the colonizing power. Tamils from Southern India were imported to work the rubber plantations, while Sikhs, a 'martial race' from Northern India according to their colonial designation, were shipped in as policemen and guards. Meanwhile the Malays were marginalized, restricted to traditional agriculture, even prevented from operating rubber smallholdings.

The tensions created by this colonial pattern led to racial strife in the years after Independence. But the ancient reflexes honed by the Islamic worldview had not disappeared entirely. The Malay majority extended full citizenship rights to the Chinese and Indians, a detail the colonial power never felt necessary. After the race riots of 1969 they also forged a new constitution. What made both Malaysia and Moorish Spain multicultural societies was that all communities participated, at least in theory if not totally in practice, in sharing political power and the economic pie. In Muslim Spain, the rise of individuals to positions of power and prestige depended on their learning and professional skills. In Malaysia, political power is distributed according to a constitutional arrangement based on communal representation and quota systems. All communities are guaranteed the continuity of their religion and languages while Islam is the official religion of the state. And the constitution has a distributive function, designed to ensure that the less privileged are provided with the educational and economic opportunities they need.

Malay Islam is often described as 'gentle', moderate and eclectic, like the Malays themselves. Much of this gentleness comes from mysticism. Islam arrived in the Archipelago in the thirteenth century, about the time of a resurgence of Islamic mysticism in the Middle East. The Sufis, reacting against the aridity of Shariah-minded legalism, preached a syncretic mix of Islamic dogma, Greek gnosis and communal spirituality, and were more than tolerant towards pre-Islamic beliefs. Their willingness to preserve continuity with the past enabled the Sufis to make deep inroads in the Archipelago and left an indelible imprint on the Malay mind. Continuity with the past is enshrined in the language of Islam in the Malay world. Sanskrit terms have been transformed to denote Islamic concepts and practices: so religion becomes '*agama*', fasting becomes '*puasa*', hell becomes '*neraka*', and heaven becomes '*syurga*' – all terms with mystical connotations in Hinduism. The combination of Sufism and Hindu practices, and a social structure that stemmed from pre-Islamic beliefs and Muslim dogma, makes Malay Islam a phenomenon unique in the Muslim world, while in no way making Malays less scrupulous or punctilious in their adherence to Islam.

Spanish Islam too was deeply influenced by mysticism. One of the greatest mystics of Islam, indeed of all time, was born in Murcia in 1165. Muhammad ibn Arabi was initiated into the Sufi way at the age of twenty and began a life of wandering when he was thirty. He made no effort to hide his disgust for the religious scholars he considered stupid and ignorant; an attitude that frequently caused tension between 'the Greatest Master' and the authorities, on occasion leading to his arrest and frequent denunciations. Despite all his travels and disputes, Ibn Arabi managed to write some 350 books. His exposition of the wisdom of the prophets of Islam, Christianity and Judaism; and his vast encyclopedia of spiritual knowledge seeking to unite tradition, reason and mysticism, are considered his greatest works. Most of Ibn Arabi's thought is impenetrable, but his most accessible books, *The Spirit of Holiness* and *The Precious Pearl*, reveal the extent to which Sufism proliferated in Muslim Spain. They provide biographical sketches and examples of the works of over seventy notable Sufis of Andalusia.

Malaysian multiculturalism had much common ground with Muslim Andalusia. But its culture of learning and intellectual energy had a long way to go to match Andalusian achievements. Some of the greatest luminaries of Muslim history were nourished by the soils of Andalusia, though their biographies demonstrate that intellectual life was not without its pitfalls. There was the twelfth-century polymath Ibn Rushd: physician, philosopher, commentator on Aristotle and Plato, author of the classic defence of philosophy *The Incoherence of the Incoherence*, and one of the greatest rationalists ever to walk this earth. A member of an old Cordoban family, he served as a Qadi, or religious judge, in Seville and Cordoba. Later, declaring 'whoever becomes fully familiar with human anatomy and physiology, his faith in Allah will increase', he became personal physician and trusted adviser to the Almohad rulers Yusuf I and Yaqub. Ibn Rushd not only imbibed Greek thought and philosophy, he elaborated and extended it. Known as the Great Commentator, he is proof of my friend Ekmeleddin Ihsanoglu's thesis of Europe's debt to Muslim civilization. Philosophers and writers such as St Thomas Aquinas and Dante learned Greek philosophy not from the Greeks, but through the commentaries and additions of Ibn Rushd. Because he was the acme of the rationalist philosopher it is often argued Ibn Rushd had no sympathy for Sufism. In fact, he was fascinated by mysticism.

But Ibn Rushd had no time for the theologians. His aim was to harmonize reason and revelation, philosophy and faith, and inquiry and values. Islam, he argued, allows latitude to competent scholars to interpret the Qur'an, and philosophers are better qualified in this regard than theologians by virtue of their understanding of the truths of science and philosophy. As truth is single, revelation and science cannot differ. But science and philosophy may contradict theology which, after all, is nothing more than the interpretation done by less than vigorous thinkers! As in the case of Ibn Arabi, his attacks on theologians led to a trial for heresy and exile. Muslim Spain, for all its tolerance and intellectual dynamism, was not a dream but a living society interwoven with complex machinations of politics, political loyalties and corresponding social, philosophical and religious tensions. It was a civilization that existed for centuries as fragmenting principalities, collectively under threat and gradually in retreat before the oncoming tide of the exclusivist, intolerant colonial settler society of Catholic Spain. And Muslim Spain shared a dilemma common to the rest of the Muslim world in its age of glories: everywhere intellectuals and thinkers benefited from the patronage of courts and their rulers, but the relationship was often fraught, always problematic. Empires and dynasties were the power system, yet they could never monopolize or hold unchallenged claim to Islamic legitimacy, they were always subject to criticism and opposition inspired by Islam. As much as scholars and thinkers participated in civil society they also sought to maintain degrees of separation from the power structure that could for its own reasons support, co-opt or as easily dispense with them.

One of Ibn Rushd's closest friends, indeed his patron, was the philosopher Ibn Tufayl, best known for his philosophical novel *The Living Son of the Awake*. The novel, which I read and reread during my youth, explores the possibility of attaining scientific, philosophical and religious knowledge by untutored natural reason. The protagonist, Hayy, is the fictional embodiment of that philosophical concept the blank slate, a character generated and appearing without antecedents on a remote island where he becomes an acute observer. Through his observations of nature, empirical reasoning, contemplation and self-discovered intellectual methods, he arrives at profound truths. Just when Hayy concludes he is alone in the world, Asal, a man brought up in religious tradition and now seeking a retreat from the world, arrives. Hayy and Asal find their philosophical positions to be identical. They set out to convert the rest of the world; only to be rejected and end up dejected. Hayy became famous in seventeenth-century Europe, when the book was translated by the English Orientalist Edward Pocock. It influenced certain sects such as the Quakers and was the model for Defoe's *Robinson Crusoe*.

My favourite Andalusian thinker is the eleventh-century writer Ibn Hazm. Parvez Manzoor describes him as 'a humanist par excellence'. Ibn Hazm was a reformer and an all-round critic who attacked the failures and excesses of religious and secular quarters with equal vigour, a combative writer who upset everyone, bar none. Not surprisingly, he was ostracized, persecuted, imprisoned, and driven into exile. His books were outlawed and burned. Even the woman he loved died young, so all in all he had a miserable life that gave him plenty of reason to mourn and moan. But the thought it produced! Ibn Hazm viewed the conventional criteria for arriving at judicial decisions, and thus shaping the Shariah, as – not to put too fine a point on it – hogwash. He argued that decisions should only be based on the Qur'an which he saw as a commentary on the life of the Prophet Muhammad. All mortals, including the companions of the Prophet and the Rightly Guided Caliphs, were subject to error. What they said or did could not be given divine sanction. In his Categories of Sciences, Ibn Hazm sets forth his criticism and suggests new ways of moving forward. Knowledge, he argues, is associated with four cardinal virtues: justice (*adl*), understanding (*fahm*), courage (*najdah*) and generosity (*jud*). Anything leading towards the capital vices of inequity, cowardice and avarice is ignorance and cannot be associated with knowledge.

But not all great scholars of Moorish Spain were Muslim. The greatest beneficiaries of Islamic rule were the Jews, for in Spain they enjoyed their finest intellectual flowering since the dispersal from Palestine. Foremost among them was Moshe ben Maimon, or Maimonides as he is generally known, born in Cordoba in 1135. As a result of Almohad policies his family had to emigrate first to Morocco and then to Cairo, where he was appointed personal physician to Sultan Saladin (the Saladin who retook Jerusalem from the Crusaders) and taught medicine at Cairo university. But Maimonides always remained in contact with Sephardic Jews. He codified Jewish doctrine in his *Mishneh Torah*; and his *Guide to the Perplexed*, written in Arabic, occupies a place in Judaism similar to that of the works of Thomas Aquinas in Catholicism. Muslims did not consider Maimonides a 'Jewish' scholar; he was an integral part of the intellectual scene of Muslim Spain, indeed the wider community of Muslim civilization.

The mysticism of Spain's Muslim community had a profound influence on Sephardic (from the Hebrew word for Spain, *Sepharad*) Jewish scholars. One such was Bahya ibn-Pakuda, who lived in the eleventh century: his *Guide to the Duties of the Heart*, written in Arabic, was an outcome of his encounter with Sufism, and became famous throughout the Jewish Diaspora. His contemporary Solomon ben Judah Ibn Gabirol, poet and neo-Platonic philosopher, also drank deep from the Sufi fountains. His famous hymn 'Keter Malkhut' (Royal Crown), adopted for the Jewish Yom Kippur (Day of Atonement) service, concludes with a confession of sin and bears strong echoes of Ibn Arabi.

In 1991 world affairs, with a gross want of *adab*, intervened to interrupt the Professor and our 'intellectual discourses'. Instead of the ferment of knowledge, the world proffered war. Iraq invaded Kuwait and forces moved to align themselves for the Gulf War. I was overwhelmed by a dread presentiment, not so much déjà vu as a mystical sense of malign prophecy being worked out on a global scale. My mind raced back to the precise moment when we started to anticipate this awful débâcle. It was 9 November 1989, our first Ijmali gathering in the aftermath of the Rushdie affair. We assembled at Merryl's flat in Golders Green for a 'way forward' meeting. By custom and tradition, the meeting started with dinner – Merryl had cooked buckets of her trademark spaghetti bolognaise. It was our obeisance to pluralism. As we twiddled our noodles we switched on the television to catch up with the news. And that was the end of our agenda for the evening, night and morning after. There before our eyes thousands upon thousands of people were milling in Friedrichstrasse, engulfing Checkpoint Charlie in Berlin. The live broadcast showed crowds pushing against the Berlin Wall. Wave upon human wave broke against the hated symbol. In disbelief we watched as it began to crumble. The more it crumbled, the more vigorously people pushed and hacked at the structure. East German border guards assisted people in crossing to the West. Strangers embraced, laughing, crying. People walked freely across the border between West and East Germany, champagne bottles in hand. The jubilation on the streets of Berlin was echoed in Merryl's living room. '*Wahnsinn*,' the crowds shouted again and again: 'ecstasy,' the television commentators translated. We shared the elation. 'At last,' shouted Parvez exultantly, 'the damn Cold War comes to an end.'

But as night turned into dawn, and the dawn eventually gave way to a reluctant sun, our mood took a different turn. It was Merryl who first raised the question. 'Now the Evil Empire's crumbled to dust, who or what will take its place?' No one answered. We looked at each other, struck dumb. To answer held the spectre of uttering self-fulfilling prophecy. Finally, Merryl answered her own question. 'It will be us. Islam will be the next bogey, the new "Evil Empire". The West, especially the military-industrial complex, still needs an evil Other to affirm its identity; to confirm its own Self and keep its political economy operating. It'll return to its original demon Other. The Rushdie affair will have been a prelude spreading all the old ideas, prejudices and language of contempt.' We all shook our heads in silent agreement. Parvez moaned aloud: 'Our sense of victimhood will increase. And Muslims will retreat further into a medieval mindset. We'll cling even more strongly to outmoded notions of the Shariah. We'll see other people demanding to return to some imagined purity of the Prophet's times as their only defence. We'll be back to square one.' More silence. We were each saying a private *kadish*, a prayer for dead hope.

During the slow inexorable gestation of war Merryl and I travelled back and forth to Malaysia. And everywhere, I remember, we had to confront questions about how the abominable psychopathic secularist Saddam Hussein was trying to play the Muslim card, rallying brainless Mullahs and politically inept critics of the West to conferences in Baghdad. But no one seemed interested in addressing the real question: what effect was all this having on the generality of Muslims? Here was the familiar pathology of contemporary Muslim existence: impotence, the victimhood of having only invidious choices. And all the while the airwaves were alive with political rhetoric, anti-Muslim sentiments, and competing often mutually contradictory emotional, political and religious views concerning the nexus of contemporary Muslim existence and the realities of the Middle East. The net effect was to render most Muslims silent, or rather inaudible because what they had to say was too involved and impenetrable to register in the mainstream western media. Who could support Saddam? Was he not the perfect pastiche of an historic despot that western rhetoric sought to portray? As the vast majority of Muslims knew, Saddam was the acme of the modern tyrant, the kind modernity offered few easy means to live with or remove.

There were equally big problems with the glib and commonly voiced dictum that the enemy of my enemy is my friend. The oil-rich states of the Middle East had few genuine friends among Muslim populations anywhere. Illiberal, undemocratic, arrogant and self-indulgent, their only motive was to perpetuate their own hold on power. The old Muslim strategy of maintaining a large degree of separation from power structures was ubiquitous and a counsel of despair. There was a lack of any global arena in which to engage with and discuss, let alone resolve by our own efforts, the problems of the *ummah*. And there was the awful realization that our impotence would produce real victims. On the fateful day when the allied forces began bombing Iraq, we worked late, not stopping to watch the news. When she got into the taxi to go home Merryl found the driver listening to live reports of the bombing of Iraq. She phoned immediately on arrival in Golders Green telling me to switch on my television. Like everyone else I watched courtesy of CNN the spectrally eerie green pictures of tracer fire and explosions over Baghdad.

While in London debilitating impotence predominated, in Malaysia the increase in anti-West and anti-Saudi sentiments was palpable. There was an emotional groundswell suggesting complexity was not an option. The honour of Islam was somehow at the heart of the war and tugging heartstrings so hard that it was turning the wits of sensible people. Even though official government policy was to support and back Saudi Arabia, the tightly controlled press and the media were awash with anti-Saudi opinions. Saudi delegations were flying in and out of Kuala Lumpur in what looked like increasingly futile attempts to change public attitudes. Abdullah Naseef came with one delegation and I went to see him at the Pan Pacific Hotel where he was staying. I remember we talked about Muslim propensity to get into impossible positions. 'Muslims lead the world in self-inflicted harm,' Naseef said. The Saudi Ambassador arrived unannounced. He started to complain about anti-Saudi feelings in the country. 'Not a single article has been written to defend our position,' he said. Then he turned towards me. 'You know Saudi Arabia well,' he said. 'Why don't you write something explaining our position?'

I did. In an op-ed article for the *New Straits Times*, Malaysia's major

English language newspaper, I argued that Muslims are trapped between two evils. On one side was Saddam Hussein, whose record of brutalities needed no elaboration. In a fit of megalomania, he had invaded and occupied Kuwait. On the other side, there was the medieval Kingdom of Saudi Arabia where foreign workers were treated as slaves and dissent was rewarded by torture. On balance, I suggested, we should side with the lesser evil of the Saudi Kingdom. Besides, they had no territorial ambitions. The Saudis were outraged. The Ambassador made an official complaint to Anwar.

A few weeks later I received a call from Naseef. 'They won't be asking you to do any more favours,' he said, laughing. 'But they do want to see you.'

'Whatever for?' I was intrigued.

'They're going to give you five million dollars,' Naseef replied in a matter-of-fact voice.

I was dumbfounded. 'FIVE MILLION DOLLARS! Whatever for?'

'To help you with your intellectual efforts,' came the answer.

'Doctor,' I replied after a long pause for thought, 'let me think about it.'

I thought seriously, talked to Merryl and other Ijmalis, and then decided not to pursue the offer from my old nemesis. Had I not been down the Saudi route and retired hurt before? A few days later, Anwar asked me to come and see him. He had moved into a new house in Damansara, an upwardly mobile residential area of Kuala Lumpur occupied by ministers, government officials and professionals. I met him, along with Merryl, in his library late at night.

'The Saudis are adamant,' Anwar said. 'I've received several calls.'

Merryl and I looked at each other. 'What's your advice, YB?' she asked.

'I think they're sincere and it's an unconditional offer,' Anwar answered. 'And their support will give a tremendous boost to our efforts to develop an intellectual *convivencia*.'

'It's settled then,' I said. 'I'll take the money.'

A week later I was in Jeddah. We were sitting in the living room of Sheikh Salah Kamel. Anwar too was there, having flown in on an official plane. En route to Sheikh Kamel's house, Naseef explained that the offer came from 'the very top'. Sheikh Kamel, as our mutual friend, had been ordered to hand over the cheque. 'No doubt,' Naseef said, grinning, 'he will be rewarded for his deed.'

On Salah Kamel's ostentatiously large sofa, I was sandwiched between Naseef and the Sheikh. Anwar sat opposite on an equally large and flamboyant settee. 'We have been asked,' the Sheikh began after a painstaking extended round of '*kahifa hal*' ('how are you') and an endless litany of *Alhamdulilllah* ('Allah be praised'), 'to give you five million dollars, Brother Zia.'

'Dollars?' I said, affecting bemused shock and surprise. 'I live in London where we deal in pounds sterling. I don't recognize dollars as a legitimate currency!'

Sheikh Kamel looked first at Naseef and then Anwar. They were smiling.

'We have been asked,' the Sheikh began again, 'to give you five million pounds.'

The Sheikh allowed a pause for the significance of his words to be appreciated. 'This money is for you to use as you wish to support your intellectual activities. Like Brother Anwar, we too would like to see a new intellectual renaissance in the Muslim world.' He made a gesture with his left hand beckoning someone. An overweight Egyptian man came running and sat on a small leather ottoman beside the Sheikh. He was carrying the largest cheque book I'd ever seen. 'Write a cheque for five million pounds sterling,' Salah Kamel instructed. The clerk opened the cheque book and, with what looked like a heavy, gold-plated Dupont fountain pen, started to write the figure in words and numbers. He lavished such time and attention on writing the cheque that it was evident he was a calligrapher.

'Who shall we make the cheque out to?' the Sheikh enquired.

'It should be made out to Dr Zia,' Anwar replied.

'No,' Naseef intervened. 'It should be made out to an institution.'

We were now joined by the roly-poly figure of Dr Abdo Yamani. He apologized for being late and sat next to Anwar.

'Let us make the cheque out to Brother Zia,' Yamani said. 'He can establish whatever intellectual institution he wants later on. After all we don't expect him to spend the money on himself!' Everyone laughed; I joined in hesitantly.

When he finished, the Egyptian clerk handed the cheque book and pen to the Sheikh.

'Before I sign,' the Sheikh said, 'Dr Yamani wishes to say something.' All eyes turned towards Abdo Yamani.

'Brother Zia,' Yamani began, 'we all love and respect you as a noble intellectual. You have strong opinions and you're not afraid to express them. We admire that.' I was in mid 'true, true' nod when his last observation struck me motionless. 'But before we hand you the money, we'd like you to consider a small stipulation.'

Now I turned in confusion to look at Naseef and Anwar; they seemed just as puzzled.

'Intellectuals should speak freely,' Yamani continued. 'But sometimes, just sometimes, they shouldn't say what they think.' Yamani paused to survey our expressions. 'For the greater good, for the sake of the Muslim *ummah*, they ought to listen occasionally and pay attention to what the authorities have to say.'

My face turned red. Anwar looked embarrassed. My immediate impulse was to grab the cheque from Salah Kamel's hand, tear it into shreds, and sprinkle it like confetti over his head. But I couldn't move. Naseef had my right arm in a vice-like grip.

'Brother Anwar,' he said, turning casually towards him and speaking with a nonchalant air, 'I don't think you've seen Sheikh Kamel's garden. Let me show it to you.' He got up, keeping my arm pinioned in his grip and bodily pulling me along with him. He led the way out of the living room, and moved swiftly through the main hall and out to the garden. Anwar followed. My departing view was of Salah Kamel and Abdo Yamani sitting still.

Salah Kamel's garden was the size of several football pitches. It was elegantly laid out, palm trees lined pathways, an artificial lake shimmered, and a string of gazebos dotted the landscape. But one's eyes were inevitably drawn to three mosques artistically integrated into the landscaped gardens to create a pleasing panorama. Doubtless the landscape artist and architect who designed them had been dreaming of the gardens of Granada. Naseef, astute, diplomatic, courteous and concerned as ever, was intent on smoothing over our embarrassment. He pointed towards the first mosque. 'Brother Anwar,' he said as if nothing was more significant, 'Sheikh Kamel made that mosque for himself.' Anwar attentively turned to admire the mosque from a distance. 'That one,' Naseef pointed in another direction, 'he made for his mother.' Anwar dutifully turned his gaze towards the second mosque. 'And the one at the end . . .'

'. . . is there for the times, just some times, when he doesn't want to pray,' I completed Naseef's sentence. The garden filled with the sound of our laughter. I left Jeddah wiser and poorer.

The Gulf War, the first virtual-reality-as-seen-on-TV war, ended. It ended as all wars do, inconclusive in victory and defeat, leaving the questions raised hanging in the air, a miasma of unresolved problems for the future. Like the ending of all wars it created the illusion for everyone, except the Iraqis, that normal life could be resumed. We could get on with things again. The BBC put away its sandpit, CNN's Christiane Amanpour descended from the roof of the Information Ministry in Baghdad. It was time to take stock of other issues suspended for the duration. The hardest thing to comprehend at the end of a war is how subtly everything has been changed, how the axis of the earth has been tilted setting normality spiralling on a slightly different trajectory into another future, not the future projected or continuing from the world ante bellum. Comprehension can take a long time after the ending of war. It takes time to notice the butterfly disturbed by the shockwaves of dropped bombs; has to flap its wings. It would be years before one sniffed the breeze and smelled the coming rains. We were heading for storms for all that.

I returned to Malaysia to continue our work. For me it was still a land of people without beards. The straggly, wispy beards of the more pious Malays are totally unconvincing. To someone like me, who is generously endowed with hair all over his body, it appeared that the Malays had an almost impossible task attempting to cultivate a beard. It had to be a providential sign, it ought to mean they were amenable to change, more open to alternative possibilities within Islam. I clung tenaciously to my belief that a true Islamic multicultural paradise could be created here.

Malaysia would once again become the fulcrum of connections by which Islam could be brought into the mainstream of world culture; it would pave the way for Muslim countries to follow. It had the preconditions, like Muslim Spain, to genuinely appreciate the alterity of others, and develop fluid notions of identity. And if five decades of so-called 'development' had taught us anything, it was self-evident that economic strength would be an essential factor in making Malaysia a model for other countries. All the right rhetoric, and the best redistributive intentions and policies, could not provide jobs, put food on the table or better the quality of life of the poor without serious, well-managed economic achievement. Before the pie can be divided among communities there has to be a pie. Here too Malaysia seemed the best candidate, blessed as it was with natural resources, location, an educated, adaptable workforce and a planned approach to economic advance. And if Anwar remained uncloned, he was still the coming man moving nearer and nearer to the centre of power. We would meet frequently in his library to discuss options and ideas. We brought him interesting projects and offered our best advice and thoughts on specific issues, contributed to speeches and researched matters that interested him.

As time passed, the limits of Malaysia gradually became harder to discern; they seemed to be simultaneously expanding and retreating. When I began to visit Kuala Lumpur it felt like a small town full of traditional enclaves. Now, before my eyes it was transformed into a global, postmodern city. Condominiums were breaking out all over, new shopping malls and office complexes were spreading like rashes. Some areas morphed in situ – old-fashioned shop houses overnight became sleek modern shops selling overpriced designer chic products or became restaurants offering international themed cuisine. The pace of life became more frenetic as it adapted to the dictates of global consumer culture. Wherever one looked tradition was in retreat, gasping for breath; modernity was on the march, turning everything, including traditional culture, into commodities – and, in the process, dispensing with depth and perspective. Within a period of five years, everything was merely surface, like the shopping mall themed on an ancient Egyptian tomb, complete with hieroglyphic daubings. The booming economy not only raised general living standards, it generated enormous wealth for some. The nouveau riche lived ostentatiously: designer clothes, expensive accessories and BMWs or Mercedes were the norm; they noisily frequented the open-galleried oyster and champagne bar in Bangsar, the fashionable district of Kuala Lumpur. The poor dressed in exactly the same way: except that their attire and accessories were fake goods, which more often than not could hardly be distinguished from the real things. Anything that could be privatized was privatized; and handed over to the same coterie of cronies clustered around the Prime Minister. Instant wealth, generated without much effort, spawned big ideas. Malaysia thought big, very big: whether it was the Petronas Towers – the tallest building in the world – or the new international airport – the most technologically advanced in the world – or the Bakun dam or hosting the Commonwealth Games, the accent was firmly on being the biggest, tallest, largest, and fastest in the world. The nation's long fascination with the *Guinness Book of Records* had finally come into its own. Michael Jackson and Madonna were everywhere. Television and cinemas were crammed with American imports. New housing developments, bought as a job lot, replaced old architecture and traditional Malay houses with a monotonous suburban modernity making no concessions to climate or to time-honoured family and communal forms of living. Everyone was running faster and faster to stand still.

The Malays never say anything directly. They do not, for example, greet you by asking 'how are you?' Instead, they ask the question that reveals all: 'Have you taken rice?' – the local equivalent of 'Have you eaten?' Malays make an art form of gossip, griping and backbiting and they do it all by telling jokes. So they never say things are getting bad, the congestion is getting worse, the pollution is escalating, shopping malls have taken over the city, western culture is displacing everything that is local and indigenous. Instead they offer hilarious asides about the time it has taken to get anywhere, pithy observations about the purchases people have made, elaborate conspiracy theories about the latest deals being cooked up. And they say, 'Things are shrinking; there's less and less space.' First, I took this to be a reference to the lack of physical space in Kuala Lumpur. But then it dawned on me: they were complaining about the loss of their own culture, which was rapidly disappearing without much trace. They were commenting on 'globalization' as cultural genocide of the world they were born into and all its remembered ways. In their Malay way they were reflecting their sense of being at one and the same time at home and homeless in a globalized domain that made the village (kampong) seem a long way ago and very far from relevant. Everyone I knew in Malaysia was born in a kampong, and it left an inedible affective mark on their sense of what and how the world should be.

'Is there a place in Malaysia untouched by globalization?' I asked a friend. 'There is,' he replied without hesitation, 'deep down in the rainforests of Sarawak.' So one day, just to get a respite from the pressure cooker of Kuala Lumpur, I took the early morning – 'red eye' – flight to Kuching, capital of Sarawak. I am not normally prone to romantic allure, but I felt the need for this experience. The rainforest bounds the Malay world, but it is also for them a place haunted by spirits. What to do about the rainforests and the people who inhabited them was a perennial issue and cause célèbre in the fashionable new-age world of global consciousness. I left early the following morning, making for the Iban longhouses on the banks of the Bunu River, deep in the interior of Borneo. The drive to the Skrang River took some five hours, much of it over a gravel road, some on no road at all. I was accompanied by two Malay friends and we navigated the Skrang River in a longboat – a voyage of about three hours through shallow waters (where I had to get out and push the boat), rocky rapids (where we had to manoeuvre and steer with skill) and gentle streams with water rippling past mossy rocks. Eventually, the Skrang opened into a lattice of tributaries, the most tame being the Bunu. Dotted on the banks of the Bunu, a few kilometres apart, were a number of Iban communities living in longhouses.

The Iban still live as they have always lived: an egalitarian, hospitable people, with a self-sufficient lifestyle relying on hill padi for cultivation and an accumulated ingenuity at making everything they need from bamboo and rattan. They measure time by the movements of the tide and by noting the main events of their own or their community's life. They have no written language and remember their history in songs handed down from generation to generation. Both men and women go naked to their waists; men cover their loins with a strip of cotton, the women wear short skirts. The longhouse in which I stayed contained forty-two families. It was a busy place: everyone was working. Some worked at weaving or preparing material for mat making, others were making mats, or strings from the inner bark of a tree, or nets for casting, or a fish-trap, or a chicken basket, or conical hats. Others were busy drying padi or pounding husks or training hornbills to be fishing birds or bringing water from the river.

We were welcomed on the communal veranda. I was greeted by Latu, a gentle but agile man of seventy. He stood about 140 centimetres, with tattooed arms and long dangling holes in the earlobes. He gave me a cigarette made of tobacco grown by the community and wrapped in a palm leaf. We spent hours sitting on the veranda, smoking, and chatting. Latu told me how he was elected *tuan rumah*, the headman of the community, and what it meant. As the evening continued, and it became darker and darker, the longhouse became colder and colder. More people gathered around us, sitting very close together for warmth and comfort. Three young men, who had joined us after dinner, whispered something to a group of young girls – flowers in their hair, glass bead collars hanging down over their shoulders. They shook with excitement. One of the girls got up, walked round the circle to Latu and whispered something in his ear. Latu seemed to disapprove. Another girl joined in and the three engaged in animated discussion. Latu agreed.

I sat silently, observing, waiting for something to happen.

A sound erupted to disturb the noise of the night forest around the longhouse, alive with insects and creatures about their own business. It was as though someone had kick-started a motor. It served as a signal. More inhabitants of the longhouse emerged from their living areas and joined the gathering crowd on the veranda. The two girls made their way forward, with elegant economy and grace of movement, and reverently set two black boxes before the assembled company. They stepped back as if swaying in a dance in honour of the shrine they had set in place. As they moved all was revealed: a television and video player could now be clearly recognized. A young man came forward and pinned a poster to one of the bamboo poles – the bones of the longhouse – next to the television. Latu looked at me, smiled, and settled himself comfortably, resting his head on his shoulders. I looked at the poster: a man sat on a motorbike, wearing a leather jacket and sunglasses, holding a shotgun; and I read the message: *Terminator 2: Judgement Day*. The *manang* (the shaman of the community) gave power to the television, slipped a cassette in the player and pressed the 'play' button. In the darkness of the rainforest, the families that constituted the Bunu longhouse settled down to watch Arnold Schwarzenegger.

You can run from globalization; but you can't hide. Its problems and predicaments in all their profusion and complexity are everywhere, even in the inner recesses of the rainforests. You can dream of making Granada live again in Malaysia, even as faux Mediterranean housing estates proliferate. But it gets harder and harder to believe the dream. Go blundering around in the rainforest and butterflies, great gorgeous creatures, beat a retreat from your approach; as you keep on wandering all the idyll of harmony you sought is stirred and flees before you.

The perturbation of wings was wreaking havoc in the air. And the air around Kuala Lumpur was getting decidedly darker. It began with the arrival in Malaysia of a sulphurous grey mist of apocalyptic proportions. There had been periods of what locals termed 'haze' before. But now when Merryl began each day with the ritual opening of all the windows of her bungalow, the air visibly insinuated itself serpent-like into each room, laden with dust and the smell of distant burning. The air made footfalls on everything, leaving telltale deposits of ash. The political atmosphere was turning just as foul. Mahathir, the undisputed leader of Malaysia, had begun to see in his deputy and protégé, Anwar Ibrahim, a major threat to the dispensation of his authority. Soon it also became clear that the much-vaunted 'Asian economic miracle' too was little more than murky air. Cut off from the sun, Kuala Lumpur was hit with a string of corporate scandals. Questions began to be asked; the professional class expressed concern and then alarm that freebooting free marketeering was going too far, too fast and relying too much on cronyism and corrupt practices. Since becoming Finance Minister in

1992, Anwar had consistently made speeches calling for corporate responsibility, and an end to corruption and complacency. He was the Cabinet Minister responsible for the Anti-Corruption Agency, a job he took seriously and worked at vigorously. Not surprisingly, Mahathir as well as his coterie of arrogant fat-cat cronies became disdainful of Anwar. When, in 1997, the Malaysian economy succumbed, along with Indonesia, Thailand and South Korea, to the Asian economic crisis that sent their currencies and stock markets into free fall, the knives were unsheathed. What followed was 'unprecedented'. From now on, the word would be on everyone's lips in Kuala Lumpur.

Wayang kulit, the traditional Malay art form of shadow puppet performance, is an apt metaphor for Malaysian politics. Behind the façade of calm and stability there exists a lively tradition of invective, a world of contending interests and perspectives, and the audience, the general public, has a keen understanding of what is going on behind the façade. After the economic collapse, the political differences between Anwar and Mahathir came out into the light and turned into open warfare. This was no fight just for authority, for control and direction of economic policy. It was a fight for the future and very soul of Malaysian society. Anwar's personality, his integrity and intellectual acumen became the focus of all issues. Mahathir's strategy to contain, and finally remove Anwar from the equation, was conjured on simple imitation. He was going to follow the model of the sex scandals that engulfed President Bill Clinton in America. But Anwar's integrity could not be impugned simply by accusing him of sexual misdemeanours with buxom office interns. Such behaviour was the norm in Malaysian political circles. No: to succeed, allegations against Anwar had to involve an enormity. They had to centre on what Malays, especially the rural Malays who formed the bulk of Anwar's supporters, found most obnoxious – homosexuality. A case against Anwar was painstakingly fabricated over two years, involving his driver, his adopted brother, and anyone else who could be framed.

Mahathir blamed an evil foreign conspiracy for bringing down the Malaysian economy out of pure envy. He accused George Soros – the American billionaire and financier of East European origins – and the Jews, the foreign press, the IMF. He expressed shock and amazement as so many of Malaysia's free marketeering corporations simply evaporated, buried under mountains of unrepayable debt. As the contagion spread there was unprecedented, virulent and open criticism of the Old Man. Throughout, the political capital of Anwar, as a safe and clean pair of hands, was relentlessly on the rise. On 2 September 1998, the storm broke. At a routine Cabinet meeting, Mahathir gave Anwar an ultimatum: resign or be sacked. Anwar chose the later. The following morning the papers were full of detailed allegations against Anwar, including sodomizing his erstwhile chauffeur. Within a week, Mahathir had Anwar expelled from UMNO, the ruling party, of which he was the elected Deputy President. Anwar declared that a 'conspiracy at the highest level' was working to destroy him.

Events moved rapidly. They always do, I have noticed, when things go from bad to worse. A week after his sacking, Anwar's adopted brother, Sukma Dermawan, and Anwar's speech writer, my Ijmali friend Munawar Ahmad Anees, were arrested. Merryl spent her days racing around Kuala Lumpur giving support to Munawar's wife and young children, helping to arrange for legal representation and trying to find out where Munawar was being held incommunicado. By the end of the week, early on Saturday morning, both Sukma and Munawar were produced in Court represented by lawyers none of their family and friends had heard of before; they insisted that guilty pleas should be entered to charges of allowing themselves to be sodomized by Anwar. Frantically summoned to get to the Court as soon as possible, Munawar's wife failed to recognize him when he was presented before the judge. His head was shaved; and his body trembling. Both men had clearly been tortured. They were convicted and led off to begin a term in jail according to Malaysian law.

As the Commonwealth Games reached its climactic closing ceremony Mahathir was booed when he drove around the stadium. In the centre of Kuala Lumpur, Merdeka (Independence) Square was the setting for an alternative ceremony, a mass public rally addressed by Anwar. That evening, when he returned to his home, masked and heavily armed police broke down the door, arrested Anwar at gunpoint and drove him to the Bukit Aman jail to be held under the Internal Security Act. Crowds still milling in Merdeka Square began to march up the hill to the Prime Minister's residence as the news spread like wildfire. Tanks appeared on the streets, helicopters whirred overhead. By the light of dawn police in riot gear and army vehicles patrolled the streets. Demonstrations were everywhere; the police used water cannons to control the crowds. But nothing could quench the anger of the populace. Mahathir complained Anwar was using 'mental telepathy' from prison to incite the crowd against him!

On Anwar's advice, I had returned to London from Kuala Lumpur a few weeks before his arrest. 'Anyone associated with me is in danger,' he had said. Immediately after his arrest, his secretaries, associates and many of his friends were rounded and locked up. I made frantic phone calls insisting Merryl leave Kuala Lumpur immediately. Unwillingly, anguished at being torn between sense and solidarity, Merryl reluctantly filled the boot of her car with what could be carried. Leaving behind all other worldly goods, she drove past the spying emissaries of the Old Man and headed for Singapore. In London, I was frantically chasing Anwar's influential friends in Europe and America, trying to get them to say and do something – anything. I was concerned not just about Anwar, who was beaten viciously in prison – by no less a person than the Chief of Police, it transpired – and appeared at his trial bearing a telltale black eye that became the symbol of a political movement born to champion his ideals. I was also beside myself with worry about Munawar Anees, haunted by the pictures of his appearance in Court looking a totally different man from the one I knew only a few days earlier. I was watching the events unfold day and night on CNN, with the telephone glued to my left ear, feeling more and more helpless.

Here was our 1492. We were being expelled from Spain. I kept on thinking about Ibn Hazm. No matter how open-minded and clever you are, he once said, authoritarianism always finds a way round. Pluralism and authoritarianism, Ibn Hazm asserted, are locked in eternal combat. A single megalomaniac can destroy a paradise it took decades or centuries to build. That's how Muslim Spain will be lost, Ibn Hazm had declared. And that's how Malaysia was dragged down. My friend and hero had fallen. The balanced individual who could constitute, nurture and build the paradise I sought so desperately was incarcerated. Maybe, I thought, paradise just does not want to be found.

Conclusion

GOING UP, OR GOING DOWN?

After the Malaysian débâcle, I began to spend a great deal of time in the small garden of my house. When we first moved in it was your average overgrown suburban garden with little form, no real identity, and not much diversity. It was a bit of grass for the kids to run around on, place for a swing and the paddling pool my daughter loved and would frequent wearing a chic black bathing suit and an ostentatious string of imitation pearls she acquired who knows where, very Côte de Colindale! As I became an upwardly mobile jobbing intellectual and the kids outgrew the paddling pool and swing, I began rebuilding the house around us and planning a proper garden. I conceived the design based on a well-known Islamic geometric pattern. The art of the Islamic garden is based on an elaborate theory that boils down to an expression of harmony, an evocation of the unity of nature with civic life and community in an urban space. I imagined the garden as a single large octagon; it would be laid to lawn with a fountain in the centre, from which would emerge other patterns, mainly triangles, to serve as flower beds. The gardener who would actually build it, known only as 'Steve', had other ideas. He modified the design to ease his burden. The perfect octagon was transformed into an irregular shape, the equilateral triangles were changed to isosceles and scalene ones, and the fountain was tucked away in a corner at the end of the garden. Steve, who seemed to be having a perpetual flaming row with his girlfriend, took an eternity to finish the job. That, I thought, is the problem with paradise. Those actually employed in building it have their own ideas; and often end up botching the grand design.

One sunny afternoon, I sat back in my garden and remembered the Awana Club, where we first met Anwar. As usual, the Ijmalis were gathered there for a conference. I woke early and decided to while away a free morning taking the cable car ride that connects the Awana complex to the nearby Genting Highland Resort, some 2,000 metres above sea level on the top of a mountain. According to a tourist brochure I picked up in the Club's Reception, at Genting 'you can taste Malaysian life, try a game with Lady Luck and watch stage shows in South-east Asia's most spectacular theatre-restaurant.' They made it sound like a millionaires' secret haunt. I discovered nothing more than a Casino populated by sundry Chinese with melancholy faces. Gamblers are sad people; once they have lost their stakes all they have to contemplate are the swirling mists that so often shroud the Genting mountaintop.

Taking the cable car back down to Awana I descended through the fumes of approaching storms and mists thick and chill as those London pea-soup smogs beloved of all Sherlock Holmes or Hammer Horror films. The cable car swung wildly on its wires as winds howled around us. Just as we approached the lower station we broke through the cloud layer, re-entered warm tropical air, a tactile medium, a tangible presence that gently envelops you in a moist blanket of humidity. By this time a few Ijmalis were gathered for lunch in the restaurant. I spotted them slumped in their chairs as I walked through Reception and went to join them. The restaurant was built in a traditional Malay style, its high roof steeply pitched mirroring the contours of the mountains encircling Awana. The roof's inverse ravines disappeared into a dense maze of exposed beams and rafters made of local wood. It rested on pillars rather than walls, for the entire construction was designed to permit window screens to be slid into the corners leaving just ornamental balustrades to provide a notional division between inside and outside while the air roamed and moulded itself around everything. We sat at a table in the centre of this space watching the storm making its way over the summits of the surrounding mountains. We watched the curtain of torrential rain move around the bowl-shaped valley occupied by Awana's golf course. Occasional bolts of lightning illuminated its path and the sound of thunder, like sharp cracks of rifle fire in the mountain valleys, rattled out its approach to our location. An outlying cloud ambled through the restaurant. I sat motionless with my Ijmali friends. For a while, it seemed it was actually raining within this dining room! The heavens matched our mood. We hardly spoke, what was there to say? The conference was a total disaster: speaker after speaker had told us how Islam had all the answers, how the religious scholars had solved all problems, and how we would all go straight to heaven if only we uttered 'the key to paradise' with certainty and sincerity: 'There is no one worthy of worship but Allah.' It was a reprise of the litany I had heard from the *Tablighi* brothers so long before. The sheer banality of contemporary Muslim thought and the plight of Muslim people had reduced us to total impotence. We sat there bemoaning our state, groaning like the storm-disturbed air around us, as Muslim intellectuals are so prone to do.

Melancholy, as it so often does, turned into nostalgia. 'What made Andalusia so successful for so long with such dazzling results?' asked Merryl.

'The coalescing of interlocking features,' Gulzar Haider answered in a matter-of-fact weary tone. 'There was ethnic pluralism, religious tolerance, an unquenchable thirst for knowledge and culture – from painting to poetry to music to philosophy. And no one thought these things to be un- or anti-Islamic. And now we lack them all.'

'Conspicuously!' I chimed in with a disconsolate tart aside.

'Of course, all these are inherently possible in Islam. We had them then; we can have them now. One might say they are inherently mandated by Islam,' Merryl observed, dragging out the words without hope or enthusiasm.

'Which Islam?' Parvez butted in. 'The Islam of the Flat Earth Society? The Islam of the religious scholars? The Islam of the Iranian revolutionaries? The Islam of Saudi Wahhabis? The Islam of the state-obsessed Muslim Brotherhood and the Jamaat-e-Islami? The simpleton Islam of Tablighi Jamaat?' He was so frustrated he did not realize he was shouting.

'Don't shout,' I said, turning towards him. 'We can hear you perfectly.'

'Ayatollah,' he shot back, 'I am only pointing out we've failed, and failed miserably. All the discourses we initiated have gone to the ground. What was your vision of Islamic science?'

I pretended to ignore the question.

'Come on, Ayatollah,' Parvez insisted in sarcastic tone. 'Do enlighten us!'

'All right,' I said irritably, annoyed to be tracked down, pinned at bay in my lair. 'All right.' I explained that the notion of Islamic science we developed would transform Muslim countries into knowledge-based societies. It would encourage research fine-tuned to solving local problems. Diarrhoea and dysentery in Pakistan, flood control in Bangladesh, tackling schistosomiasis (bilharzia) in Egypt and the Sudan would have replaced the international agenda dominated by the predilections of western science and blindly adopted by Muslim nations. I also thought that certain problems specific to Muslim societies would get priority in research. Considering almost three-quarters of all political refugees in the world are Muslims, Centres of Excellence devoted to the problems of refugees could be established to develop materials for quick, clean temporary housing, efficient and cheap ways of supplying emergency water, better techniques for providing basic healthcare and so on, ad infinitum. And I thought indigenous knowledge, too, would receive a tremendous boost. Traditional medicine, healthcare systems, agriculture and water management would be researched, built upon and improved in collaboration with a new outlook on science. I imagined certain big philosophical issues would be addressed: What happens to modern science if its basic metaphysical assumptions about nature, time, the universe, logic and the nature of humanity are replaced with those of Islam? What if nature, for example, is seen not as a resource to be exploited but instead as a trust to be nursed and nourished? What would then replace vivisection as the basic methodology of biology? How would science itself change when we consider human values, moral and ethical principles to be integral to the process of doing science? '*There*,' I said, when I finished, having worked myself into a fine passion. 'That's what I imagined and believed would happen.'

'And what did you get?' Parvez shouted. 'Your idea of Islamic science has been hijacked by fundamentalists and mystics. The fundamentalists are looking for scientific miracles in the Qur'an. Everything from relativity, quantum mechanics, big bang theory to the entire field of embryology and much of modern geology has been "discovered" in the Qur'an. They're experimenting on jinn in Pakistan!' He laughed. 'The mystics have reduced the discourse to a quest for numinous understanding of the Absolute. Everywhere, mystical cults have subordinated conjecture and hypothesis to supernatural experience. All is sacred; and knowledge has no social function. There's no correlation between what you envisioned and what actually happened.'

Parvez surveyed the devastating gloom around him. No one said anything.

'And what of your discourse of Islamic futures? The vision of a dynamic, thriving future civilization of Islam? Or your attempts to develop a contemporary classification of Islam; and evolve new disciplines reflecting the hopes and aspirations of Muslim people?'

Still, no one replied. Parvez, moved by the force of his anger, got up. 'The *ummah*'s not worth it,' he said, storming out of the restaurant. 'I'm retiring from the *ummah*. I will have nothing to do with these people' – his parting words trailing after him.

I contemplated the papaya sitting in front of Anwar Nasim, prodded the neatly cut rhomboids of its delicate perfumed warm terracotta-coloured flesh aimlessly around the plate with a fork and then pronged one, slowly delivering it to my mouth. The energy this movement required was almost too much. I felt exhausted, more tired and emotional, more spent and deflated than I could ever remember being. I looked up at Anwar Nasim and groaned aloud: 'Parvez is right. We've failed miserably. If all the versions of Islam out there are so truncated and deeply authoritarian, what hope can there be for the likes of us – Muslim intellectuals?' Nasim was shrouded in deep thought, introspective. He shook his head. 'I am not an intellectual,' he said eventually in a portentous tone, sonorous with seriousness, paused and added, 'and I have doubts about you.' Laughter cracked, rattled, volleyed and ricocheted around the group. The rifle burst petered to a few single shots of deep-throated chuckles as we began to get up and make our way out of the dining room heading for the lift. 'Seriously though,' I said, recalling the group to a semblance of order as we assembled before the lift door, 'if all the versions of Islam on offer are so truncated, what can we do to improve the situation? Especially when all the power is in the hands of the dehumanized bearded ones?'

A sprightly ping announced the arrival of the lift, and with a mechanical sigh its doors swished open. 'I need to collect my key,' someone said as the rest of us jostled, trying to arrange the right formation to insinuate ourselves into the lift. We were perhaps too many. Everyone breathed in to make themselves very small to permit the dragon lady to wriggle out of the lift. 'I'll just go get a packet of cigarettes from the . . .' her remaining words were lost as the lift doors swooshed shut. A hand emerged from the compressed mass of bodies and pressed the 'Open Door' button. We exhaled and exited the lift in a jumble. Gulzar intercepted our dismount, brandishing his room key. We re-entered the lift in an even more amorphous mass. 'Wait, here comes Merryl,' someone observed. There was a fumbling of hands attempting to reach the 'Open Door' button. For some reason once the doors opened we all exited the lift in solidarity. Merryl marched straight past our unruly mob into the empty cavern of the lift and turned to look quizzically at the befuddled assemblage without. 'Isn't anyone else coming?' she enquired. There was a general movement to comply, resulting in Zaffar and Munawar becoming lodged in the insufficient space of the doorway. More writhing, wriggling, jostling and insinuating with sucking in of breath ensued.

Parvez had rejoined the company and resumed his tirade. We were trying not to listen while attempting to reorganize the internal arrangement of bodies within this confined space. The lift doors twitched nervously open and then swooshed shut disconsolately a few times. Parvez kept up his monologue, oblivious of the noises off questioning 'Which floor do you want?', observing 'No, that's the door button', suggesting 'No, now close the door first', and asking plaintively 'Whose floor is first?' The last was no idle question. The Awana Club is curiously configured. Its Reception and public rooms are, as one would expect, on ground level. But all the guest suites are built down the side of the mountain, fanning out below the level of Reception like a flounced skirt arranged around the contours of the land till it meets the valley floor below. Hence getting to one's floor is in inverse relation to the increase in the numerical value of the number. Discussions were breaking out about who was going to whose suite for a coffee, on which floor and should therefore get off first. Above the canned muzak, disparate negotiations, whooshing and swooshing of the doors we could not prevent engaging in erotic tantalizing embraces Parvez kept up a muzak of his own. 'We must confront the power structures directly,' he boomed above the hubbub as a sinking sensation indicated we had attained lift-off in a downward direction.

'Be realistic,' Anwar Nasim shot back. 'If a group of Muslim intellectuals can't even manage a lift, what chance of confronting power structures directly or otherwise?' Laughter rocked the lift wildly on its cable setting up a general turbulence among the bodies within. We all spilled out in an untidy heap as the lift doors opened somewhere between heaven and hell. We panted, gasping for breath as we laughed and laughed. The lift gathered its doors together in a huff and shuffled off in disgust at our behaviour. We laughed even more. As the laughter tittered down to chuckles Nasim, ever the showman, resumed. 'It reminds me of the Marxist who went to the chemist to get some medication for his dying father. On his return he encountered some street people, and stirred by their plight he began haranguing them, urging them to organize and stand up to the bourgeoisie. "You must break the class structure, confront the establishment," he declaimed. "Power comes from the barrel of the gun," he declared. "Organize and fight for your rights," he exhorted. After several hours of heated political debate he was joined by his brother. "While you've been discussing the finer points of dialectical materialism," the brother announced, "our father has died."'

Anwar Nasim stood silent to permit the moral of his story to find its level. 'You see, brothers,' he resumed, 'confronting the power structures at this stage would be suicidal; it will only produce deaths in the family. The odds against us are greater than those in the Genting Casino. On all sides they're summoning people to die for Islam, mobilizing people to run headlong into the power structure. All it does is test the fitness and resilience of the power structure which spits out more and more corpses and flattened bodies with the life, physical and intellectual, squeezed out of them. Oh, you can call them all martyrs and heroes for the cause of Islam. But dying for Islam like that changes nothing.'

'Quite right,' I said defiantly, 'it's high time some of us demanded to live for Islam, unfashionable as that may sound. Martyrdom has its uses, but right now living for Islam takes more courage and more effort. You don't have to think to offer yourself for death, in fact thinking is the last thing you'd want to do. But to live, by God, you've got to think all the unthinkables and face all the slings, arrows, brickbats and siren songs of the entire gamut from the West to the Rest, from without and within, and then come up with a way forward worth travelling. Life! You can't beat it! If only we could bottle it, Milk Marketing Board style, and give it to everyone!'

We went to our rooms. I didn't know it then, but this was the last meeting of the Ijmalis. Our group dispersed in an atmosphere of despair, disillusion and dejection; and never met again. Back in my room I wandered through the patio door onto the balcony and looked to the distant horizon of the encircling mountains. A dark but friendly cloud was hovering nearby. There seemed to be words inscribed on the cloud. I narrowed my eyes and peered harder. Indeed, there were words. I squinted even harder to make out what was written: 'Despair is sin. There *is* a cure for impotence.' My eyes opened wide in mystical wonder. I saw an advertising blimp hovering over the golf course proclaiming hope for functionally challenged executives in mid life! Ah well. I flopped in the chair gazing at nothing. The Muslims, I reflected. If only we could convince them of the truth of Dorothy Parker's experiments with suicide – 'You might as well live.'

On 11 September 2001, it became intolerably clear that Muslim civilization was being offered suicide, both as method and metaphor. It was a warm and sunny Tuesday. In the morning, I received a postcard from my nephew, the one training to become a stockbroker. 'This building is where I am working now,' read the message. I turned the card over and glanced fleetingly at the glossy photograph of the World Trade Center illuminated at night rearing above the lesser lights of the Manhattan skyline. In the afternoon, I attended the graduation ceremony for law students at University College London. After the ceremony, we joined the queue for the obligatory photograph of the new graduate, my daughter, in her cap and gown, proudly holding her degree certificate in her hand. As we waited we became aware of a commotion behind us. Someone was crying, and not tears of joy and celebration. An American student, standing a few steps behind us, was holding a mobile phone in the open palm of her hand as if it were a live grenade or a diseased rodent. Her whole body was racked with sobs. Everyone clustered around, anxious and alarmed. 'Whatever's the matter, dear?' someone's mother cooed and clucked. Through her sobs confused, bemused, jumbled, tumbled down the news. 'Oh no!' 'My God!' 'No! No!' Our collective hearts sank.

We rushed home and switched on the television. Again and again the unfathomable disaster replayed itself before our eyes. The awful, incomprehensible moment when the second plane describes an elegant arc, tilting like a swooping bird, then plunges into the second tower of the World Trade Center emerging as a vibrant ball of flame from the other side is forever lodged in my memory. 'Atif! Atif! Hana! Hana!' My mother began to sob. No one reads postcards with such attention or holds them as fondly in mind as a grandmother. Atif: the nephew training to be a stockbroker. Oh, my God! Atif! The postcard! And Hana, why Hana? Where's Hana? Atif's young sister, the one I persuaded my reluctant sister to allow to take up postgraduate studies at a New York university! Oh, God! Where's Hana's university? I couldn't think. Oh, no! In downtown Manhattan! It's just two blocks from the World Trade Center! We lived the fear and the panic. We fumbled with the phone. We dialled and dialled with rising desperation. Atif's number, Hana's number, my sister's number. Rude noises, failed connections, no dial tone, bleeps, static white noise and no way through. My mother was inconsolable; she sobbed as she prayed and read the Qur'an fearing and preparing herself for the worst. No one thought of sleep.

Early Wednesday morning, finally, we had some news after hours and hours of listening and watching nothing but the news. My nephew Atif left New York on Monday! Blessed Monday! On leave, he flew off to visit his mum in San Francisco. His sister, sleeping on the thirty-first floor of her apartment building, was woken up by the first explosion and just managed to escape before the first tower imploded. As the massive dust cloud made its way towards her apartment, a fireman grabbed her hand and led her away to one of the refuge stations in New York.

It made no more sense as I watched the pictures again and again over the coming days. The terrorist in general, and the suicide bomber in particular, I remember thinking, are a special breed. They stand outside normality, beyond reason. They justify their rage and actions with perverse self-righteousness and twisted religious notions – utterances and pieties as impenetrable to me as they are to so many Muslims. Yet the community of believers must take some responsibility for their actions. Did I not witness the planting of the seeds that produced these bitter fruits in Saudi Arabia, Iran and Pakistan, in the eyes of the Shariah-obsessed champions of the Islamic movement and the authoritarian thought of the mystic gurus who so dominate the Muslim world?

Literalism. Literally taken. When metaphors are taken literally, should it surprise us that they lead to madness? It was hardly a revelation to me that Osama bin Laden was behind all this. It was the glint in his eyes, all those years ago, when I first caught sight of him in that fateful meeting of Mujahidin groups in Peshawar. The insistent refrain at that meeting was 'impossible'. Nothing could be negotiated. Everything was impossible. To make the Word flesh one must have the power of God. The literalists had assumed that impossible power. They had ceased to ask the fundamental questions of existence: 'Who are we?' 'Why are we?' 'Where are we going?' 'What is the purpose of humanity?' Their literalism provided ready-made answers to everything. It was impossible for them to do otherwise.

On 9 March 2002, a Palestinian suicide bomber blew himself up in a crowded café-bar in West Jerusalem, killing twelve other people and injuring fifty-two. The following day, televisions across the world broadcast his video testament. A bearded young man, Kalashnikov in hand, stands in front of a green flag. The writing on the flag is clear: '*Allahu Akbar*' (God is Great). 'By the Grace of Allah,' says the young man, 'I am the living martyr, Mohammed Bakri Farahat, the son of the Battalions of Izz-a-din al-Qassam. I ask Almighty Allah to accept this work of mine. I ask him to join me with my brother martyrs. I ask him to join me with the Prophet, peace and blessings upon him, in the highest of paradise.' The video sent a shiver through my body. It was a chilly day; but I went out into the garden anyway.

The description of paradise in the Qur'an, my mother had said all those years before, was a parable; the Qur'an itself tells us its description of paradise is a 'similitude', metaphor, a springboard to be used by the imagination. The 'houris' of paradise – frequently and erroneously rendered as 'virgins' – derive their name from the eyes of the gazelle with their large black irises and contrasting whites. They personify beauty and total innocence: these eyes have never cast their gaze on sin. In classical Arabic, Persian and Urdu poetry, the houri often signifies the sun or the moon: those celestial eyes, one shining and the other reflecting, their beneficial gaze on the dwellers in earthly existence. In the gardens of paradise, the Qur'an says, houris with 'wide eyes . . . hear no idle talk, no cause of sin, only the saying, "Peace, Peace!"'. So in the domains of the earth: innocence, beauty and peace must prevail. But the houris are only a sideshow. The central metaphor, I learned from my mother, is the garden which the Qur'an mentions 130 times in its descriptions of paradise. But paradise is not any garden. It is a specially landscaped garden, with 'fountains of gushing water' and 'rivers of milk unchanging in flavour, and rivers of wine – a delight to the drinkers – rivers too of honey purified'. It is a garden well endowed 'with every fruit two kind'. It is a place of 'immortal youth' and eternal bliss. It is a world of beauty and freedom (from physical desires and moral ineptitude) and synthesis and diversity (apart from men and women, it is the habitat of angels, jinn, houris, as well as all manner of flora and fauna!). Above all, it is a place of protection. The Qur'anic word for paradise, *janna*, contains the root meaning of 'veiling, covering'. Just as the garden veils us from the harshness of the built environment, so paradise protects from the heat of hell.

To the Qur'anic description of paradise, we must add the arresting detail of the Hadith, the traditions of the Prophet. Here too metaphors abound. One Hadith describes a tree so huge one can ride for a century in its shade and not reach its end, another tells of the blessed sweet musk, yet another talks of a garden with silver and gold bricks glued together with mortar of pungent musk. The Prophet, aware we can grasp only what we can perceive with our limited earthly vision, uses analogies from this world and the human body – and then deliberately subverts the lush detail to make the point that analogies are, after all, analogies, and no metaphor can portray the real thing. He thus tells us there is nothing in the garden that is on earth except the name of things: for what is in the garden, no eye has seen, no ear has heard, no nose has smelled, no body has experienced, no mind has perceived. What appears at first to be straight literalism is in fact an illustration of the limitation of language, a demonstration of the ineffability of the world to come.

One way to appreciate paradise is to think of its exact opposite: hell. The Qur'an describes hell in just such oppositional terms. Here, fire provides the fundamental metaphor. Whereas paradise is cool, hell is hot; paradise is water, hell a place of perishing thirst; hell is hunger, paradise a place of delicious fulfilment; paradise is contentment, hell is eternal regret. But, most important of all: hell is separation from God, while paradise is the grace of His (although 'He' has no gender!) company.

Paradise and hell, the two sides of the same coin: that is the Islamic notion of the Hereafter. In the Hereafter, such concerns of life as sickness, hardship, agony, love, happiness, death, as well as time and change, cease: pleasure and pain go their separate ways, one to the garden, the other to the fire. In between, the fulcrum on the plane of time between the here and now and the Hereafter, is the Day of Judgement, when each will be held responsible for their actions in life.

The actions of our earthly existence must stand the test of that day. They must be measured against the ideal life of prayer, devotion to humility, equality, pursuit of knowledge and justice. It is the image one confronts when one stands on a prayer mat to offer supplication to God. Most carpets in the mosques, and individual prayer mats people keep in their homes, are decorated with heavenly symbols and metaphors. I remember visiting an exhibition at the Hood Museum of Art of Dartmouth College in Hanover, New Hampshire entitled 'Images of Paradise in Islamic Art'. It was composed of carpets and prayer mats, all silently conveying the message of metaphors. The centrepiece of the exhibition was a large 'Garden Carpet with Chahar Bagh Design' – a design reflecting the Muslim idea of *firdous* or walled garden. Other prayer rugs from Persia, Turkey and Mughal India, with their profusion of flowers seen through an arch and flanked by the mystical Lote Tree, present worshippers with an image of paradise that can be given earthly dimension, through enlightened actions. Some works present the viewer with multiple layers of metaphorical meaning, not all of which are obvious at first glance. A mosque lamp included in the exhibition, for example, was not just an exquisite practical object: made of glass, with a round belly, a flare at the top and a small round foot, it symbolized divine light; indeed, the omnipresence of God. The Qur'anic inscriptions on its surface explicated its metaphorical connection:

> *Allah is the Light of the heavens and the earth.*
> *The similitude of His light is as a niche wherein is a lamp.*
> *The lamp is in a glass. The glass is as it were a shining star.*
> *(This lamp is) kindled from a blessed tree, an olive neither of*
> *the East nor of the West, whose oil would almost glow forth*
> *(of itself) though no fire touched it. Light upon light, Allah*
> *guides unto His Light whom He will.*
> (24: 35)

The same repertoire of metaphors can be read in all forms of Islamic art: from pottery to paintings, bookbinding to metalwork, ceramic tiles to architecture, calligraphy to textiles. Yet contemporary Muslims seem incapable of reading these metaphors. Determined, as so many are, to declare art *haram*, prohibited, forbidden, a distraction. And that inability and unwillingness to read has deep historic roots.

Of all the objects in the Hood museum exhibition, one stands out in my mind. A miniature entitled 'allegory of heavenly and earthly drunkenness'. It is an illustration, painted in the sixteenth century, from a manuscript of *Dewan-e-Hafiz*, the anthology of poetry by the great fourteenth-century Persian lyric poet, Hafiz. A drunken poet, a book in hand, reclining in his balcony, looks down on a scene of merry-making. A band of twisted religious scholars, an assembly of senseless musicians, a group of travelling mystics with grotesque faces, and an assorted number of other people, dance, sing and fall about in a stupor. On the roof top, five angels are engaged in their own form of drinking. Hafiz's couplet, at the top of the painting, reads:

> *The angel of mercy took the revelling cup,*
> *and tossed it down*
> *As rose-water, on the cheeks of houris and angels.*

Wine is a recurrent metaphor for mystical elevation in Sufi poetry. But 'good times' in heaven are clearly not the same thing as a good time on this earth. Drunkenness on earth signifies something quite different. The mystic intoxicated with the love of God is on a different plain. The painter, however, had managed to subvert the clearly mystical intent of the poet. For him the one-dimensional mystical intoxication signified by the grotesque faces of the mystics is not much different from earthly drunkenness or the intoxication with rigid rules of the literalist religious scholars: the stupefied expressions on their faces speak volumes. The search for paradise on earth lies neither in the direction of literalism nor mystical incantations, the painter indicates. Oh, I am with the artist there. His figurative metaphor and all my journeys lead to one overriding conclusion: we ought to be looking elsewhere.

And yet the contemporary Muslim world is dominated by an array of mystical cults and an equally banal variety of literalism. The world of the Muslim mystic, as I had discovered, is selfish (mysticism is the ultimate ego trip), sanctimonious (mystics are amongst the most authoritarian figures around), a silhouette, a figure seen only in darkness, of what we could be. The world of pure literalism is dry, dreadful, and totally dead. One drowns in Selfhood, the other fries in a medieval mindset – both are fatally flawed, dangerously drunk.

The 'allegory of heavenly and earthly drunkenness' points us towards a different world: the balanced world of metaphor, marvellous, mature, a meaningful world. It is a world of multiple dimensions: the two-dimensional representation of the 'allegory' communicates several levels. A world where intrinsic values combine with freedom to engender beauty and creativity, where Islam is expressed as an open system flowering with diversity. It is the vision of the 'earthly paradise' I set out to discover.

What I found was something quite different. Most Muslims think of paradise as a piece of property one can purchase by accumulating the right amount of Islamic deeds: imposing outmoded concepts of the Shariah, banning all varieties of art, literature and culture, killing and being killed in the name of Islam. The accumulation of this supposed wealth has become an end in itself! So the Qur'anic vision of paradise has been turned into an earthly vision of hell: an enclave of bloodbath and bigotry, suppression and severity, censorship and castration. Evil often thrives in those who constantly proclaim 'evil doesn't live here any more'. What could be further from the spirit of the Qur'an, so far removed from its description of paradise?

My journeys led me to one unavoidable conclusion: the Muslim paradise is not a place of arrival but a way of travelling. Just as we cannot stop living, we cannot stop searching for our paradise. But the search is for a continual kind of becoming. All the failed paradises I discovered were founded on the misguided belief of arrival. All people are left with then is to live out a set of unquestioning certainties. But the journey, the way to the watering hole that measures out each day's travel, itself is a way of thinking and questioning. In particular, making the journey requires constant attention, observation and questioning to ensure the right path is being taken as the landscape and surroundings continually change. So the route map is constantly amended, adjusted; and the precise direction of travel regularly modified as circumstances indicate shifts in the water table, new freshets and springlets bursting forth in previously unexplored or unsuspected locations. The potent and protean metaphors of the Qur'an served as guides to shape my journeys. They provided images and ideas within which I moved and acted; metaphors with which I imagined and reflected; allegories with which I sought comprehension, association and appreciation. They furnished me with visions of better worlds to build. They gave me warnings of what can be and hope of what could be. And even though I failed, the journeys continue. I still seek 'wide-eyed houris', my reward 'of goodness for goodness'; and I repeat after them, 'Peace, Peace!'

Failure makes us human. To accept that you have erred and failed is a good basis on which to build the future. A few weeks after the tragedy of 11 September 2001, I received a telephone call from my old FOSIS friend, Ghayasuddin Siddiqui. We hadn't spoken to each other for almost twenty years. And for good reason. Ghayasuddin had joined Kalim Siddiqui at the Muslim Institute as his Deputy Director. The two Siddiquis were fervent supporters of the Iranian Revolution. When Kalim Siddiqui cynically asked me to go and preach democracy to the Iranians and threw me out of the Muslim Institute, with the refrain 'if you come here again, I will have your legs broken', Ghayasuddin had stood there, visibly upset but unable to do anything except passively observe the proceedings. After Kalim Siddiqui's death in 1996, he became the Director of the Muslim Institute. 'Look!' he said. 'We've had our differences. But now I want to say one thing. We were wrong, terribly, terribly wrong.' Ghayasuddin had always struck me as a hesitant man. He hesitated before saying anything. But now I could detect no hesitation at all. He was speaking with total confidence. 'We've done incalculable damage to ourselves. Our literalist, fundamentalist and revolutionary interpretations were all based on exceptionally arrogant notions of truth and certainty,' he confessed. There was a long silence. I tried to say something but words escaped me. 'Look,' Ghayasuddin continued, 'you were correct. And we, with our sense of moral superiority, were wrong. I apologize for what happened to you in the Muslim Institute.' So the impasse of decades was broken. We met several times after that brief but ground-breaking telephone conversation, refugees from innumerable failures.

Ghayasuddin had changed. Rigidity, intolerance, impatience, and an unbecoming sense of moral superiority had evaporated. He smiled a lot; and even laughed occasionally. I looked into his eyes. There was warmth and humanity there. But there was also awareness – the tempering awareness that comes from participating in something detestable and accepting that one has made a serious mistake. Ghayasuddin had become human again. Given half a chance, I thought, humanity always reasserts itself. 'Look,' he said, when we met at the Muslim Heritage Centre in Kensington, London, one Saturday afternoon. 'We can't resign our membership of the *ummah*. We'll always belong to the Muslim community. And while running away from the "flame of fire and molten brass" of *jahanna* [hell], we can't stand idly by and watch the combustion of this world. As Muslim intellectuals and thinkers, it falls to us to redouble our efforts to reconstruct a Muslim civilization of the future where, like in the Qur'anic paradise, synthesis and diversity, beauty and imagination, green pastures and freedom are the basic norms.' He persuaded me to join the circle of concerned Muslims he was establishing who would meet on a monthly basis to rethink and re-imagine Islam.

The diverse group turned out to include many of my old friends as well as younger intellectuals and scholars who became my new friends. We quickly established a common distaste for all forms of oppression, slogans and platitudes, mass hysteria and Messianism, medieval jurisprudence and obsolete conventions. We shared a passion for humanity, a vision deeply rooted in Islamic history and tradition where literary, artistic, scientific and moral concerns drew their basic sustenance from the central metaphor of the garden as paradise, and sought a fresh understanding of the revealed text – the Qur'an – based on conceptual analysis and an understanding of the modern world. Each month there were heated discussions aimed at painting pictures of what a future civilization based on the Qur'anic idea of paradise would look like. What would be the nature of governance in such a civilization? How would cultural diversity and ethnic autonomy be ensured? How would a garden-civilization promote genuine freedom? What would be the style and content of science and technology in this civilization? And, how can we get from here – where the Muslim world is buried so deep in despotism and despondency – to there, a world of cultural authenticity and dynamic tolerant pluralism? What can we do to achieve the transition? These are not new questions. We merely approached them again in the light of new experiences.

Last summer, I spent a sunny Sunday morning in my customary perusal of the newspapers. I read a story about Hashem Aghajari, a history lecturer at Tehran University and a war veteran who had lost a leg in the Iran–Iraq war. In a speech, Aghajari had argued that each generation of Muslims should reinterpret Islam for itself rather than blindly follow the Mullahs. It was the selfsame argument I had advanced over twenty-five years before in *The Future of Muslim Civilisation*. Aghajari was accused of blasphemy and sentenced to death. In another story, I read that a Shariah court in Katsina, Nigeria, had upheld the appeal of a Muslim woman, Safiya Hsuaini, who had been convicted of adultery and sentenced to death by stoning. The original ruling was declared unsound because the alleged act had taken place before Shariah law was introduced in Nigeria. But a second Shariah court in Katsina State sentenced another woman, Amina Lawal, to die after she confessed to having a child while divorced.

I wandered into the conservatory and stopped before the bookshelf. I needed some diversion from all this too-distressing news. My eye lighted on a copy of *The Best of Dorothy Parker*, the Folio Society edition with charming illustrations by Helen Smithson. It has a flashy silver cover showing the Manhattan skyline in silhouette, dotted with flying objects – a hat, an armchair, a pair of gloves, a chic shoe, a teapot. Strangely, there is also a two-seater, pre-Second World War plane which seems to be heading straight for a skyscraper. I went back into the garden and fell to reading the essay 'A Telephone Call', when Merryl rang. She posed the question of the day: 'What are we going to do now?' she enquired. 'We will do what we have always done,' I replied. 'Smile and struggle. And, as usual, our struggle will be a fight through books.' 'And,' Merryl added, 'I suppose we'll have to find a new bunch of beardless characters.' Before I could give a reply, I was summoned by the sound of the doorbell.

I opened the door to be greeted by two young men: one clean-shaven, the other with a beard so faintly furred I had to strain to notice it. '*Salamu 'alaykum*,' they said as I ushered them towards the garden. I knew them well. Ehsan Masood, a slim handsome man in his mid-thirties who wore thick glasses, had followed a journalistic career similar to mine. I got to know him when he was news editor of *Q News*, a British Muslim youth magazine. After finishing university, he joined *Nature* as a science reporter, moving later to *New Scientist* as 'Opinion' editor. His companion, Shamim Miah, was a short stocky man with an infectious laugh. I met him on the streets of Oldham, in the aftermath of the race riot, that broke out in the city in June 2001. He taught sociology at Oldham College while working for his doctorate on 'motivating young people' at Manchester University. The three of us sat in the garden, talking, drinking tea and sharing samosas.

'Brother Zia,' Shamim said after the polite conversation dried up, 'we are here to ask you to help us.'

'Help you do what?' I asked, pretending to be surprised.

'Change the Muslims,' Ehsan shot back.

I thought for a moment; and looked at their faces. I recognized the passion, the devotion, the concern, the perplexity, and all the expectation I had known when I too considered myself to be a young man.

Off on the road again, I thought. I can do nothing but live by my metaphors. Paradise awaits. And once again, in the company of new and old friends, I set off on a new departure.

But that's another story.

Index